CHOCOLAT

vol.1

Shin JiSang ·Geo

ice
Kunion

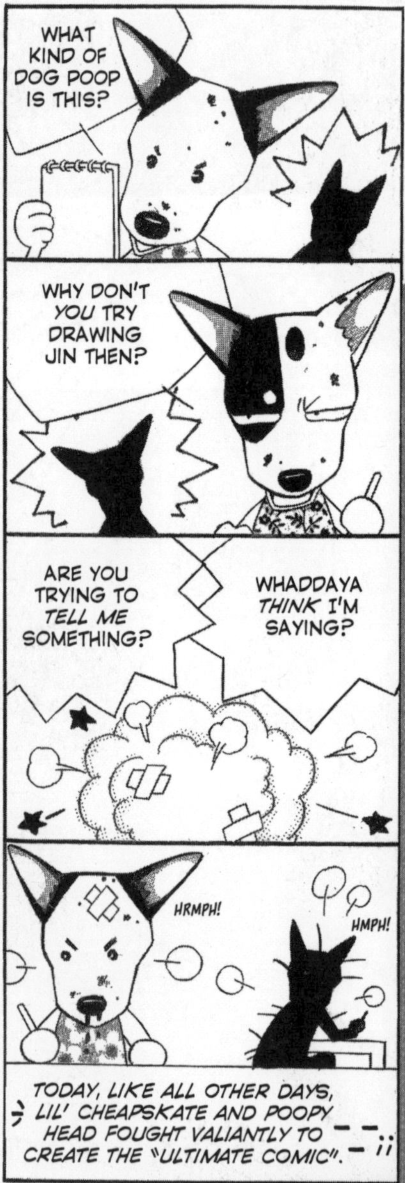
WHAT KIND OF DOG POOP IS THIS?
WHY DON'T *YOU* TRY DRAWING JIN THEN?
ARE YOU TRYING TO *TELL ME* SOMETHING?
WHADDAYA *THINK* I'M SAYING?
HRMPH!
HMPH!
TODAY, LIKE ALL OTHER DAYS, LIL' CHEAPSKATE AND POOPY HEAD FOUGHT VALIANTLY TO CREATE THE "ULTIMATE COMIC".

WORDS FROM THE CREATORS

HEE HEE...

IT IS ALREADY OUR FOURTH SERIES TOGETHER!

IT'S BEEN AWHILE SINCE WE'VE BEEN PUBLISHED IN MAGAZINES, SO THERE WERE A LOT OF THINGS WE FORGOT ABOUT AND HAD TO RE-LEARN...BUT... LIKE ALWAYS...WE HAVE JUST ONE SINGLE WISH: THAT YOU ENJOY OUR WORK TO THE FULLEST! (WELL, WHO DOESN'T WISH FOR THAT, RIGHT?)

AS THE VOLUMES GO BY, WE WILL DO OUR BEST TO CREATE THE SEXY AND SIZZLING CHARACTERS WITH A COOL AND REFRESHING STORY.

JI-SANG SHIN & GEO

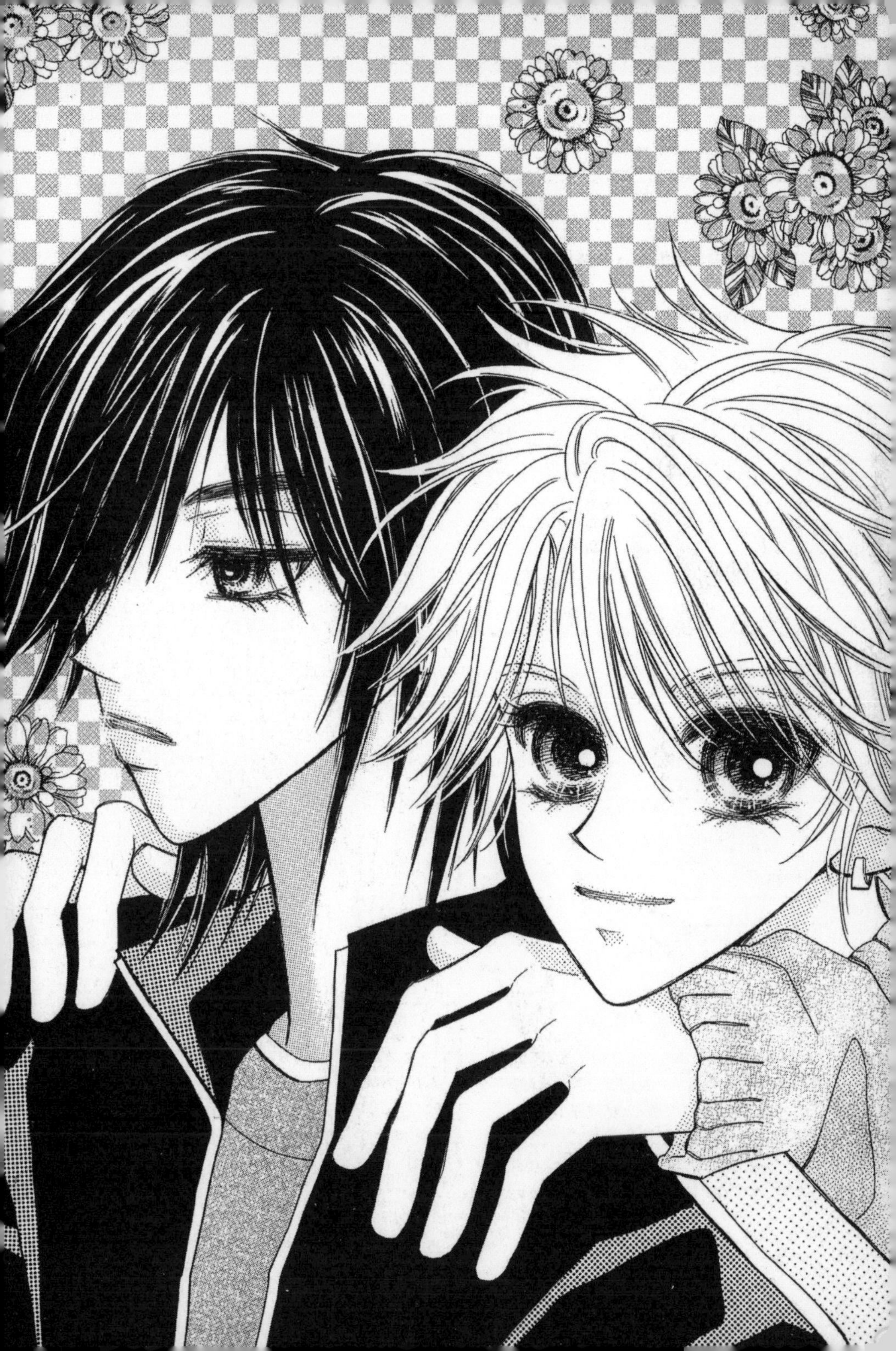

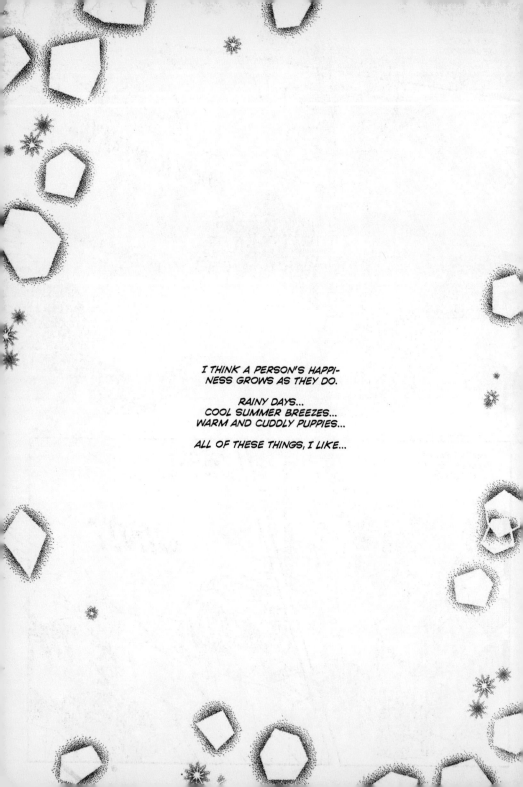

I THINK A PERSON'S HAPPI-
NESS GROWS AS THEY DO.

RAINY DAYS...
COOL SUMMER BREEZES...
WARM AND CUDDLY PUPPIES...

ALL OF THESE THINGS, I LIKE...

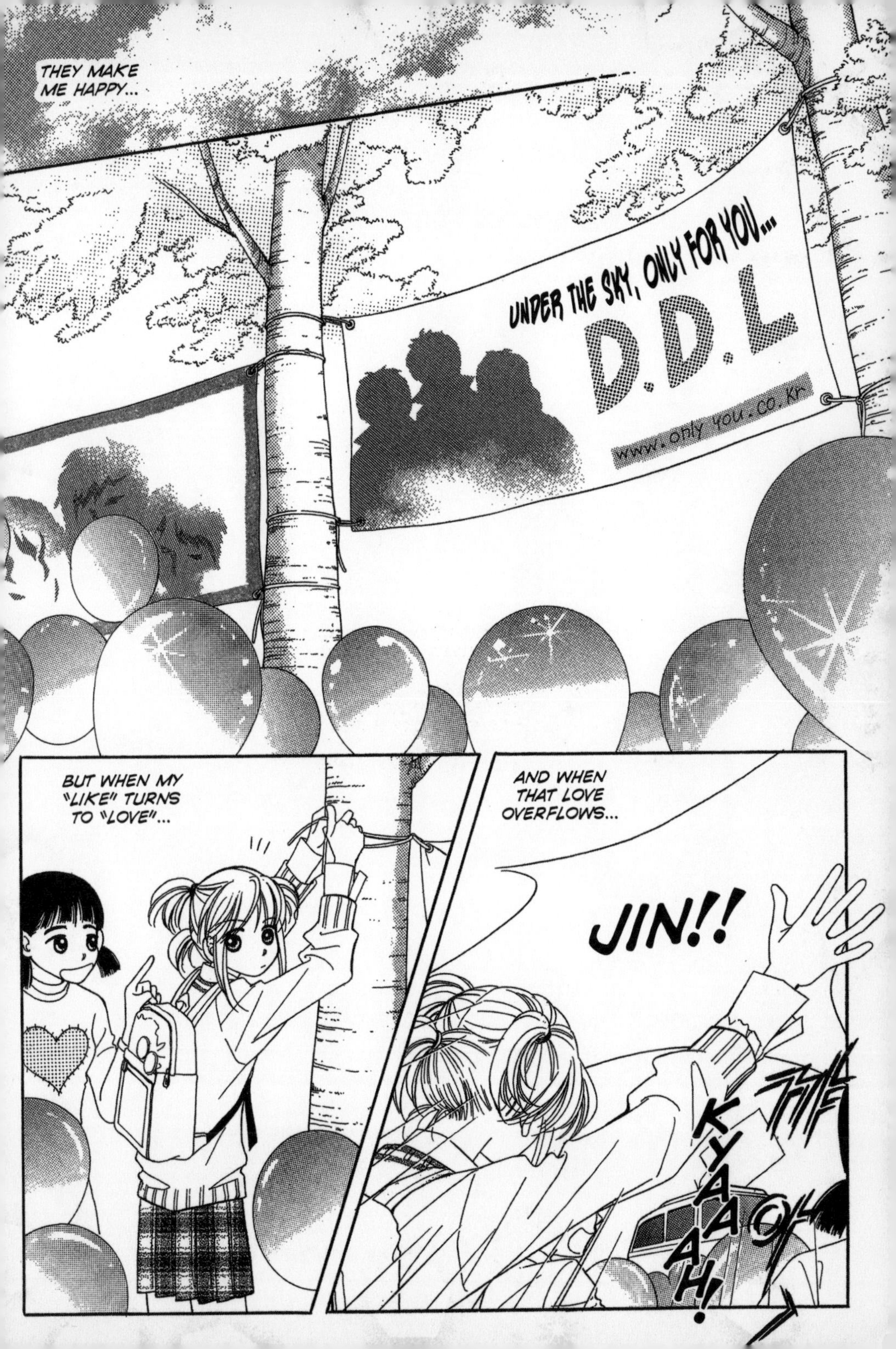
THEY MAKE ME HAPPY...
UNDER THE SKY, ONLY FOR YOU...
D.D.L
www.only you.co.kr
BUT WHEN MY "LIKE" TURNS TO "LOVE"...
AND WHEN THAT LOVE OVERFLOWS...
JIN!!
KYAAAAH!

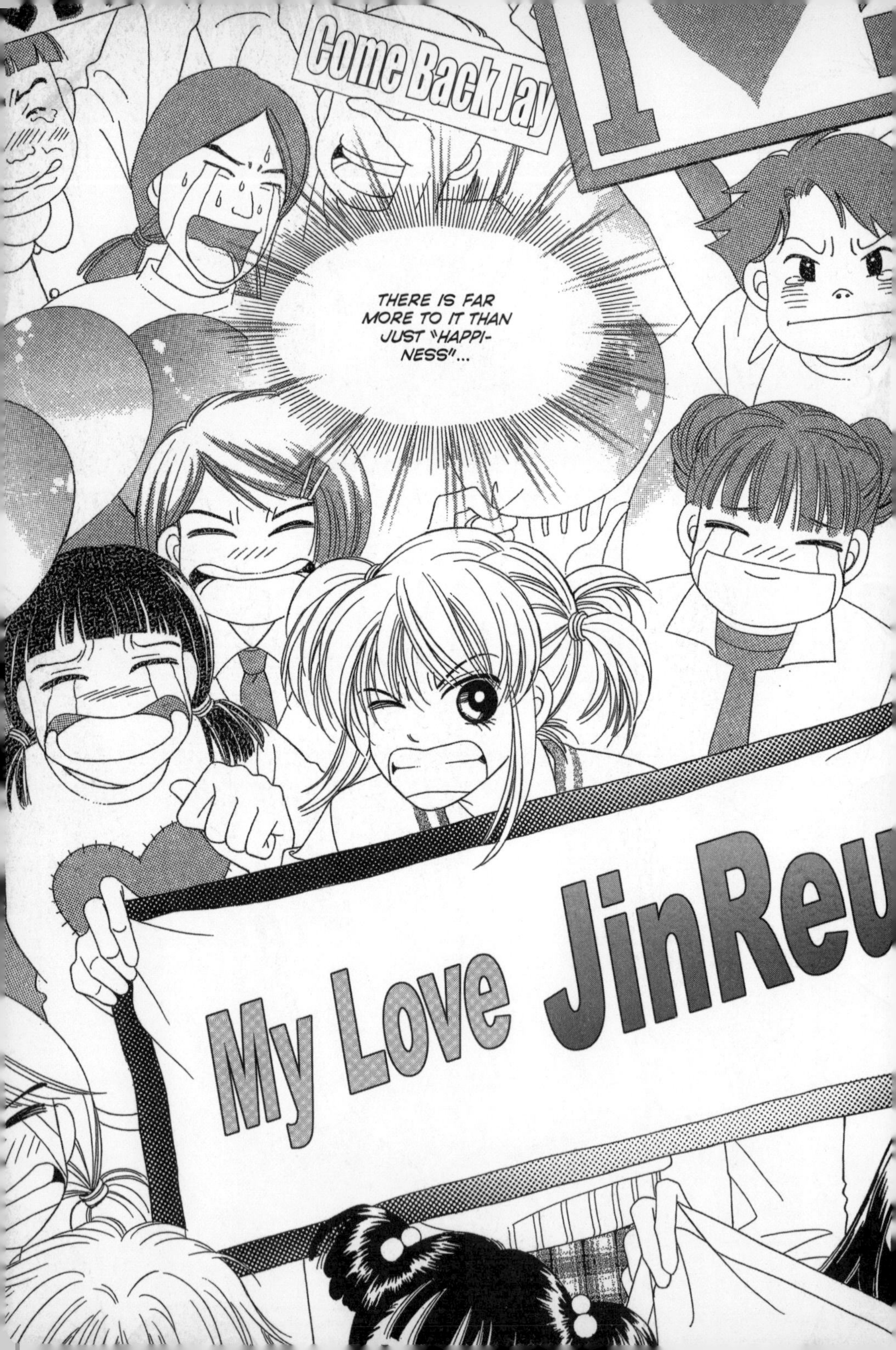
Come Back Jay
THERE IS FAR MORE TO IT THAN JUST "HAPPI-NESS"...
My Love JinReu

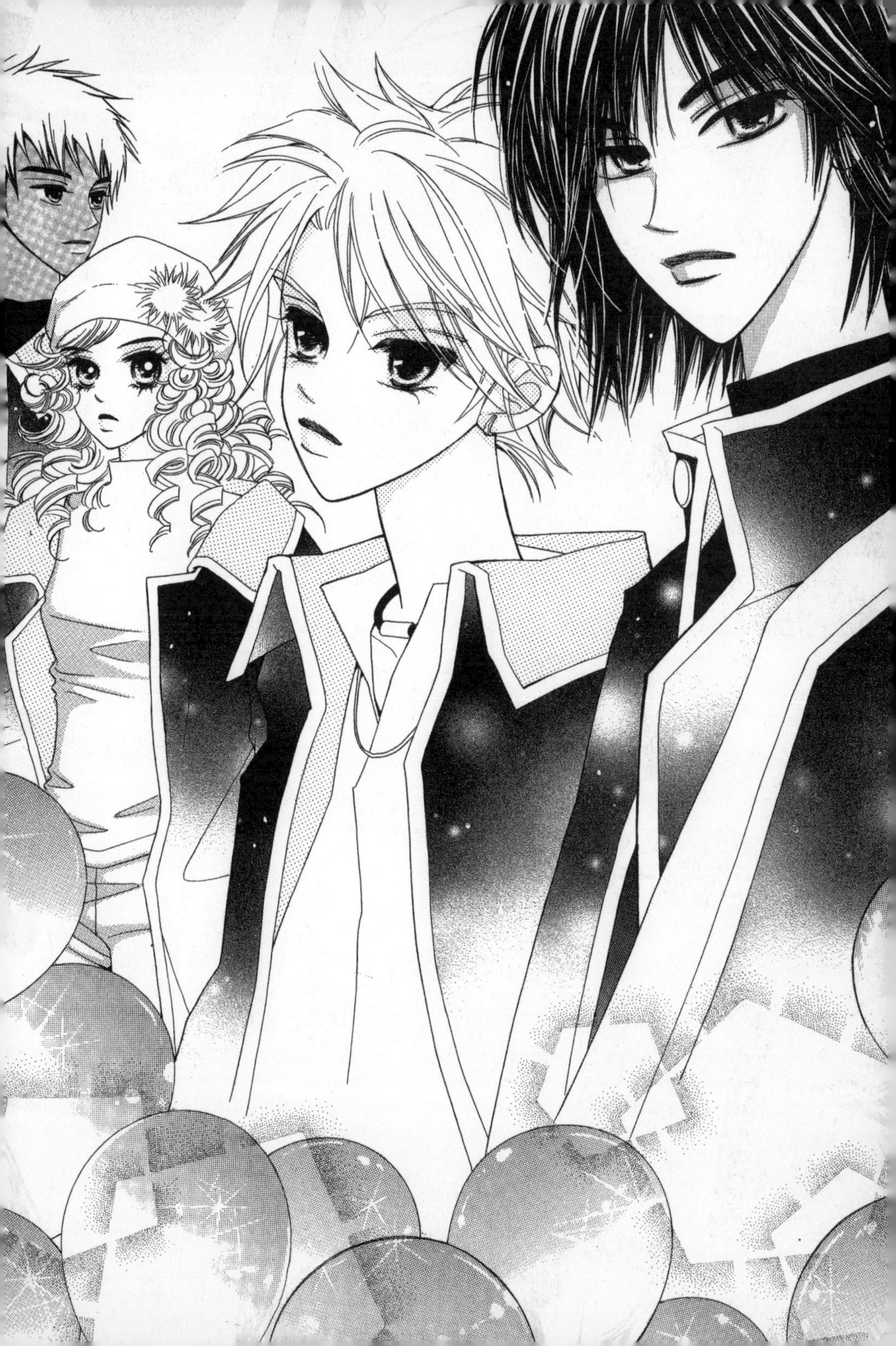

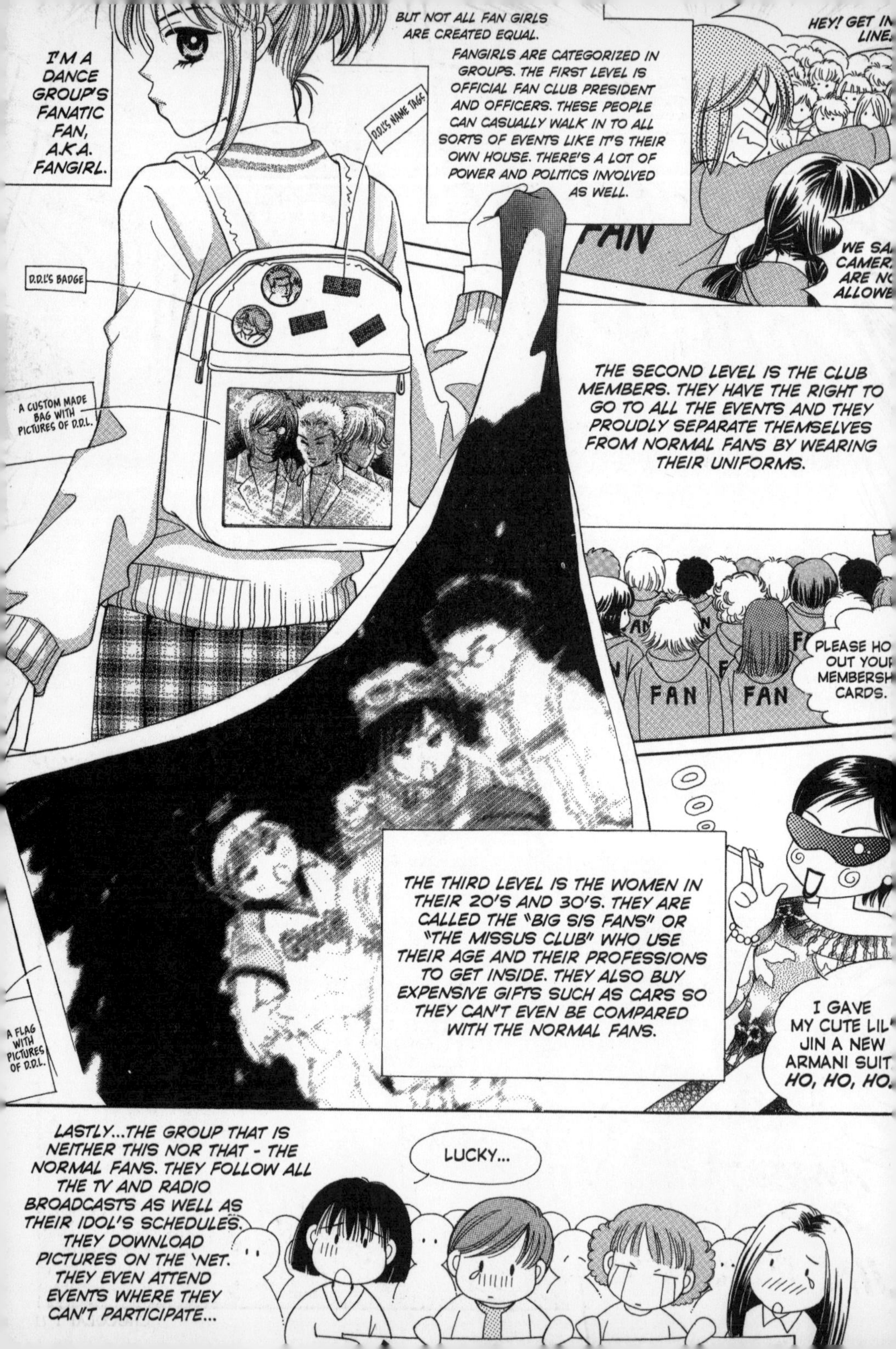
I'M A DANCE GROUP'S FANATIC FAN, A.K.A. FANGIRL.
D.D.L'S NAME TAGS
D.D.L'S BADGE
A CUSTOM MADE BAG WITH PICTURES OF D.D.L.
A FLAG WITH PICTURES OF D.D.L.
BUT NOT ALL FAN GIRLS ARE CREATED EQUAL.
FANGIRLS ARE CATEGORIZED IN GROUPS. THE FIRST LEVEL IS OFFICIAL FAN CLUB PRESIDENT AND OFFICERS. THESE PEOPLE CAN CASUALLY WALK IN TO ALL SORTS OF EVENTS LIKE IT'S THEIR OWN HOUSE. THERE'S A LOT OF POWER AND POLITICS INVOLVED AS WELL.
HEY! GET IN LINE.
FAN
WE SA CAMER ARE NO ALLOWE
THE SECOND LEVEL IS THE CLUB MEMBERS. THEY HAVE THE RIGHT TO GO TO ALL THE EVENTS AND THEY PROUDLY SEPARATE THEMSELVES FROM NORMAL FANS BY WEARING THEIR UNIFORMS.
FAN FAN
PLEASE HO OUT YOUR MEMBERSH CARDS.
THE THIRD LEVEL IS THE WOMEN IN THEIR 20'S AND 30'S. THEY ARE CALLED THE "BIG SIS FANS" OR "THE MISSUS CLUB" WHO USE THEIR AGE AND THEIR PROFESSIONS TO GET INSIDE. THEY ALSO BUY EXPENSIVE GIFTS SUCH AS CARS SO THEY CAN'T EVEN BE COMPARED WITH THE NORMAL FANS.
I GAVE MY CUTE LIL JIN A NEW ARMANI SUIT HO, HO, HO.
LASTLY...THE GROUP THAT IS NEITHER THIS NOR THAT - THE NORMAL FANS. THEY FOLLOW ALL THE TV AND RADIO BROADCASTS AS WELL AS THEIR IDOL'S SCHEDULES. THEY DOWNLOAD PICTURES ON THE 'NET. THEY EVEN ATTEND EVENTS WHERE THEY CAN'T PARTICIPATE...
LUCKY...

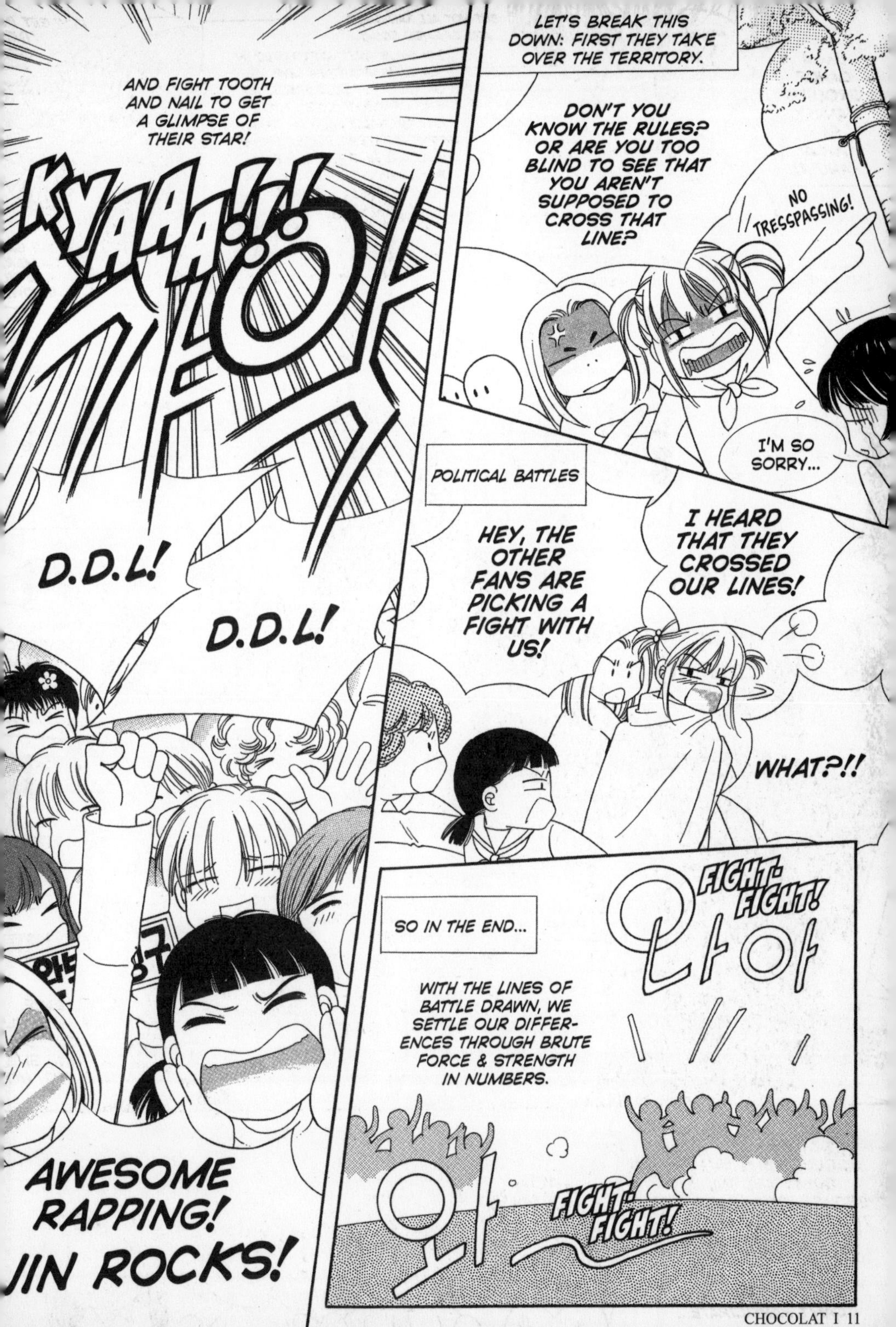
AND FIGHT TOOTH AND NAIL TO GET A GLIMPSE OF THEIR STAR!
KYAA!!!
D.D.L!
D.D.L!
AWESOME RAPPING! JIN ROCKS!
LET'S BREAK THIS DOWN: FIRST THEY TAKE OVER THE TERRITORY.
DON'T YOU KNOW THE RULES? OR ARE YOU TOO BLIND TO SEE THAT YOU AREN'T SUPPOSED TO CROSS THAT LINE?
NO TRESSPASSING!
I'M SO SORRY...
POLITICAL BATTLES
HEY, THE OTHER FANS ARE PICKING A FIGHT WITH US!
I HEARD THAT THEY CROSSED OUR LINES!
WHAT?!!
SO IN THE END...
WITH THE LINES OF BATTLE DRAWN, WE SETTLE OUR DIFFERENCES THROUGH BRUTE FORCE & STRENGTH IN NUMBERS.
FIGHT-FIGHT!
FIGHT-FIGHT!

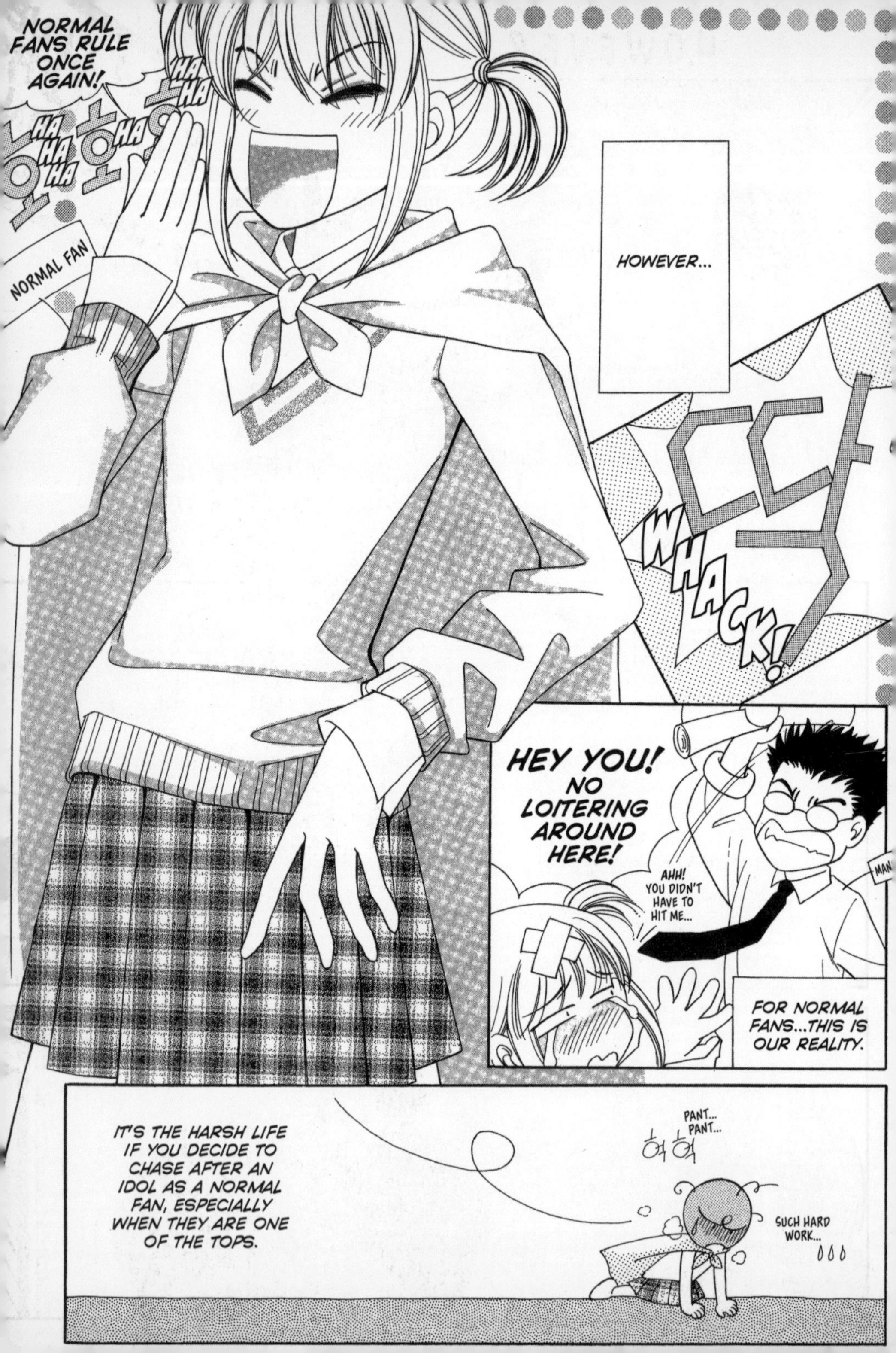
NORMAL FANS RULE ONCE AGAIN!
HA HA HA HA HA HA
NORMAL FAN
HOWEVER...
WHACK!
HEY YOU! NO LOITERING AROUND HERE!
AHH! YOU DIDN'T HAVE TO HIT ME...
FOR NORMAL FANS...THIS IS OUR REALITY.
IT'S THE HARSH LIFE IF YOU DECIDE TO CHASE AFTER AN IDOL AS A NORMAL FAN, ESPECIALLY WHEN THEY ARE ONE OF THE TOPS.
PANT... PANT...
헉헉
SUCH HARD WORK...

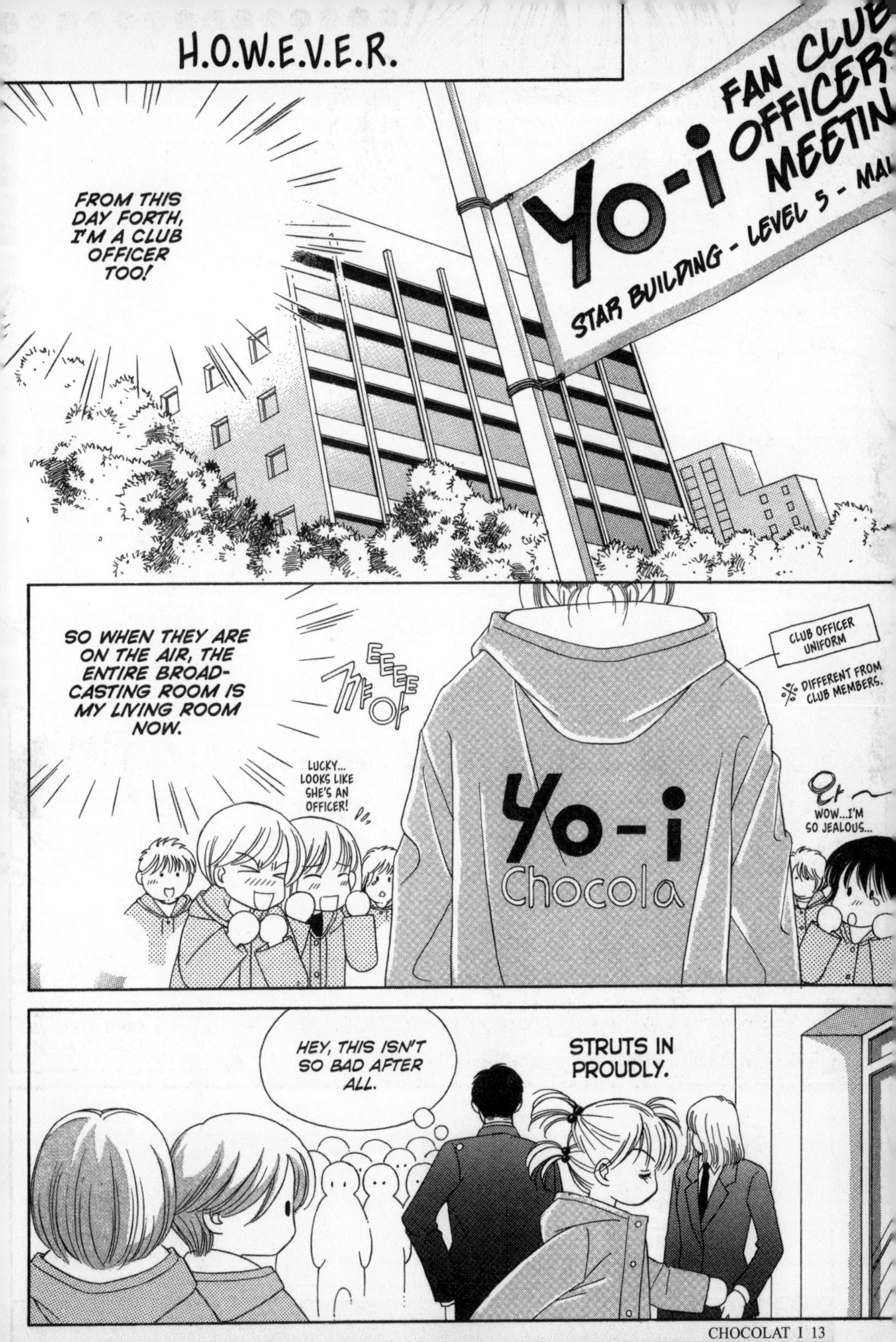
H.O.W.E.V.E.R.
FROM THIS DAY FORTH, I'M A CLUB OFFICER TOO!
Yo-i FAN CLUB OFFICERS MEETIN
STAR BUILDING - LEVEL 5 -
SO WHEN THEY ARE ON THE AIR, THE ENTIRE BROAD-CASTING ROOM IS MY LIVING ROOM NOW.
꺄아 EEEEE
CLUB OFFICER UNIFORM
※ DIFFERENT FROM CLUB MEMBERS.
LUCKY... LOOKS LIKE SHE'S AN OFFICER!
Yo-i Chocola
으냐~
WOW...I'M SO JEALOUS...
HEY, THIS ISN'T SO BAD AFTER ALL.
STRUTS IN PROUDLY.

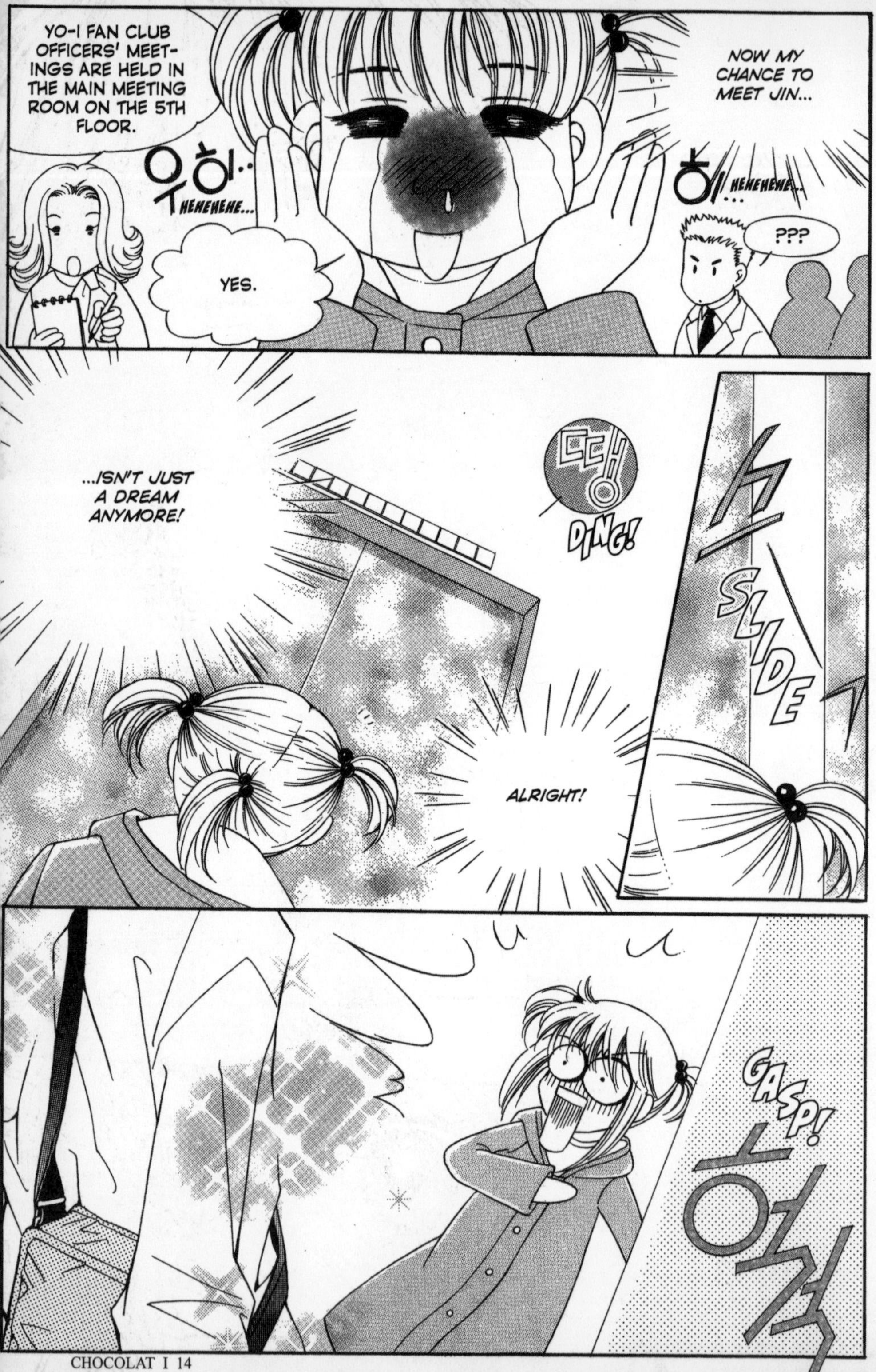
YO-I FAN CLUB OFFICERS' MEETINGS ARE HELD IN THE MAIN MEETING ROOM ON THE 5TH FLOOR.
우히..
HEHEHEHE...
YES.
NOW MY CHANCE TO MEET JIN...
히...
HEHEHEHE...
???
...ISN'T JUST A DREAM ANYMORE!
띵
DING!
스
SLIDE
ALRIGHT!
GASP!
헉

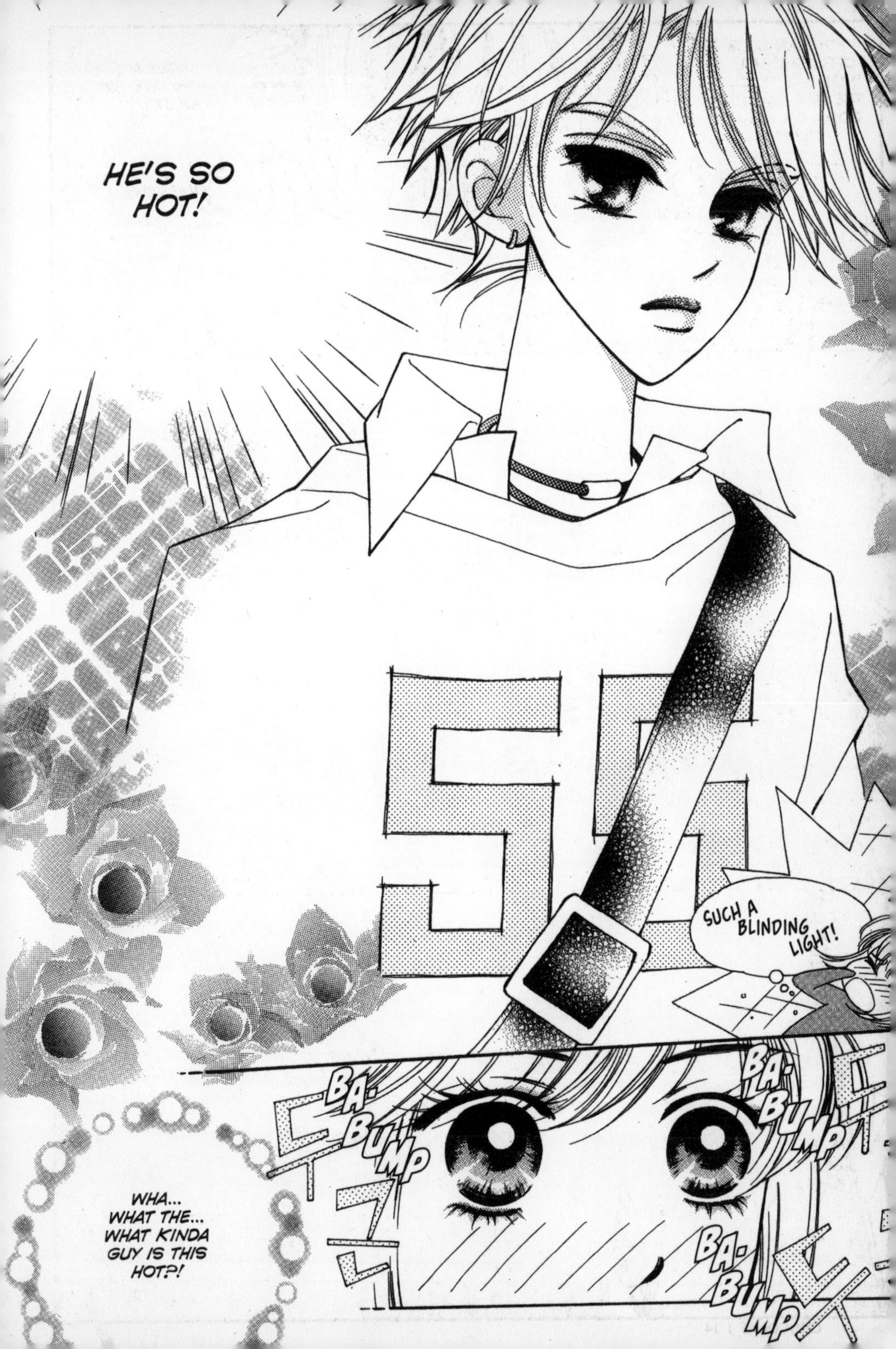
HE'S SO HOT!
SUCH A BLINDING LIGHT!
WHA... WHAT THE... WHAT KINDA GUY IS THIS HOT?!
BA-BUMP
BA-BUMP
BA-BUMP

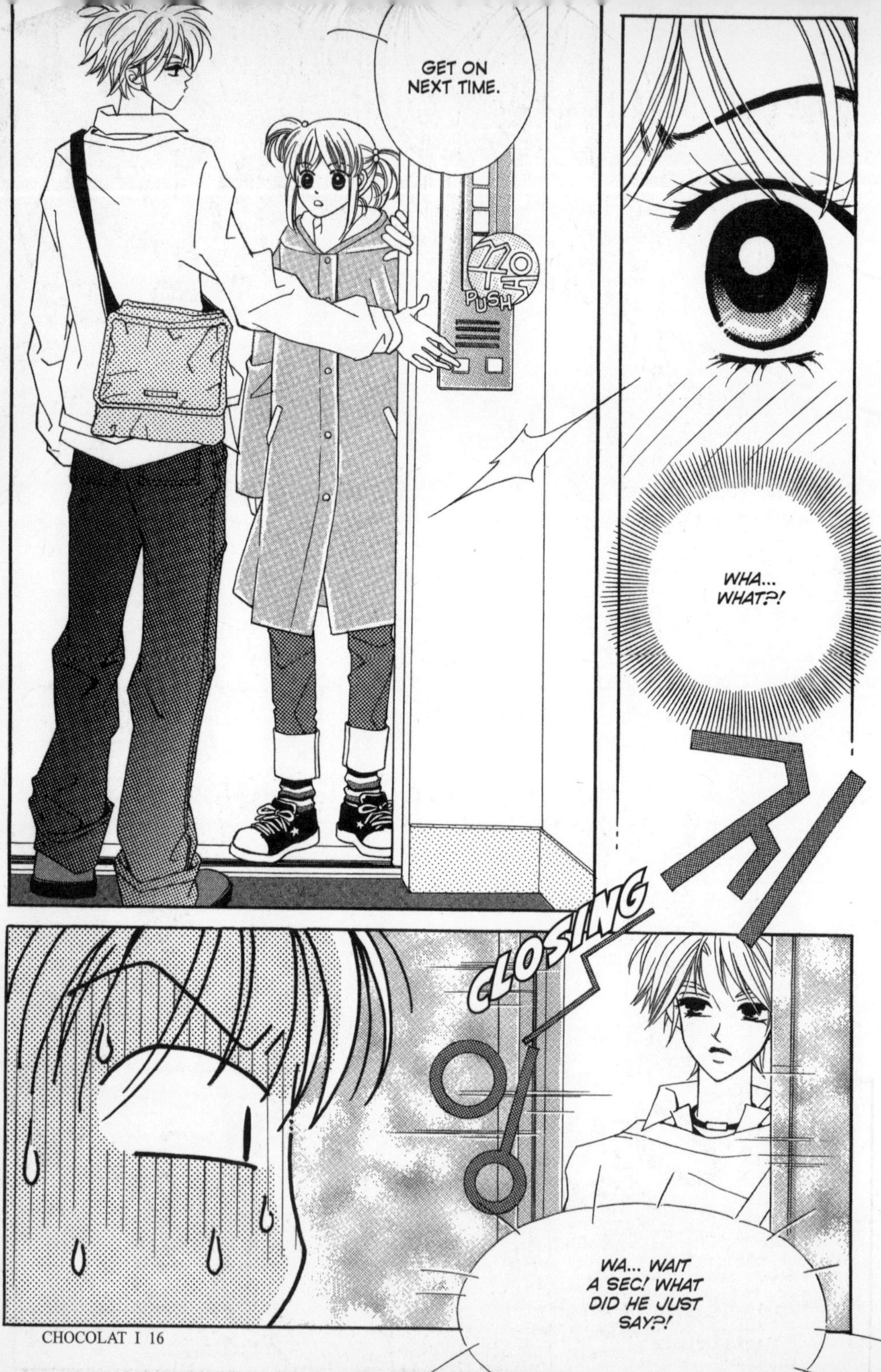
GET ON
NEXT TIME.
PUSH
WHA...
WHAT?!
CLOSING
WA... WAIT
A SEC! WHAT
DID HE JUST
SAY?!

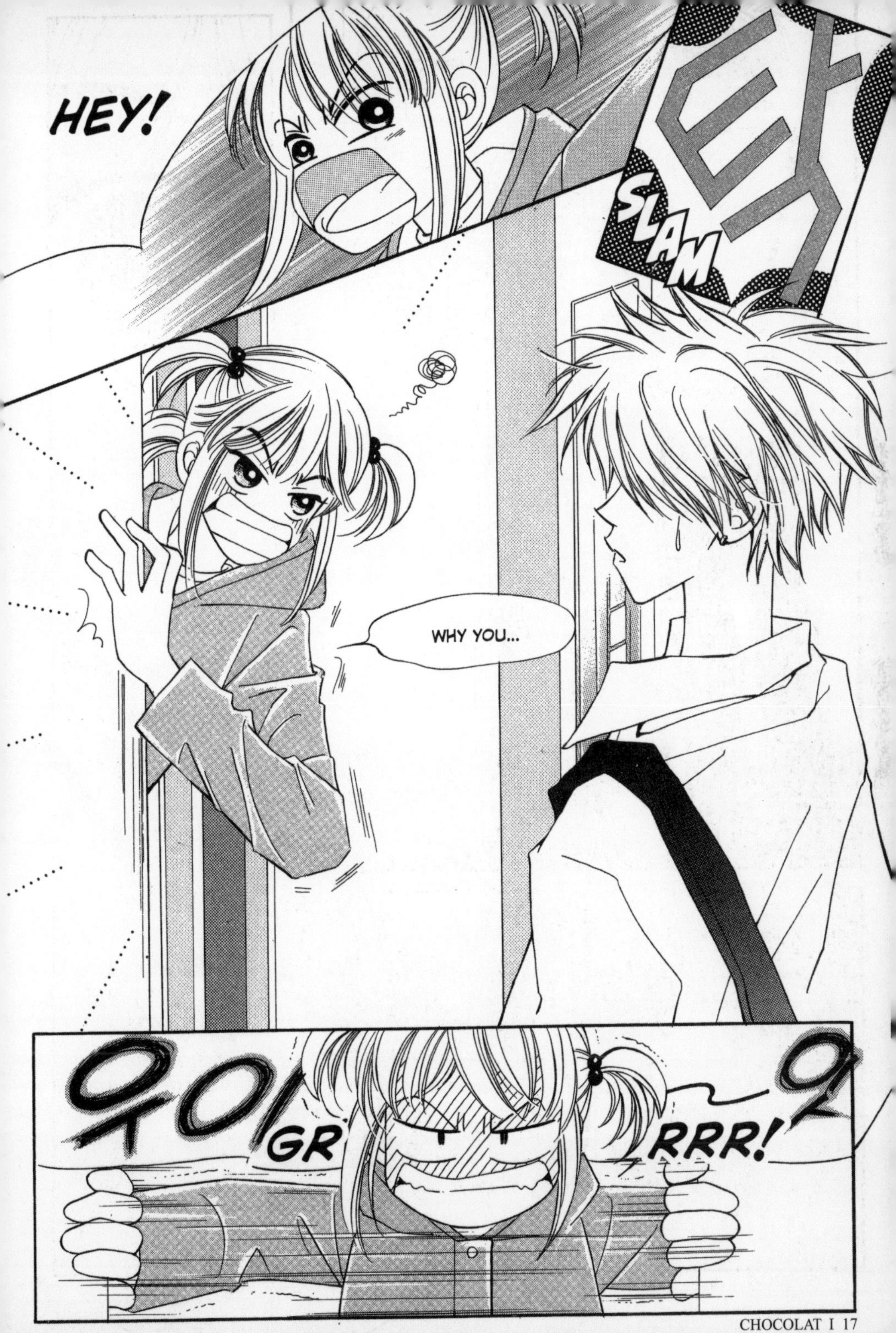
HEY!
SLAM
WHY YOU...
GR
RRR!

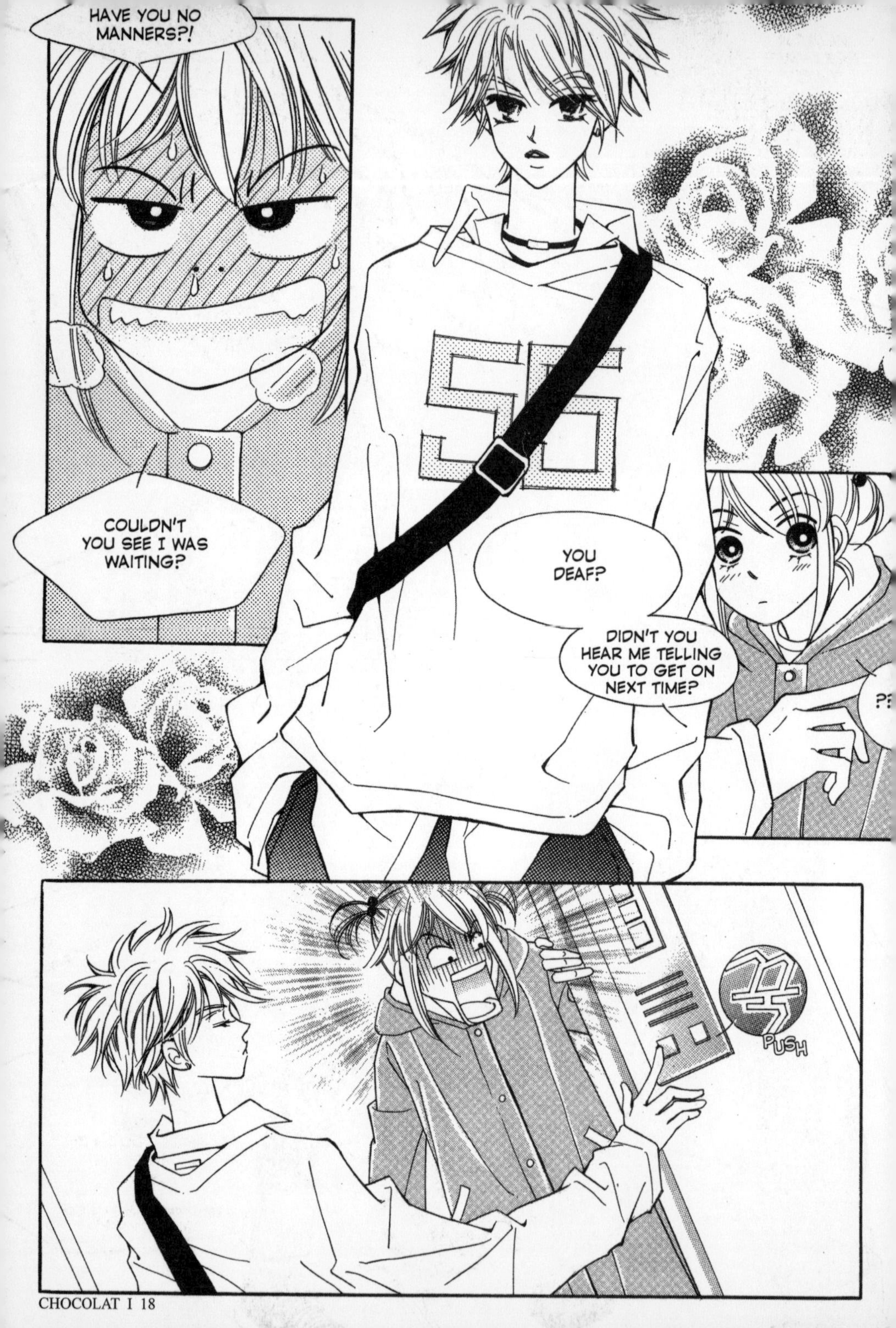
HAVE YOU NO MANNERS?!
COULDN'T YOU SEE I WAS WAITING?
YOU DEAF?
DIDN'T YOU HEAR ME TELLING YOU TO GET ON NEXT TIME?
?!
PUSH

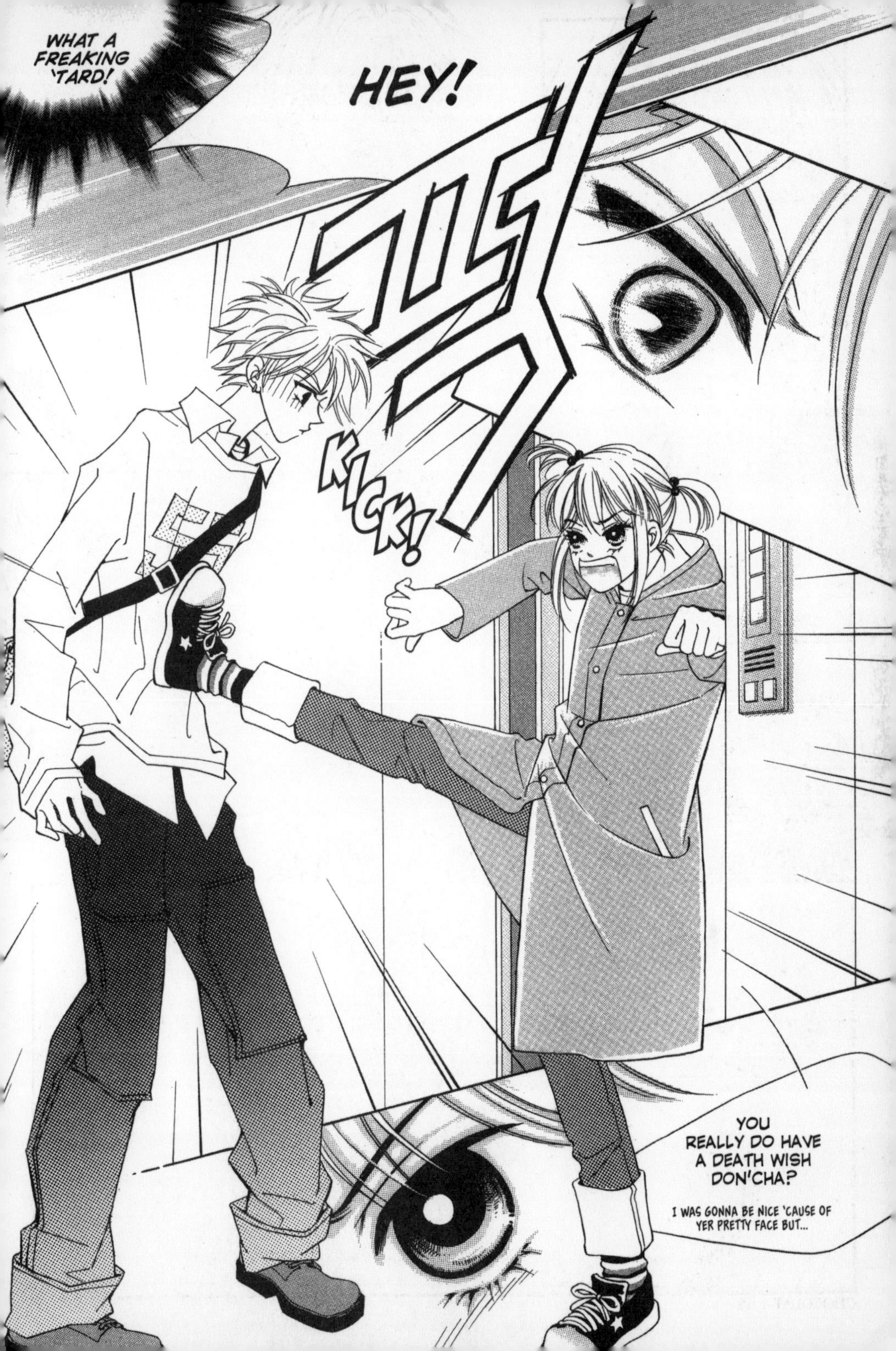
WHAT A FREAKING 'TARD!
HEY!
KICK!
YOU REALLY DO HAVE A DEATH WISH DON'CHA?
I WAS GONNA BE NICE 'CAUSE OF YER PRETTY FACE BUT...

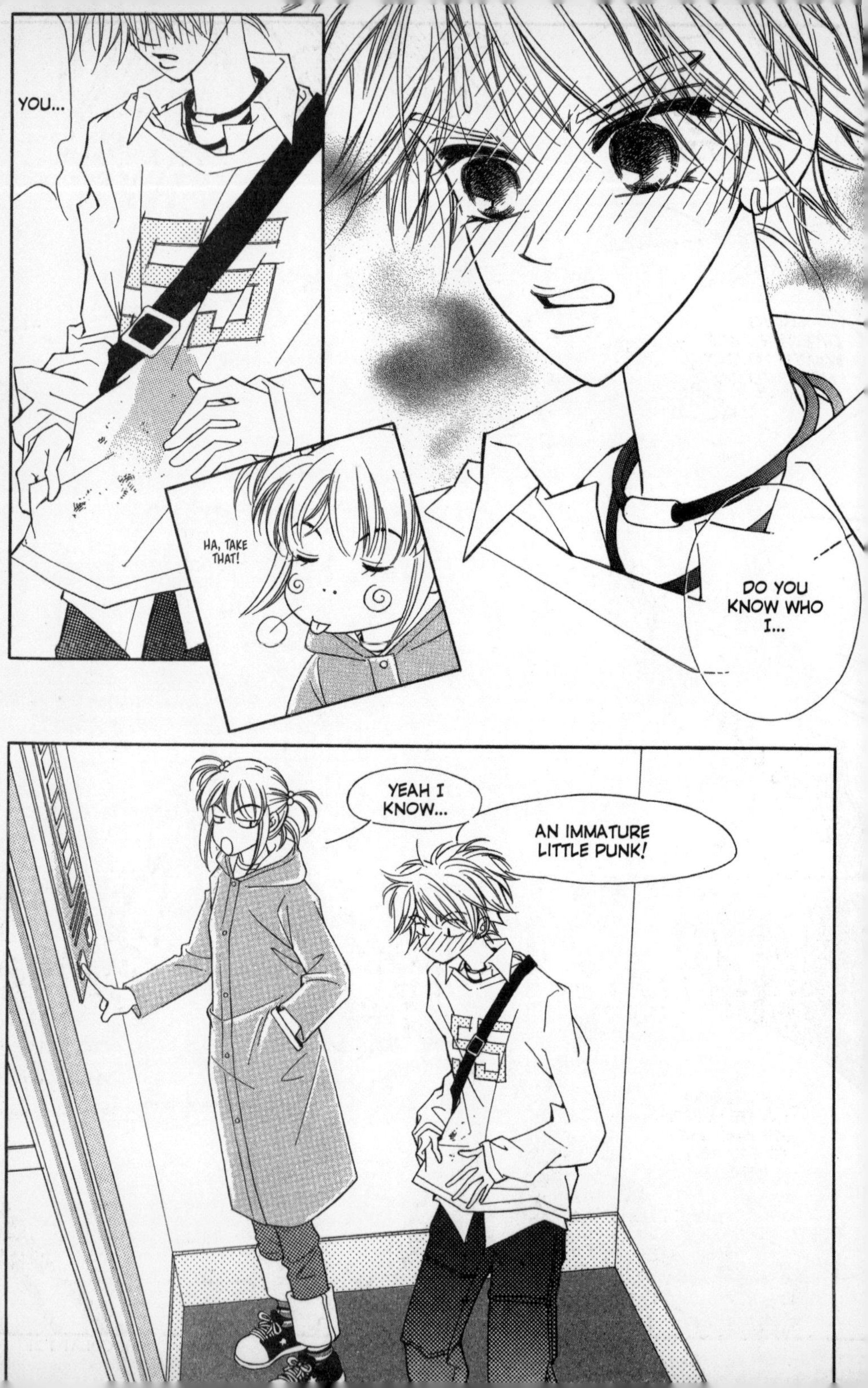

YOU...
HA, TAKE THAT!
DO YOU KNOW WHO I...
YEAH I KNOW...
AN IMMATURE LITTLE PUNK!

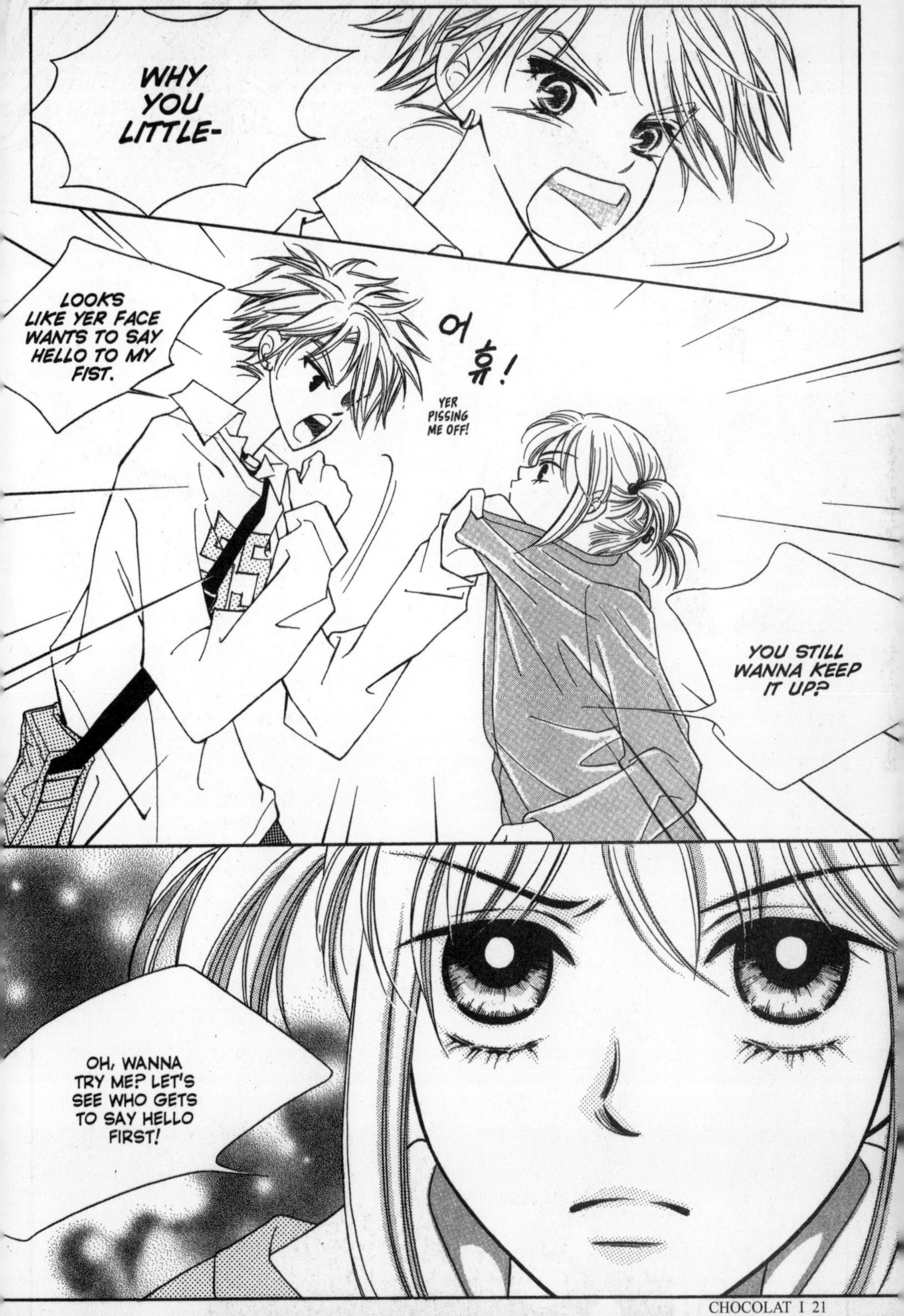
WHY YOU LITTLE-
LOOKS LIKE YER FACE WANTS TO SAY HELLO TO MY FIST.
어휴!
YER PISSING ME OFF!
YOU STILL WANNA KEEP IT UP?
OH, WANNA TRY ME? LET'S SEE WHO GETS TO SAY HELLO FIRST!

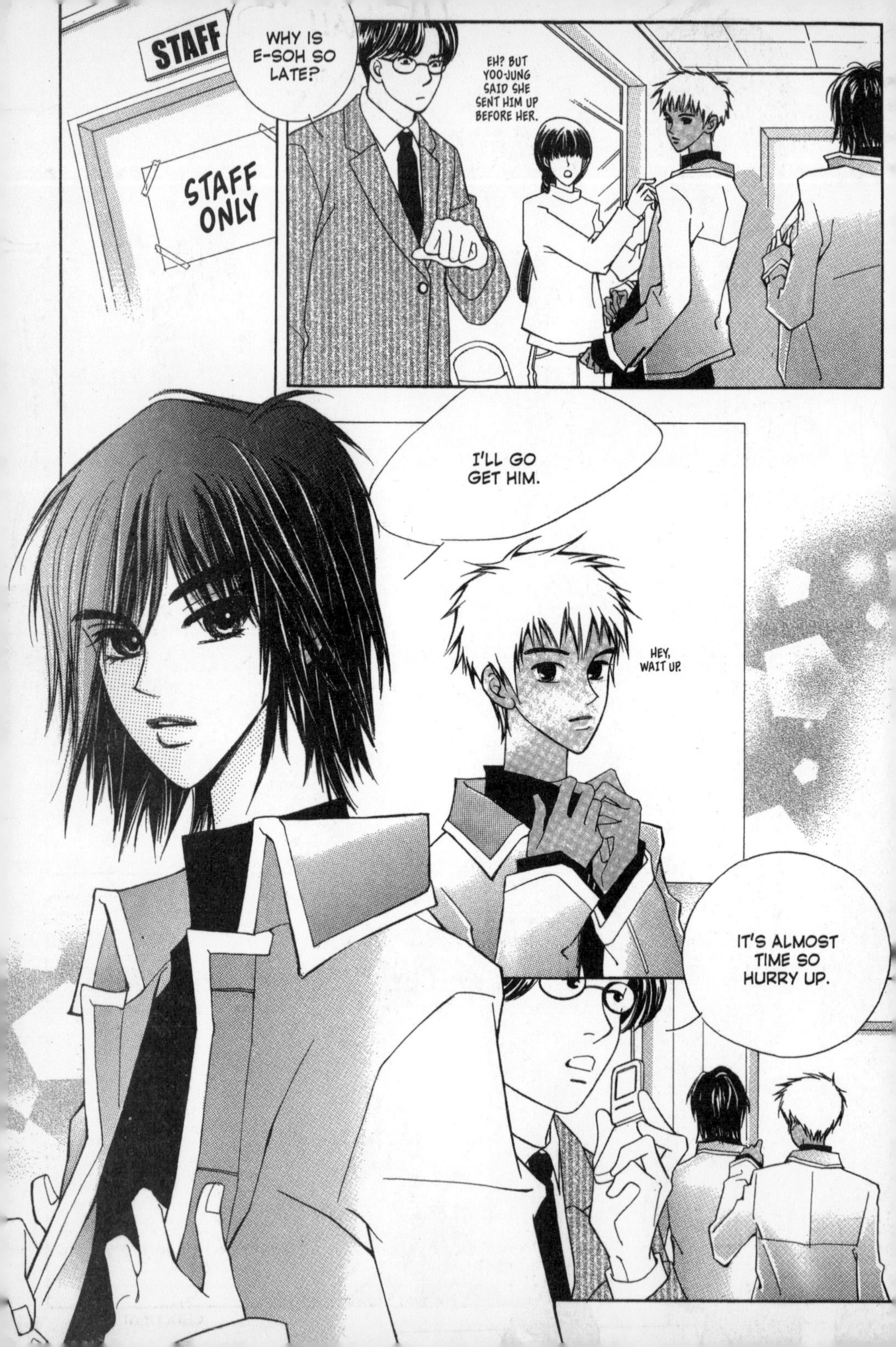
STAFF
STAFF ONLY
WHY IS E-SOH SO LATE?
EH? BUT YOO-JUNG SAID SHE SENT HIM UP BEFORE HER.
I'LL GO GET HIM.
HEY, WAIT UP.
IT'S ALMOST TIME SO HURRY UP.

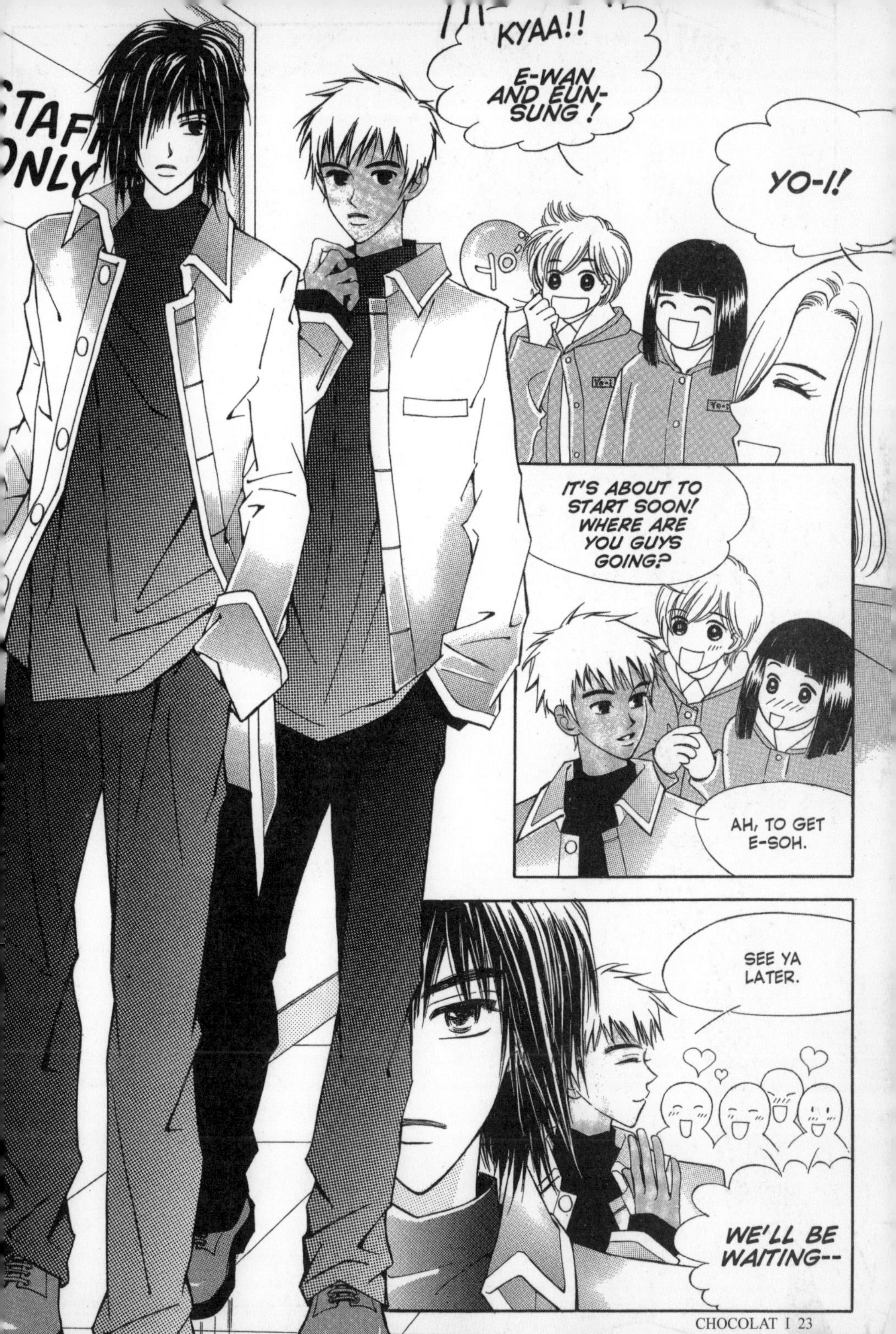
ONLY
KYAA!! E-WAN AND EUN-SUNG !
YO-I!
IT'S ABOUT TO START SOON! WHERE ARE YOU GUYS GOING?
AH, TO GET E-SOH.
SEE YA LATER.
WE'LL BE WAITING--

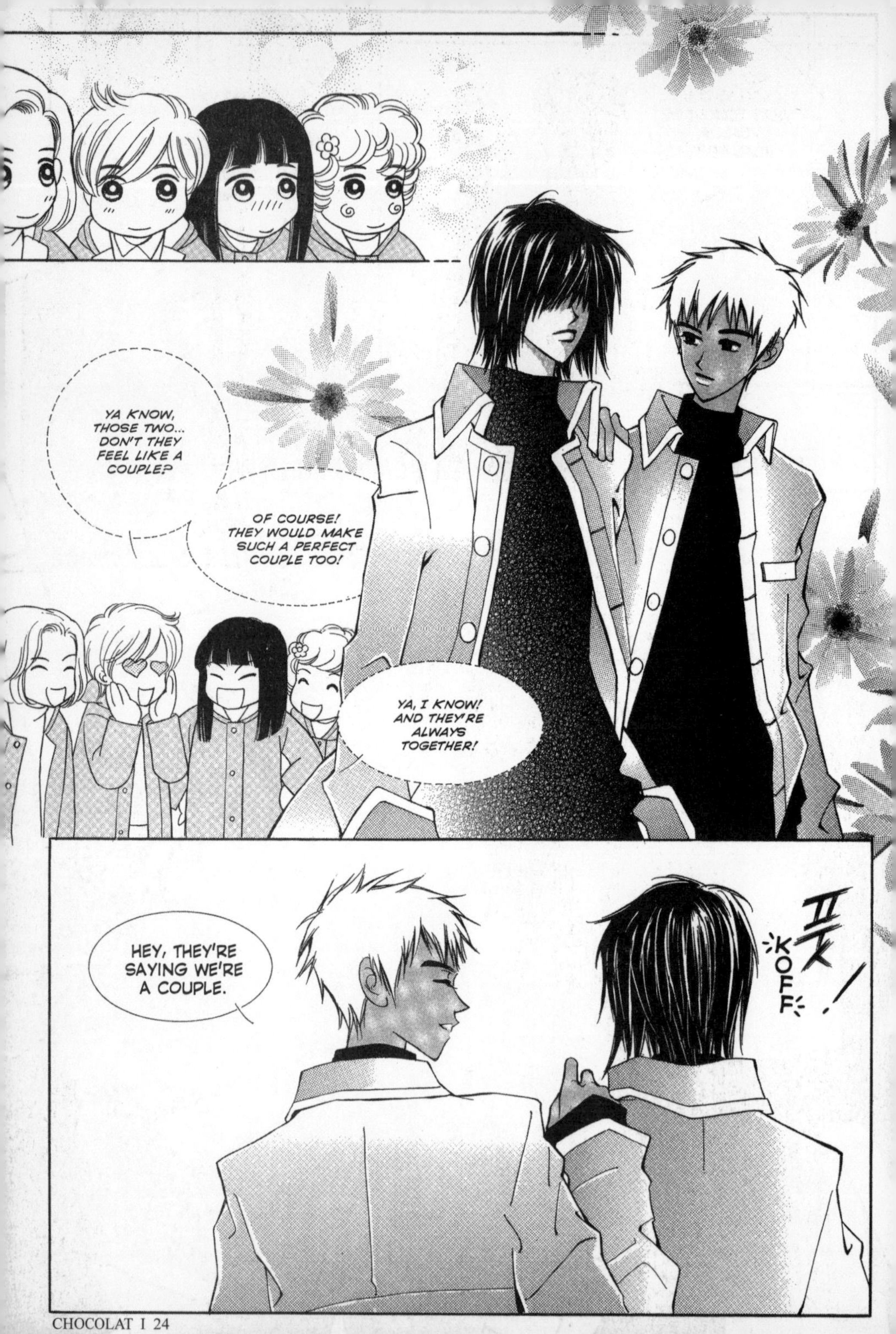
YA KNOW, THOSE TWO... DON'T THEY FEEL LIKE A COUPLE?
OF COURSE! THEY WOULD MAKE SUCH A PERFECT COUPLE TOO!
YA, I KNOW! AND THEY'RE ALWAYS TOGETHER!
HEY, THEY'RE SAYING WE'RE A COUPLE.
KOFF
!

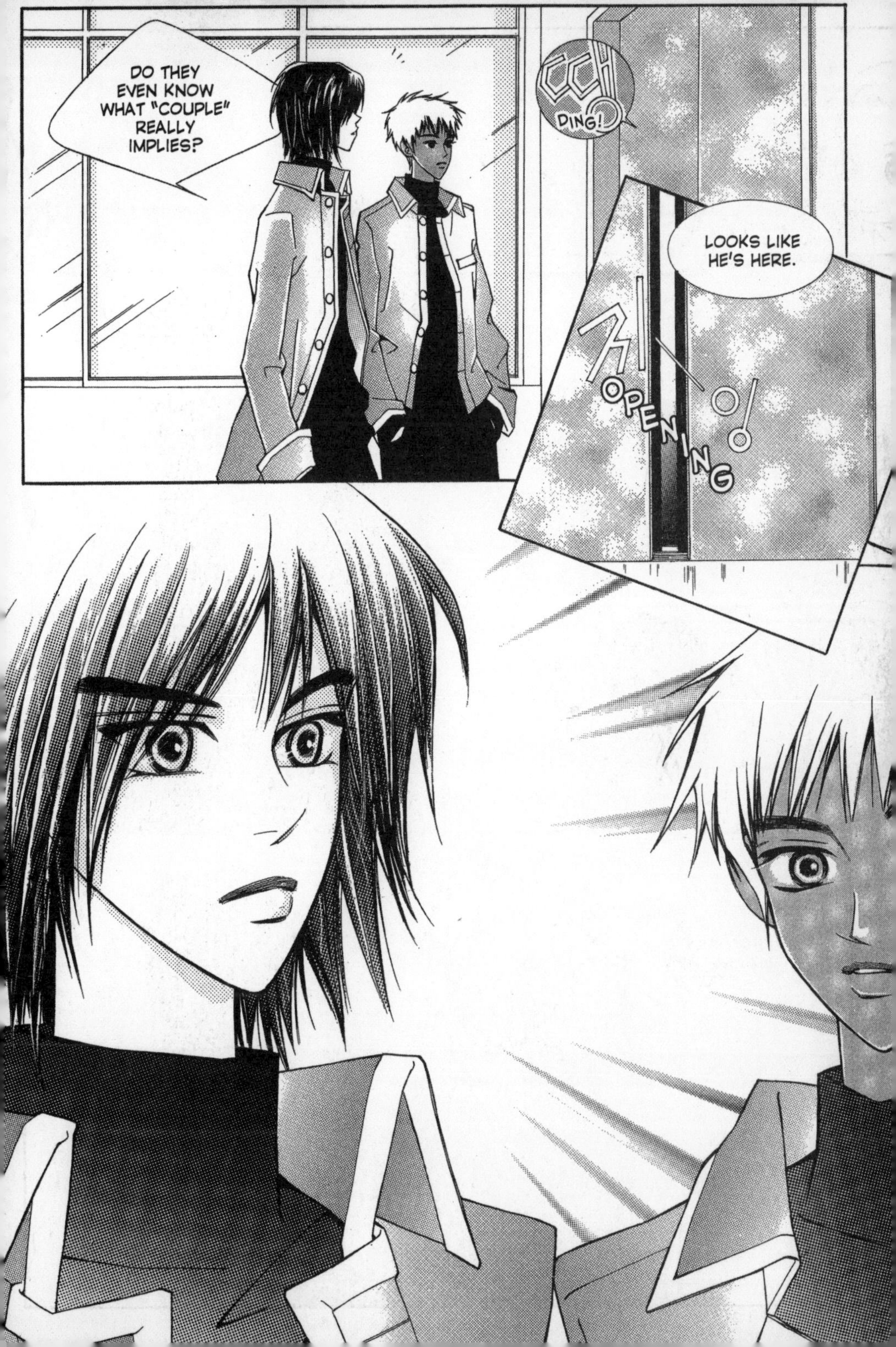
DO THEY EVEN KNOW WHAT "COUPLE" REALLY IMPLIES?
DING!
LOOKS LIKE HE'S HERE.
OPENING

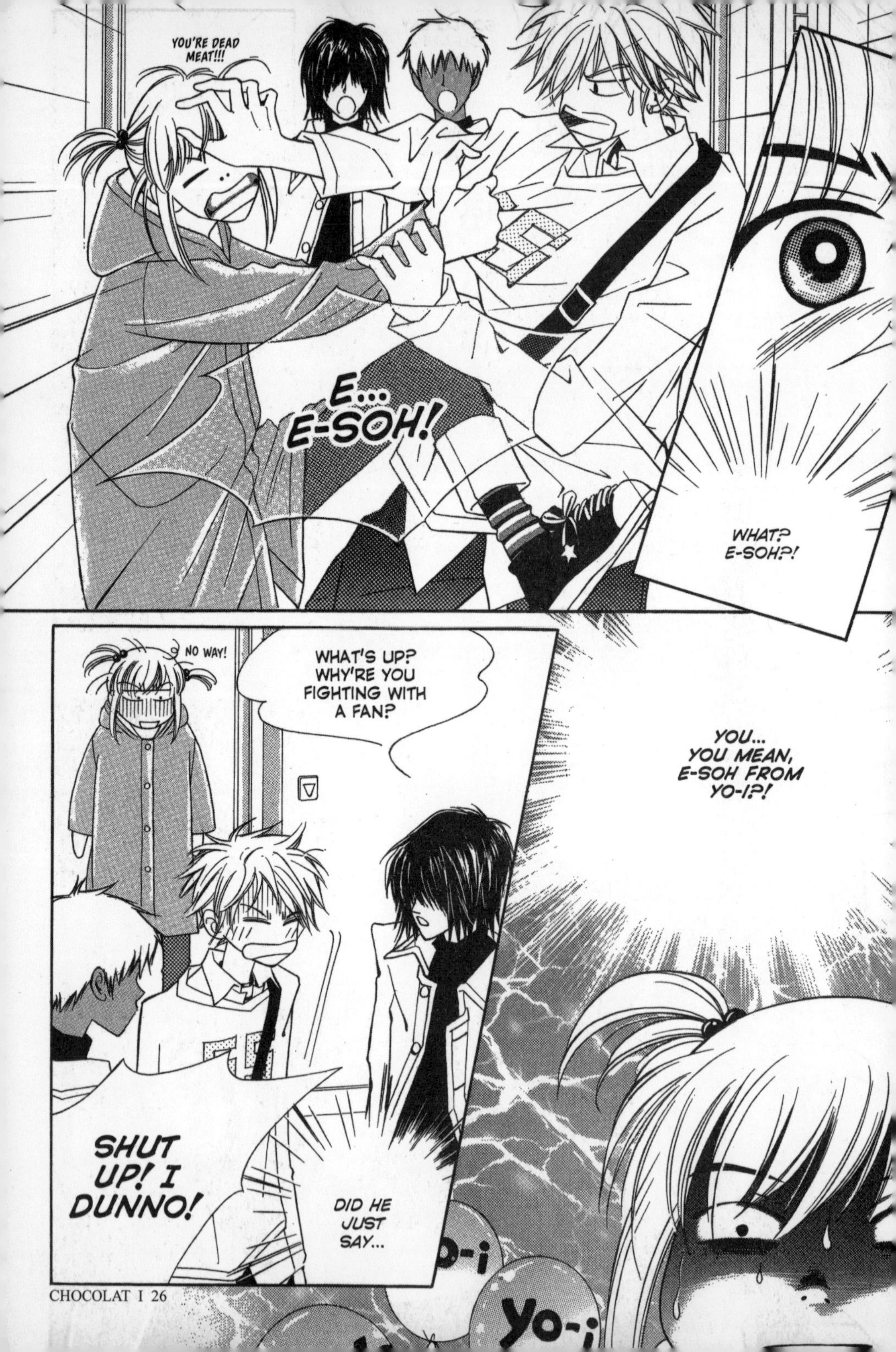
YOU'RE DEAD MEAT!!!
E... E-SOH!
WHAT? E-SOH?!
NO WAY!
WHAT'S UP? WHY'RE YOU FIGHTING WITH A FAN?
SHUT UP! I DUNNO!
DID HE JUST SAY...
YOU... YOU MEAN, E-SOH FROM YO-I?!
yo-i

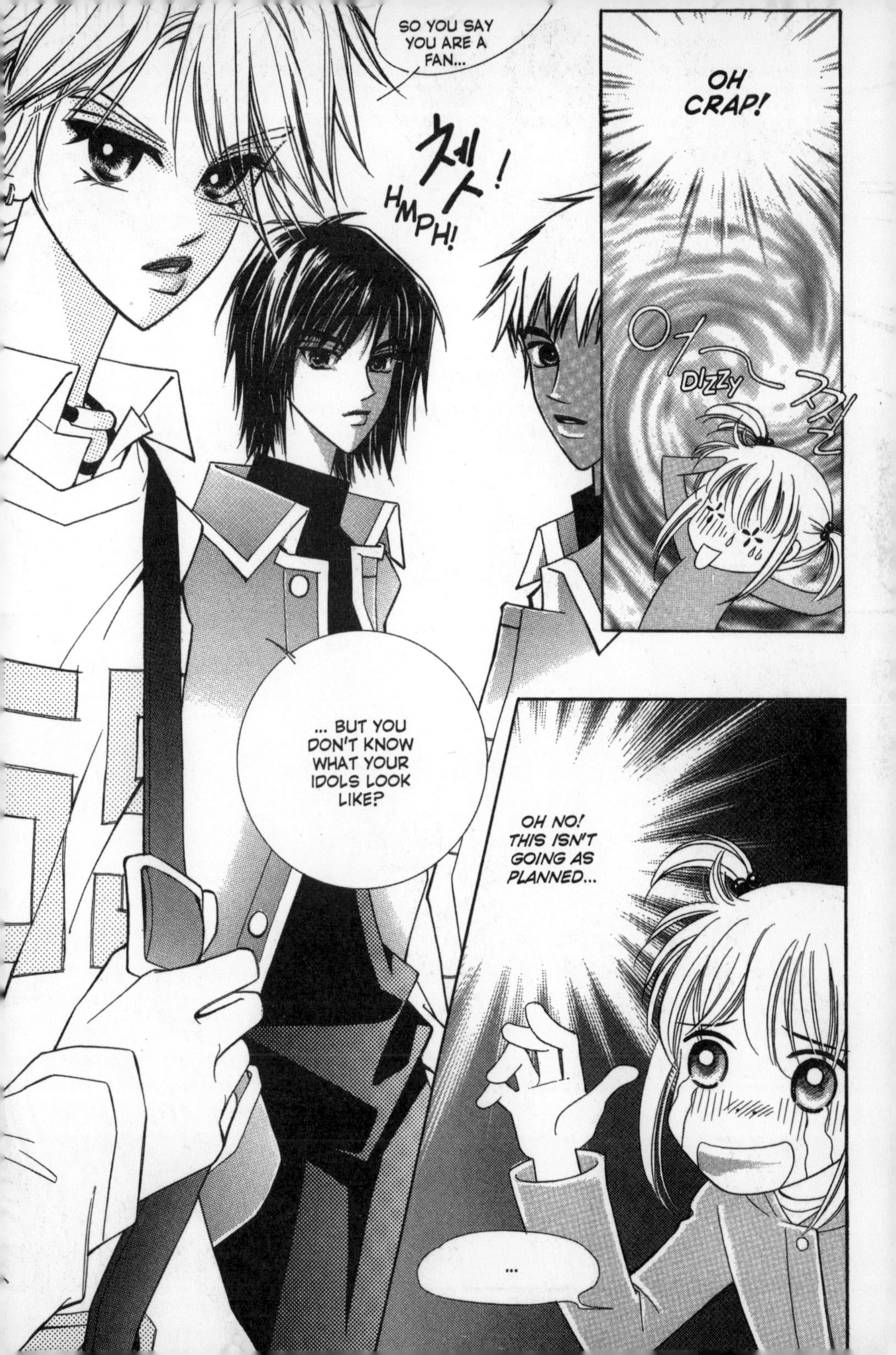
SO YOU SAY YOU ARE A FAN...
췟!
HMPH!
... BUT YOU DON'T KNOW WHAT YOUR IDOLS LOOK LIKE?
OH CRAP!
DIZZY
OH NO! THIS ISN'T GOING AS PLANNED...
...

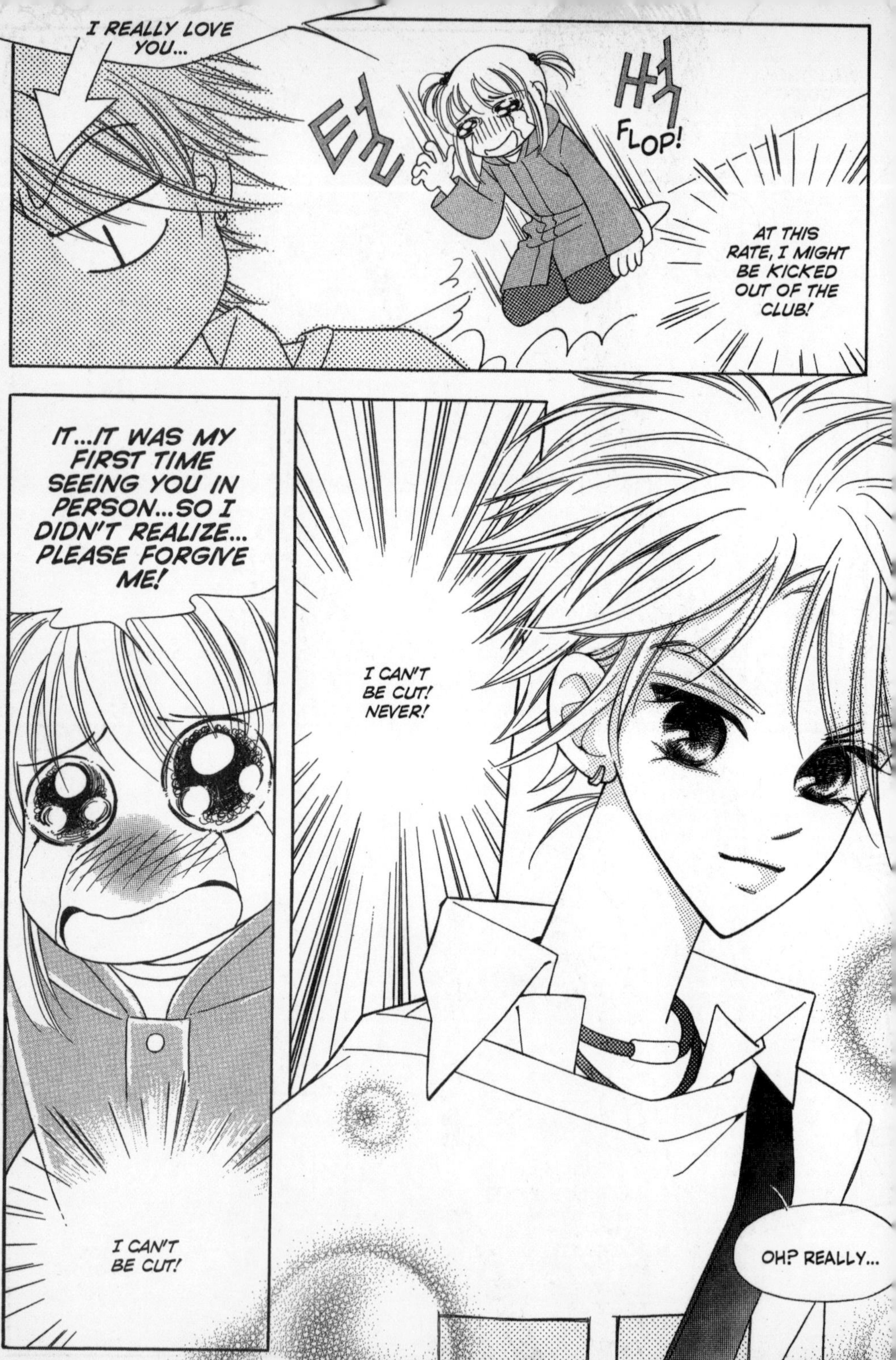
I REALLY LOVE YOU...
털
썩
FLOP!
AT THIS RATE, I MIGHT BE KICKED OUT OF THE CLUB!
IT...IT WAS MY FIRST TIME SEEING YOU IN PERSON...SO I DIDN'T REALIZE... PLEASE FORGIVE ME!
I CAN'T BE CUT!
I CAN'T BE CUT! NEVER!
OH? REALLY...

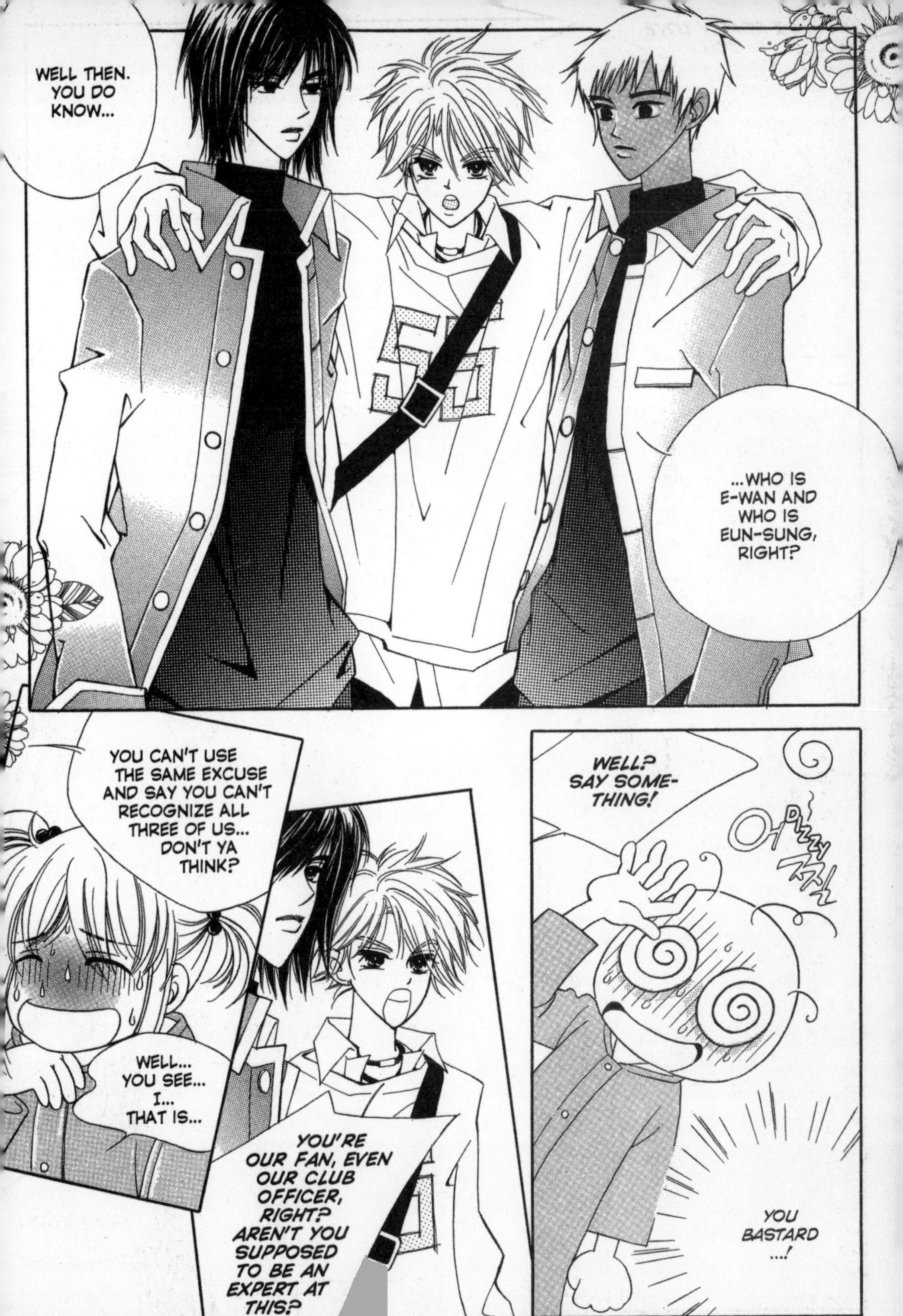
WELL THEN. YOU DO KNOW...
...WHO IS E-WAN AND WHO IS EUN-SUNG, RIGHT?
YOU CAN'T USE THE SAME EXCUSE AND SAY YOU CAN'T RECOGNIZE ALL THREE OF US... DON'T YA THINK?
WELL... YOU SEE... I... THAT IS...
YOU'RE OUR FAN, EVEN OUR CLUB OFFICER, RIGHT? AREN'T YOU SUPPOSED TO BE AN EXPERT AT THIS?
WELL? SAY SOME-THING!
DIZZY
YOU BASTARD ...!

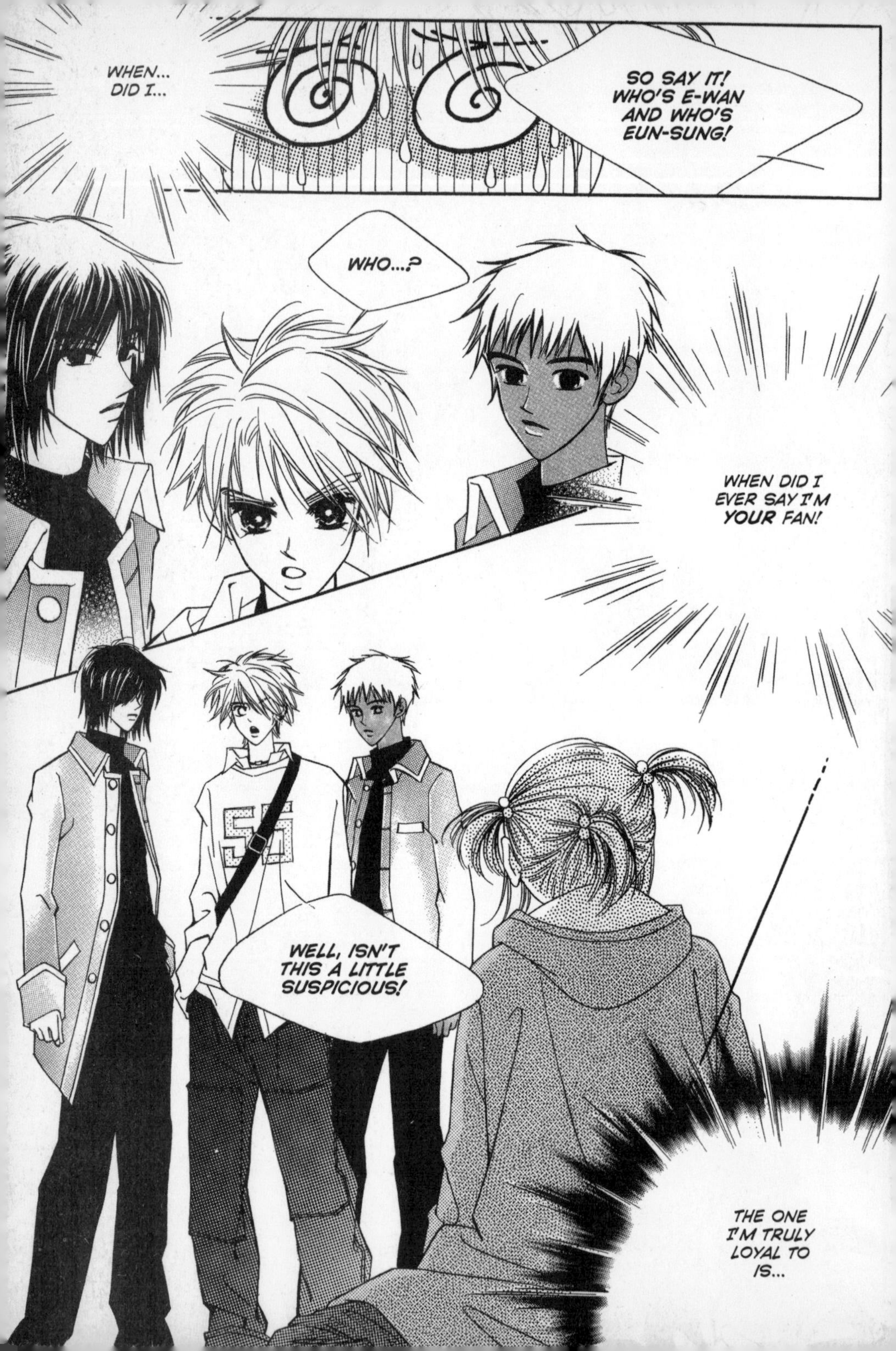
WHEN... DID I...
SO SAY IT! WHO'S E-WAN AND WHO'S EUN-SUNG!
WHO...?
WHEN DID I EVER SAY I'M YOUR FAN!
WELL, ISN'T THIS A LITTLE SUSPICIOUS!
THE ONE I'M TRULY LOYAL TO IS...

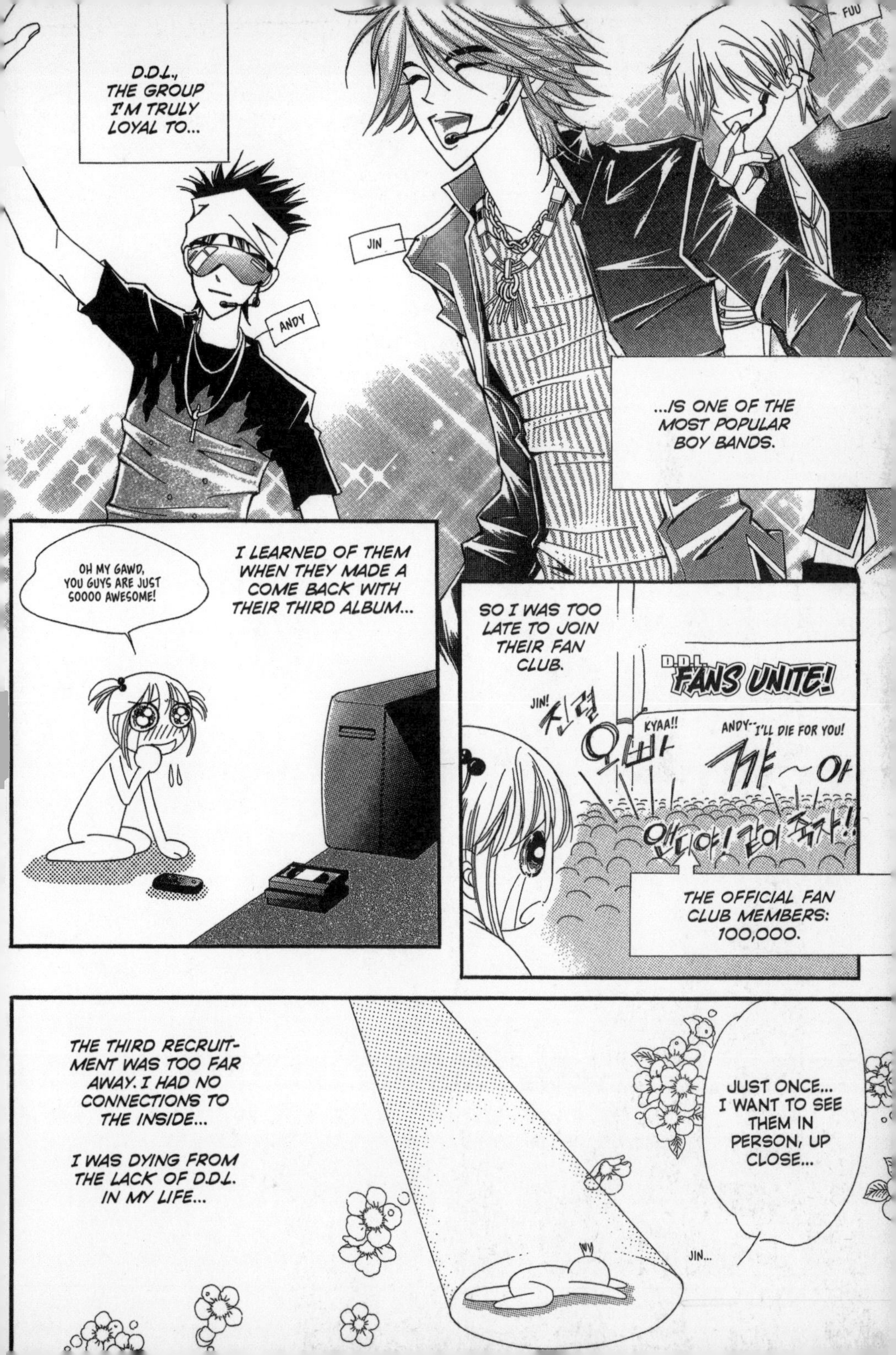

D.D.L., THE GROUP I'M TRULY LOYAL TO...
FUU
JIN
ANDY
...IS ONE OF THE MOST POPULAR BOY BANDS.
OH MY GAWD, YOU GUYS ARE JUST SOOOO AWESOME!
I LEARNED OF THEM WHEN THEY MADE A COME BACK WITH THEIR THIRD ALBUM...
SO I WAS TOO LATE TO JOIN THEIR FAN CLUB.
D.D.L. FANS UNITE!
JIN!
오빠
KYAA!!
ANDY-- I'LL DIE FOR YOU!
꺄~아
앤디야! 같이 죽자!!
THE OFFICIAL FAN CLUB MEMBERS: 100,000.
THE THIRD RECRUIT-MENT WAS TOO FAR AWAY. I HAD NO CONNECTIONS TO THE INSIDE...
I WAS DYING FROM THE LACK OF D.D.L. IN MY LIFE...
JUST ONCE... I WANT TO SEE THEM IN PERSON, UP CLOSE...
JIN...

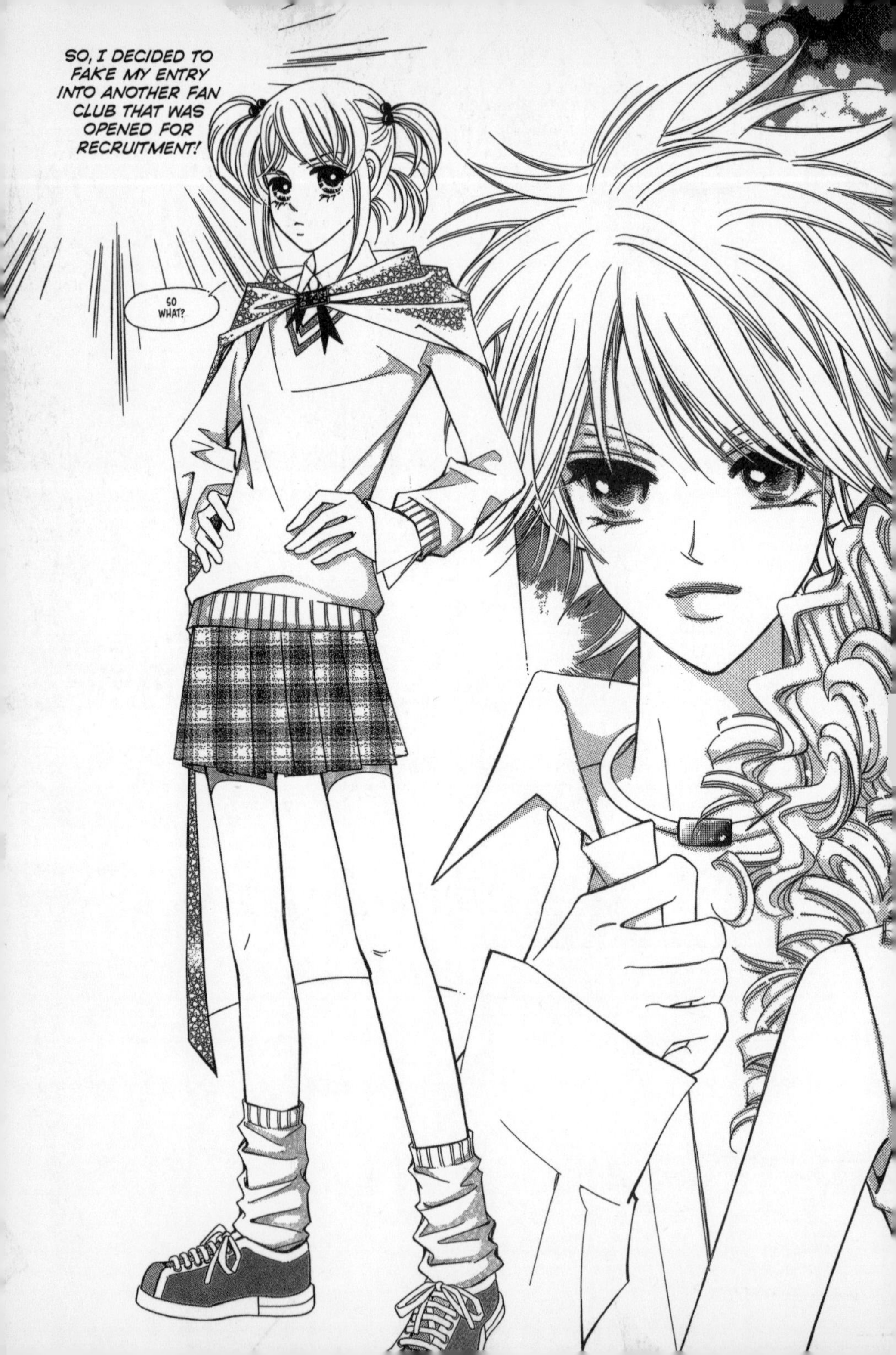
SO, I DECIDED TO FAKE MY ENTRY INTO ANOTHER FAN CLUB THAT WAS OPENED FOR RECRUITMENT!
SO WHAT?

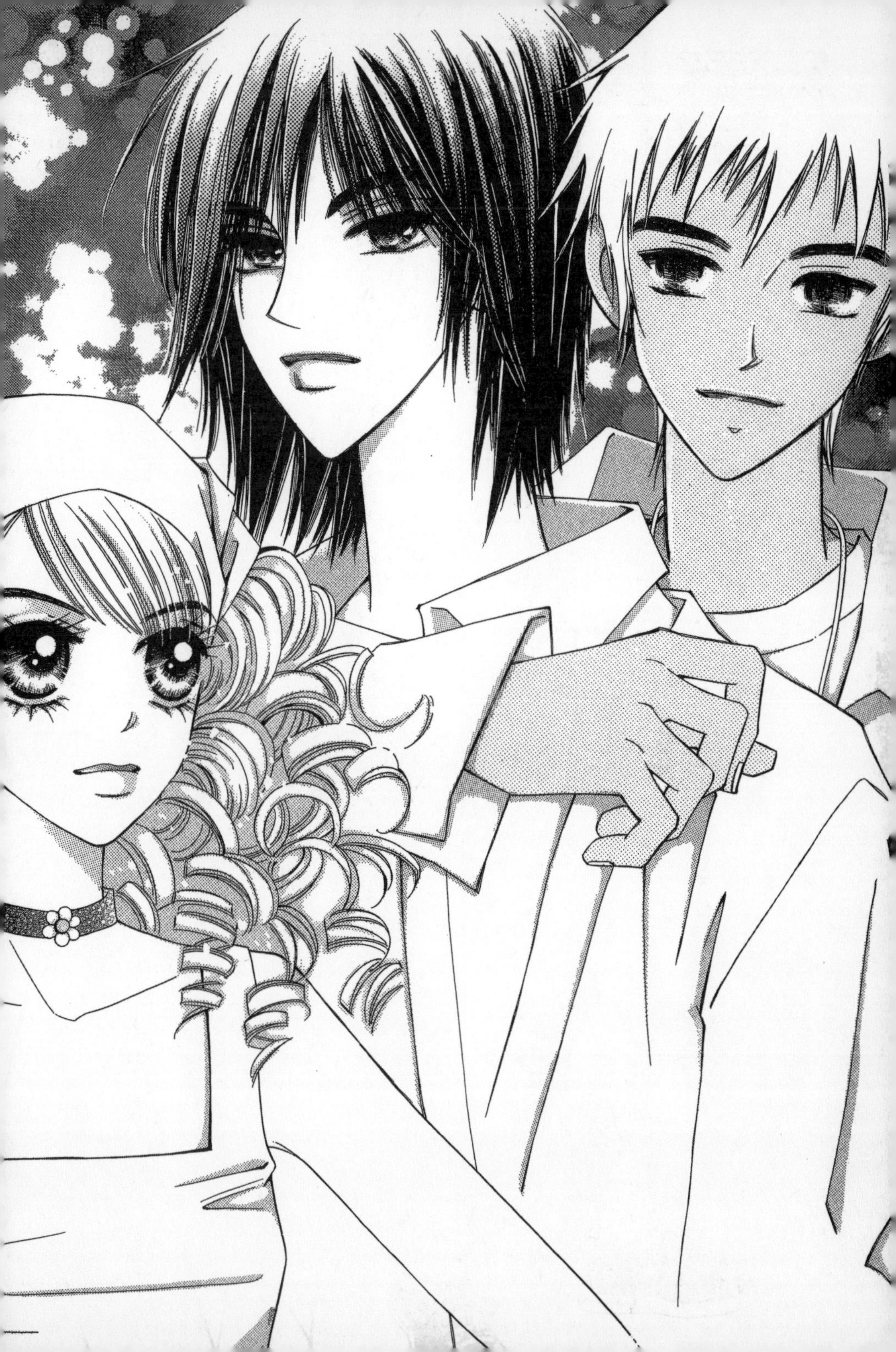

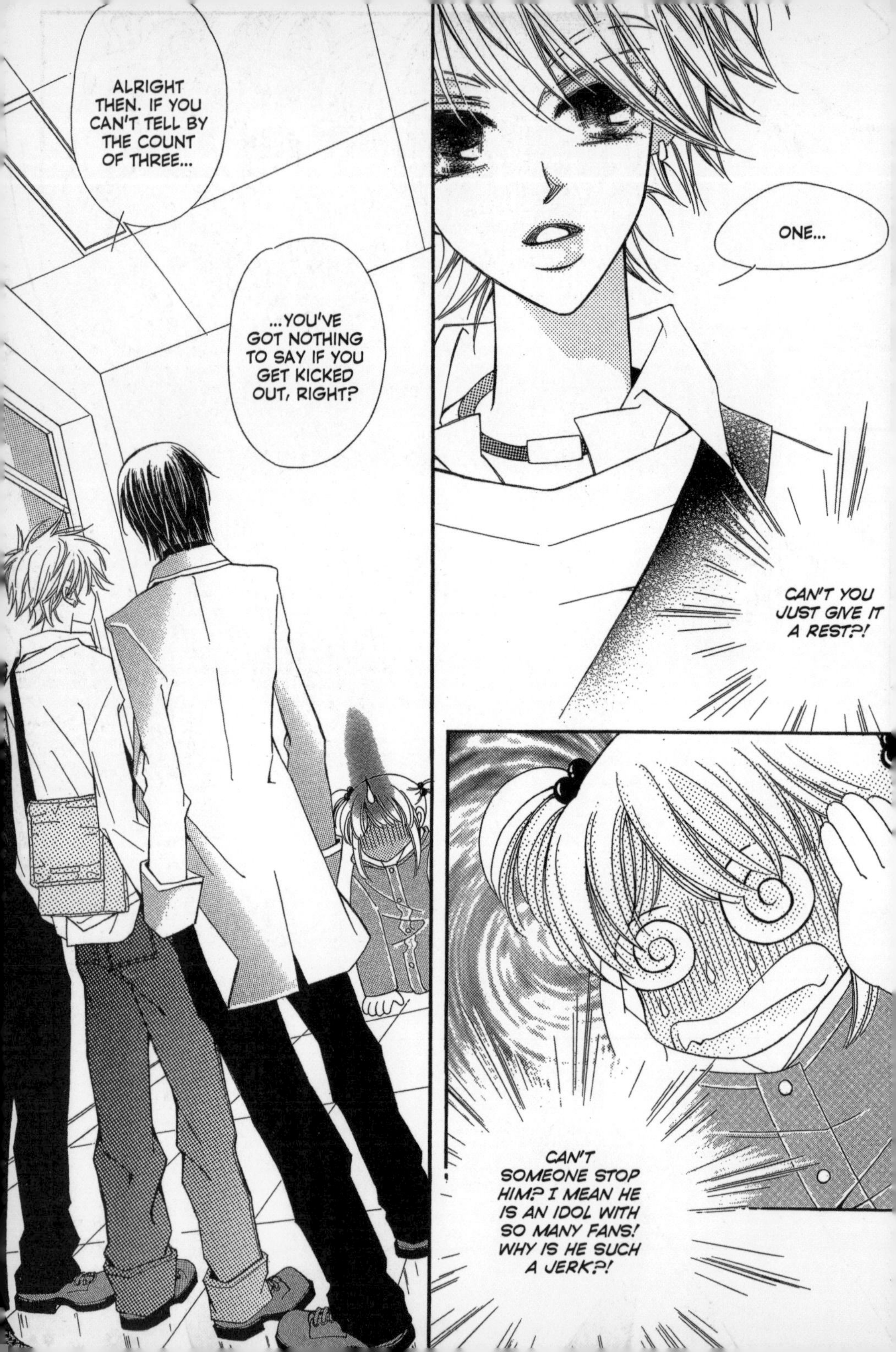
ALRIGHT THEN. IF YOU CAN'T TELL BY THE COUNT OF THREE...
...YOU'VE GOT NOTHING TO SAY IF YOU GET KICKED OUT, RIGHT?
ONE...
CAN'T YOU JUST GIVE IT A REST?!
CAN'T SOMEONE STOP HIM? I MEAN HE IS AN IDOL WITH SO MANY FANS! WHY IS HE SUCH A JERK?!

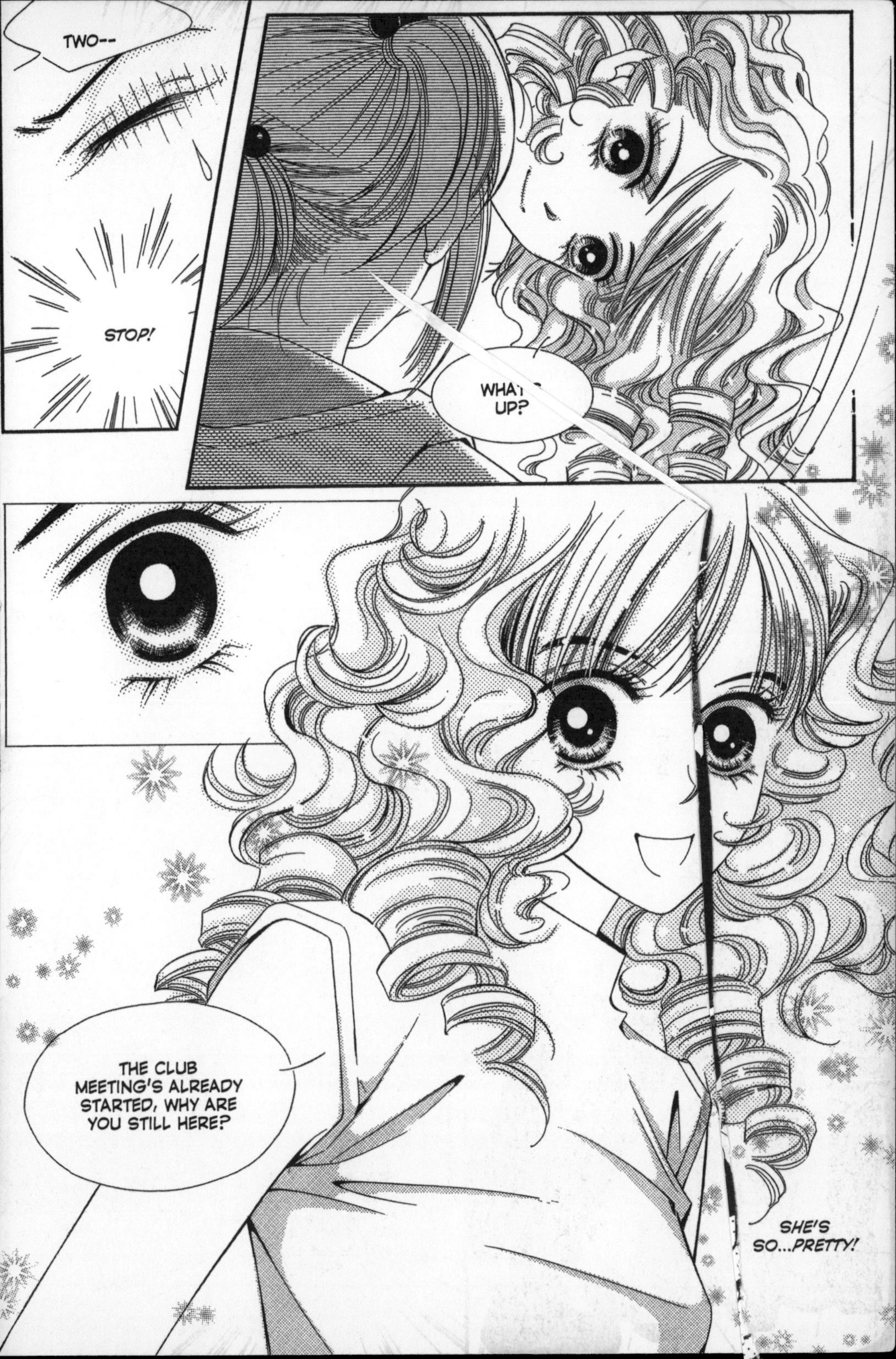
TWO--
STOP!
WHAT'S UP?
THE CLUB MEETING'S ALREADY STARTED, WHY ARE YOU STILL HERE?
SHE'S SO...PRETTY!

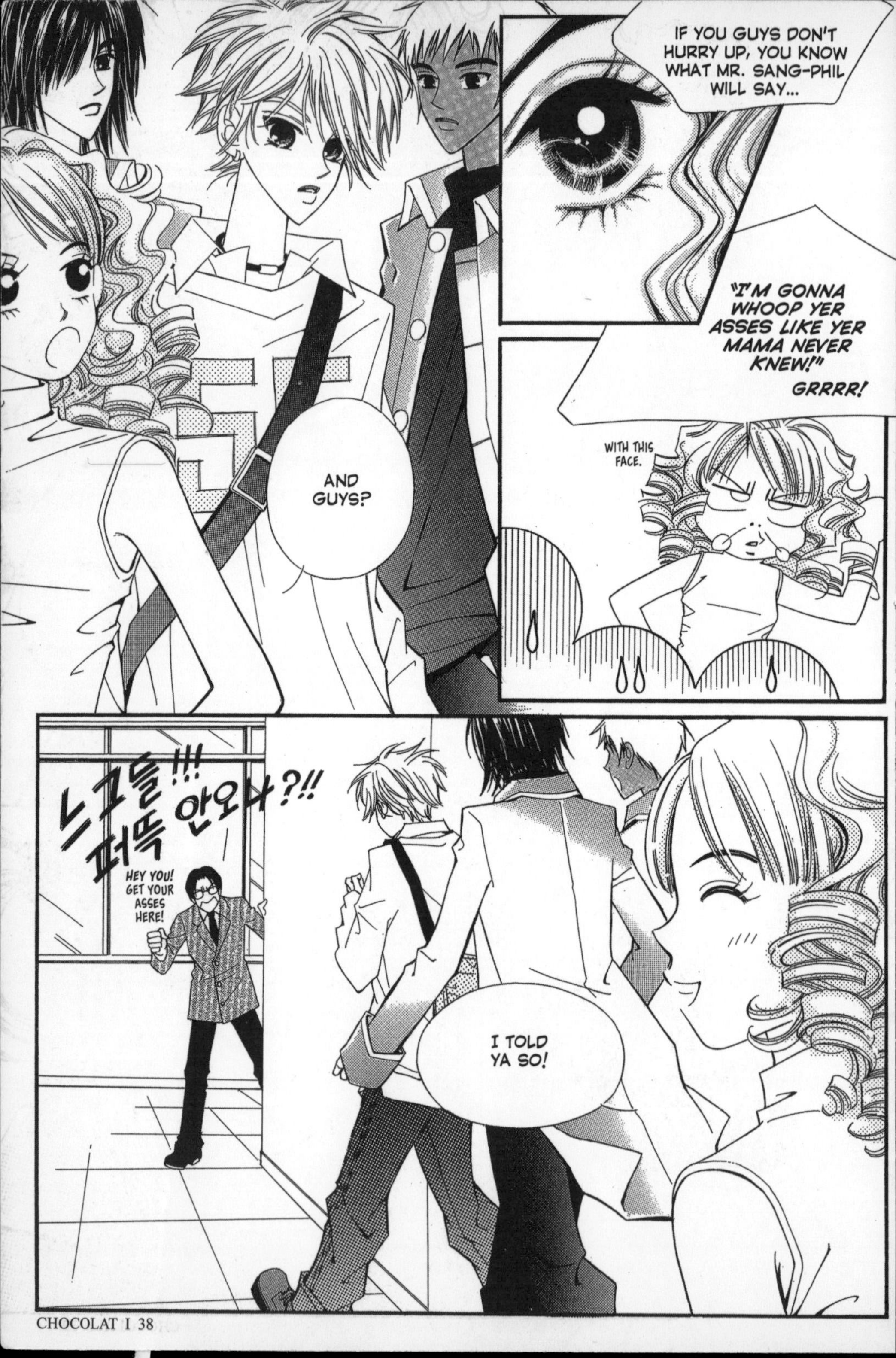
AND GUYS?
IF YOU GUYS DON'T HURRY UP, YOU KNOW WHAT MR. SANG-PHIL WILL SAY...
"I'M GONNA WHOOP YER ASSES LIKE YER MAMA NEVER KNEW!"
GRRRR!
WITH THIS FACE.
느그들!!! 퍼뜩 안오나?!!
HEY YOU! GET YOUR ASSES HERE!
I TOLD YA SO!

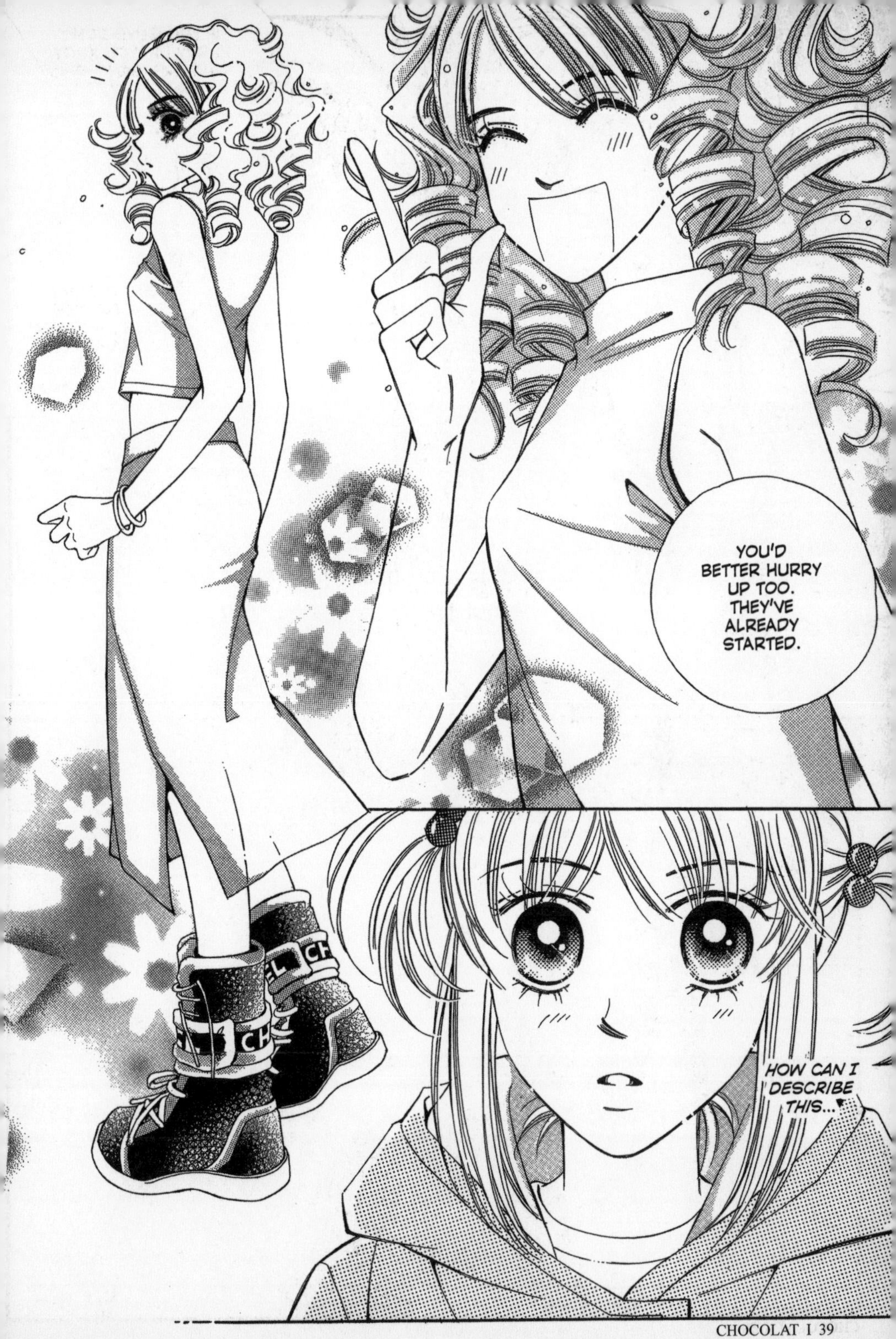
YOU'D BETTER HURRY UP TOO. THEY'VE ALREADY STARTED.
HOW CAN I DESCRIBE THIS...

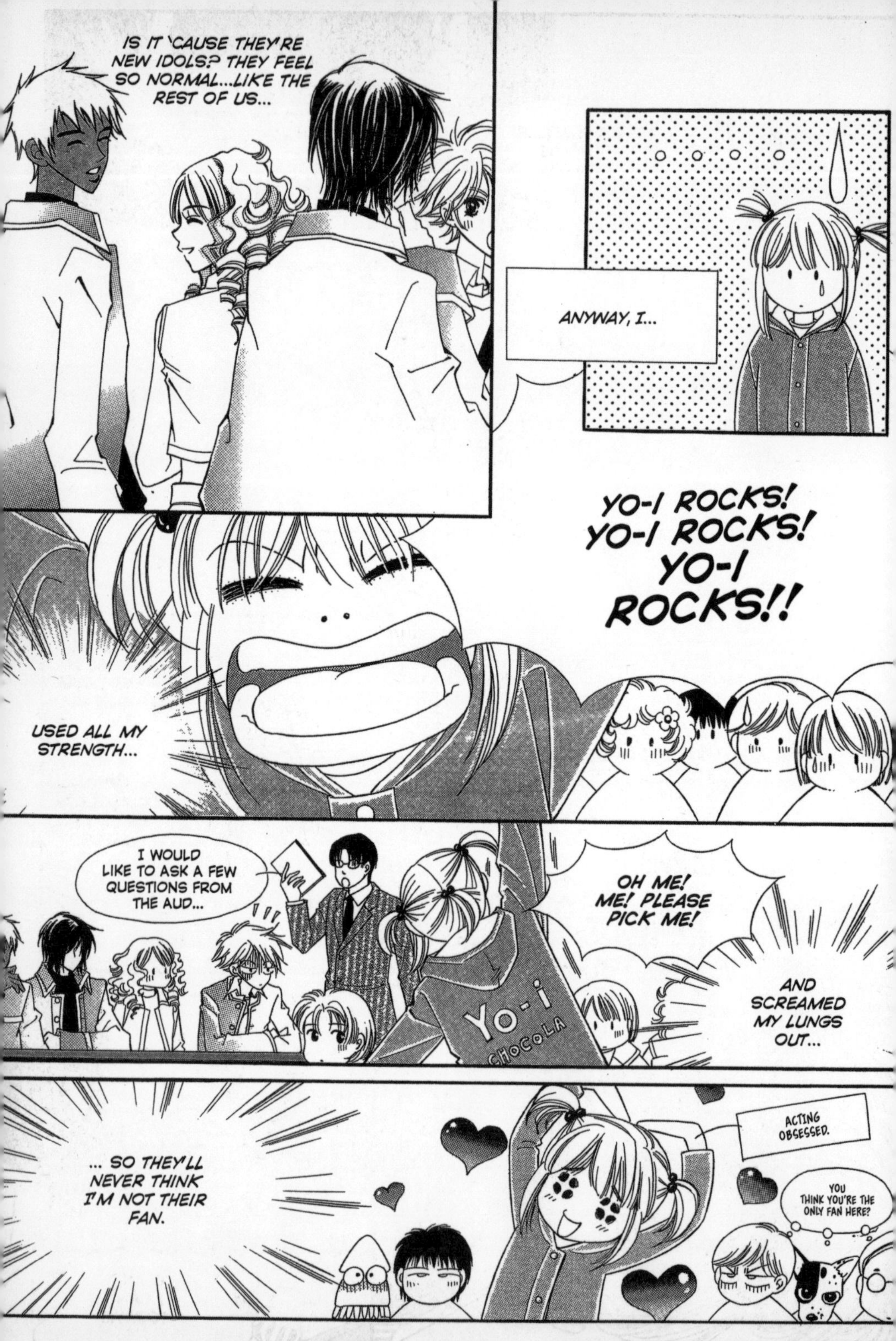
IS IT 'CAUSE THEY'RE NEW IDOLS? THEY FEEL SO NORMAL...LIKE THE REST OF US...
ANYWAY, I...
YO-I ROCKS! YO-I ROCKS! YO-I ROCKS!!
USED ALL MY STRENGTH...
I WOULD LIKE TO ASK A FEW QUESTIONS FROM THE AUD...
OH ME! ME! PLEASE PICK ME!
YO-i CHOCOLA
AND SCREAMED MY LUNGS OUT...
... SO THEY'LL NEVER THINK I'M NOT THEIR FAN.
ACTING OBSESSED.
YOU THINK YOU'RE THE ONLY FAN HERE?

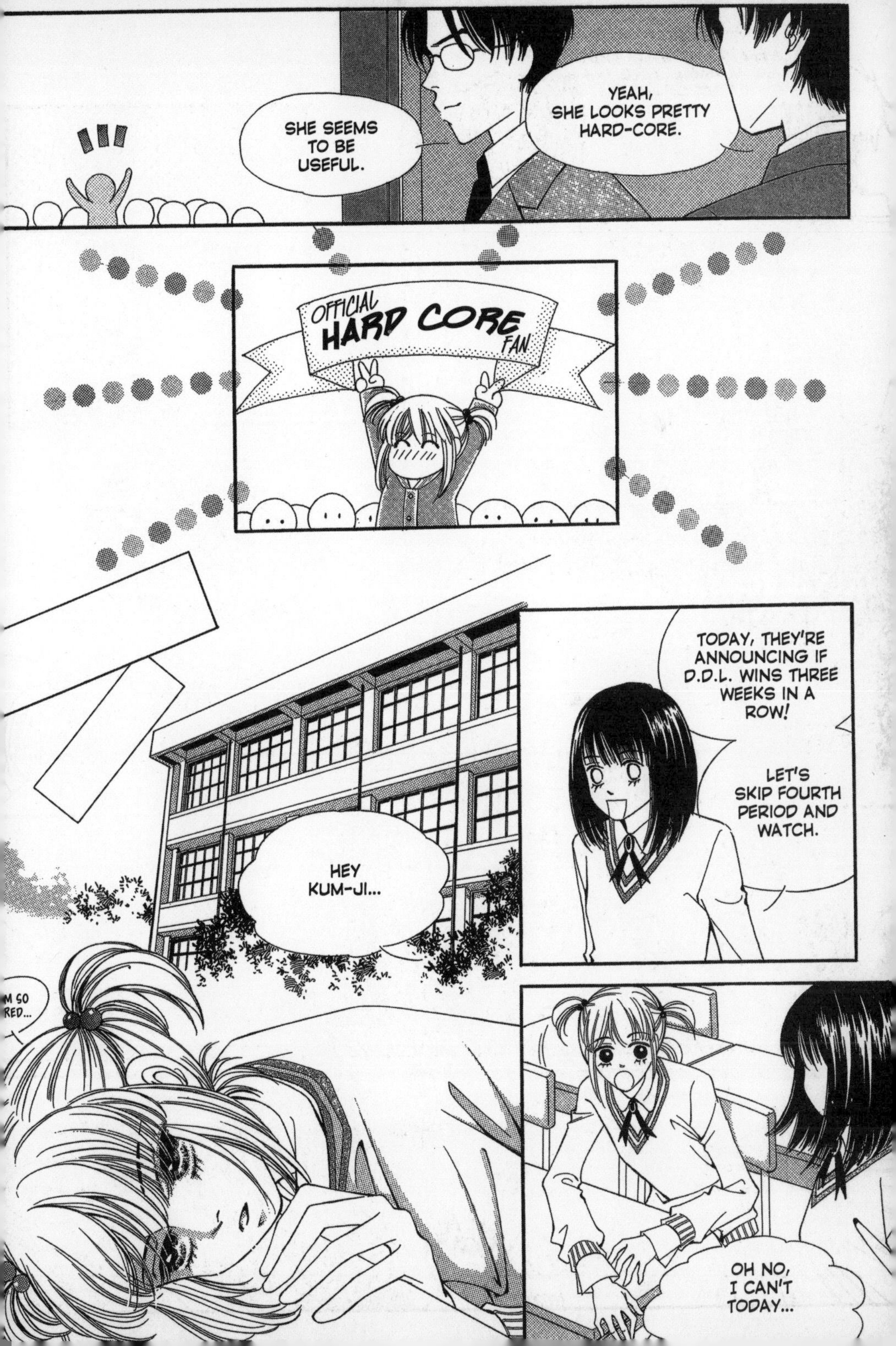
SHE SEEMS TO BE USEFUL.
YEAH, SHE LOOKS PRETTY HARD-CORE.
OFFICIAL HARD CORE FAN
HEY KUM-JI...
TODAY, THEY'RE ANNOUNCING IF D.D.L. WINS THREE WEEKS IN A ROW!
LET'S SKIP FOURTH PERIOD AND WATCH.
OH NO, I CAN'T TODAY...

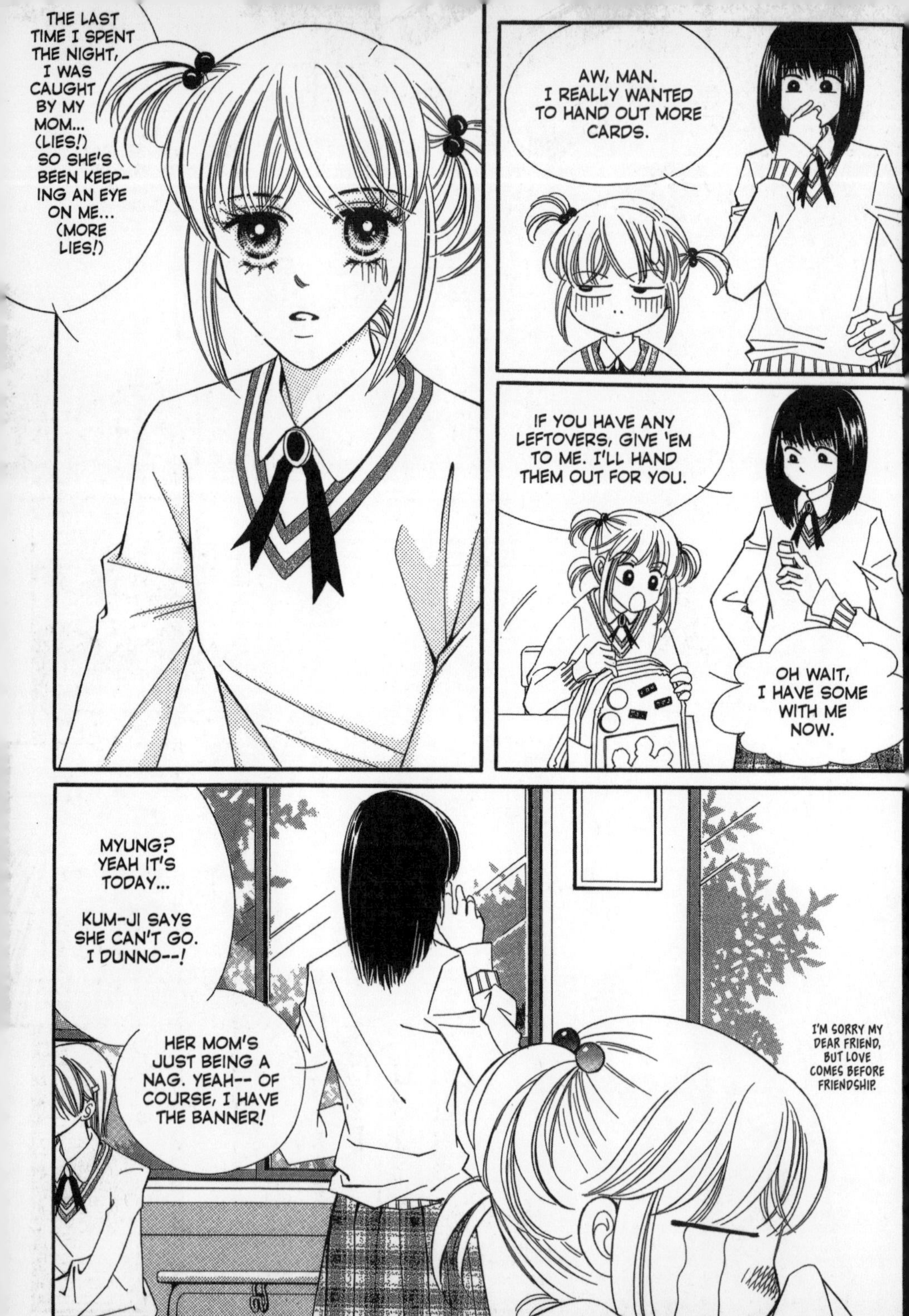
THE LAST TIME I SPENT THE NIGHT, I WAS CAUGHT BY MY MOM... (LIES!) SO SHE'S BEEN KEEPING AN EYE ON ME... (MORE LIES!)
AW, MAN. I REALLY WANTED TO HAND OUT MORE CARDS.
IF YOU HAVE ANY LEFTOVERS, GIVE 'EM TO ME. I'LL HAND THEM OUT FOR YOU.
OH WAIT, I HAVE SOME WITH ME NOW.
MYUNG? YEAH IT'S TODAY...
KUM-JI SAYS SHE CAN'T GO. I DUNNO--!
HER MOM'S JUST BEING A NAG. YEAH-- OF COURSE, I HAVE THE BANNER!
I'M SORRY MY DEAR FRIEND, BUT LOVE COMES BEFORE FRIENDSHIP.

NOTE ABOUT "CARDS": THOSE WITH ACTIVE HOMEPAGES ON THE 'NET PRINT THEIR ADDRESS AND OTHER INFO ON BUSINESS CARDS. THEY SCOUT OUT OFFLINE FANS AND ADVERTISE WITH THEM. SOMETIMES, THEY JUST TRADE AND COLLECT THEM.

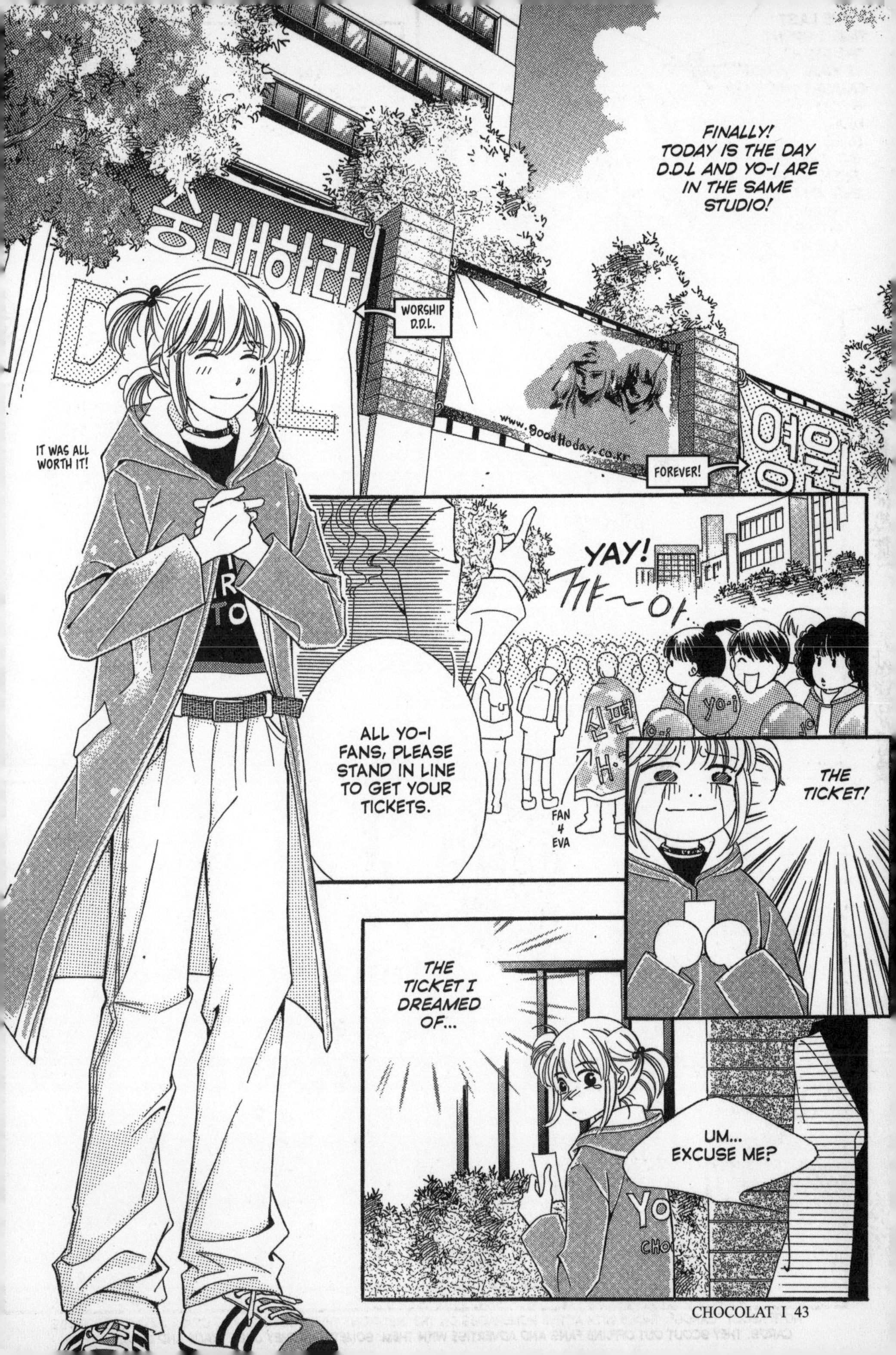

FINALLY! TODAY IS THE DAY D.D.L AND YO-I ARE IN THE SAME STUDIO!
WORSHIP D.D.L.
www.good4today.co.kr
FOREVER!
IT WAS ALL WORTH IT!
YAY!
ALL YO-I FANS, PLEASE STAND IN LINE TO GET YOUR TICKETS.
FAN 4 EVA
THE TICKET!
THE TICKET I DREAMED OF...
UM... EXCUSE ME?

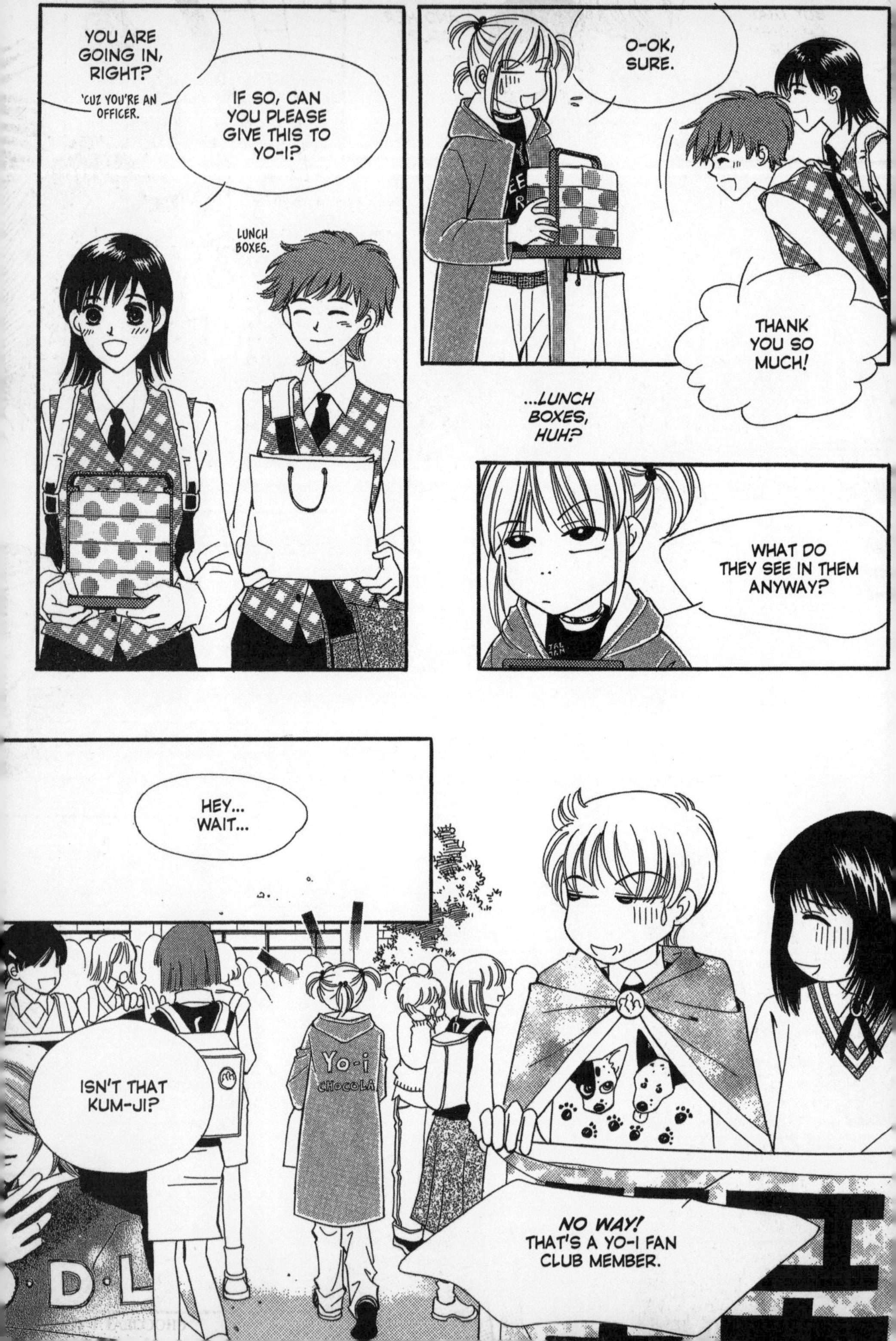
YOU ARE GOING IN, RIGHT?
'CUZ YOU'RE AN OFFICER.
IF SO, CAN YOU PLEASE GIVE THIS TO YO-I?
LUNCH BOXES.
O-OK, SURE.
THANK YOU SO MUCH!
...LUNCH BOXES, HUH?
WHAT DO THEY SEE IN THEM ANYWAY?
HEY... WAIT...
ISN'T THAT KUM-JI?
NO WAY! THAT'S A YO-I FAN CLUB MEMBER.
Yo-i CHOCOLA

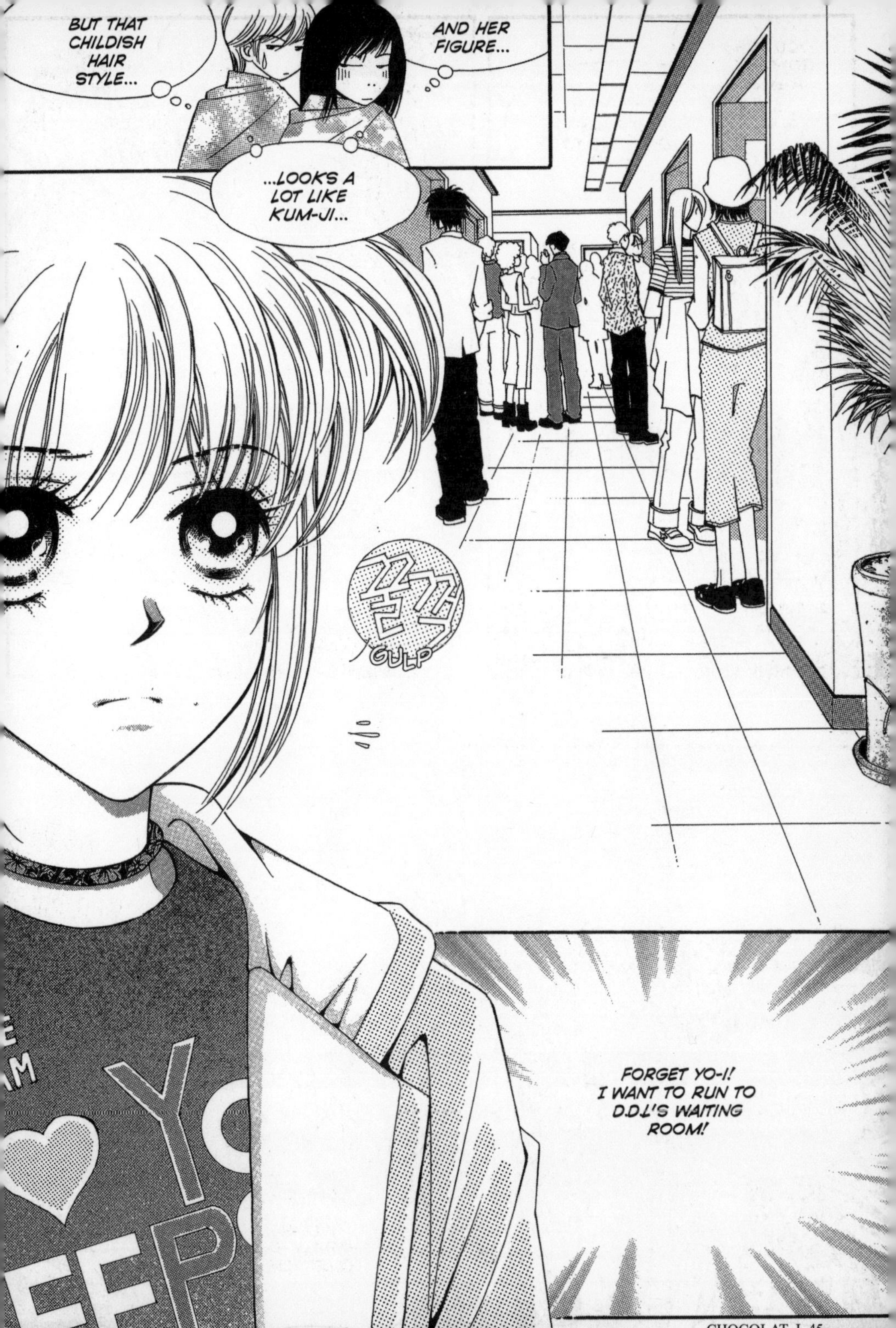
BUT THAT CHILDISH HAIR STYLE...
AND HER FIGURE...
...LOOKS A LOT LIKE KUM-JI...
GULP
FORGET YO-I! I WANT TO RUN TO D.D.L'S WAITING ROOM!

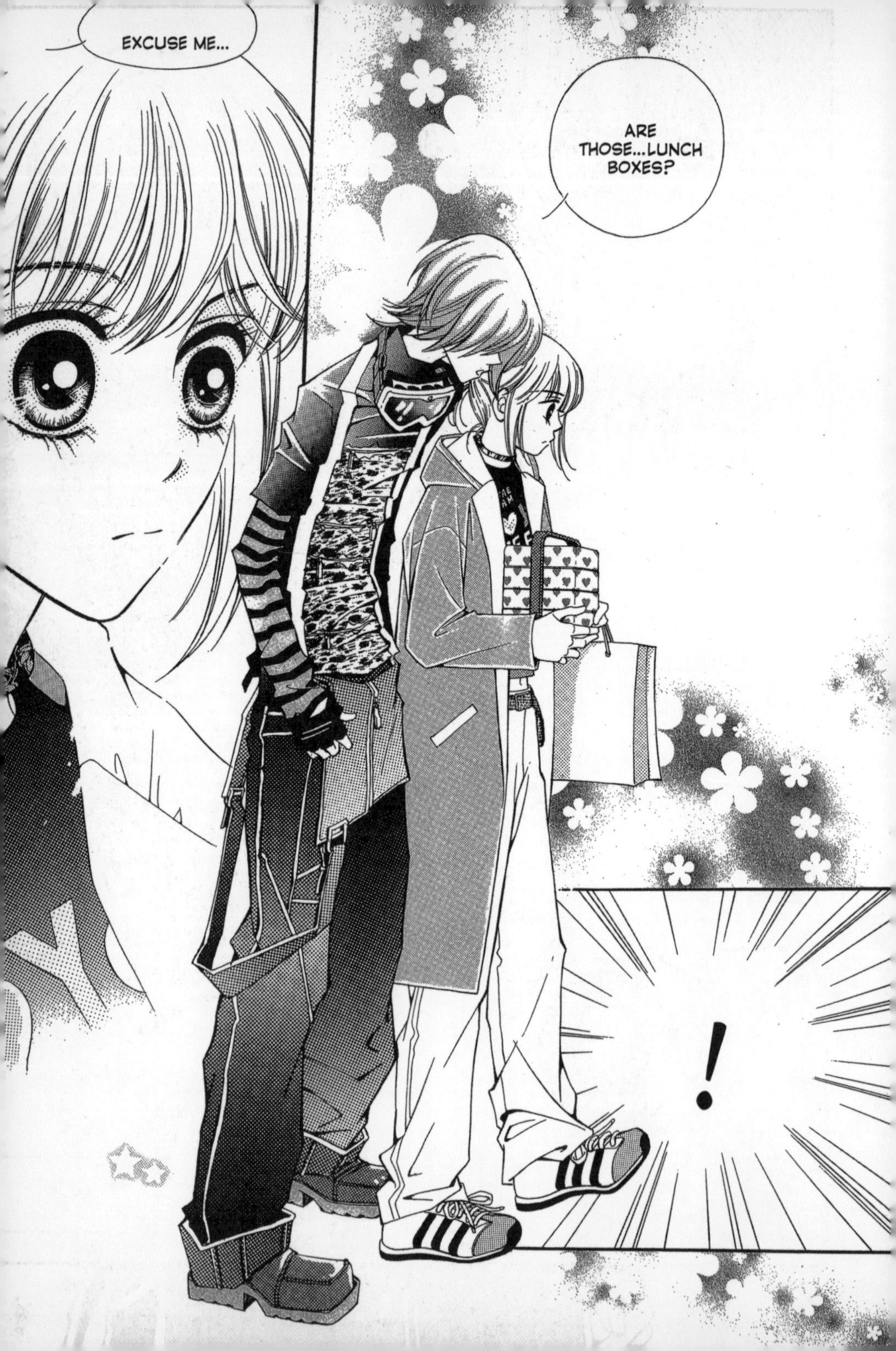
EXCUSE ME...
ARE THOSE...LUNCH BOXES?
!

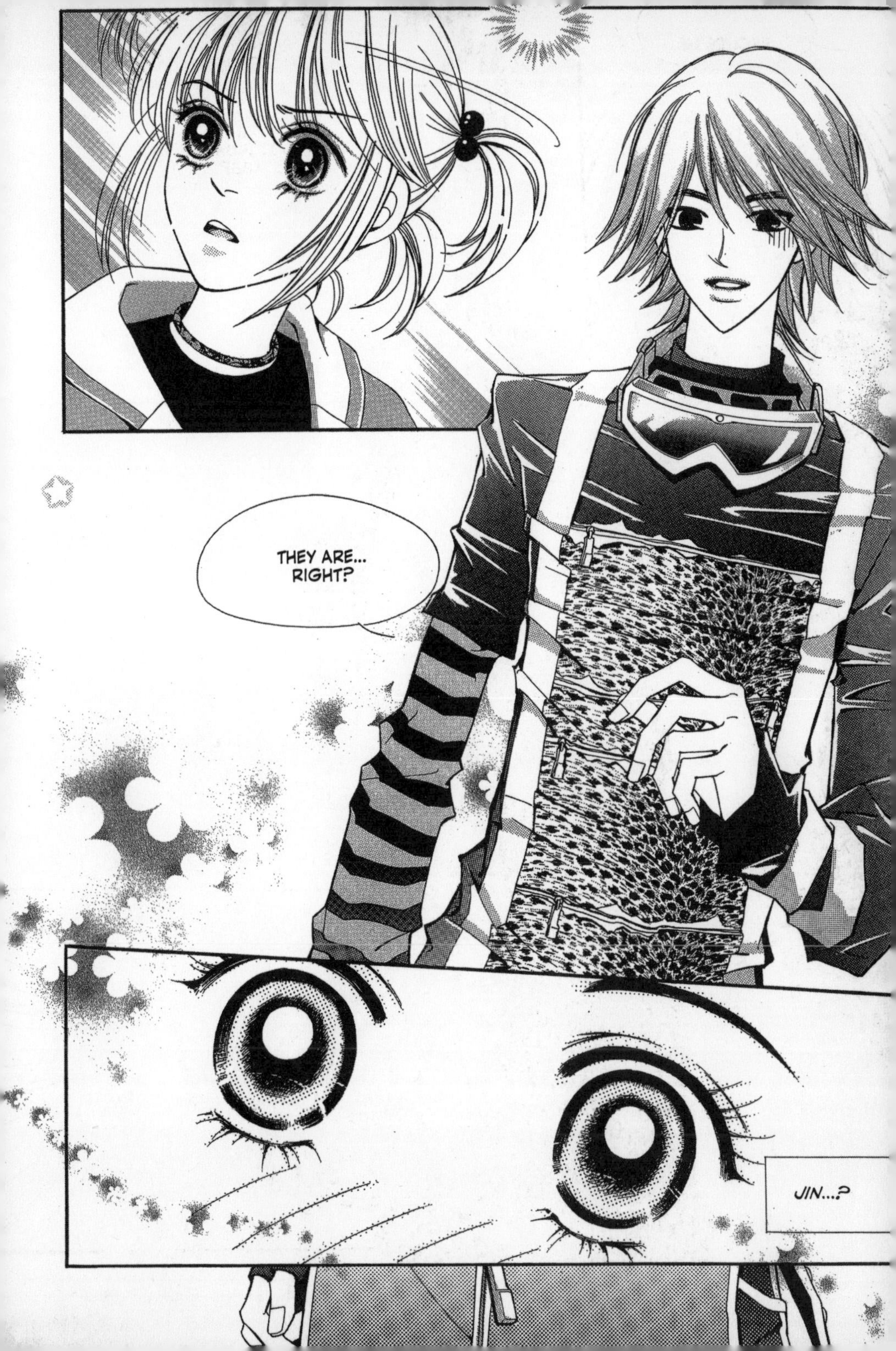
THEY ARE... RIGHT?
JIN...?

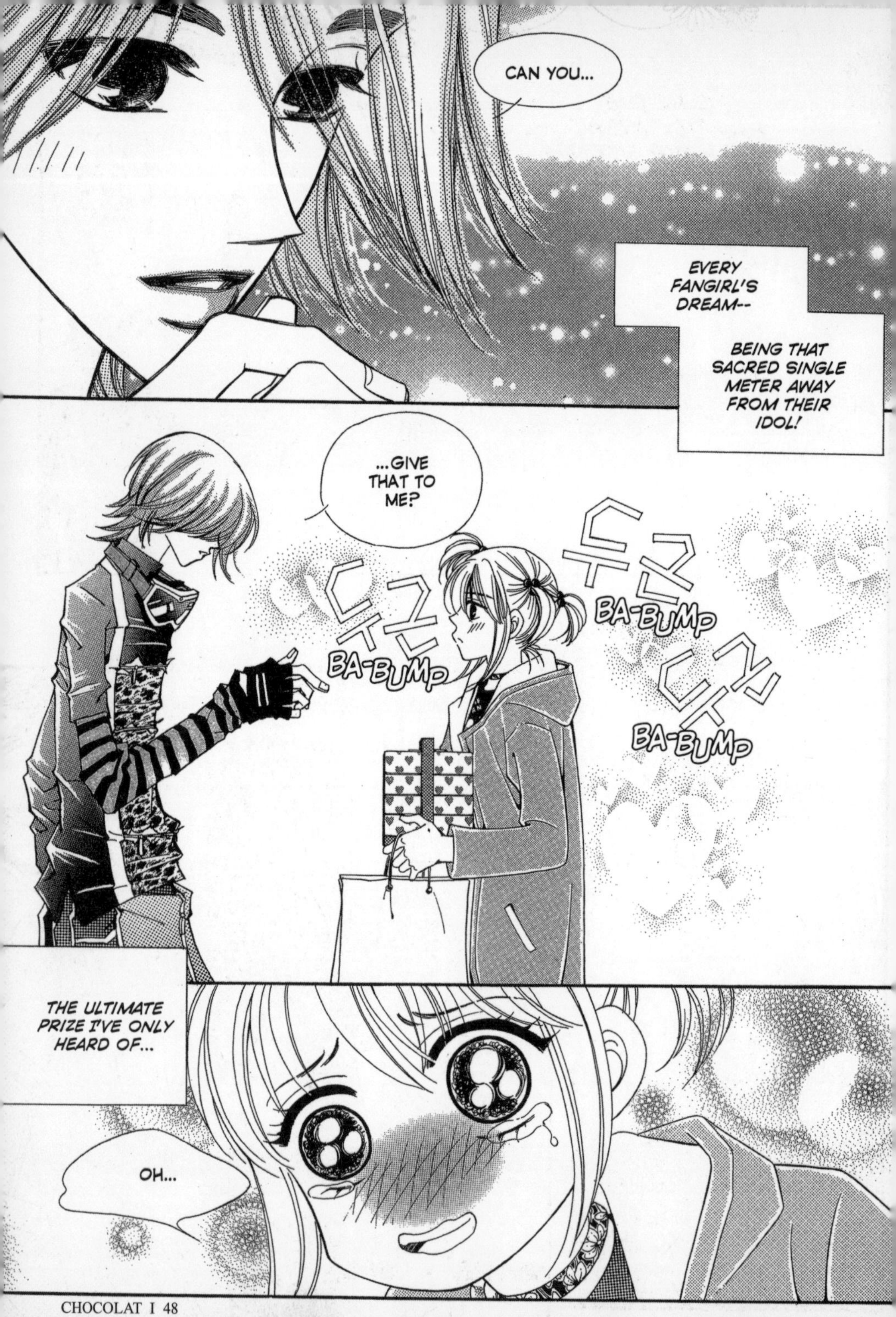
CAN YOU...
EVERY FANGIRL'S DREAM--
BEING THAT SACRED SINGLE METER AWAY FROM THEIR IDOL!
...GIVE THAT TO ME?
BA-BUMP
BA-BUMP
BA-BUMP
THE ULTIMATE PRIZE I'VE ONLY HEARD OF...
OH...

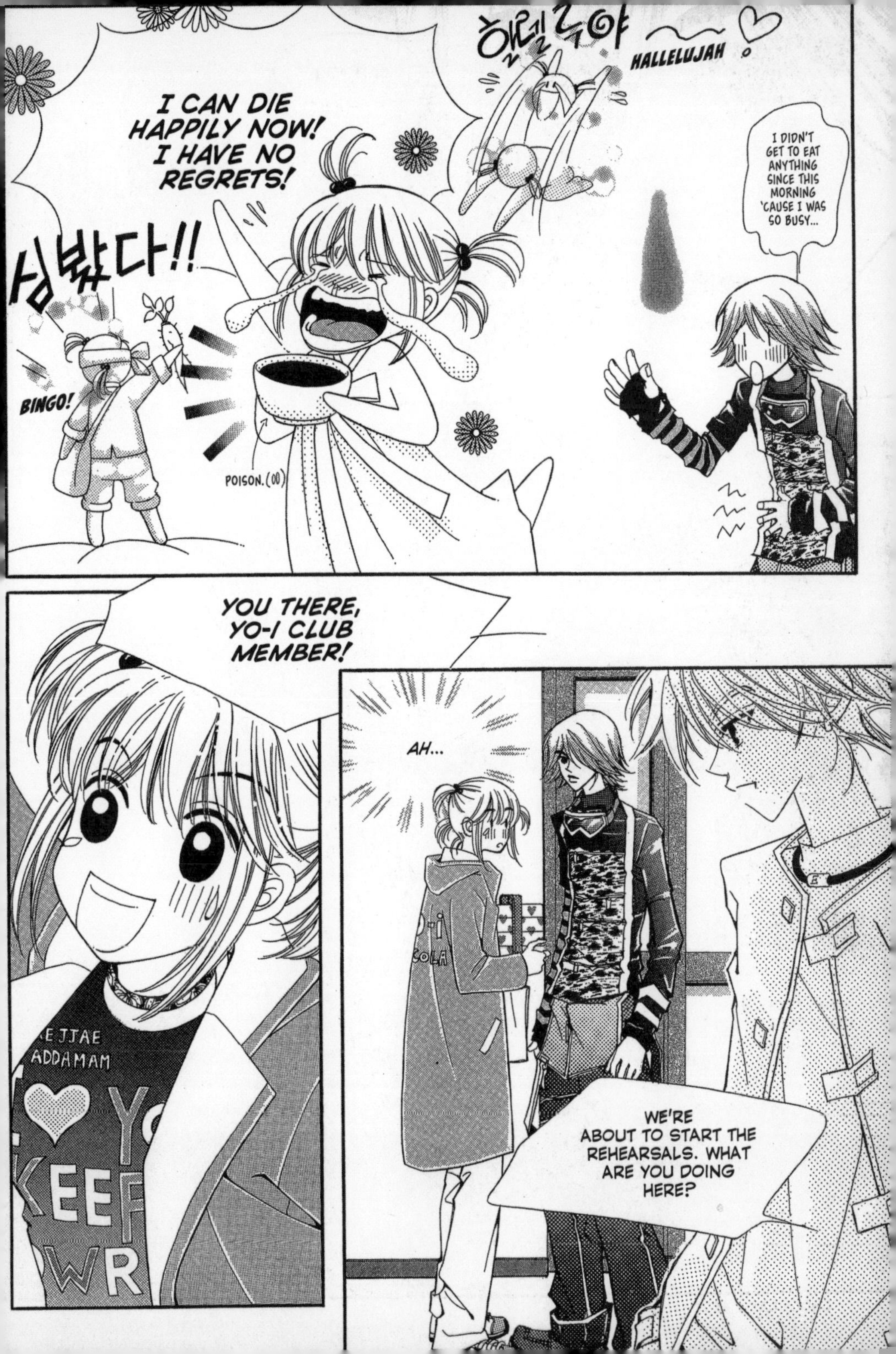
I CAN DIE HAPPILY NOW! I HAVE NO REGRETS!
심봤다!!
BINGO!
POISON.(00)
할렐루야
HALLELUJAH
I DIDN'T GET TO EAT ANYTHING SINCE THIS MORNING 'CAUSE I WAS SO BUSY...
YOU THERE, YO-I CLUB MEMBER!
AH...
WE'RE ABOUT TO START THE REHEARSALS. WHAT ARE YOU DOING HERE?

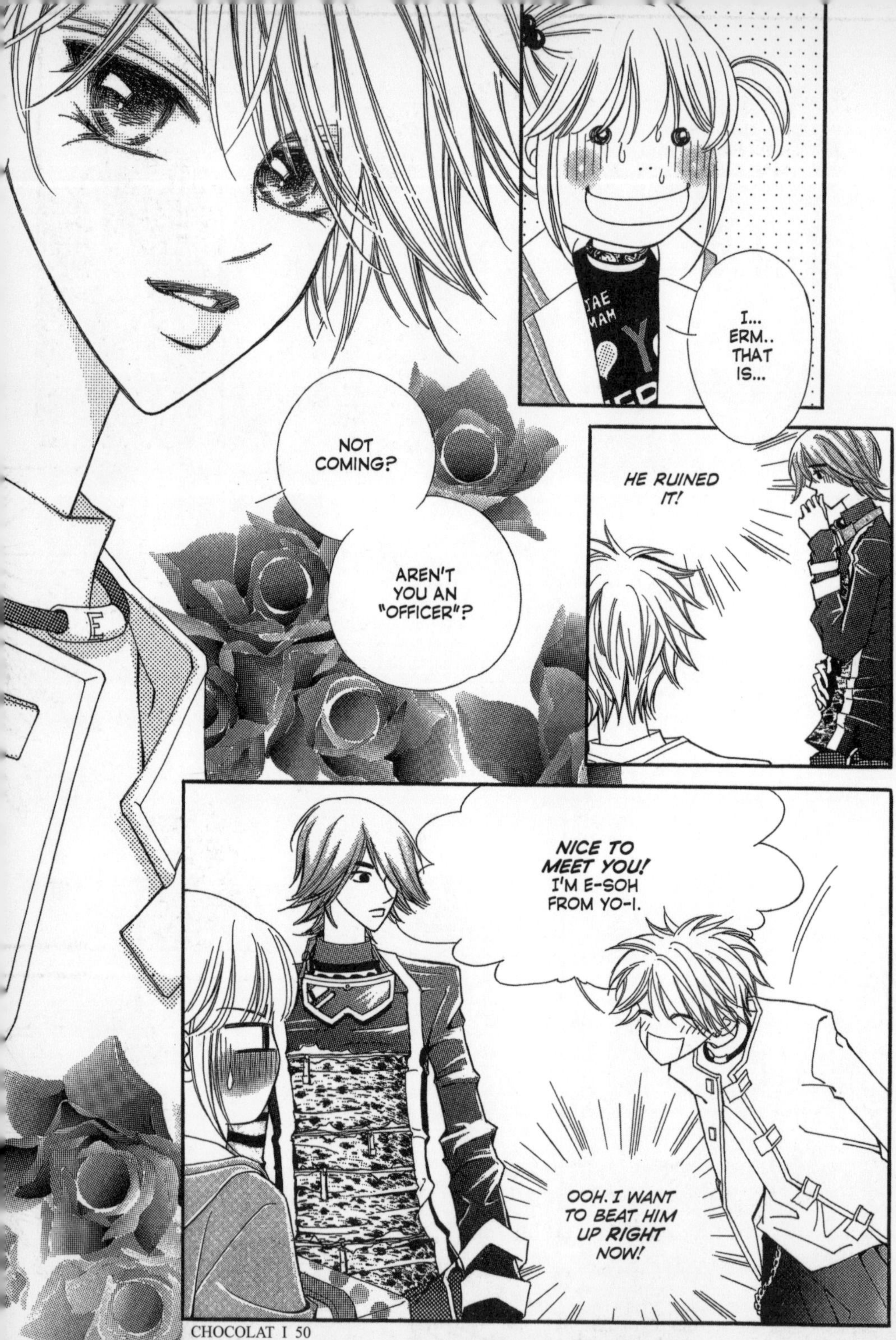

I... ERM.. THAT IS...
NOT COMING?
AREN'T YOU AN "OFFICER"?
HE RUINED IT!
NICE TO MEET YOU! I'M E-SOH FROM YO-I.
OOH. I WANT TO BEAT HIM UP RIGHT NOW!

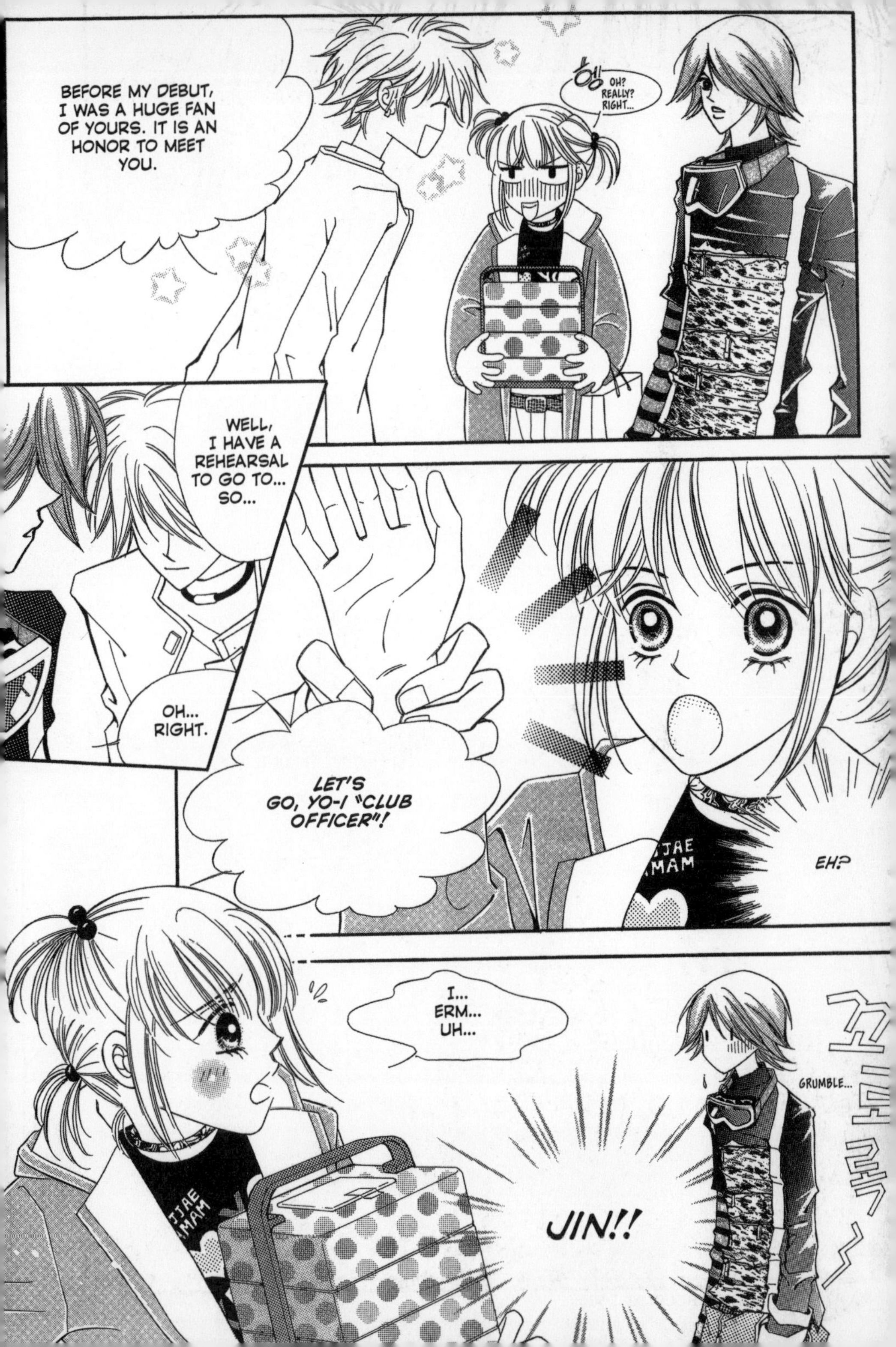
BEFORE MY DEBUT, I WAS A HUGE FAN OF YOURS. IT IS AN HONOR TO MEET YOU.
OH? REALLY? RIGHT...
WELL, I HAVE A REHEARSAL TO GO TO... SO...
OH... RIGHT.
LET'S GO, YO-I "CLUB OFFICER"!
EH?
I... ERM... UH...
JIN!!
GRUMBLE...

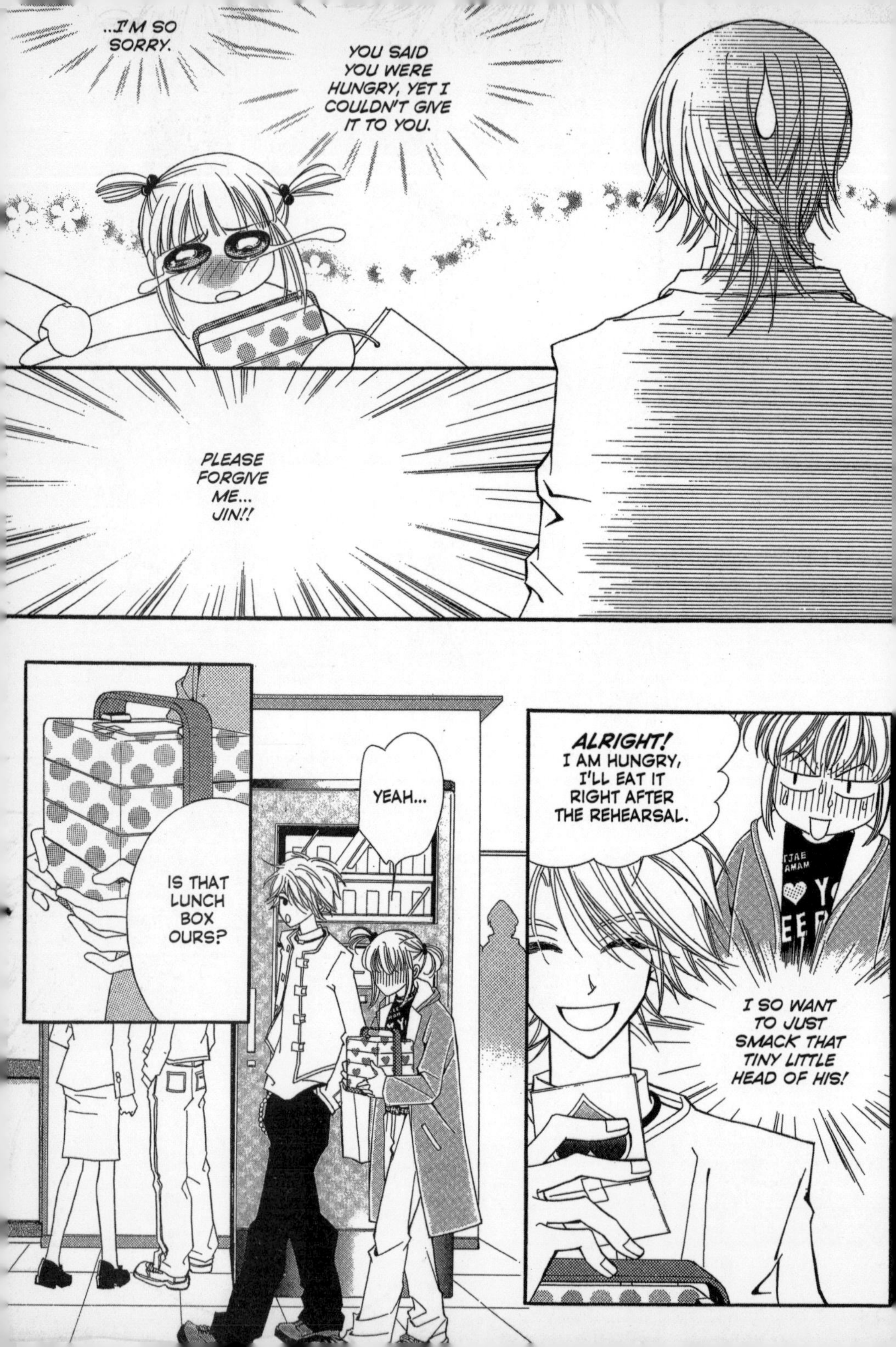

...I'M SO SORRY.
YOU SAID YOU WERE HUNGRY, YET I COULDN'T GIVE IT TO YOU.
PLEASE FORGIVE ME... JIN!!
IS THAT LUNCH BOX OURS?
YEAH...
ALRIGHT! I AM HUNGRY, I'LL EAT IT RIGHT AFTER THE REHEARSAL.
I SO WANT TO JUST SMACK THAT TINY LITTLE HEAD OF HIS!

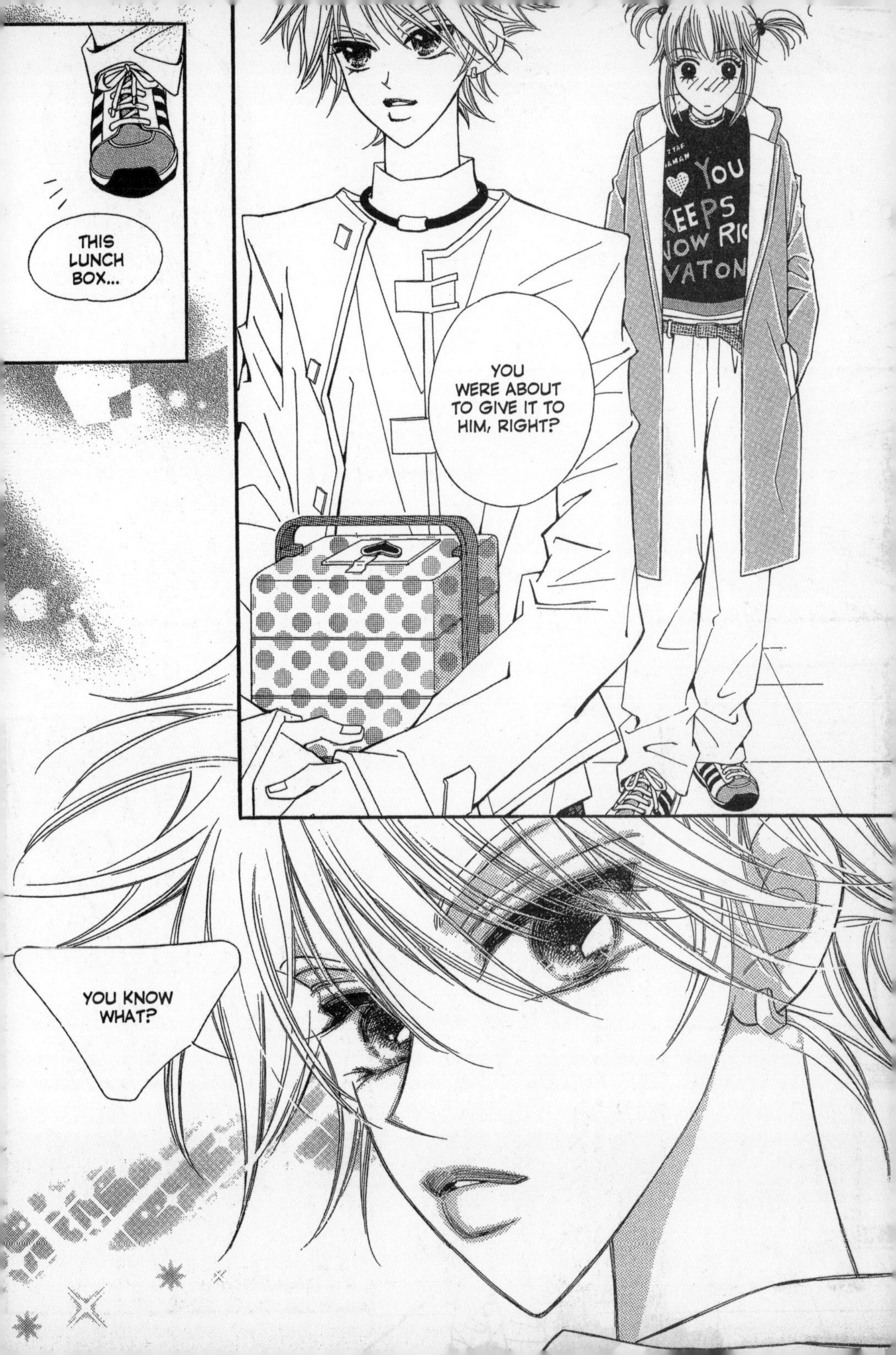
THIS LUNCH BOX...
YOU WERE ABOUT TO GIVE IT TO HIM, RIGHT?
YOU KNOW WHAT?

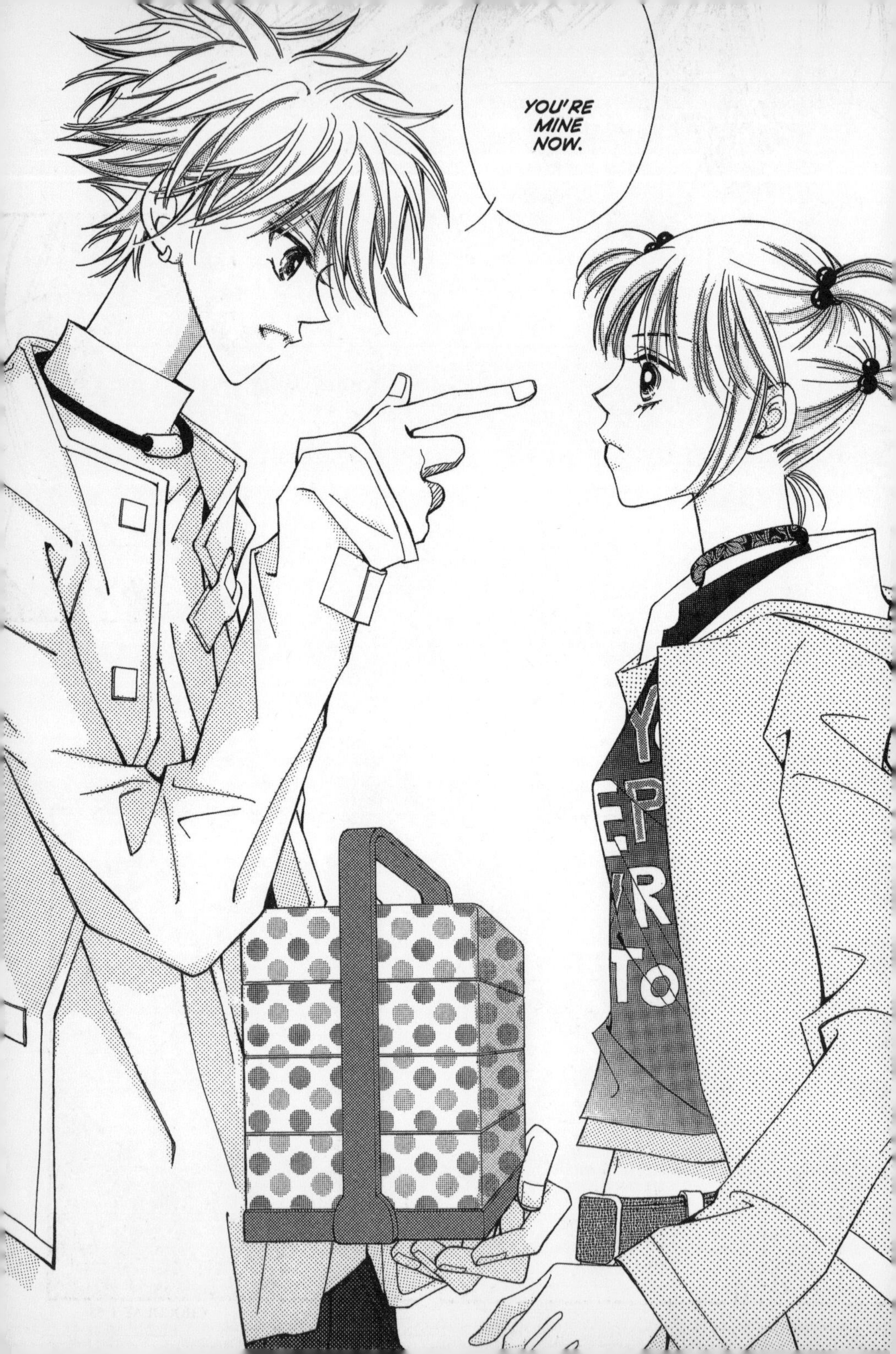
YOU'RE MINE NOW.

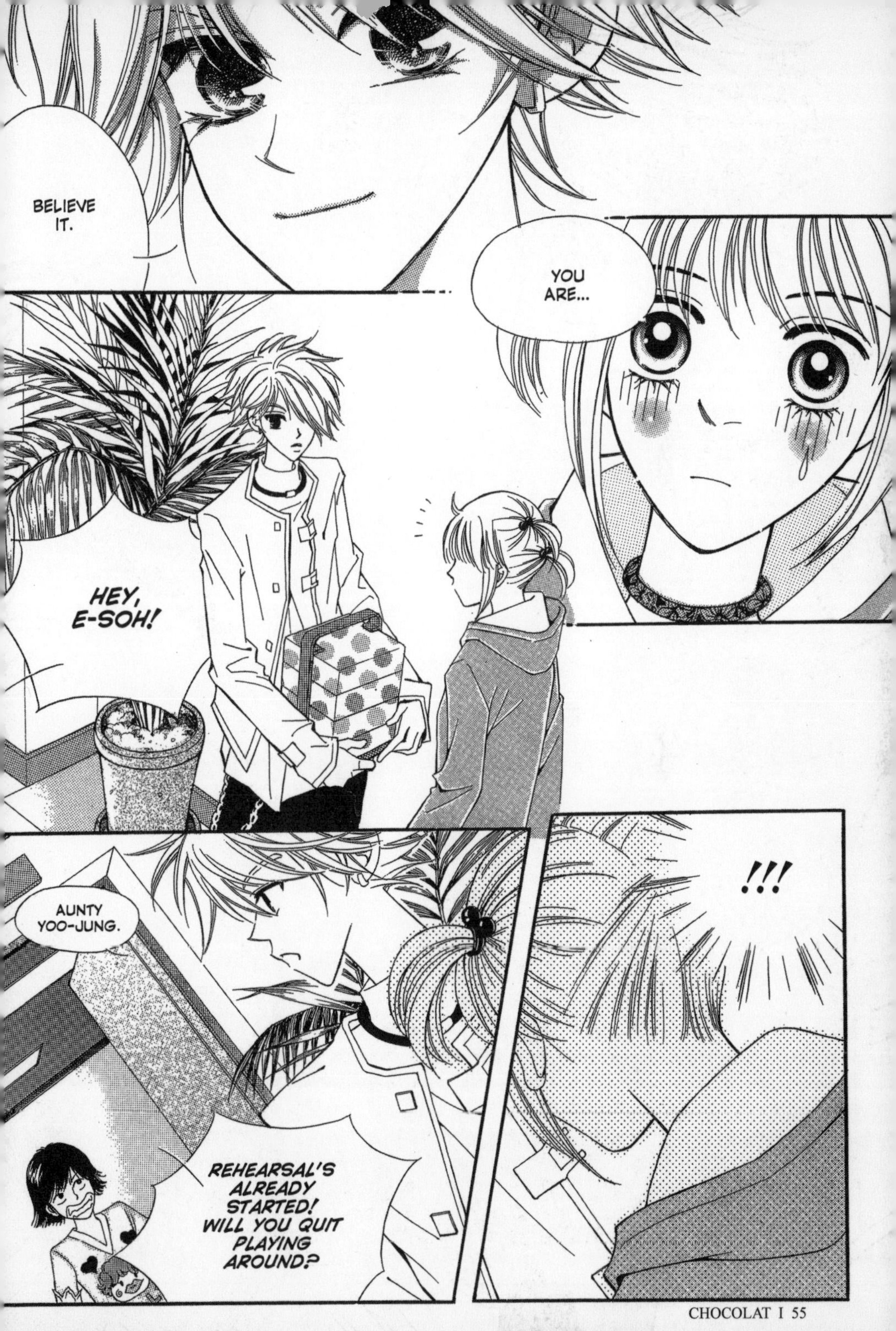
BELIEVE IT.
YOU ARE...
HEY, E-SOH!
AUNTY YOO-JUNG.
!!!
REHEARSAL'S ALREADY STARTED! WILL YOU QUIT PLAYING AROUND?

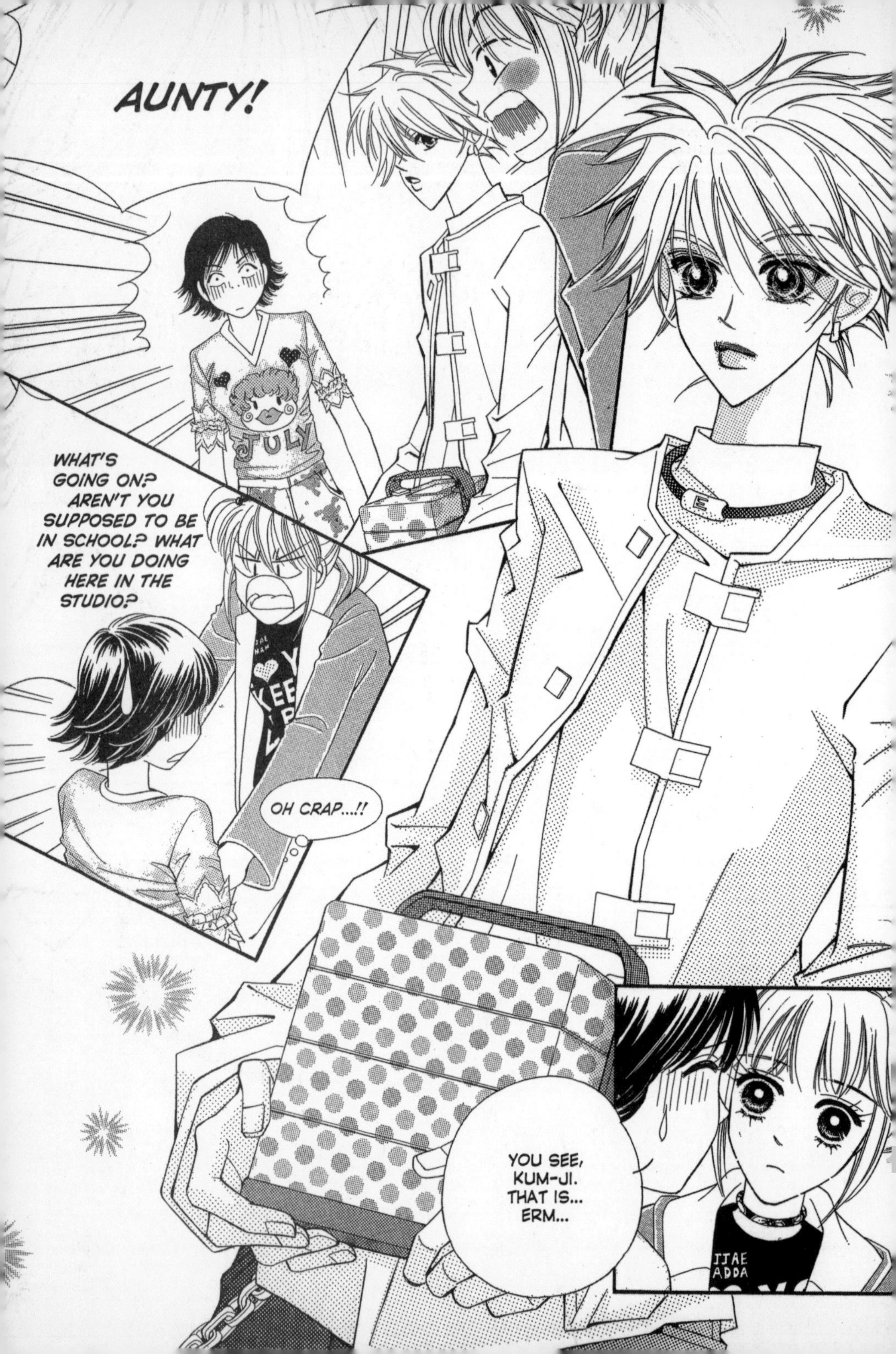
AUNTY!
WHAT'S GOING ON? AREN'T YOU SUPPOSED TO BE IN SCHOOL? WHAT ARE YOU DOING HERE IN THE STUDIO?
OH CRAP...!!
YOU SEE, KUM-JI. THAT IS... ERM...

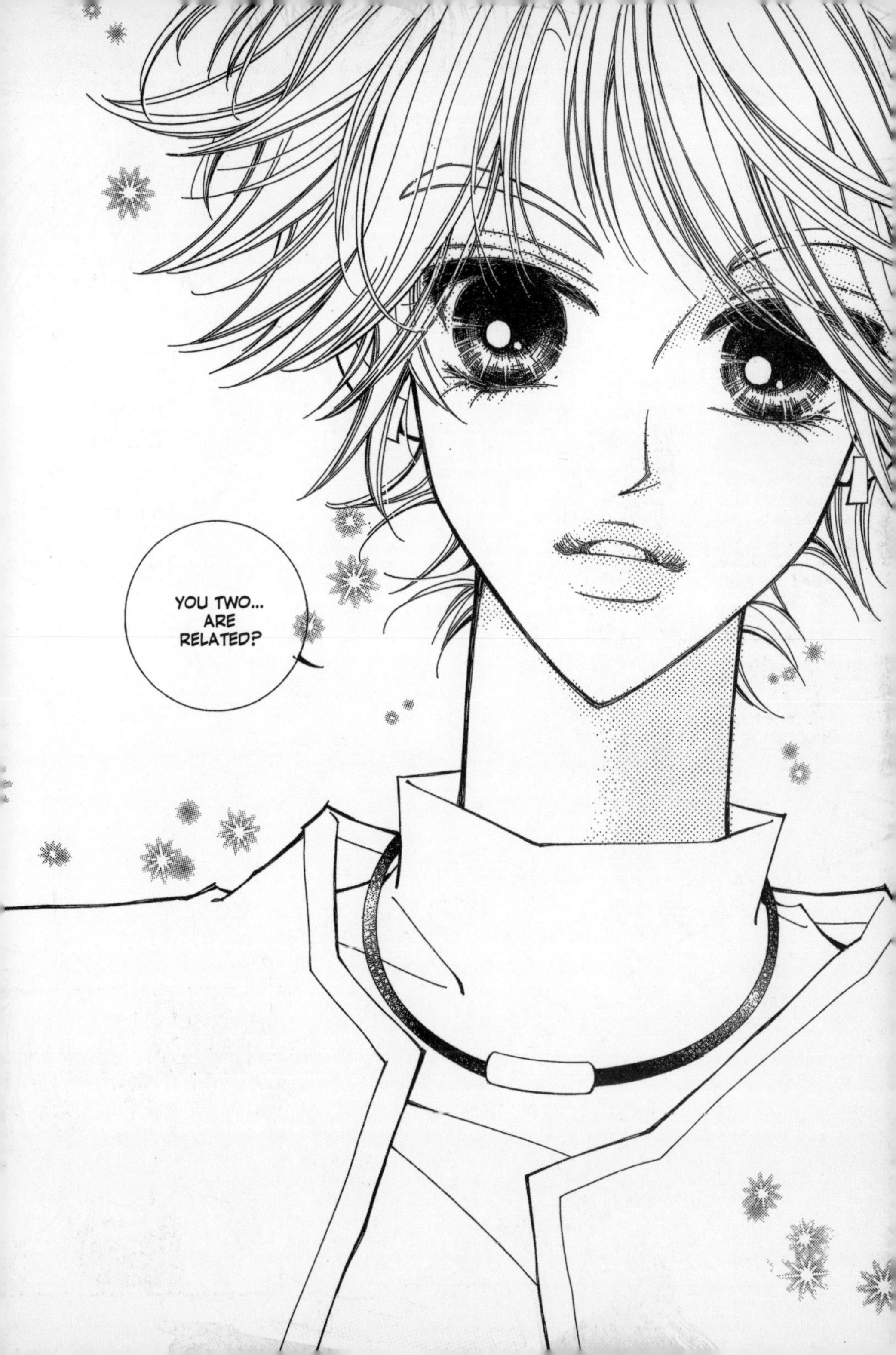
YOU TWO... ARE RELATED?

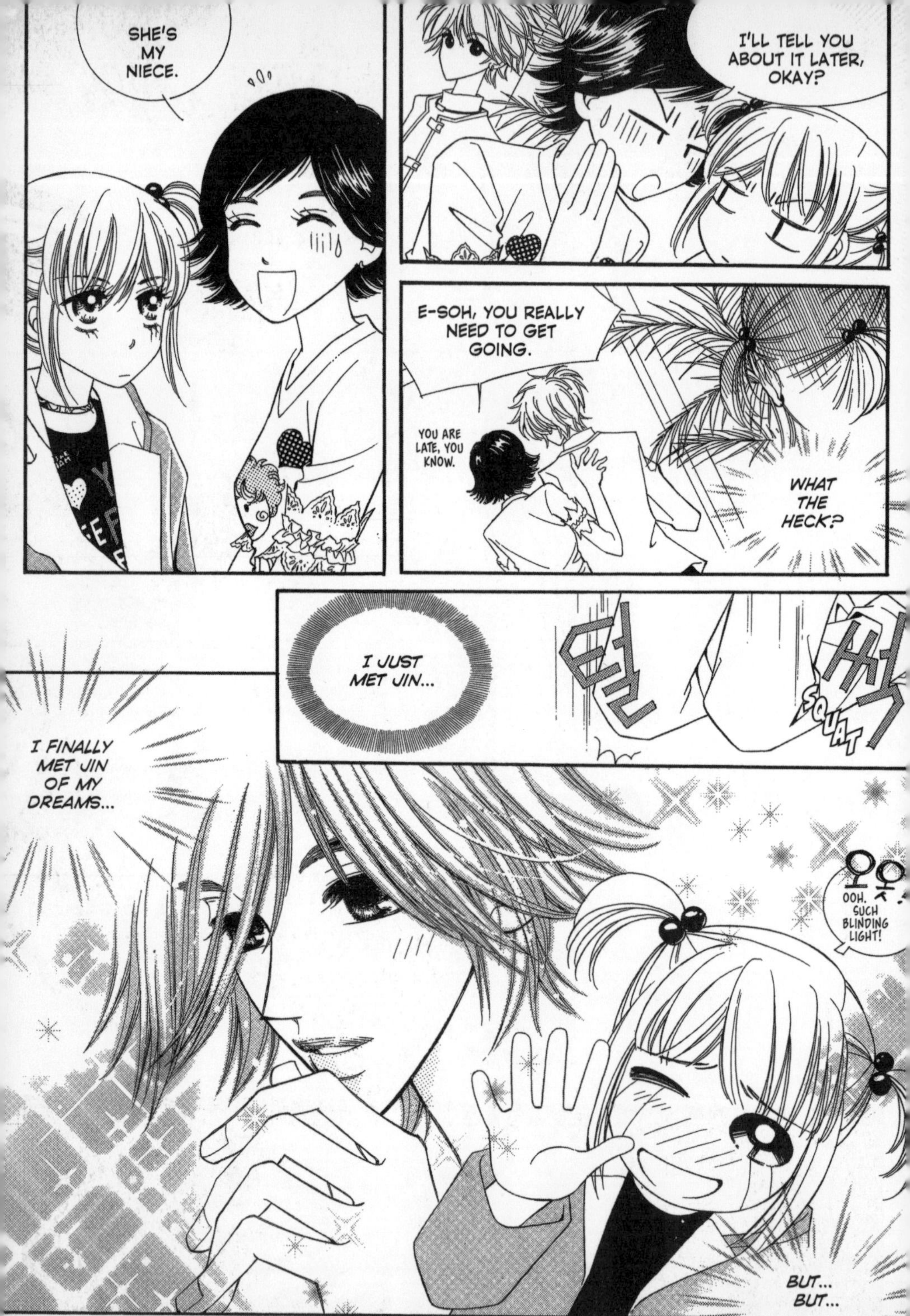
SHE'S MY NIECE.
I'LL TELL YOU ABOUT IT LATER, OKAY?
E-SOH, YOU REALLY NEED TO GET GOING.
YOU ARE LATE, YOU KNOW.
WHAT THE HECK?
I JUST MET JIN...
털썩
SQUAT
I FINALLY MET JIN OF MY DREAMS...
OOH, SUCH BLINDING LIGHT!
BUT... BUT...

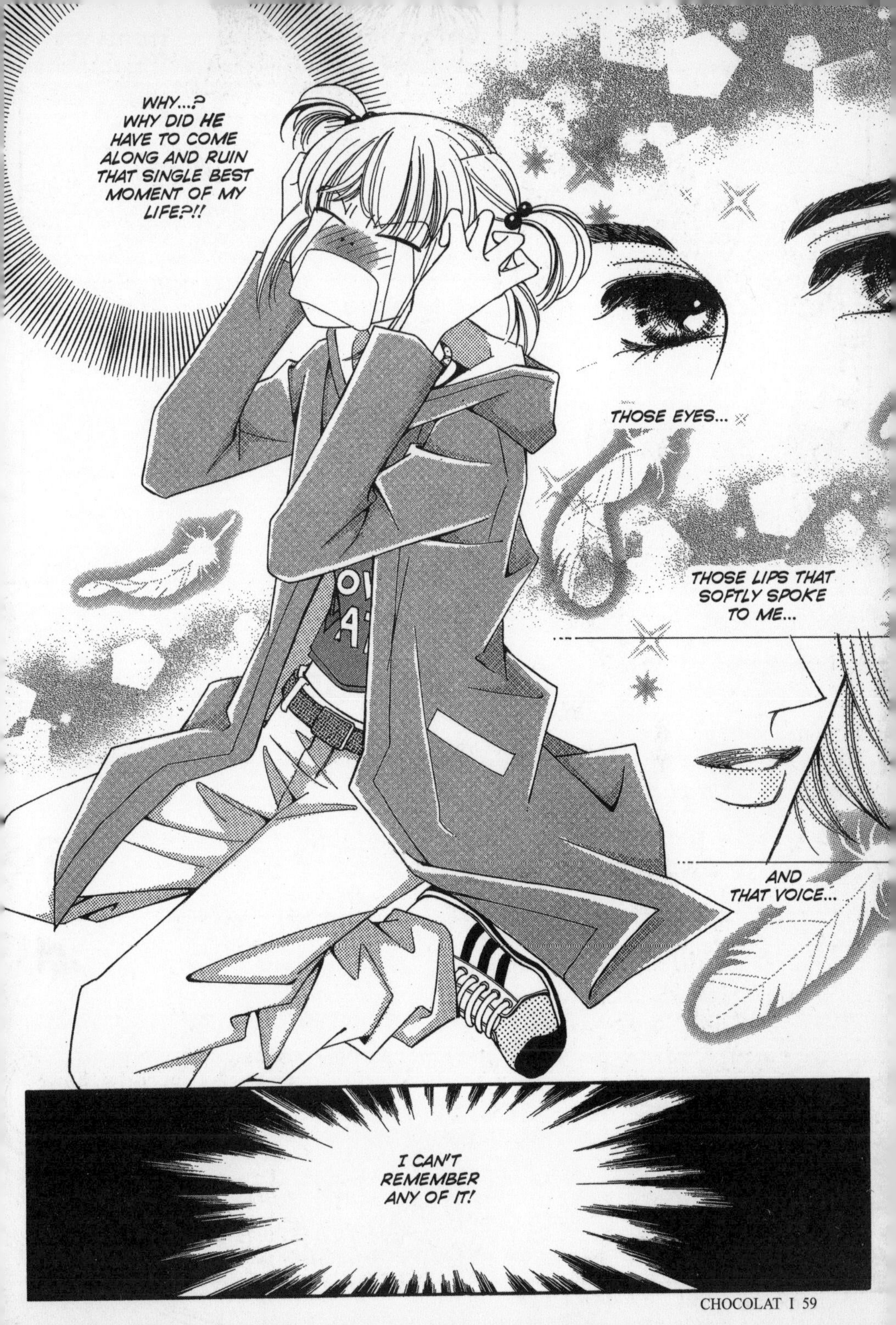

WHY...? WHY DID HE HAVE TO COME ALONG AND RUIN THAT SINGLE BEST MOMENT OF MY LIFE?!!
THOSE EYES...
THOSE LIPS THAT SOFTLY SPOKE TO ME...
AND THAT VOICE...
I CAN'T REMEMBER ANY OF IT!

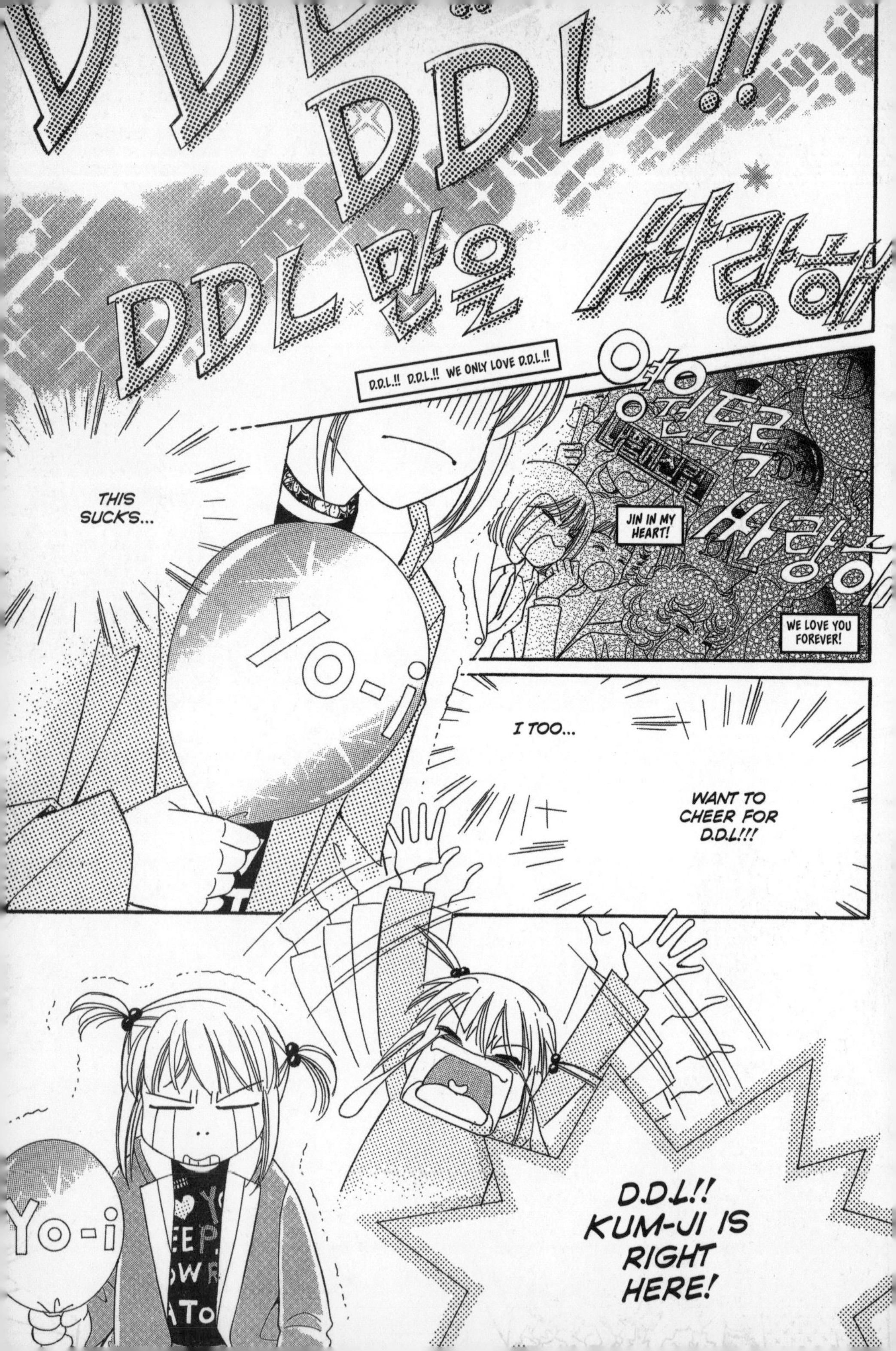
DDL!!
DDL만을 사랑해
D.D.L.!! D.D.L.!! WE ONLY LOVE D.D.L.!!
THIS SUCKS...
YO-i
영원토록 사랑해
JIN IN MY HEART!
WE LOVE YOU FOREVER!
I TOO...
WANT TO CHEER FOR D.D.L!!!
Yo-i
D.D.L!! KUM-JI IS RIGHT HERE!

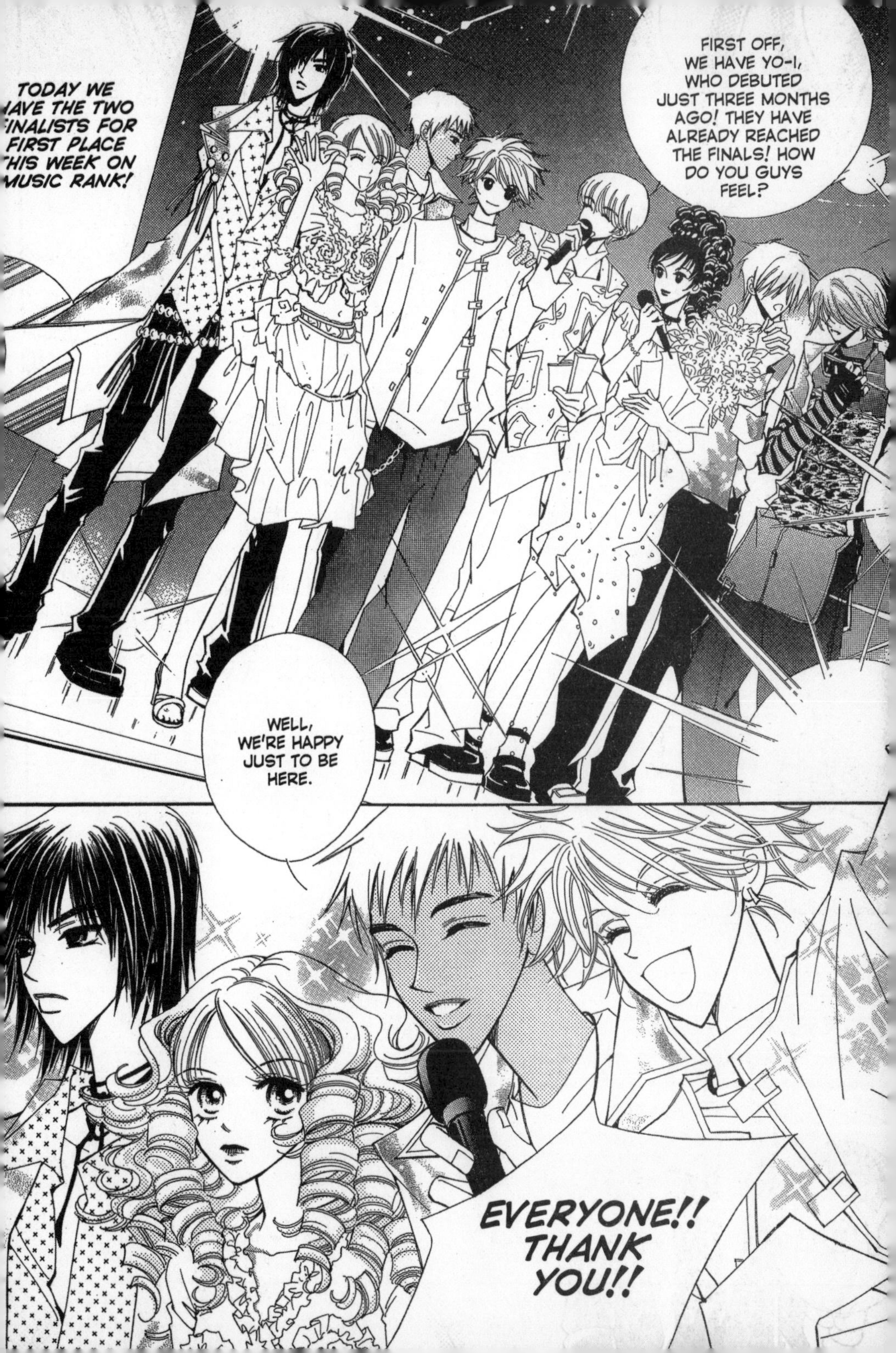
TODAY WE HAVE THE TWO FINALISTS FOR FIRST PLACE THIS WEEK ON MUSIC RANK!
FIRST OFF, WE HAVE YO-I, WHO DEBUTED JUST THREE MONTHS AGO! THEY HAVE ALREADY REACHED THE FINALS! HOW DO YOU GUYS FEEL?
WELL, WE'RE HAPPY JUST TO BE HERE.
EVERYONE!! THANK YOU!!

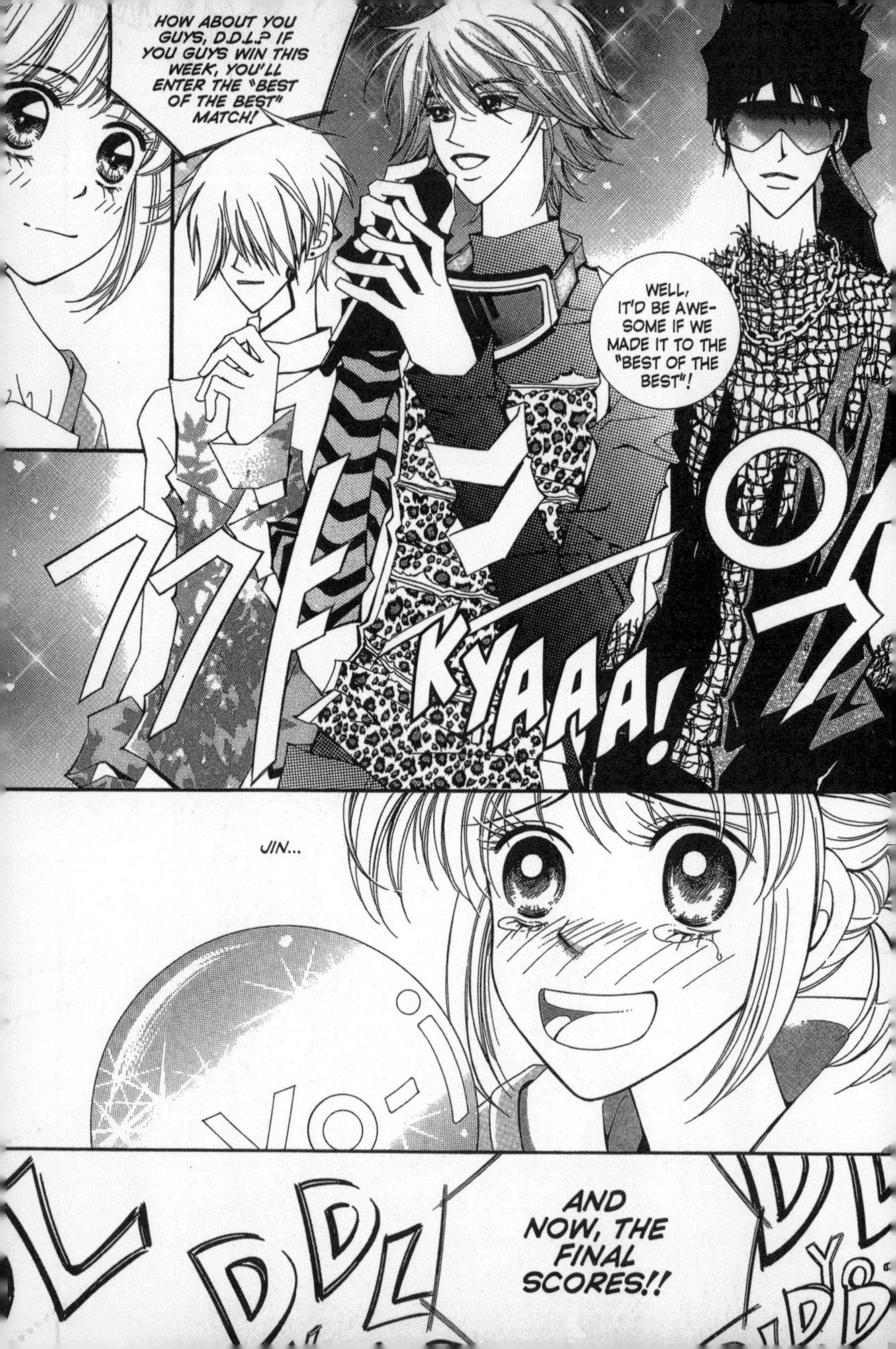
HOW ABOUT YOU GUYS, D.D.L.? IF YOU GUYS WIN THIS WEEK, YOU'LL ENTER THE "BEST OF THE BEST" MATCH!
WELL, IT'D BE AWE-SOME IF WE MADE IT TO THE "BEST OF THE BEST"!
KYAAA!
JIN...
AND NOW, THE FINAL SCORES!!

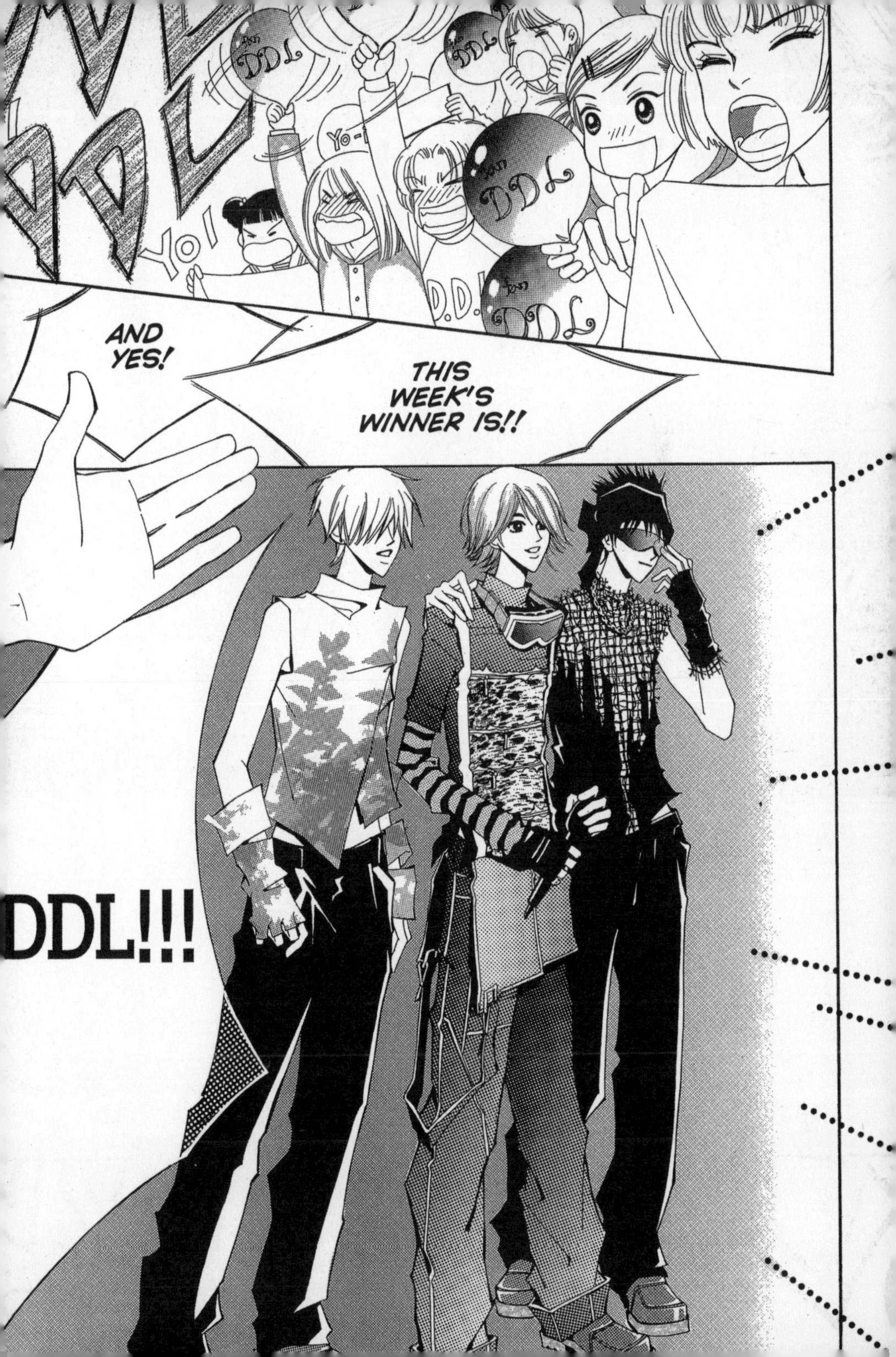

AND YES!
THIS WEEK'S WINNER IS!!
DDL!!!

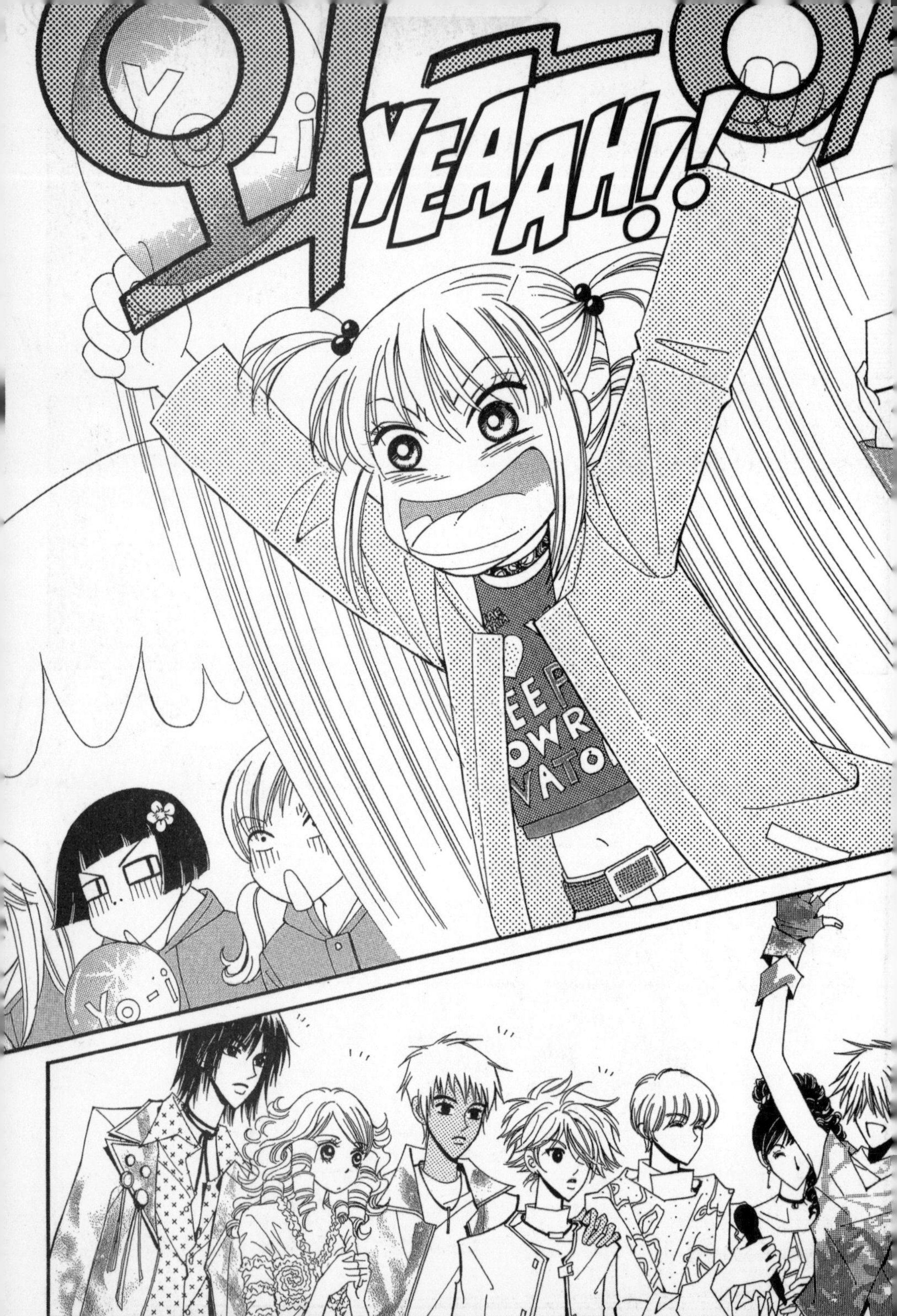
Yo-i
YEAAH!!
Yo-i

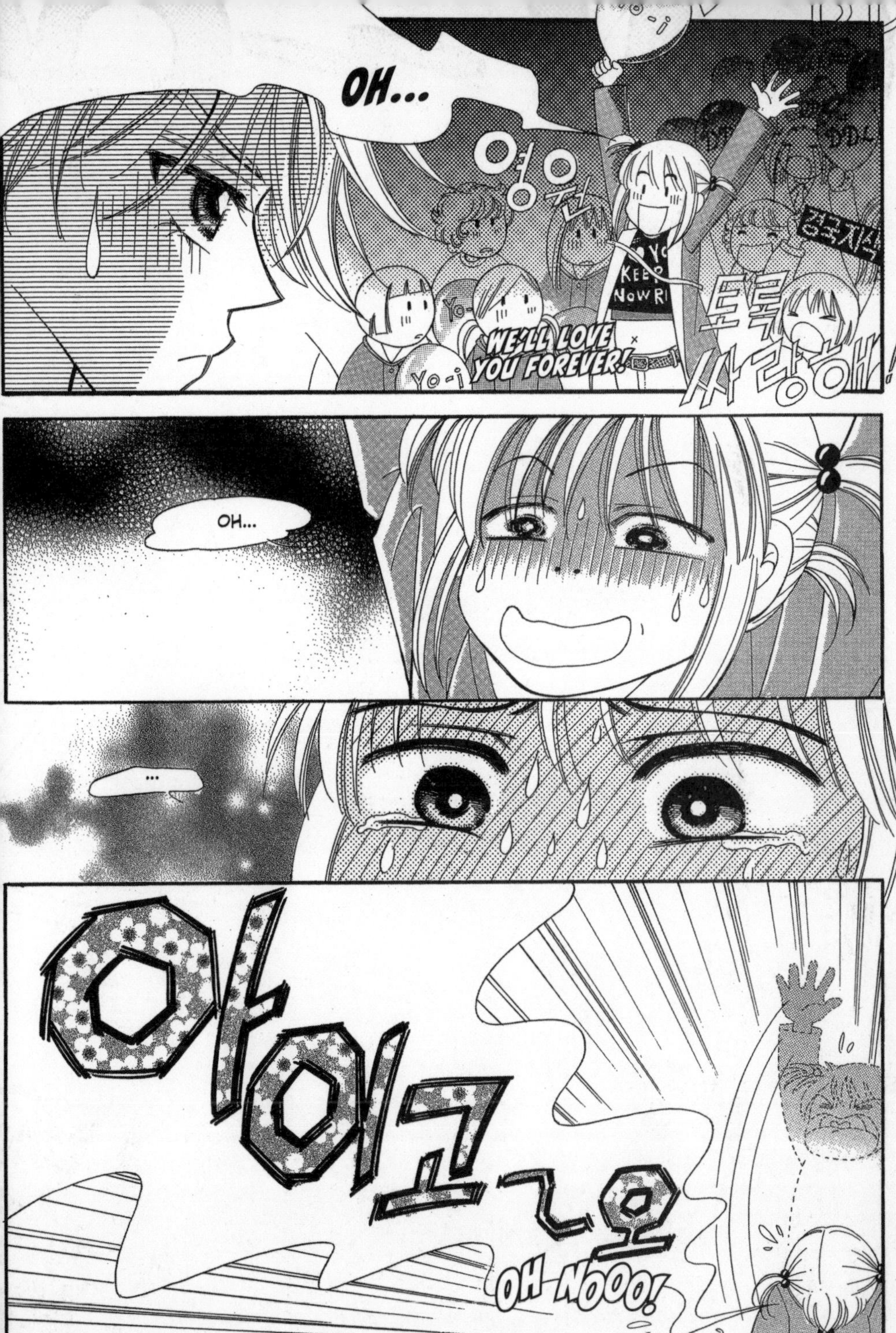
OH...
WE'LL LOVE YOU FOREVER!
사랑해!!
OH...
...
아이고오
OH NOOO!

I THOUGHT YO-I WOULD WIN FIRST PLACE...

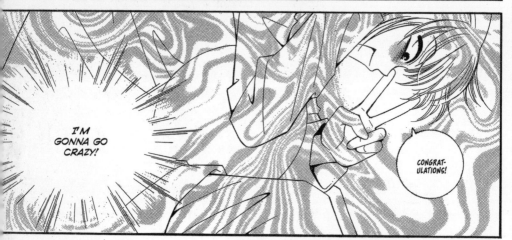

I'M GONNA GO CRAZY!

CONGRAT-ULATIONS!

AT THIS RATE, I'M GONNA BE ADMITTED TO THE MENTAL HOSPITAL...

FOR BEING SCHIZO...

THAT GIRL...

PRINCE E-WAN

YO-I CLUB

YO-I!

E-SOH! OVER HERE!

TODAY YOU GUYS WERE AWESOME!!

EUN-SUNG!!

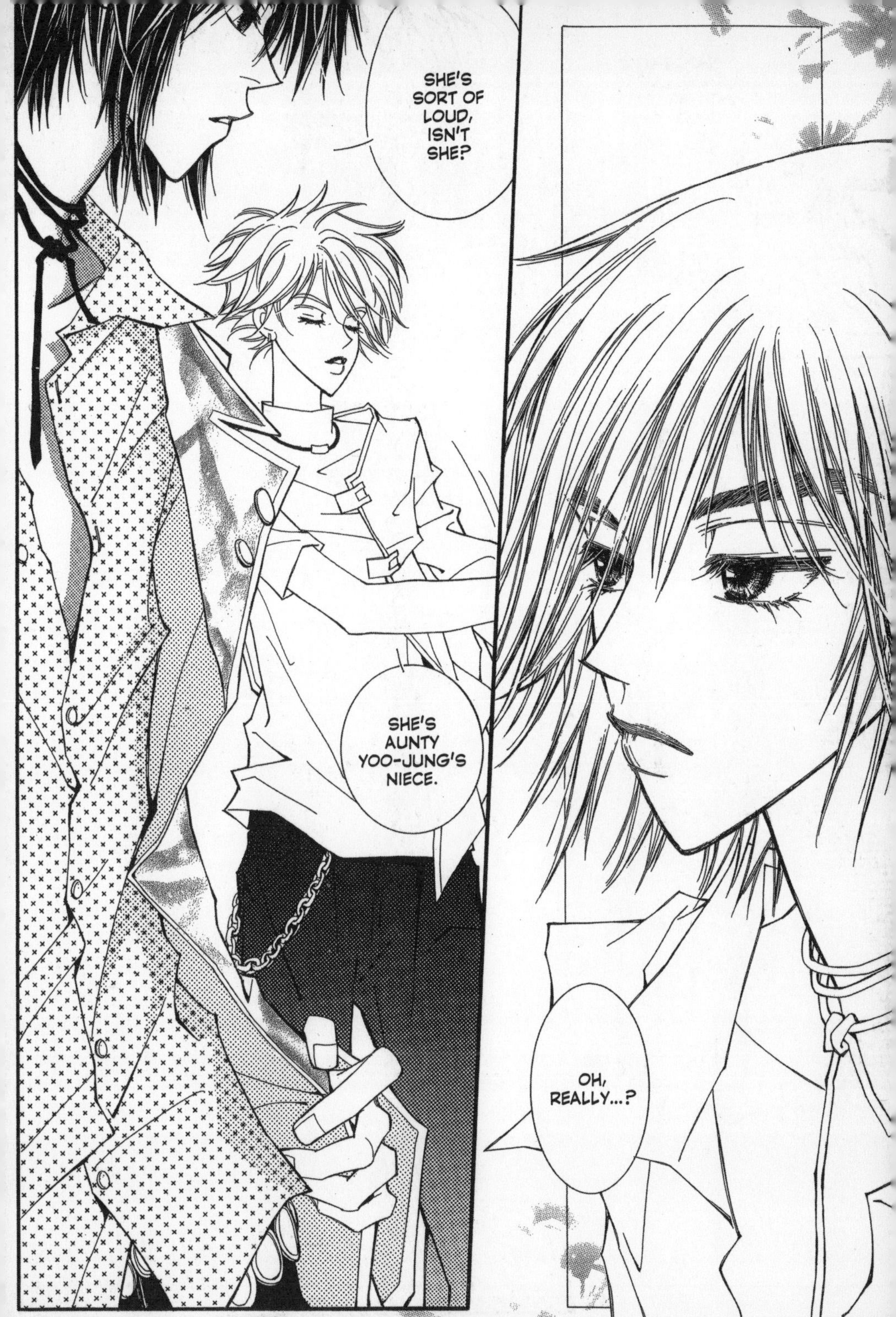
SHE'S SORT OF LOUD, ISN'T SHE?
SHE'S AUNTY YOO-JUNG'S NIECE.
OH, REALLY...?

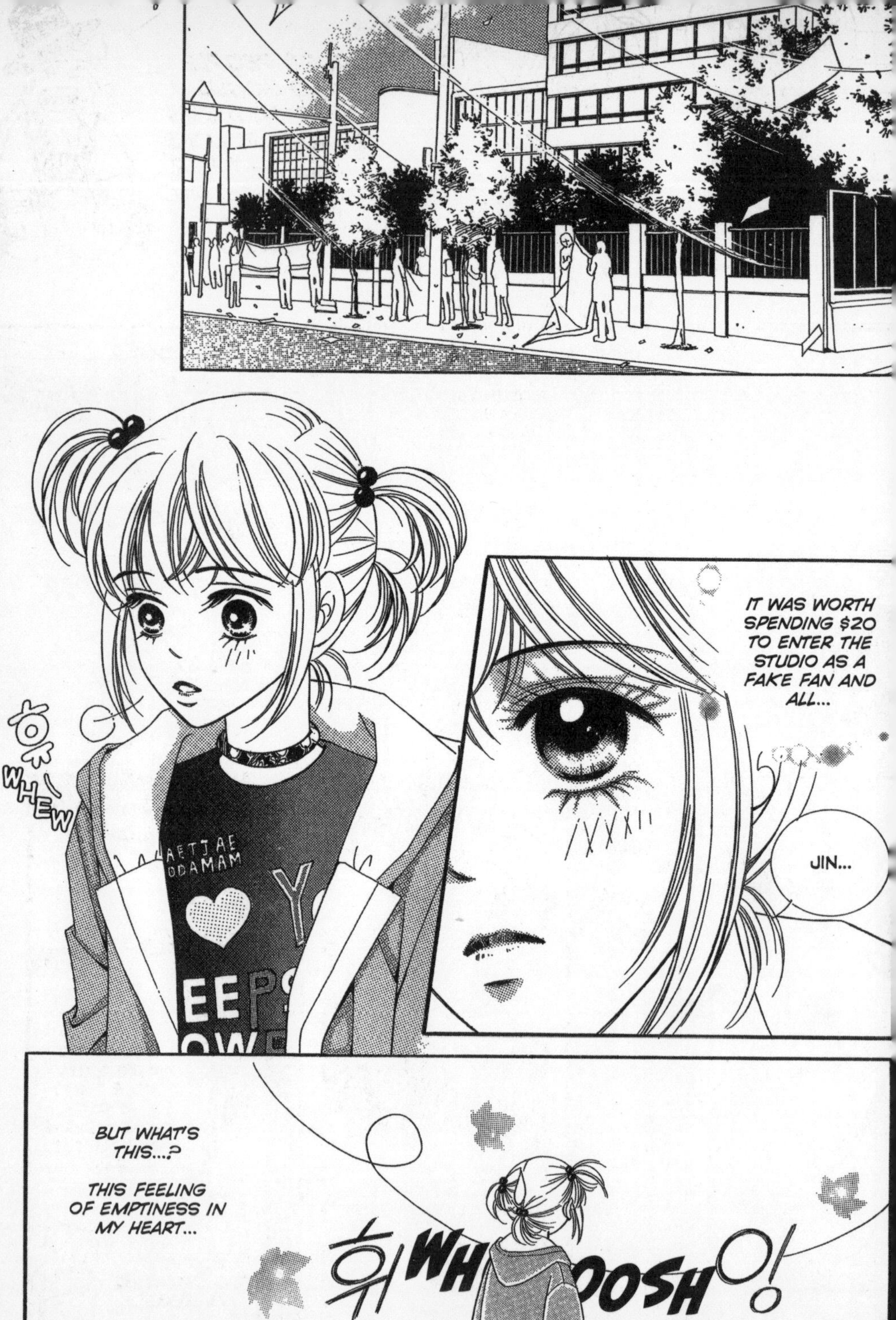
WHEW
IT WAS WORTH SPENDING $20 TO ENTER THE STUDIO AS A FAKE FAN AND ALL...
JIN...
BUT WHAT'S THIS...?
THIS FEELING OF EMPTINESS IN MY HEART...
WH OOSH

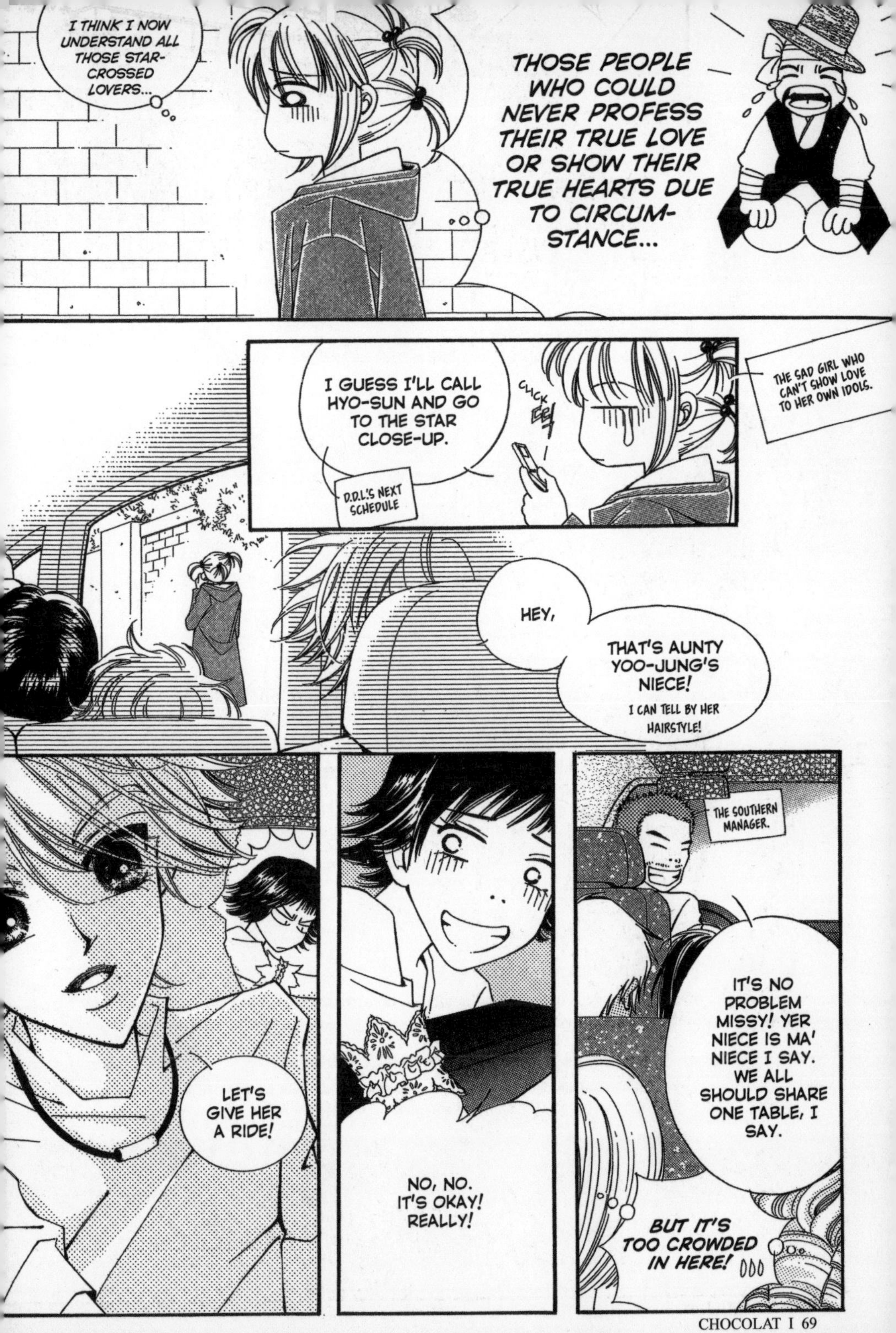
I THINK I NOW UNDERSTAND ALL THOSE STAR-CROSSED LOVERS...
THOSE PEOPLE WHO COULD NEVER PROFESS THEIR TRUE LOVE OR SHOW THEIR TRUE HEARTS DUE TO CIRCUM-STANCE...
I GUESS I'LL CALL HYO-SUN AND GO TO THE STAR CLOSE-UP.
D.D.L.'S NEXT SCHEDULE
CLICK
THE SAD GIRL WHO CAN'T SHOW LOVE TO HER OWN IDOLS.
HEY,
THAT'S AUNTY YOO-JUNG'S NIECE!
I CAN TELL BY HER HAIRSTYLE!
LET'S GIVE HER A RIDE!
NO, NO. IT'S OKAY! REALLY!
THE SOUTHERN MANAGER.
IT'S NO PROBLEM MISSY! YER NIECE IS MA' NIECE I SAY. WE ALL SHOULD SHARE ONE TABLE, I SAY.
BUT IT'S TOO CROWDED IN HERE!

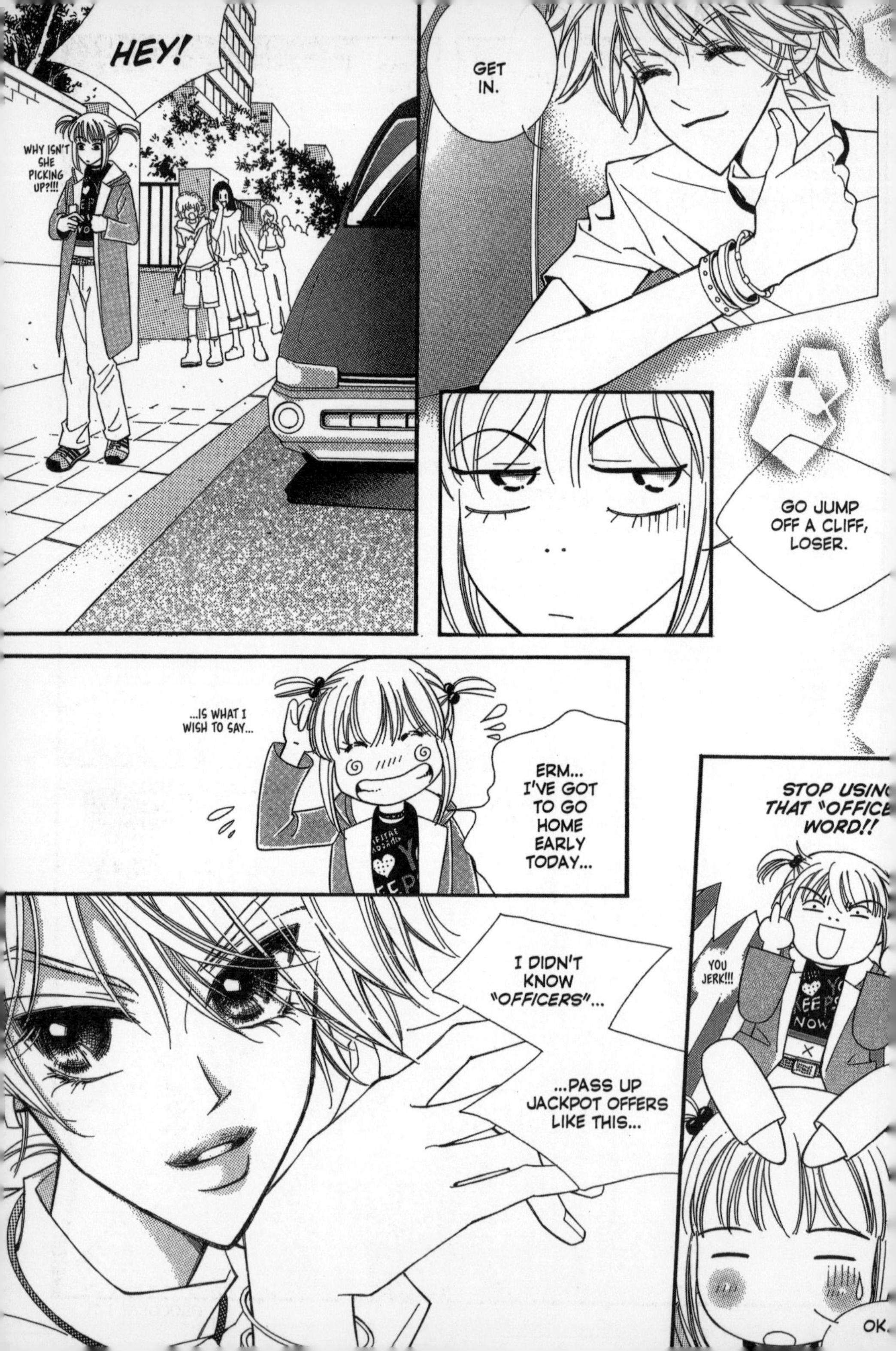
HEY!
WHY ISN'T SHE PICKING UP?!!!
GET IN.
GO JUMP OFF A CLIFF, LOSER.
...IS WHAT I WISH TO SAY...
ERM... I'VE GOT TO GO HOME EARLY TODAY...
I DIDN'T KNOW "OFFICERS"...
...PASS UP JACKPOT OFFERS LIKE THIS...
STOP USIN THAT "OFFICE WORD!!
YOU JERK!!!
OK.

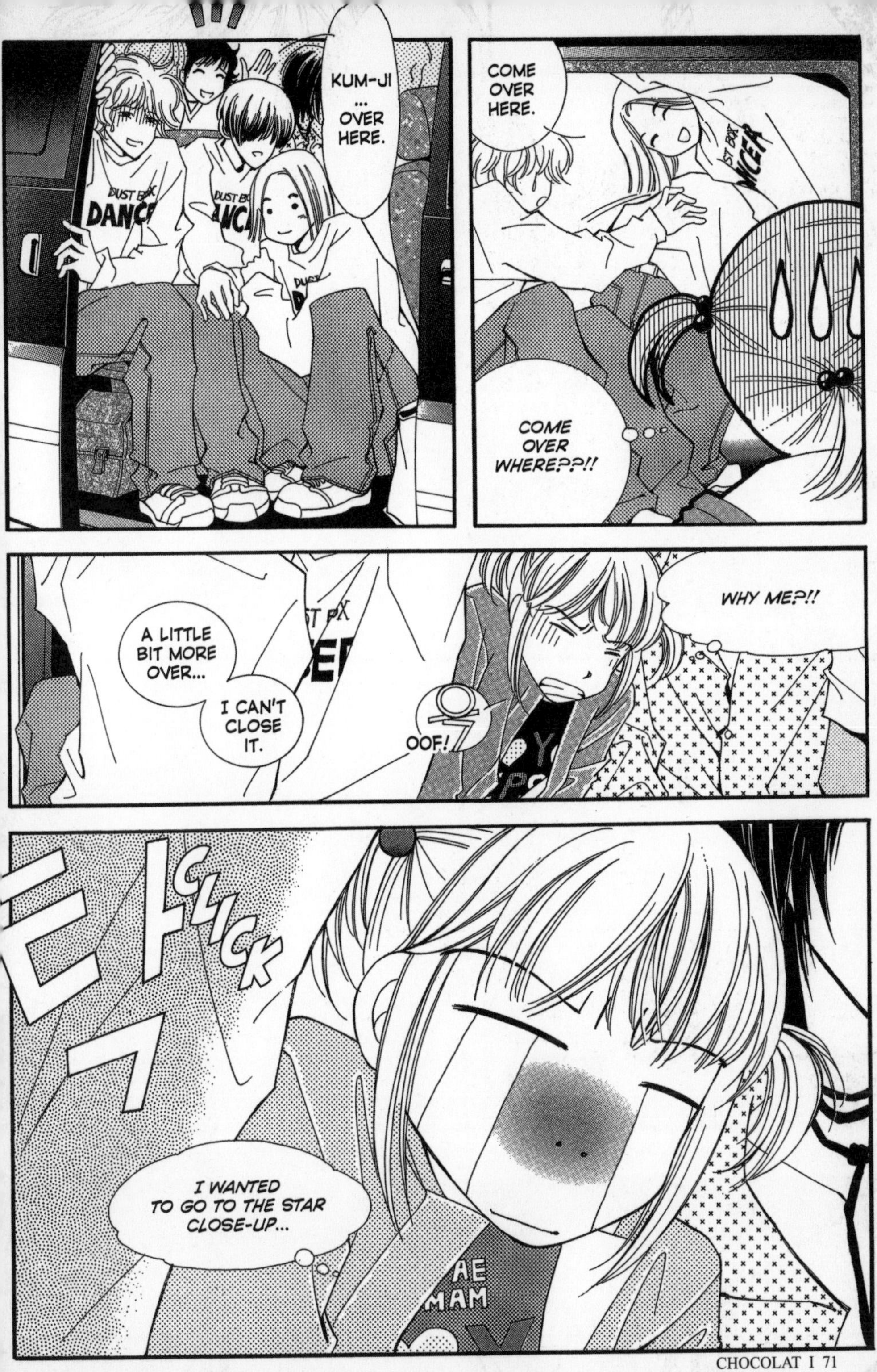
KUM-JI ... OVER HERE.
COME OVER HERE.
COME OVER WHERE??!!
A LITTLE BIT MORE OVER...
I CAN'T CLOSE IT.
OOF!
WHY ME?!!
CLICK
I WANTED TO GO TO THE STAR CLOSE-UP...

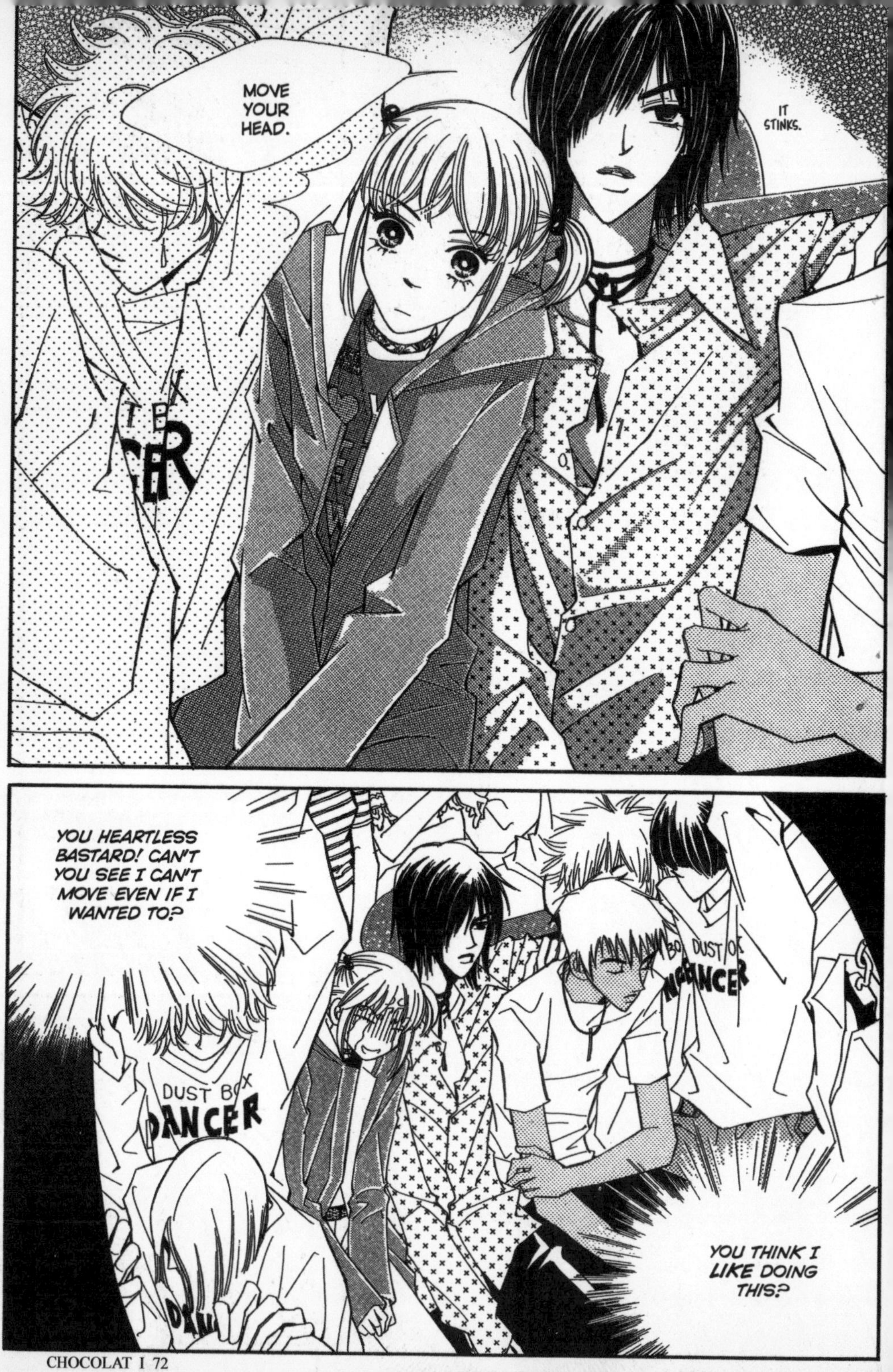
MOVE YOUR HEAD.
IT STINKS.
YOU HEARTLESS BASTARD! CAN'T YOU SEE I CAN'T MOVE EVEN IF I WANTED TO?
DUST BOX DANCER
YOU THINK I LIKE DOING THIS?

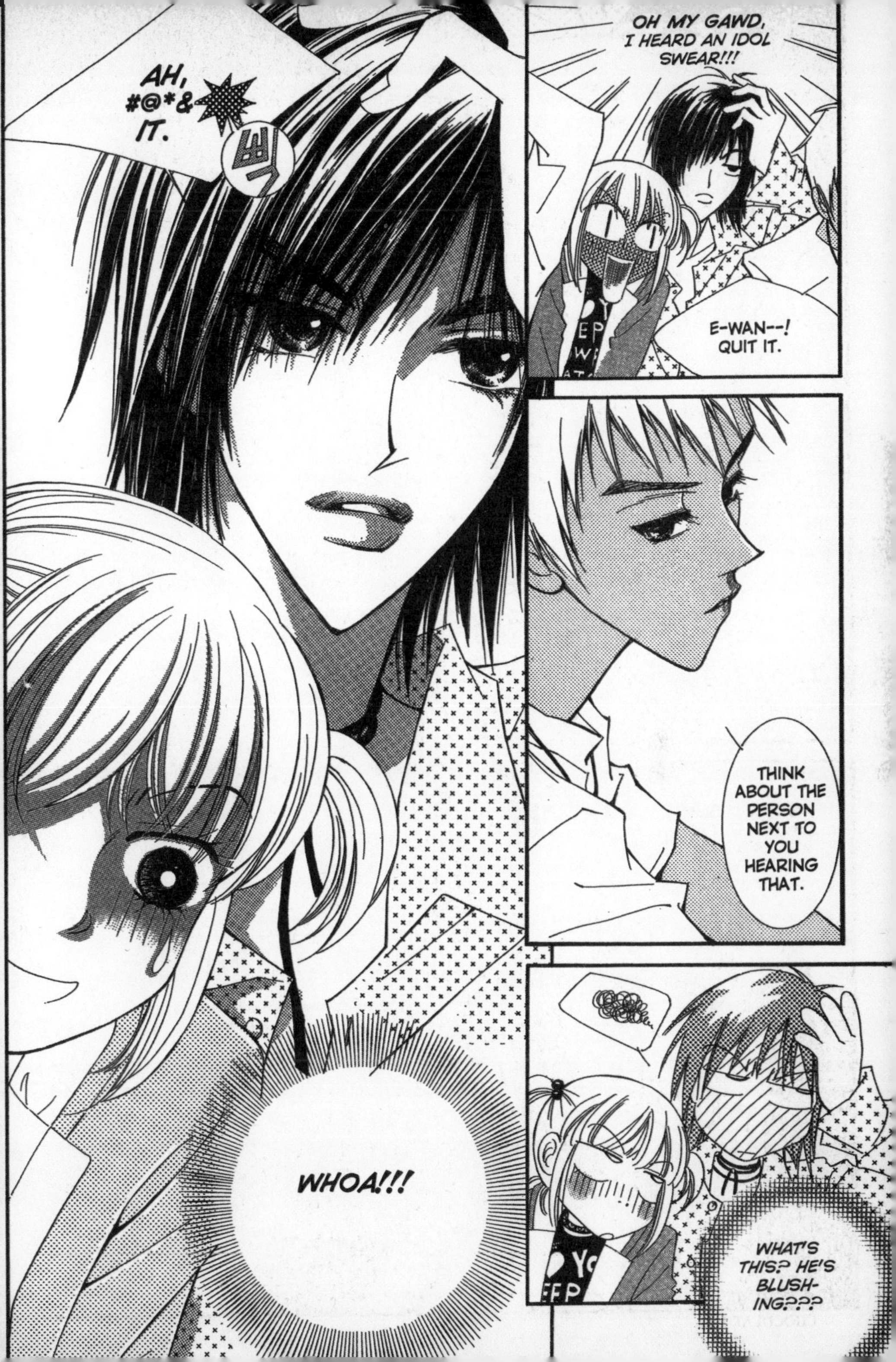
AH, #@*& IT.
WHOA!!!
OH MY GAWD, I HEARD AN IDOL SWEAR!!!
E-WAN--! QUIT IT.
THINK ABOUT THE PERSON NEXT TO YOU HEARING THAT.
WHAT'S THIS? HE'S BLUSH-ING???

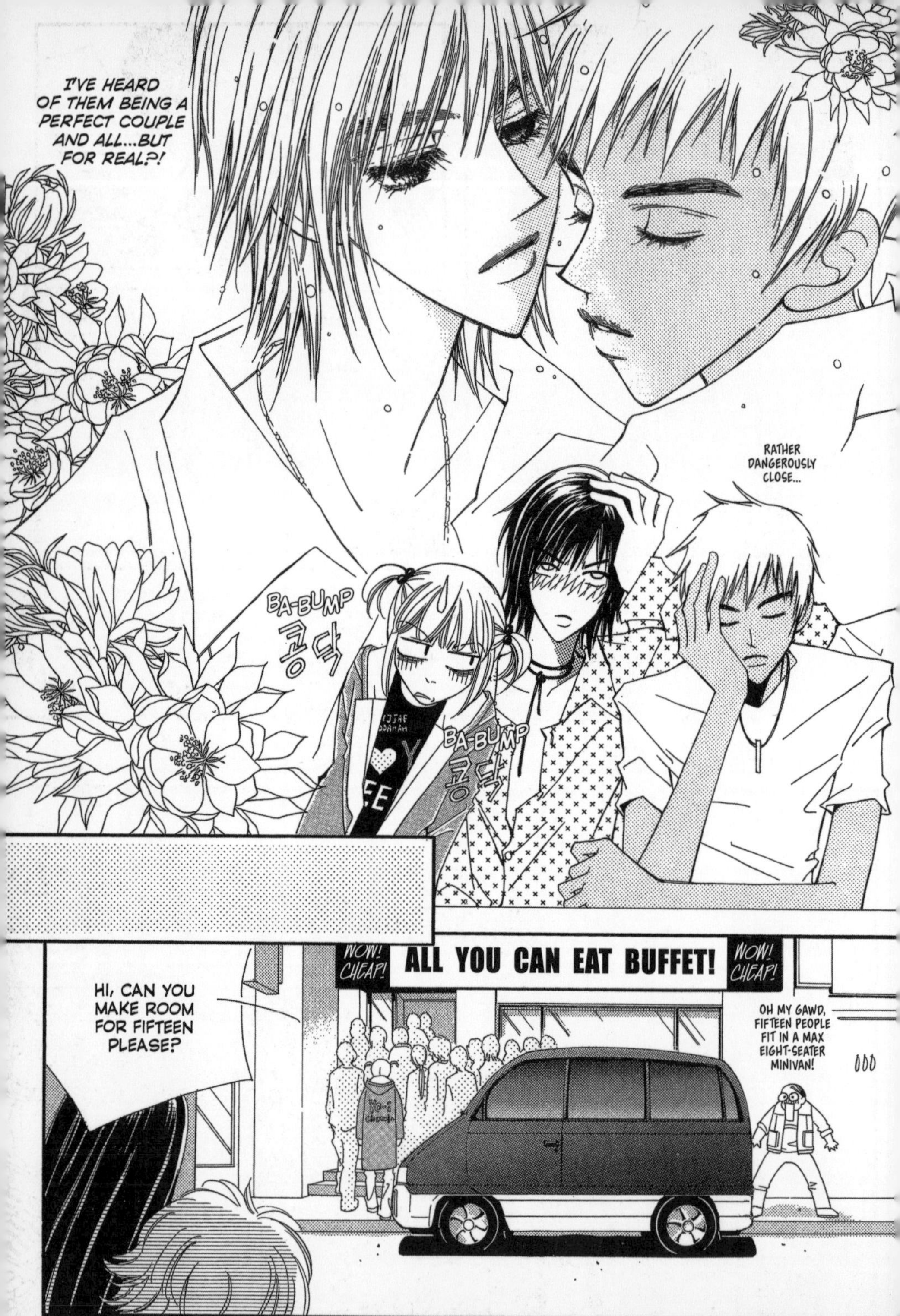
I'VE HEARD OF THEM BEING A PERFECT COUPLE AND ALL...BUT FOR REAL?!
RATHER DANGEROUSLY CLOSE...
BA-BUMP
콩닥
BA-BUMP
콩닥
WOW! CHEAP!
ALL YOU CAN EAT BUFFET!
WOW! CHEAP!
HI, CAN YOU MAKE ROOM FOR FIFTEEN PLEASE?
OH MY GAWD, FIFTEEN PEOPLE FIT IN A MAX EIGHT-SEATER MINIVAN!

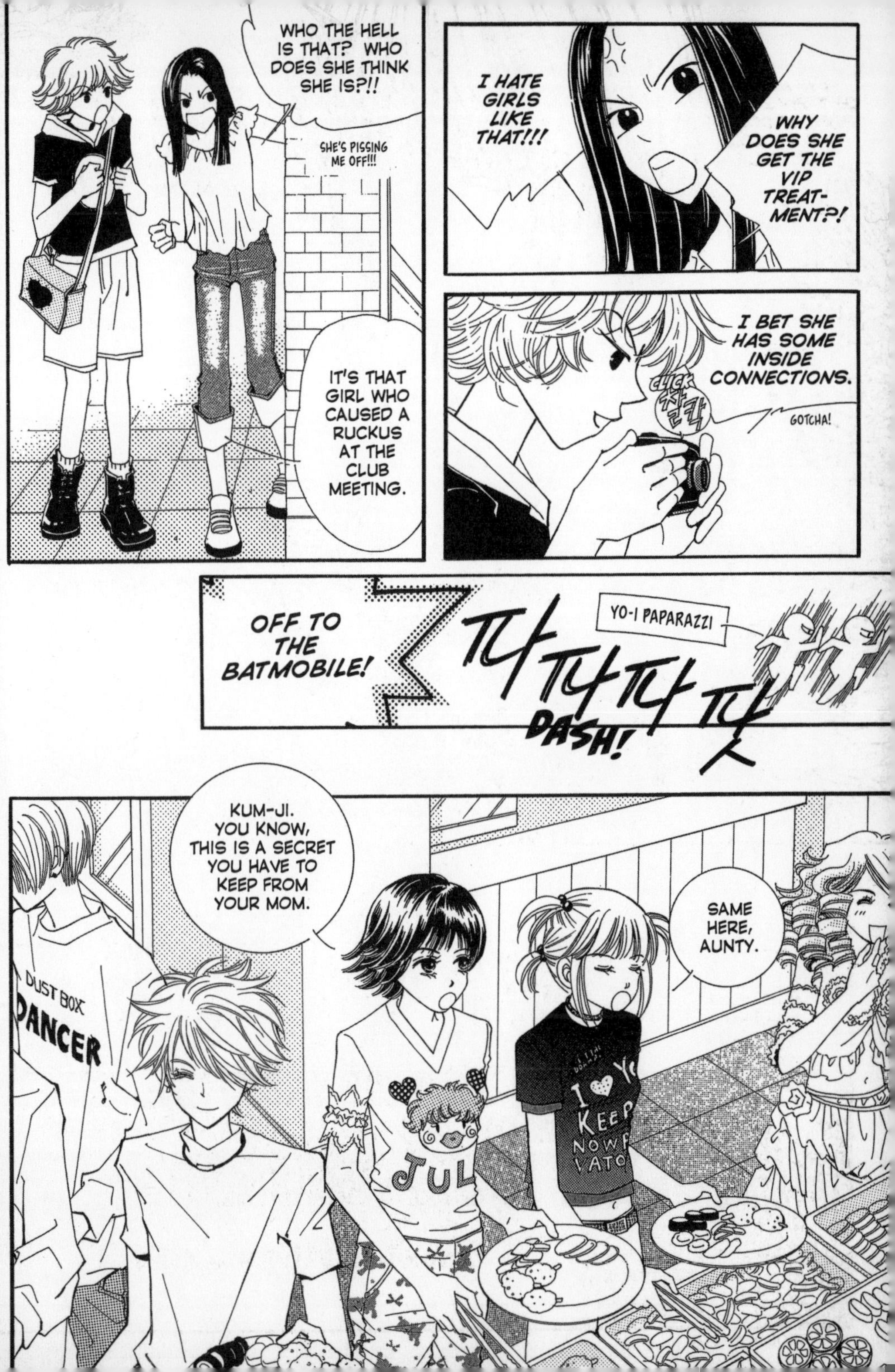
WHO THE HELL IS THAT? WHO DOES SHE THINK SHE IS?!!
SHE'S PISSING ME OFF!!!
IT'S THAT GIRL WHO CAUSED A RUCKUS AT THE CLUB MEETING.
I HATE GIRLS LIKE THAT!!!
WHY DOES SHE GET THE VIP TREATMENT?!
I BET SHE HAS SOME INSIDE CONNECTIONS.
CLICK
찰칵
GOTCHA!
OFF TO THE BATMOBILE!
YO-I PAPARAZZI
DASH!
KUM-JI. YOU KNOW, THIS IS A SECRET YOU HAVE TO KEEP FROM YOUR MOM.
SAME HERE, AUNTY.
DUST BOX DANCER

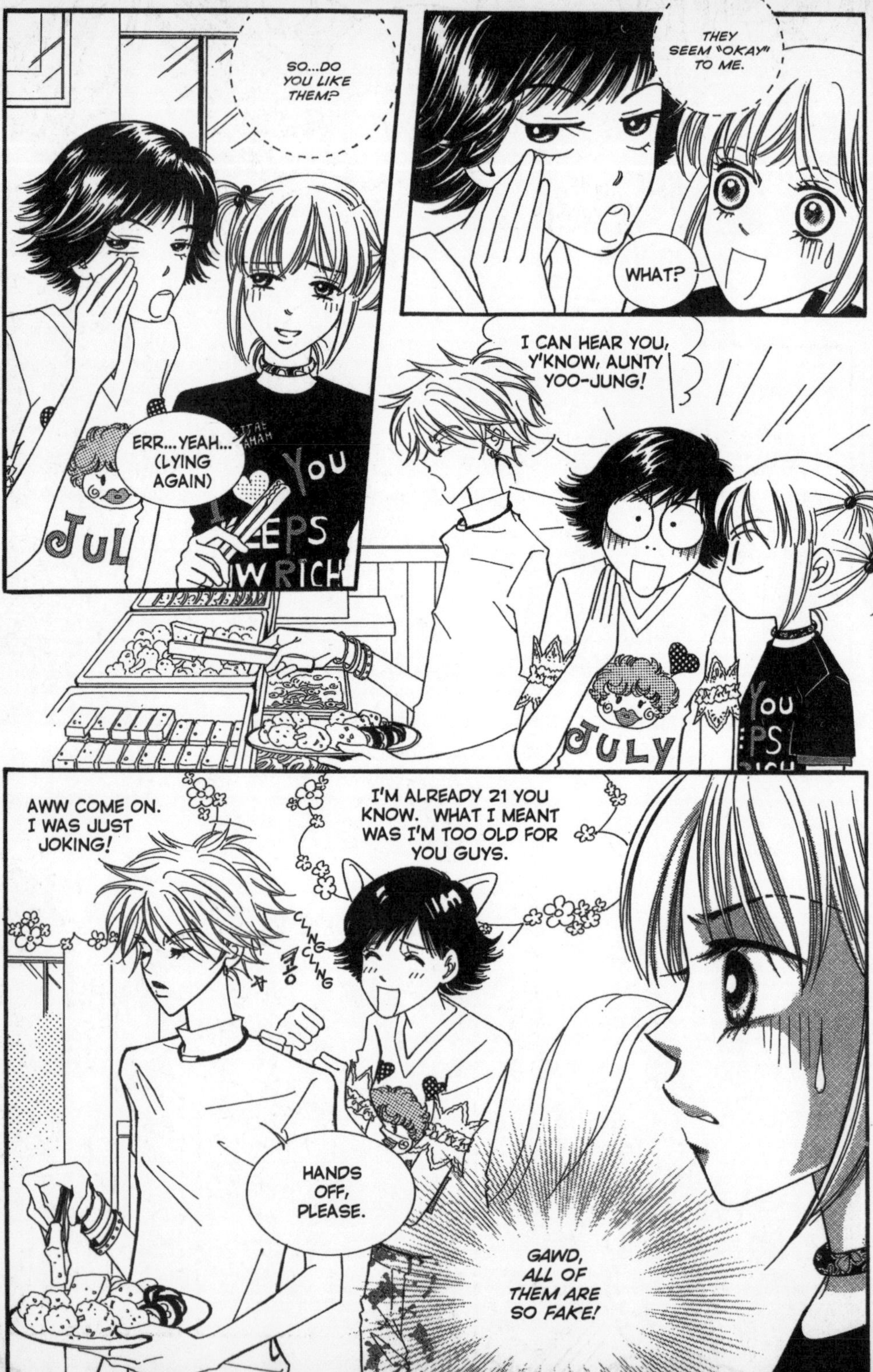
SO...DO YOU LIKE THEM?
ERR...YEAH... (LYING AGAIN)
THEY SEEM "OKAY" TO ME.
WHAT?
I CAN HEAR YOU, Y'KNOW, AUNTY YOO-JUNG!
AWW COME ON. I WAS JUST JOKING!
I'M ALREADY 21 YOU KNOW. WHAT I MEANT WAS I'M TOO OLD FOR YOU GUYS.
CLING CLING
HANDS OFF, PLEASE.
GAWD, ALL OF THEM ARE SO FAKE!

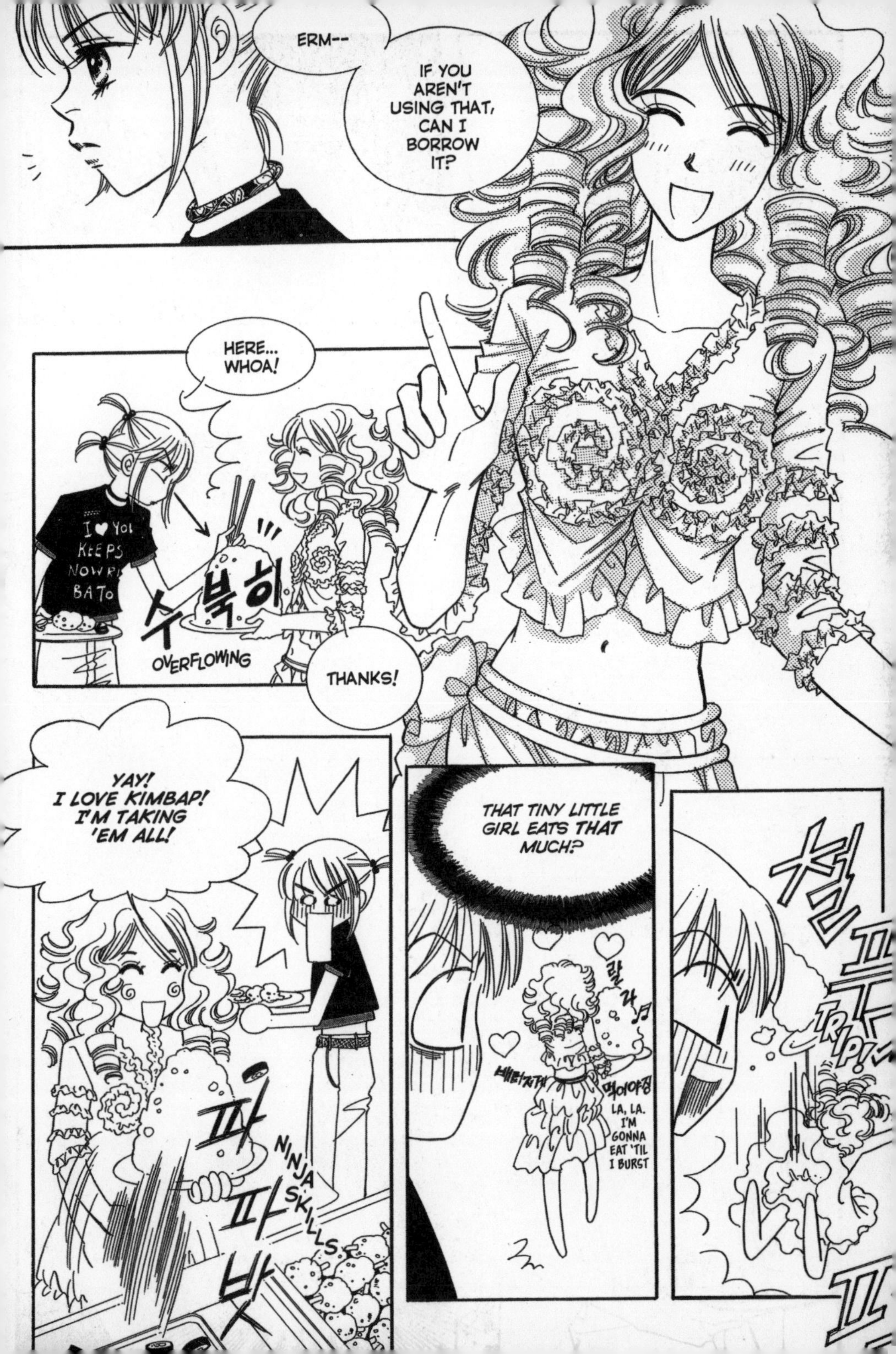
ERM--
IF YOU AREN'T USING THAT, CAN I BORROW IT?
HERE... WHOA!
수북히
OVERFLOWING
THANKS!
YAY! I LOVE KIMBAP! I'M TAKING 'EM ALL!
파파바
NINJA SKILLS
THAT TINY LITTLE GIRL EATS THAT MUCH?
랄라
배터지게 먹어야징
LA, LA. I'M GONNA EAT 'TIL I BURST
TRIP!

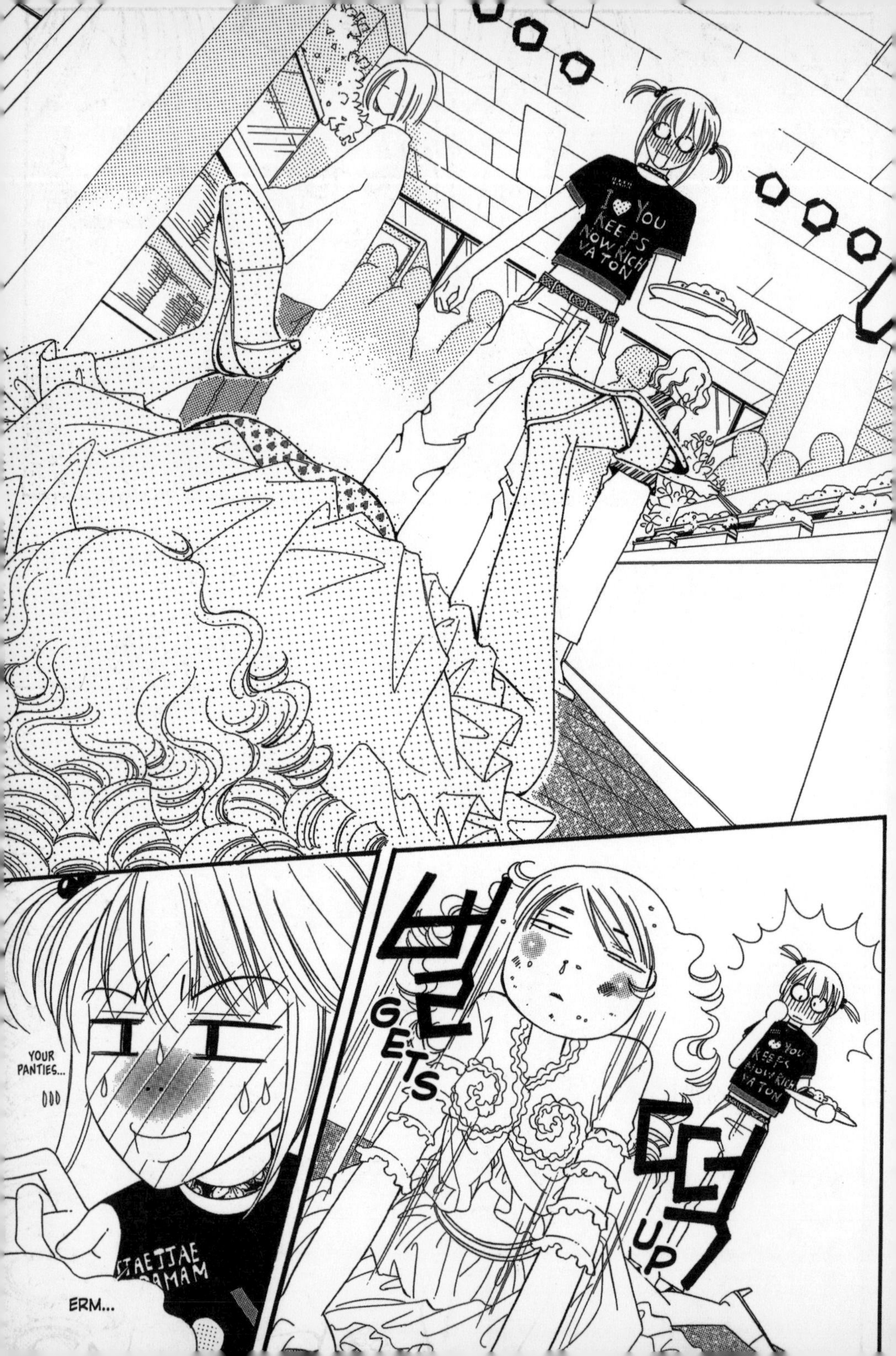
I ♥ YOU
KEEPS
NOW RICH
VA TON
YOUR PANTIES...
ERM...
GETS
UP

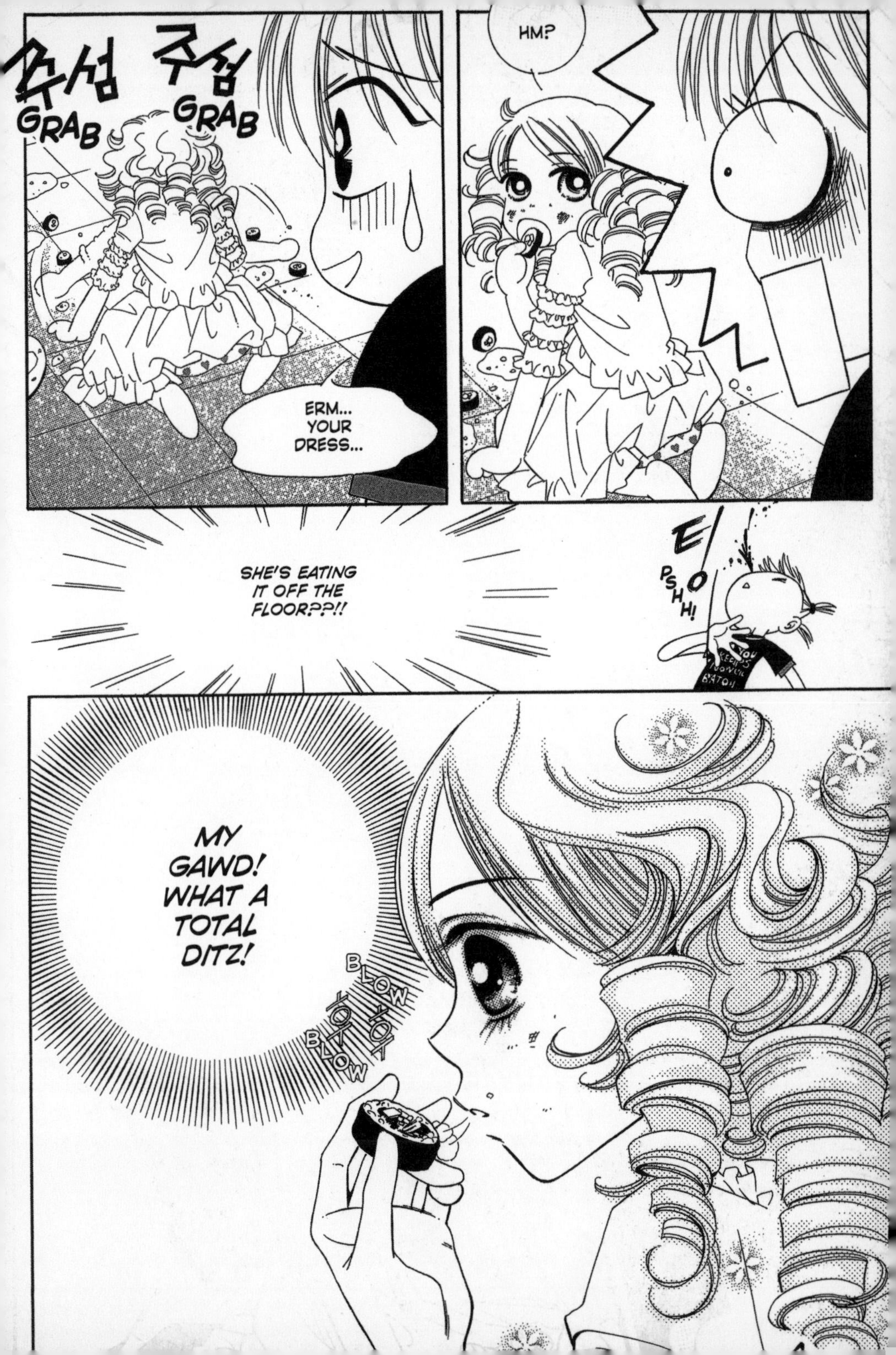
주섬 주섬
GRAB GRAB
ERM... YOUR DRESS...
HM?
SHE'S EATING IT OFF THE FLOOR??!!
PSHH!
MY GAWD! WHAT A TOTAL DITZ!
BLOW BLOW

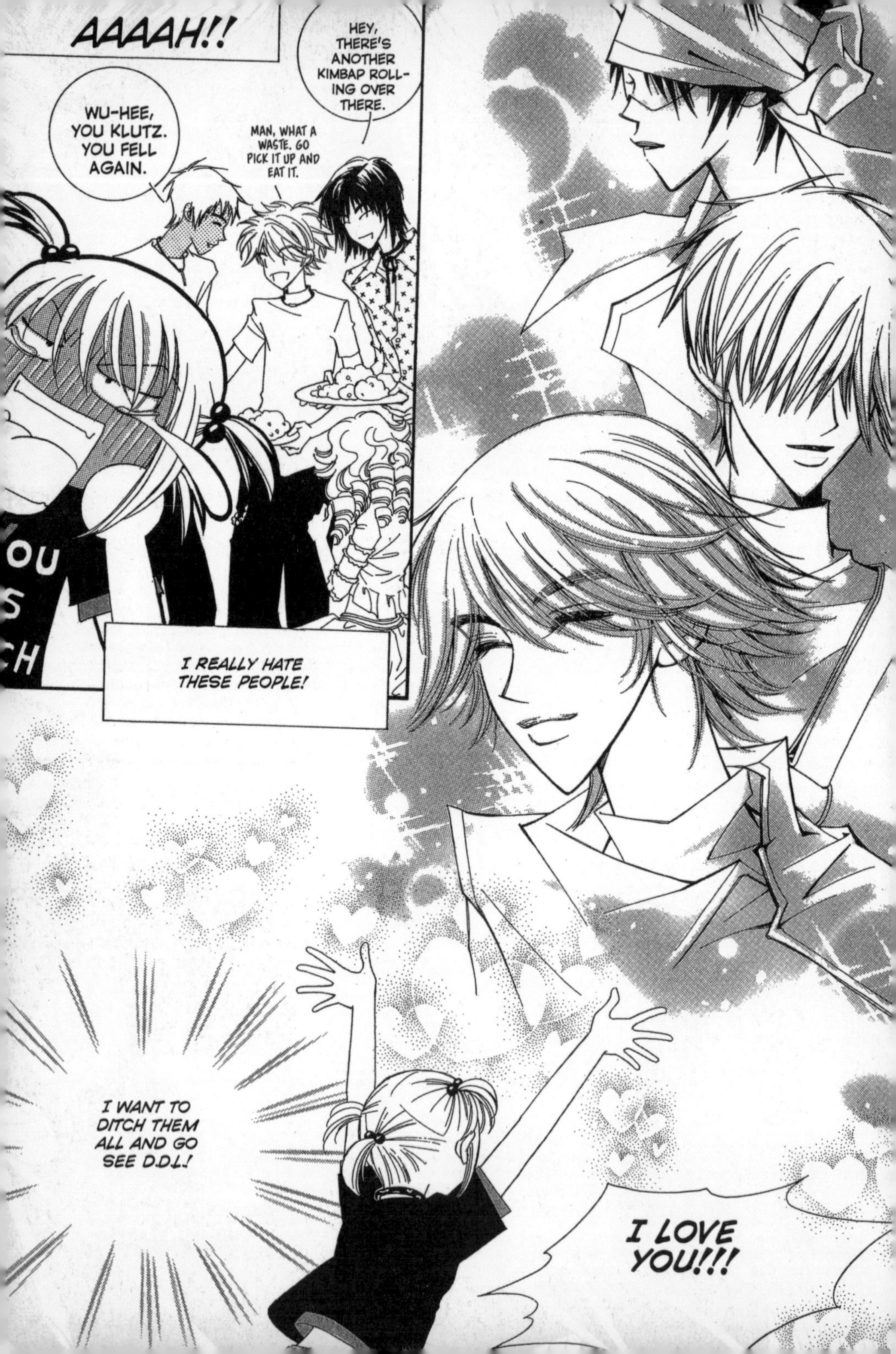
AAAAH!!
WU-HEE, YOU KLUTZ. YOU FELL AGAIN.
MAN, WHAT A WASTE. GO PICK IT UP AND EAT IT.
HEY, THERE'S ANOTHER KIMBAP ROLLING OVER THERE.
I REALLY HATE THESE PEOPLE!
I WANT TO DITCH THEM ALL AND GO SEE D.D.L!
I LOVE YOU!!!

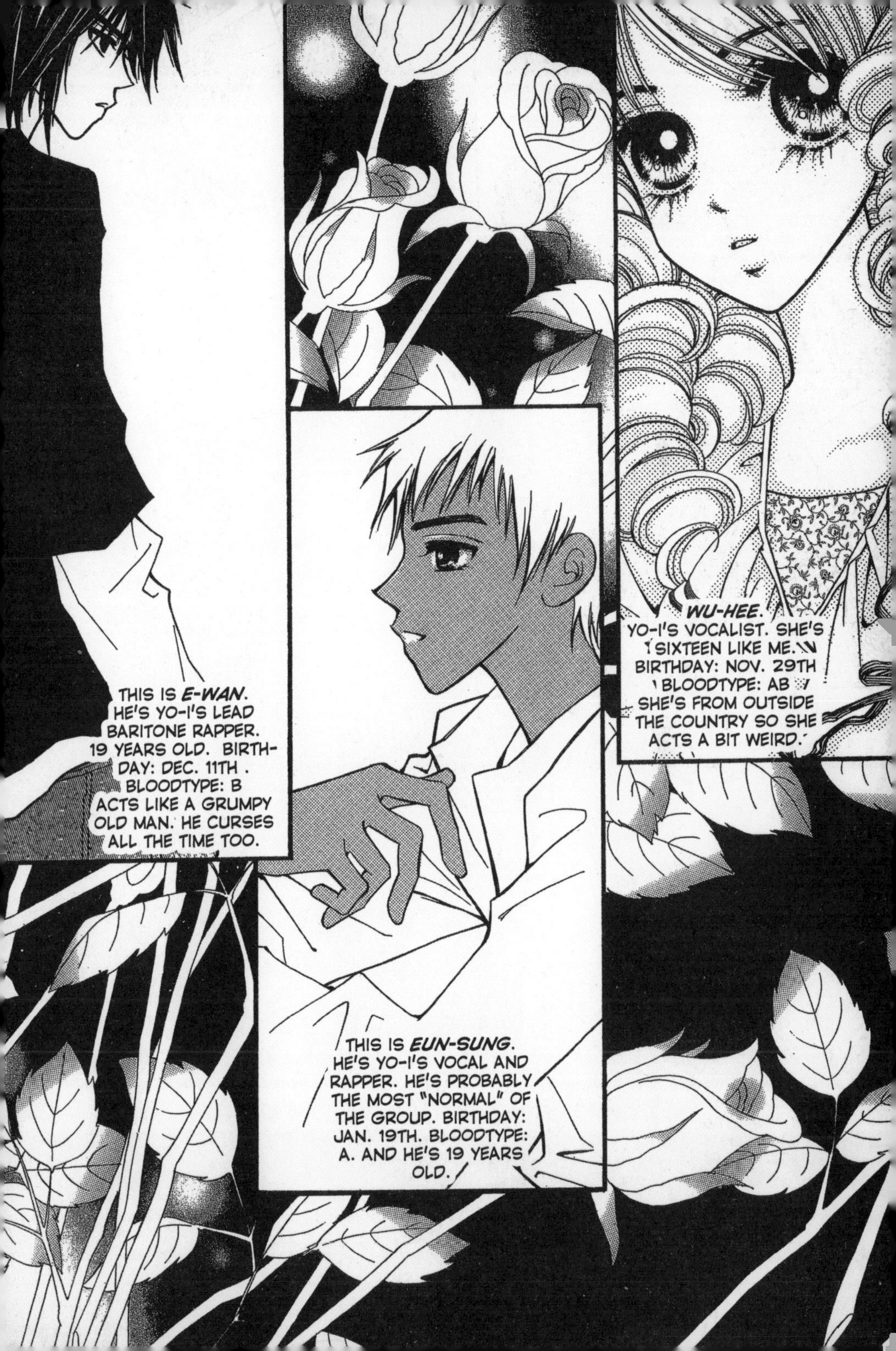
THIS IS E-WAN. HE'S YO-I'S LEAD BARITONE RAPPER. 19 YEARS OLD. BIRTH-DAY: DEC. 11TH. BLOODTYPE: B ACTS LIKE A GRUMPY OLD MAN. HE CURSES ALL THE TIME TOO.
WU-HEE. YO-I'S VOCALIST. SHE'S SIXTEEN LIKE ME. BIRTHDAY: NOV. 29TH BLOODTYPE: AB SHE'S FROM OUTSIDE THE COUNTRY SO SHE ACTS A BIT WEIRD.
THIS IS EUN-SUNG. HE'S YO-I'S VOCAL AND RAPPER. HE'S PROBABLY THE MOST "NORMAL" OF THE GROUP. BIRTHDAY: JAN. 19TH. BLOODTYPE: A. AND HE'S 19 YEARS OLD.

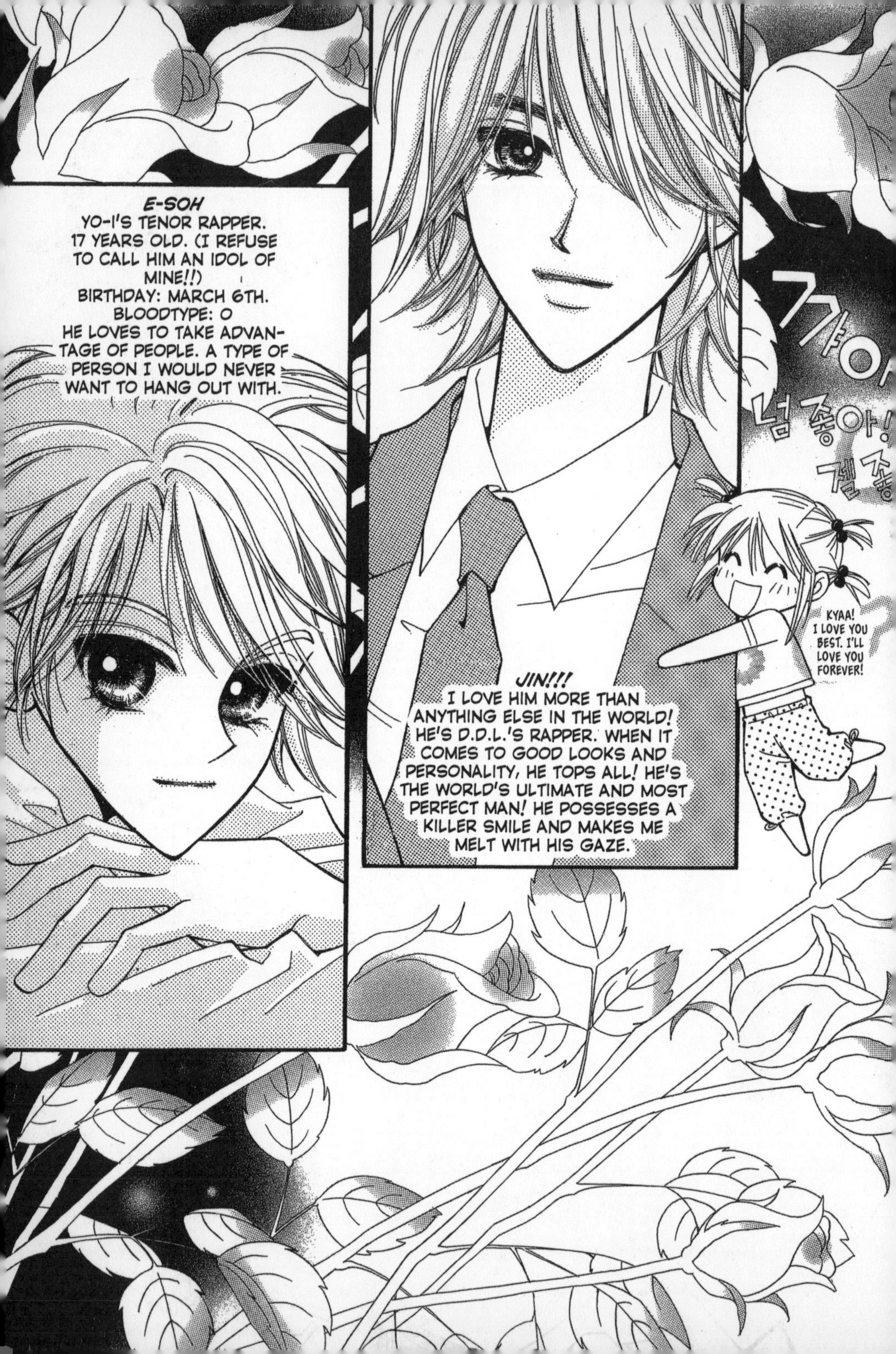
E-SOH
YO-I'S TENOR RAPPER.
17 YEARS OLD. (I REFUSE TO CALL HIM AN IDOL OF MINE!!)
BIRTHDAY: MARCH 6TH.
BLOODTYPE: O
HE LOVES TO TAKE ADVANTAGE OF PEOPLE. A TYPE OF PERSON I WOULD NEVER WANT TO HANG OUT WITH.
JIN!!!
I LOVE HIM MORE THAN ANYTHING ELSE IN THE WORLD! HE'S D.D.L.'S RAPPER. WHEN IT COMES TO GOOD LOOKS AND PERSONALITY, HE TOPS ALL! HE'S THE WORLD'S ULTIMATE AND MOST PERFECT MAN! HE POSSESSES A KILLER SMILE AND MAKES ME MELT WITH HIS GAZE.
KYAA! I LOVE YOU BEST. I'LL LOVE YOU FOREVER!

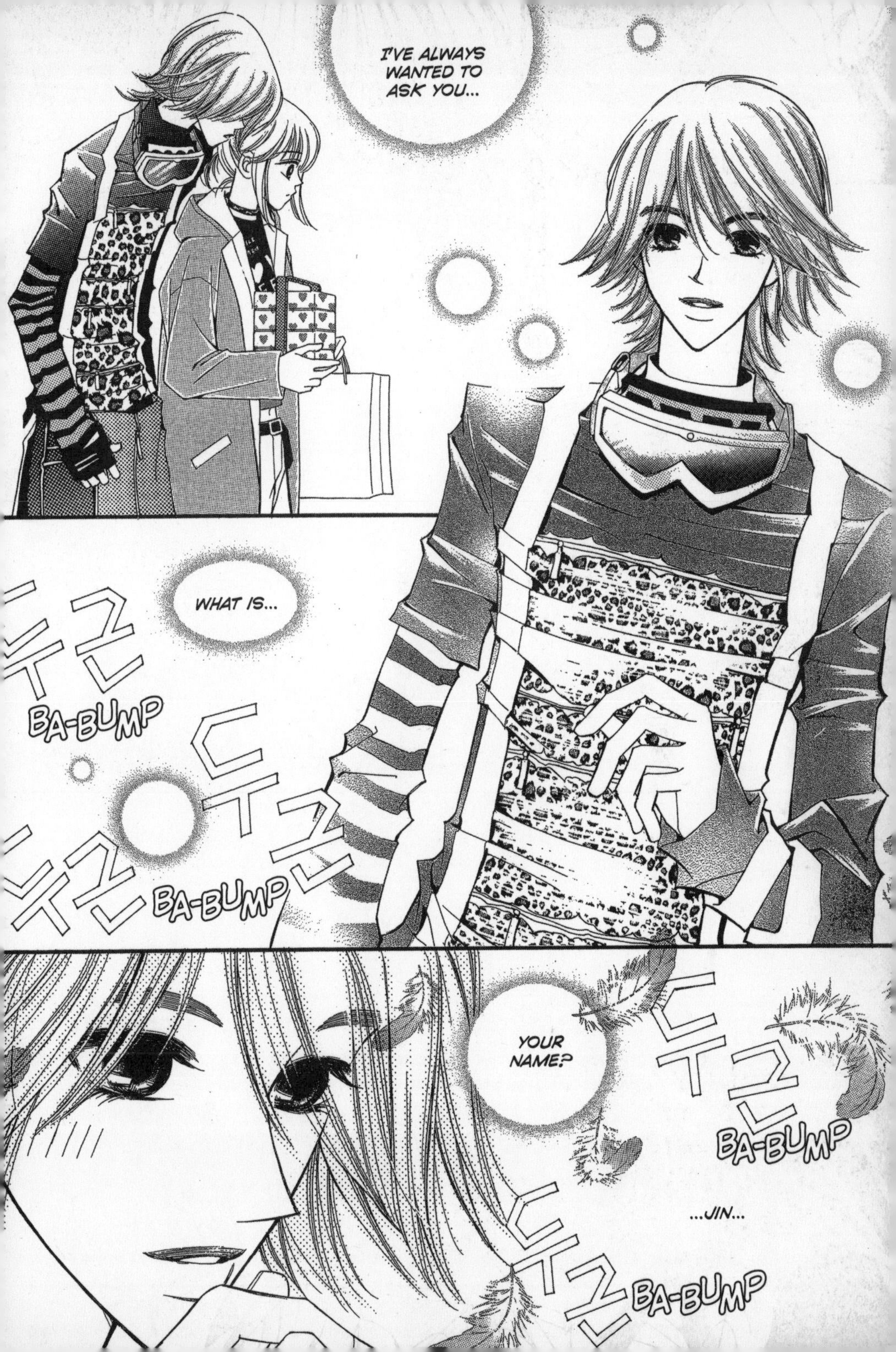
I'VE ALWAYS WANTED TO ASK YOU...
WHAT IS...
BA-BUMP
BA-BUMP
YOUR NAME?
BA-BUMP
...JIN...
BA-BUMP

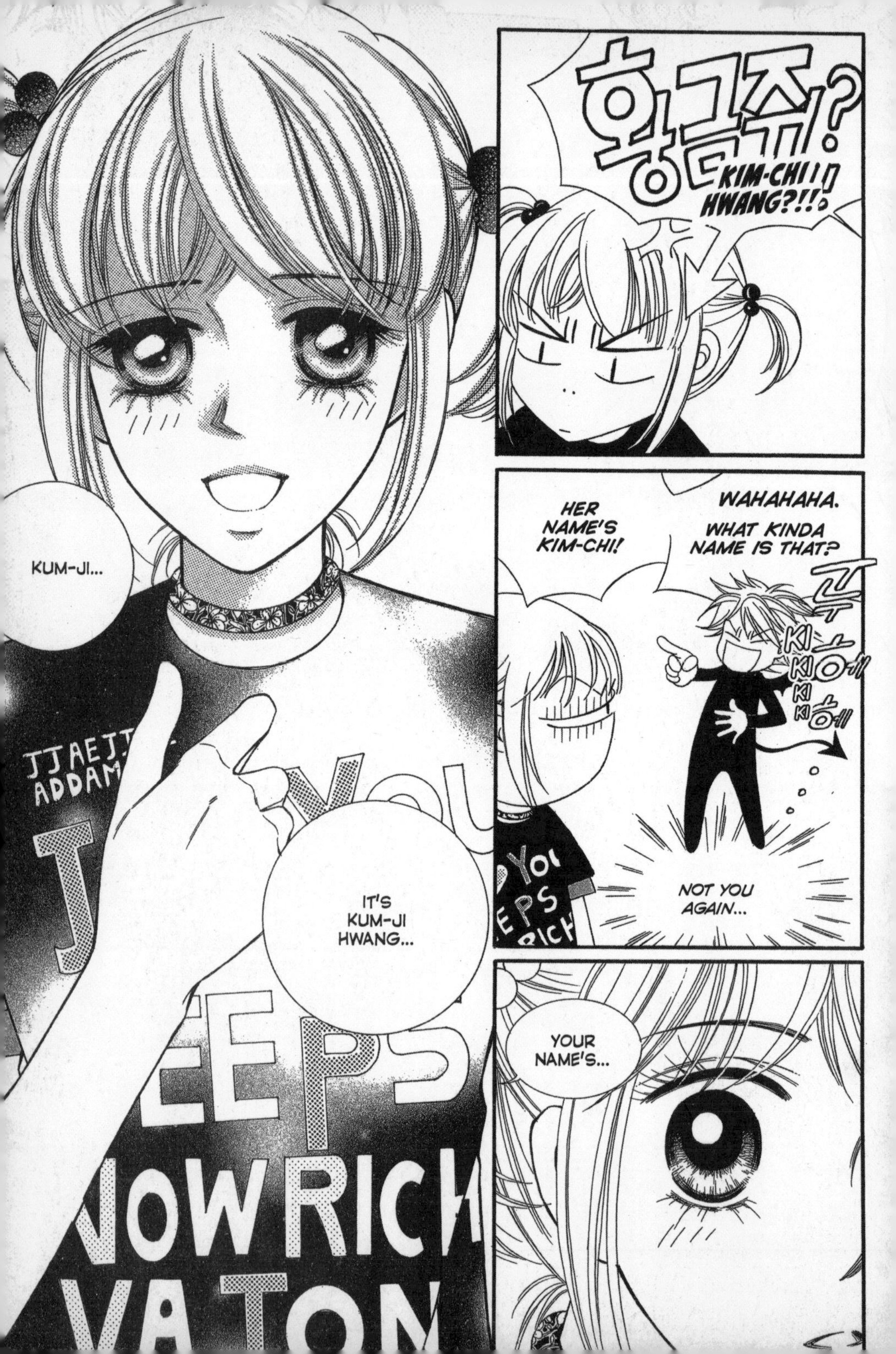
KUM-JI...
IT'S KUM-JI HWANG...
황금쥐?
KIM-CHI!! HWANG?!!
HER NAME'S KIM-CHI!
WAHAHAHA.
WHAT KINDA NAME IS THAT?
KI KI KI KI
NOT YOU AGAIN...
YOUR NAME'S...

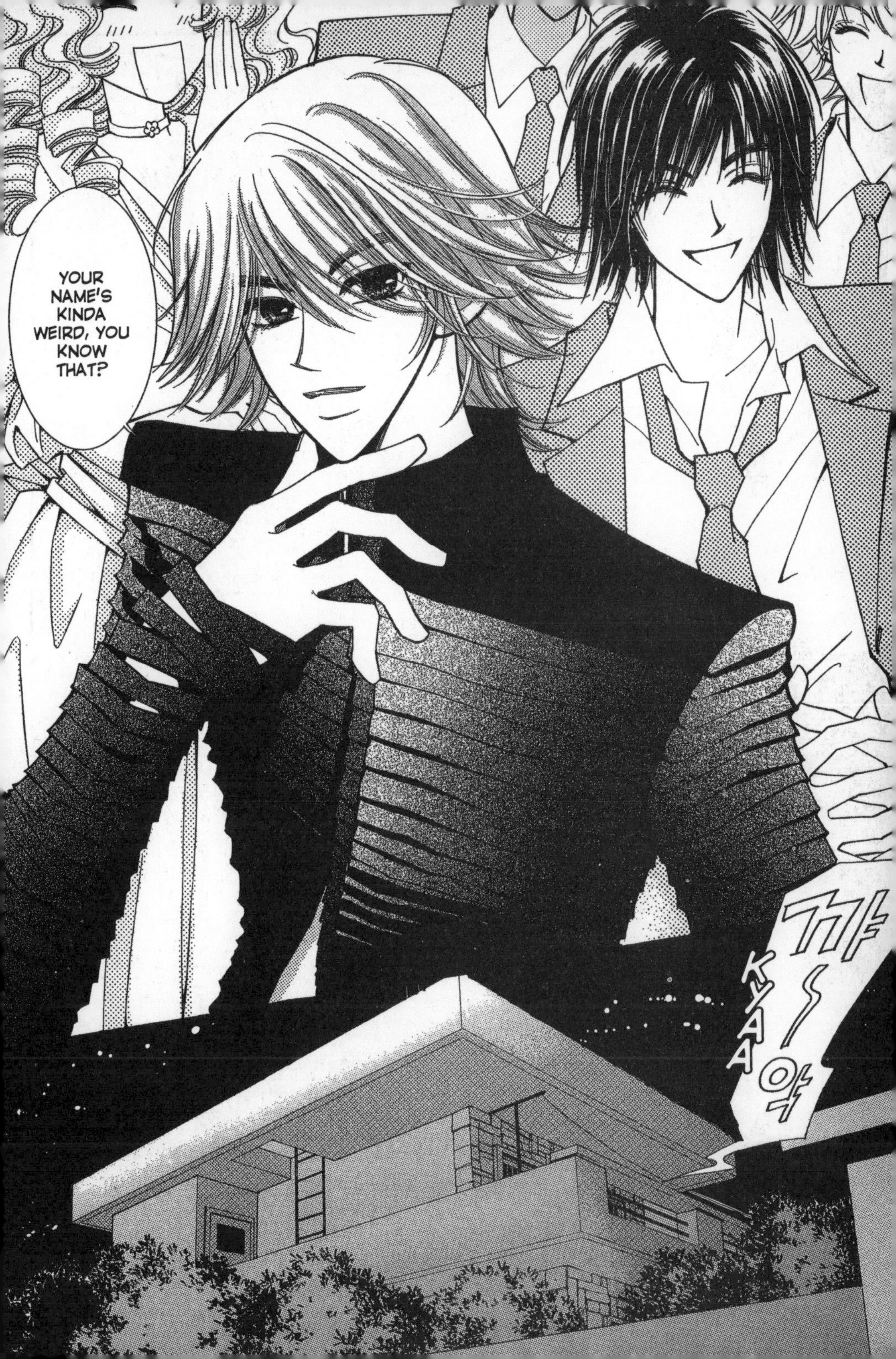
YOUR NAME'S KINDA WEIRD, YOU KNOW THAT?
꺄~약
KYAAA

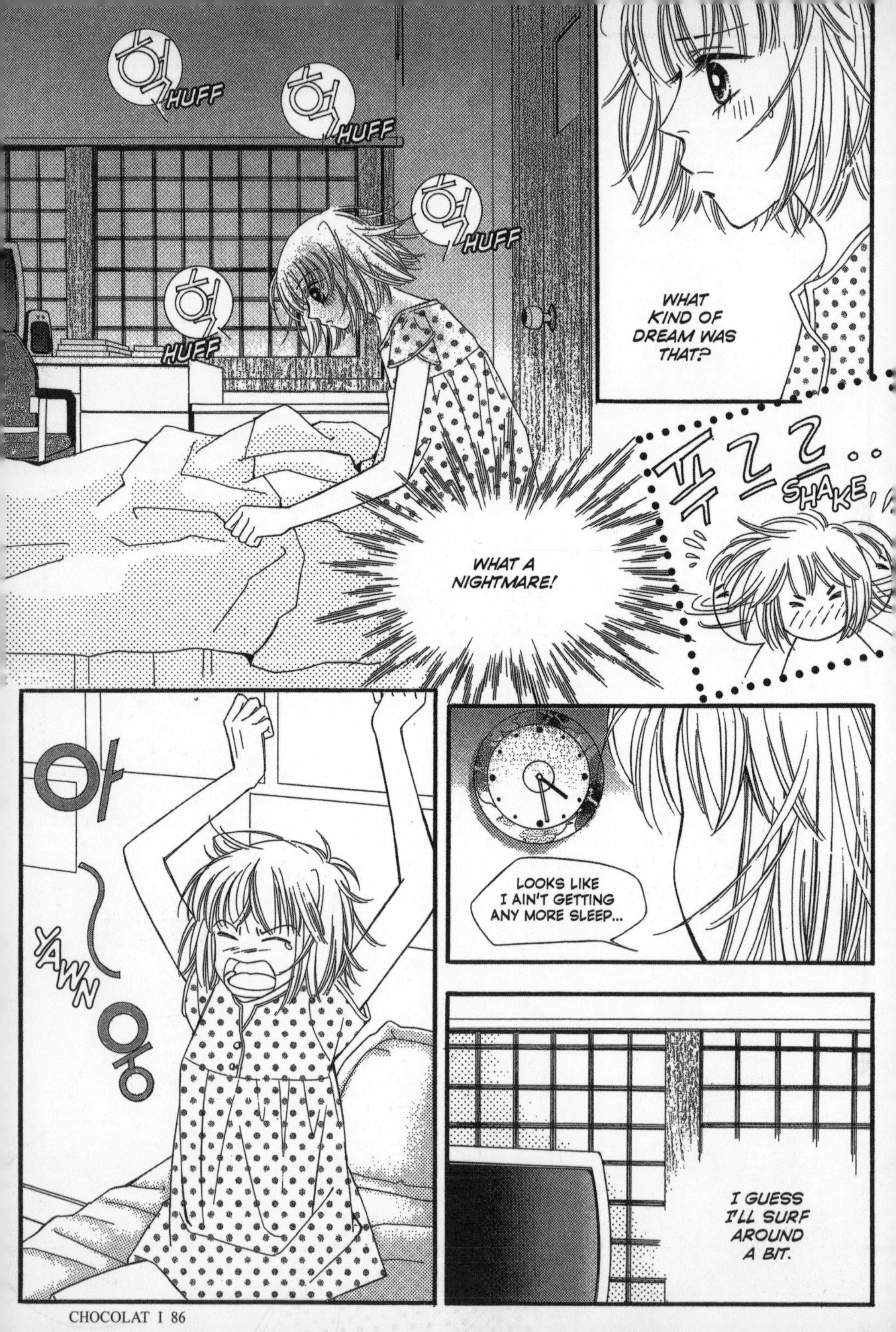
헉 HUFF
헉 HUFF
헉 HUFF
헉 HUFF
WHAT KIND OF DREAM WAS THAT?
WHAT A NIGHTMARE!
SHAKE,
YAWN
LOOKS LIKE I AIN'T GETTING ANY MORE SLEEP...
I GUESS I'LL SURF AROUND A BIT.

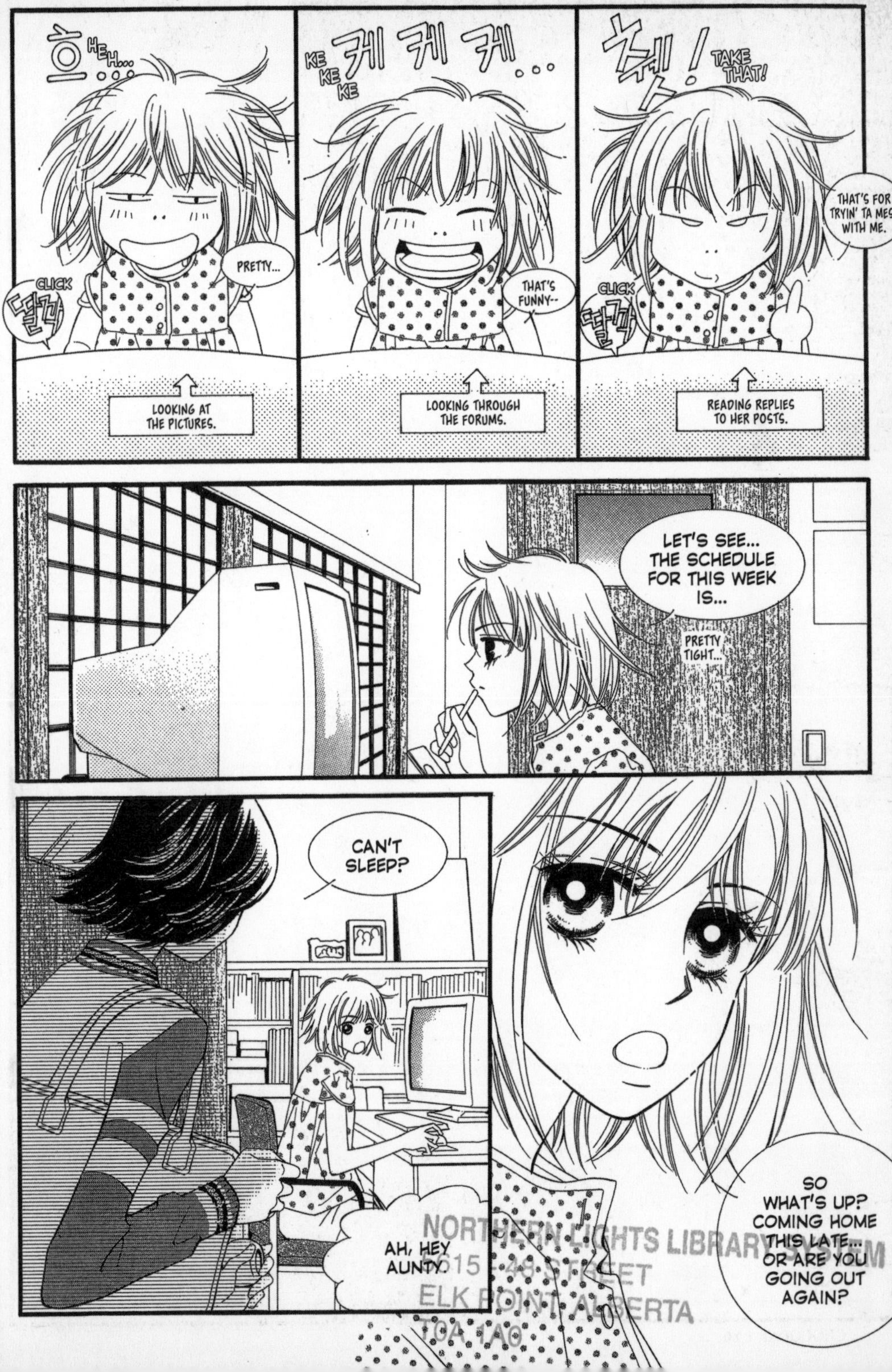
흐
HEH...
PRETTY...
CLICK
LOOKING AT THE PICTURES.
KE KE KE
케 케 케...
THAT'S FUNNY--
LOOKING THROUGH THE FORUMS.
TAKE THAT!
THAT'S FOR TRYIN' TA MESS WITH ME.
CLICK
READING REPLIES TO HER POSTS.
LET'S SEE... THE SCHEDULE FOR THIS WEEK IS...
PRETTY TIGHT...
CAN'T SLEEP?
AH, HEY AUNTY.
SO WHAT'S UP? COMING HOME THIS LATE... OR ARE YOU GOING OUT AGAIN?

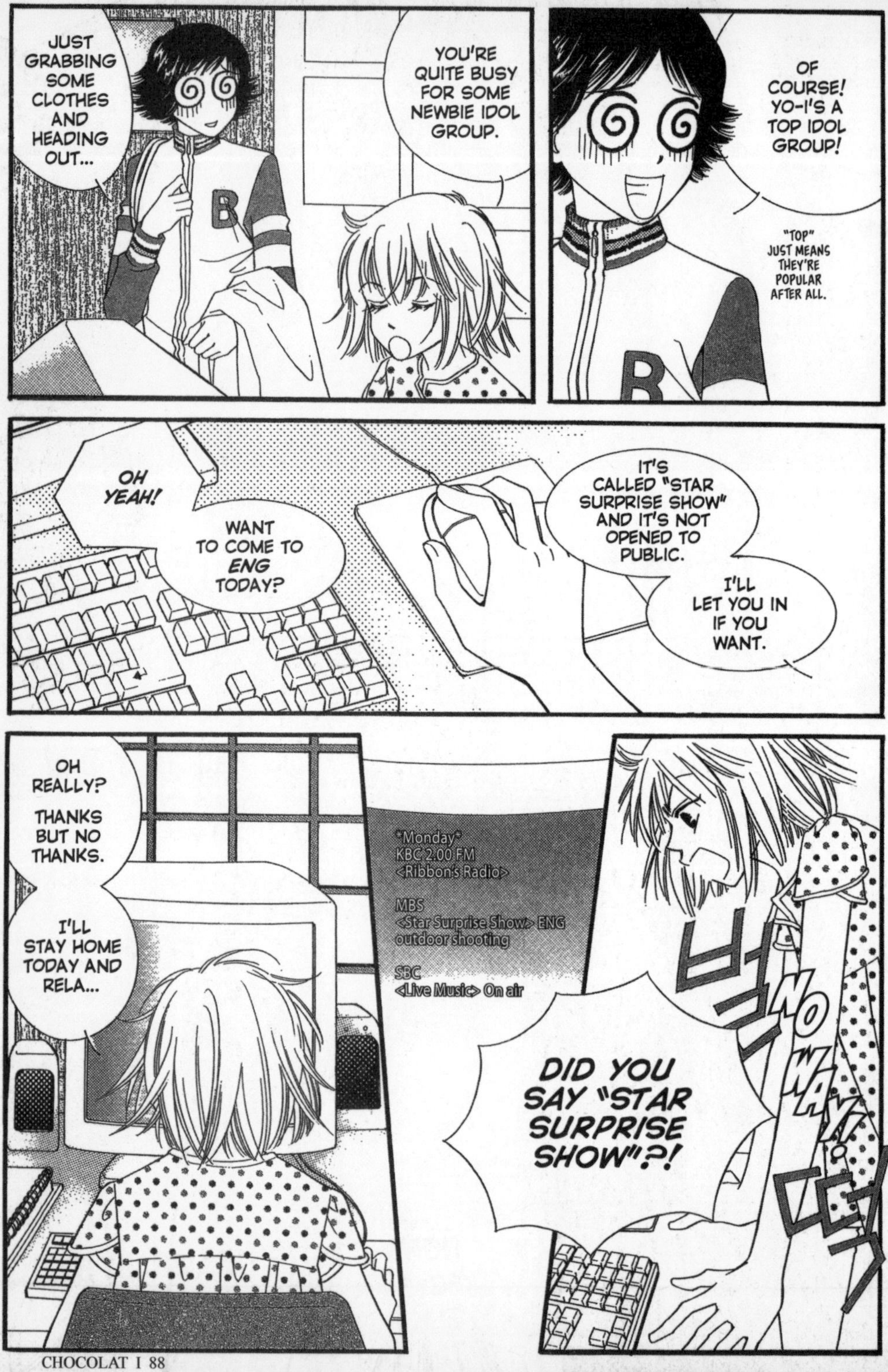
JUST GRABBING SOME CLOTHES AND HEADING OUT...
YOU'RE QUITE BUSY FOR SOME NEWBIE IDOL GROUP.
OF COURSE! YO-I'S A TOP IDOL GROUP!
"TOP" JUST MEANS THEY'RE POPULAR AFTER ALL.
OH YEAH!
WANT TO COME TO ENG TODAY?
IT'S CALLED "STAR SURPRISE SHOW" AND IT'S NOT OPENED TO PUBLIC.
I'LL LET YOU IN IF YOU WANT.
OH REALLY?
THANKS BUT NO THANKS.
I'LL STAY HOME TODAY AND RELA...
Monday
KBC 2.00 FM
<Ribbon's Radio>
MBS
<Star Surprise Show> ENG
outdoor shooting
SBC
<Live Music> On air
DID YOU SAY "STAR SURPRISE SHOW"?!
NO WAY!

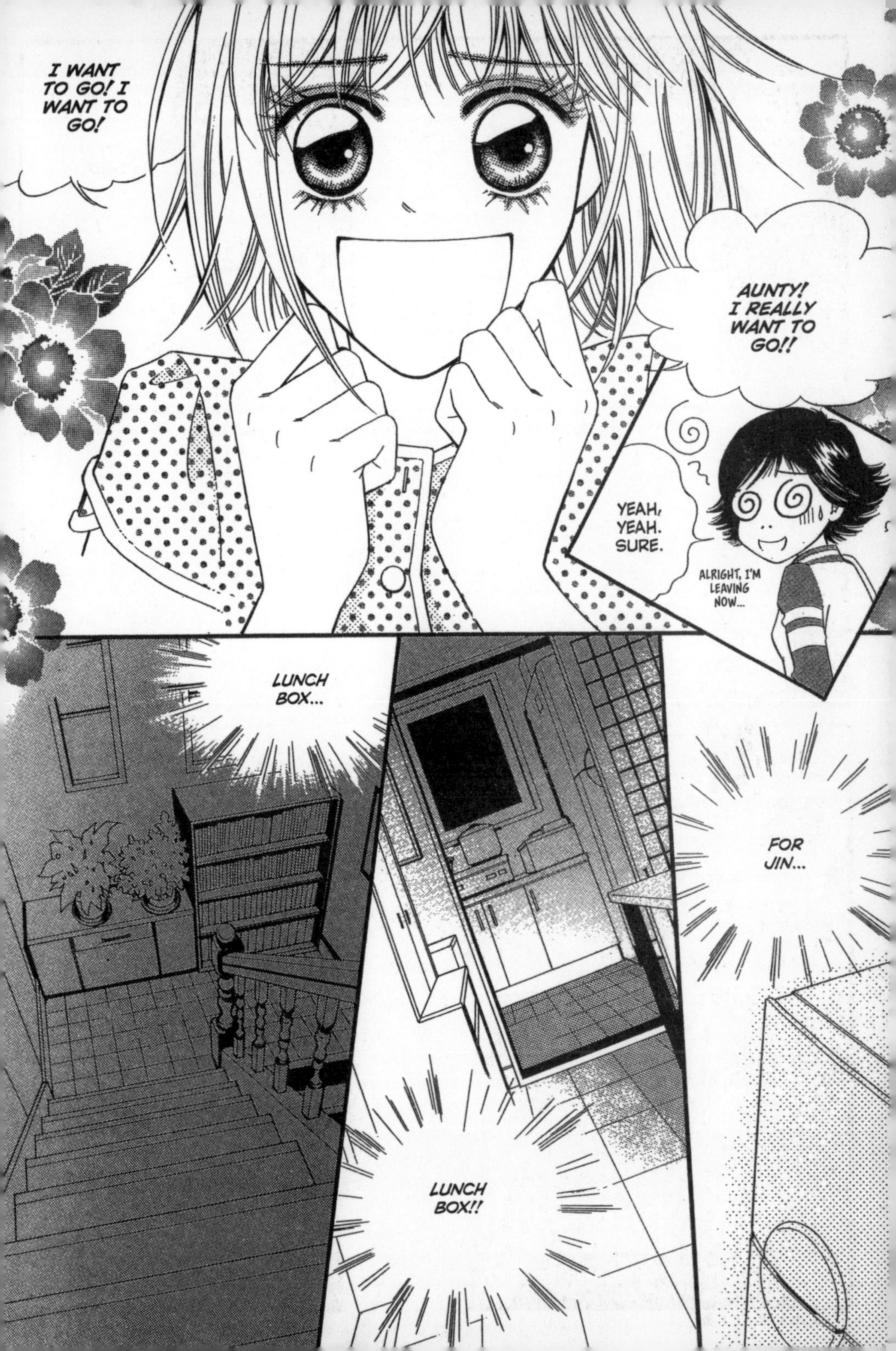

I WANT TO GO! I WANT TO GO!
AUNTY! I REALLY WANT TO GO!!
YEAH, YEAH. SURE.
ALRIGHT, I'M LEAVING NOW...
LUNCH BOX...
LUNCH BOX!!
FOR JIN...

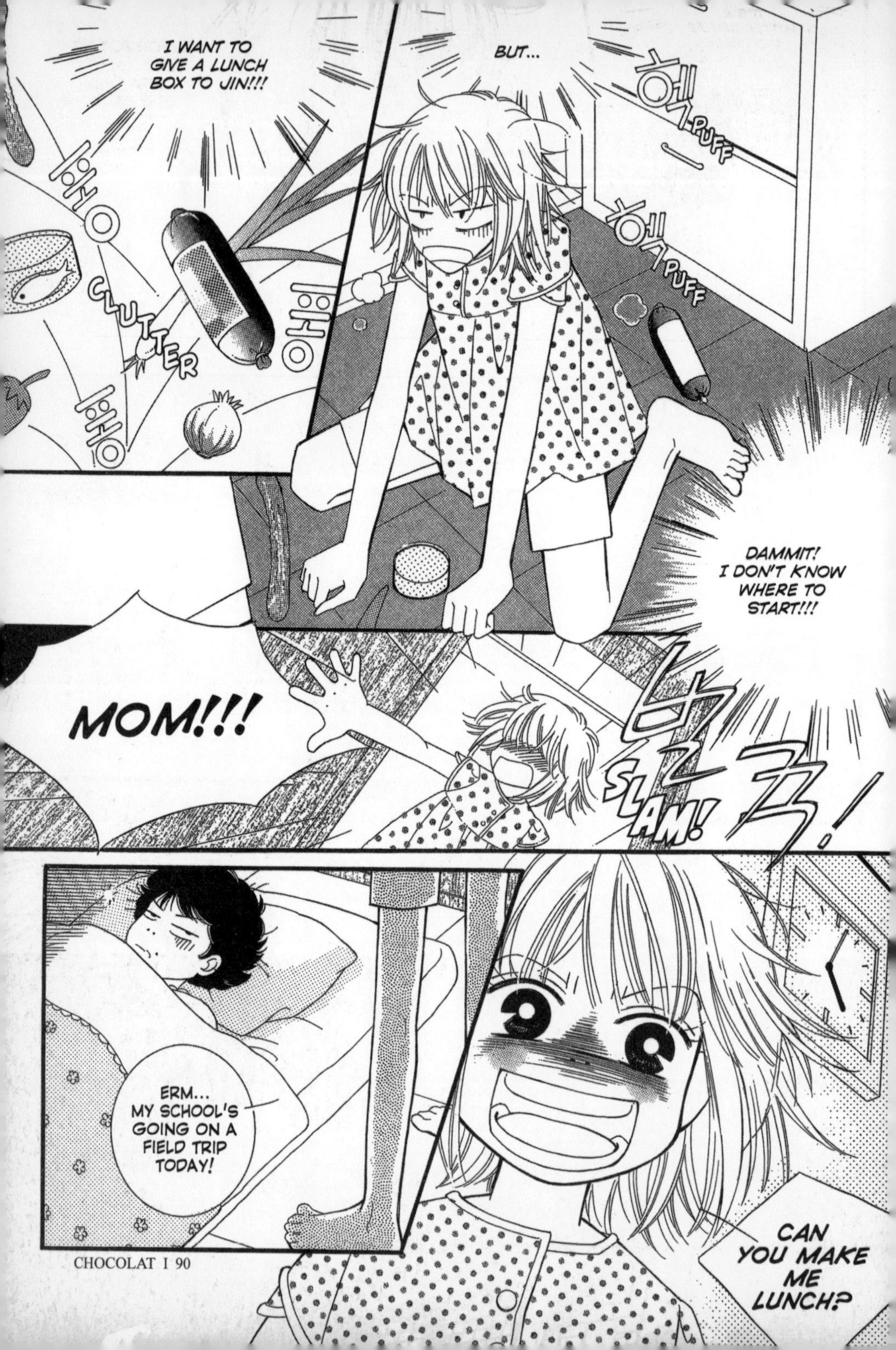
I WANT TO GIVE A LUNCH BOX TO JIN!!!
CLUTTER
BUT...
PUFF
PUFF
DAMMIT! I DON'T KNOW WHERE TO START!!!
MOM!!!
SLAM!
ERM... MY SCHOOL'S GOING ON A FIELD TRIP TODAY!
CAN YOU MAKE ME LUNCH?

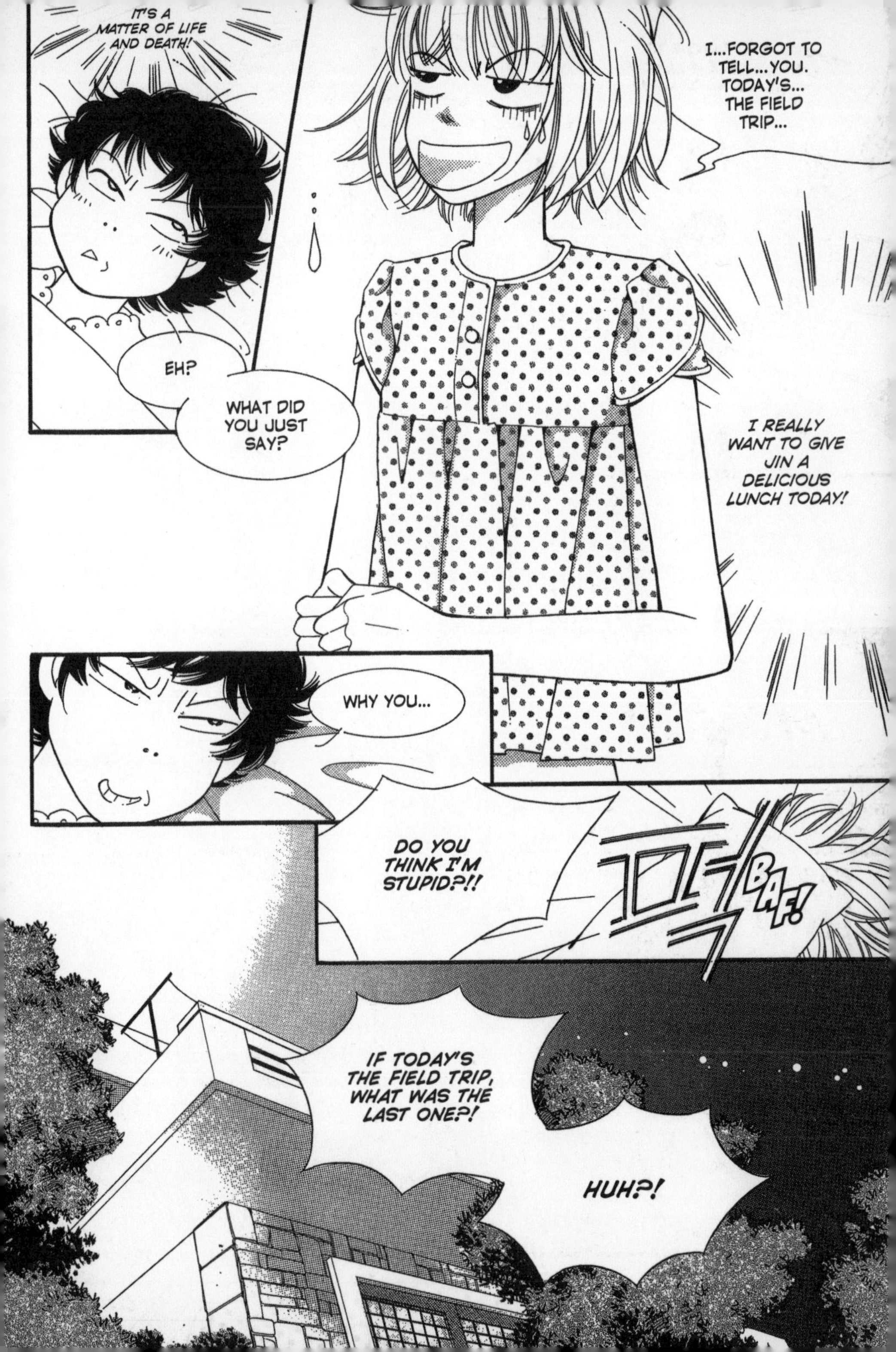
IT'S A MATTER OF LIFE AND DEATH!
EH?
WHAT DID YOU JUST SAY?
I...FORGOT TO TELL...YOU. TODAY'S... THE FIELD TRIP...
I REALLY WANT TO GIVE JIN A DELICIOUS LUNCH TODAY!
WHY YOU...
DO YOU THINK I'M STUPID?!!
BAF!
IF TODAY'S THE FIELD TRIP, WHAT WAS THE LAST ONE?!
HUH?!

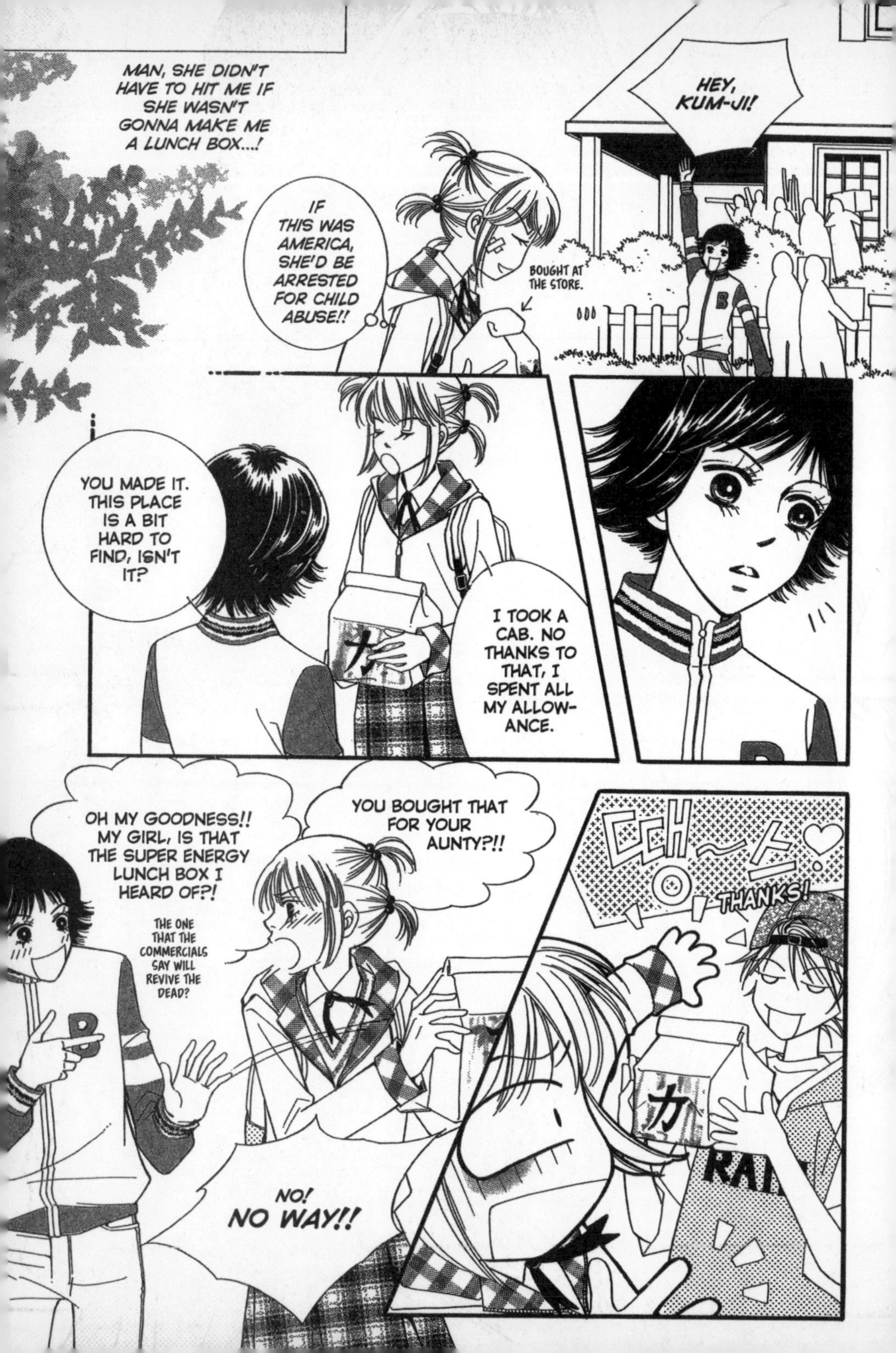
MAN, SHE DIDN'T HAVE TO HIT ME IF SHE WASN'T GONNA MAKE ME A LUNCH BOX...!
IF THIS WAS AMERICA, SHE'D BE ARRESTED FOR CHILD ABUSE!!
BOUGHT AT THE STORE.
HEY, KUM-JI!
YOU MADE IT. THIS PLACE IS A BIT HARD TO FIND, ISN'T IT?
I TOOK A CAB. NO THANKS TO THAT, I SPENT ALL MY ALLOW-ANCE.
OH MY GOODNESS!! MY GIRL, IS THAT THE SUPER ENERGY LUNCH BOX I HEARD OF?!
THE ONE THAT THE COMMERCIALS SAY WILL REVIVE THE DEAD?
YOU BOUGHT THAT FOR YOUR AUNTY?!!
NO! NO WAY!!
THANKS!

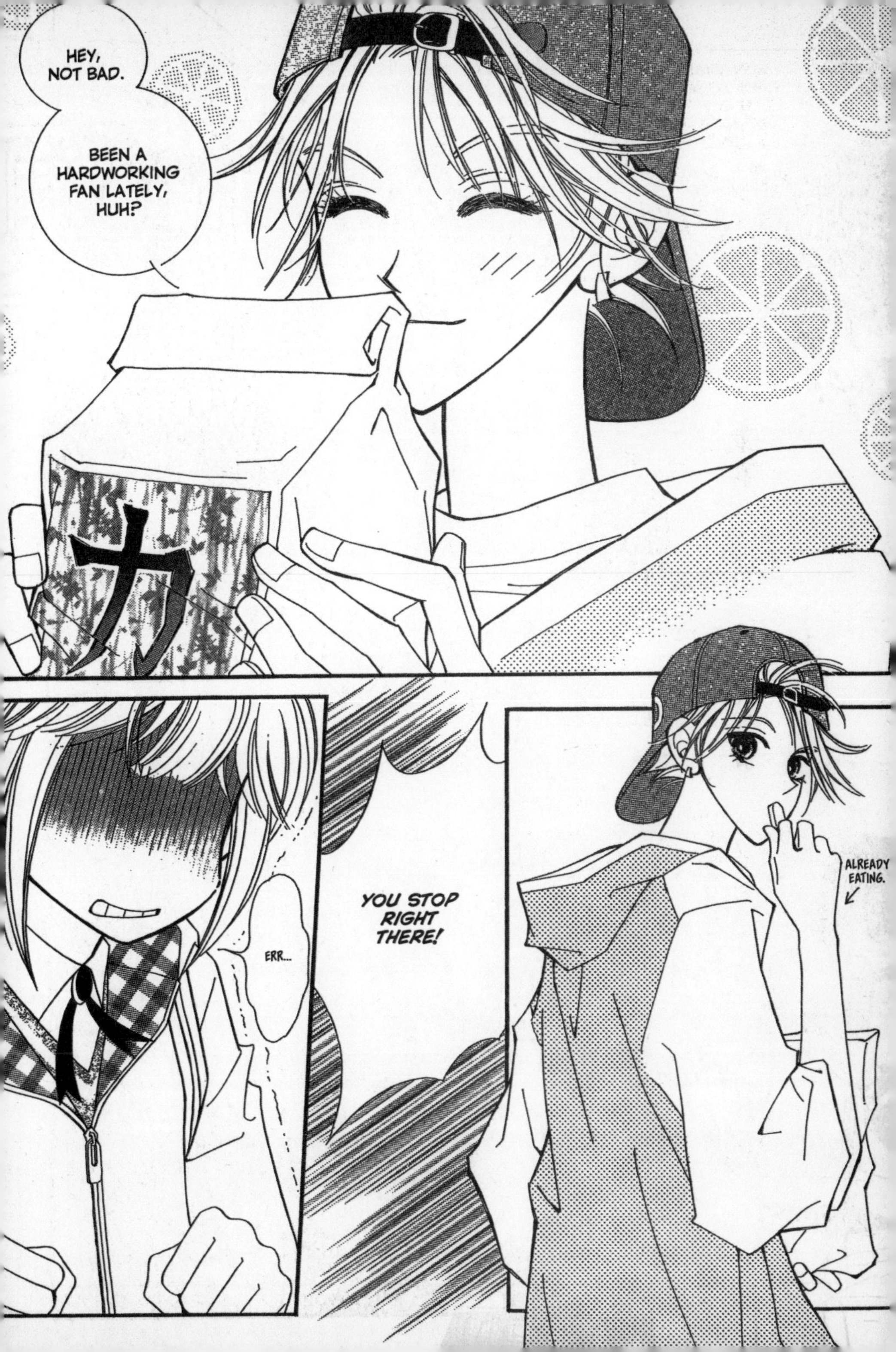
HEY, NOT BAD.
BEEN A HARDWORKING FAN LATELY, HUH?
ERR...
YOU STOP RIGHT THERE!
ALREADY EATING.

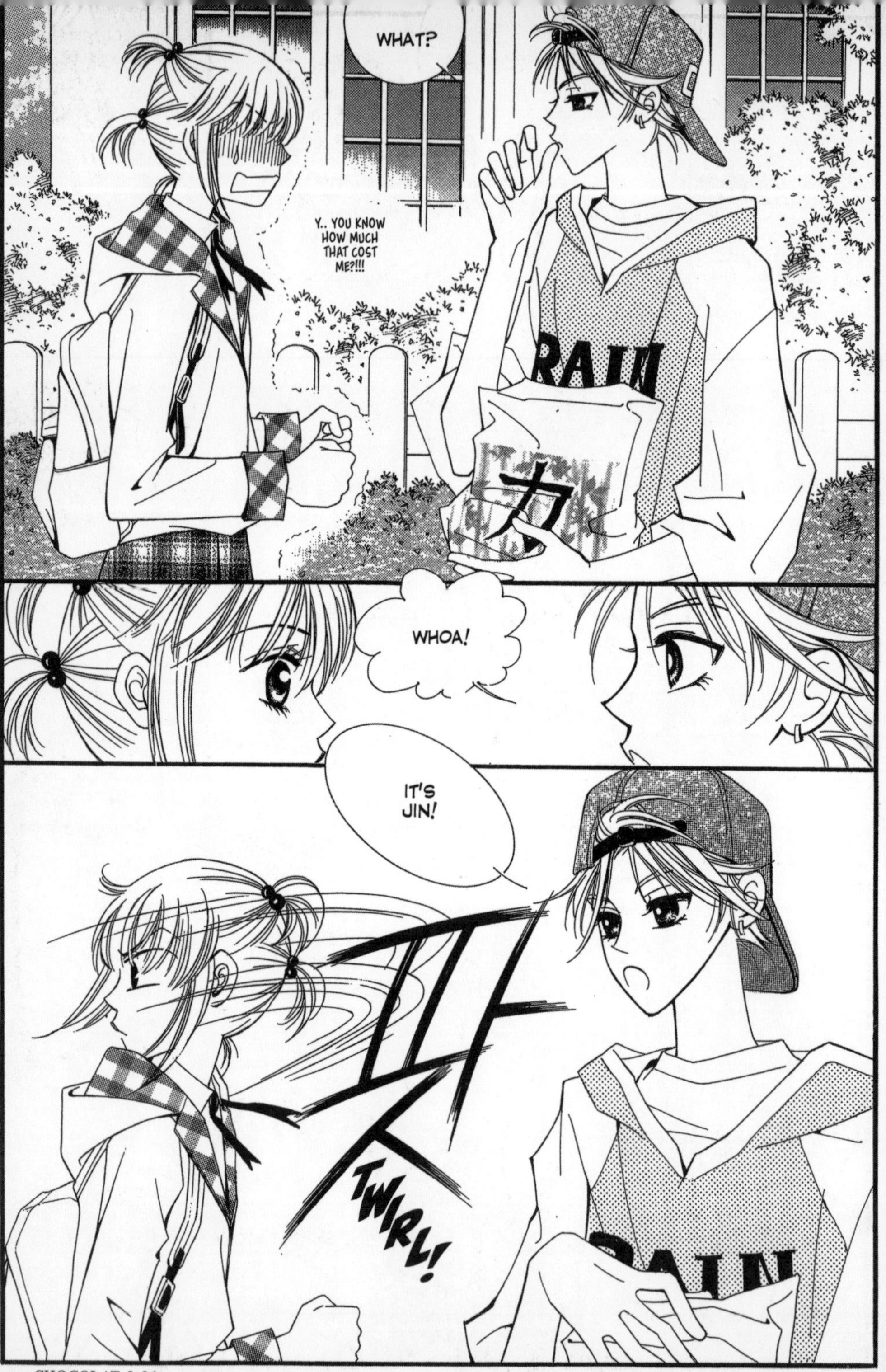
WHAT?
Y.. YOU KNOW HOW MUCH THAT COST ME?!!!
WHOA!
IT'S JIN!
TWIRL!

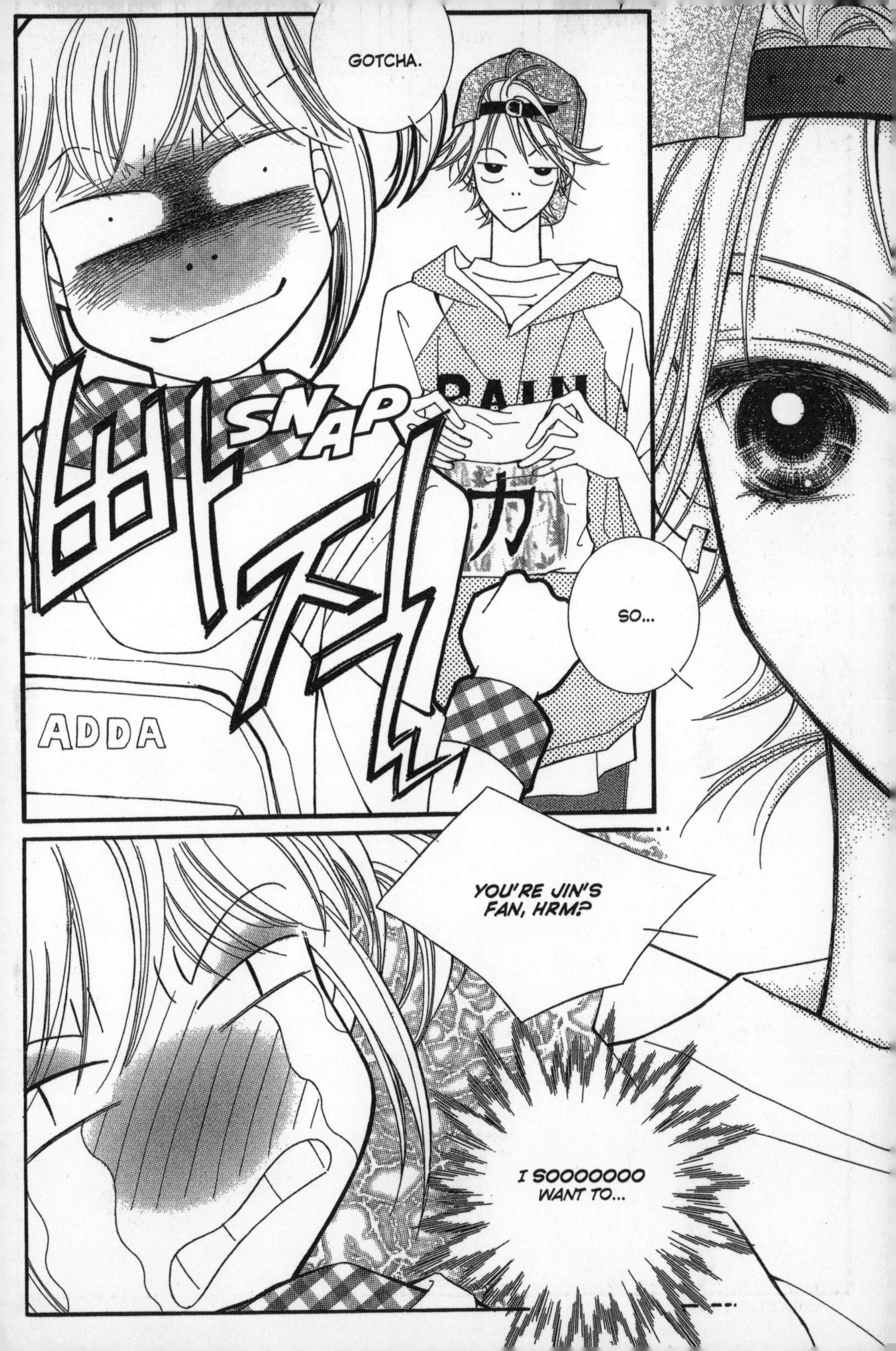
GOTCHA.
SNAP
ADDA
SO...
YOU'RE JIN'S FAN, HRM?
I SOOOOOOO WANT TO...

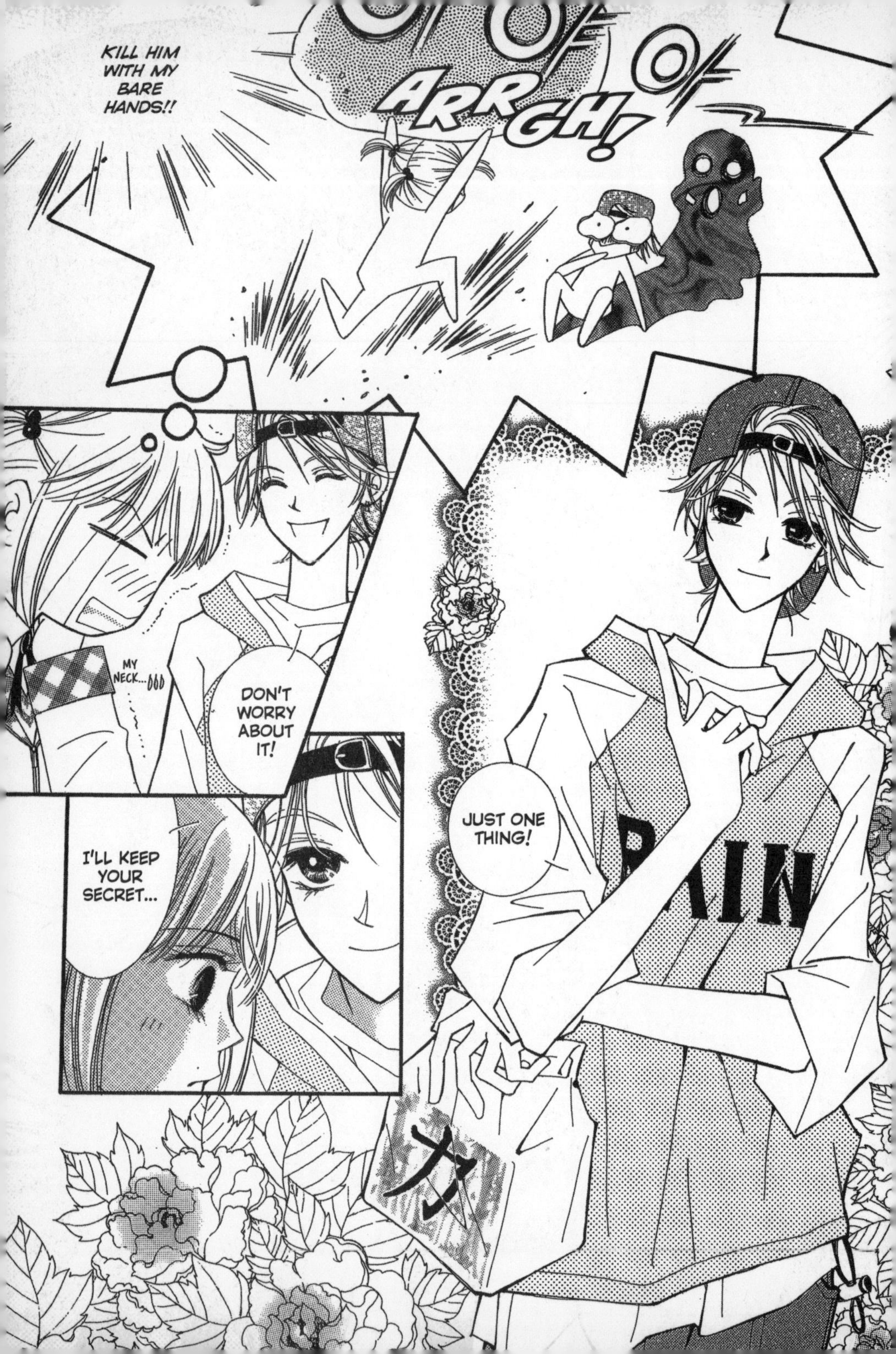
KILL HIM WITH MY BARE HANDS!!
ARRGH!
MY NECK...
DON'T WORRY ABOUT IT!
I'LL KEEP YOUR SECRET...
JUST ONE THING!

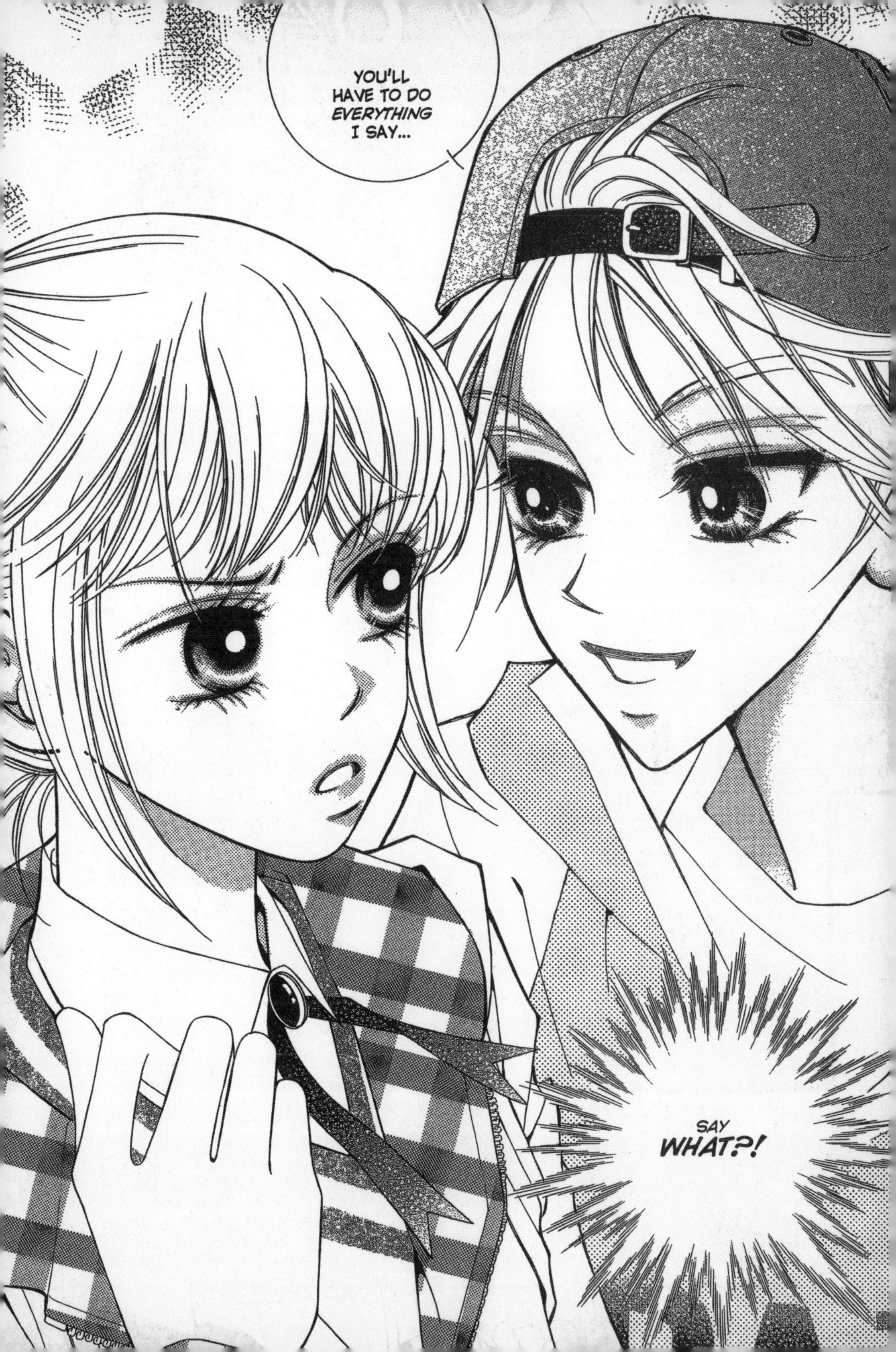
YOU'LL HAVE TO DO *EVERYTHING* I SAY...
SAY **WHAT?!**

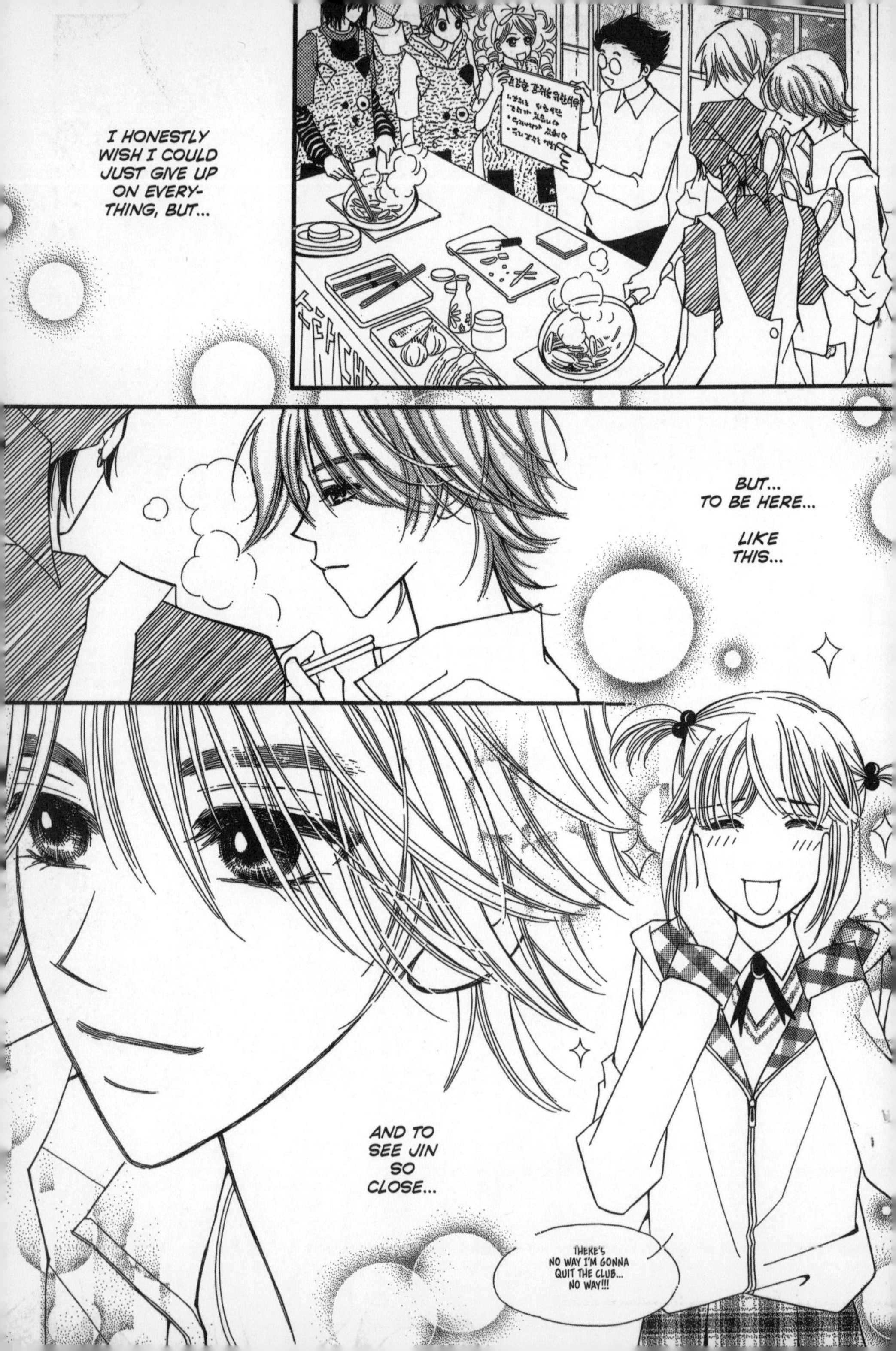
I HONESTLY WISH I COULD JUST GIVE UP ON EVERY-THING, BUT...
BUT... TO BE HERE...
LIKE THIS...
AND TO SEE JIN SO CLOSE...
THERE'S NO WAY I'M GONNA QUIT THE CLUB... NO WAY!!!

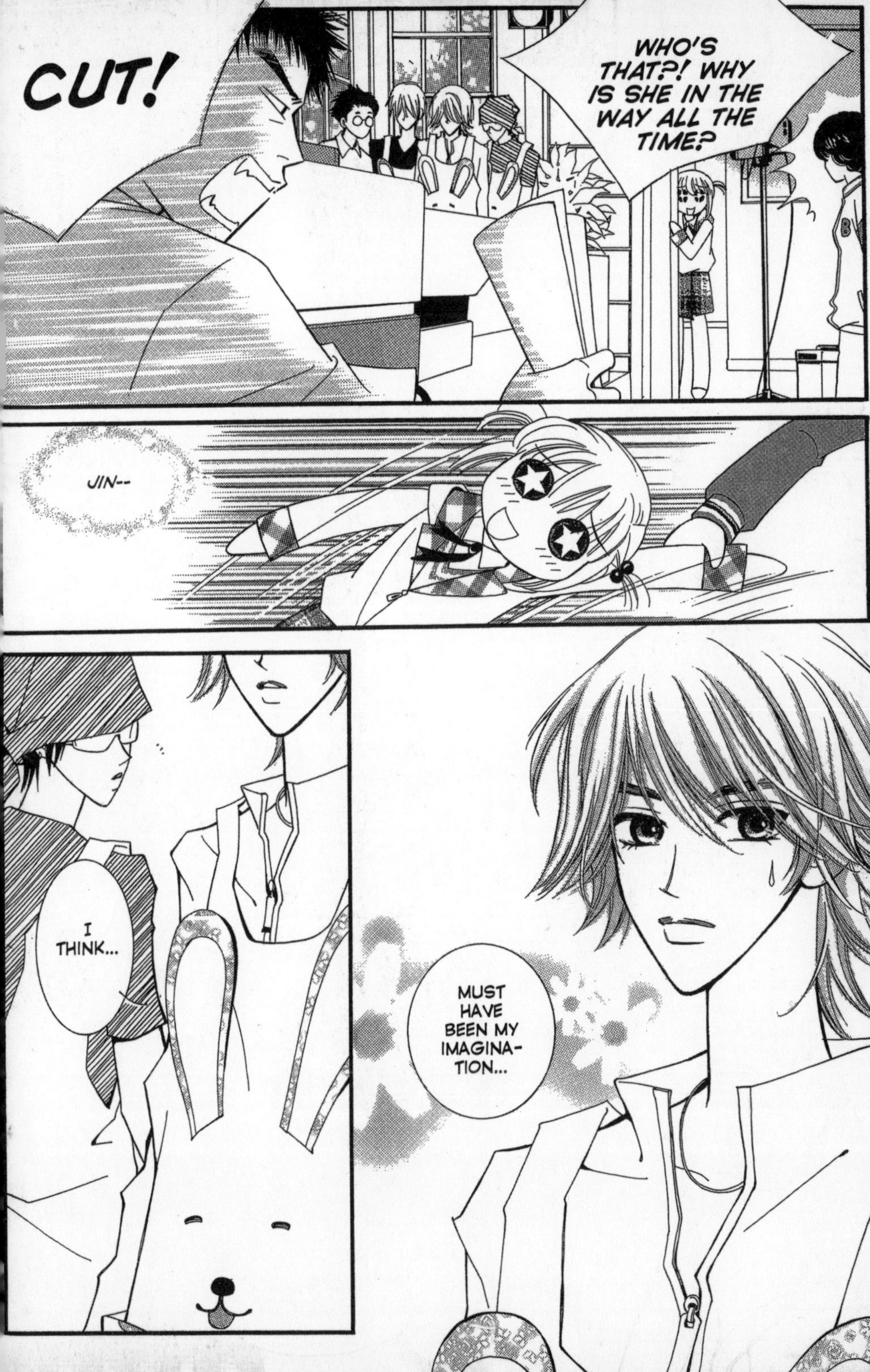
CUT!
WHO'S THAT?! WHY IS SHE IN THE WAY ALL THE TIME?
JIN--
I THINK...
MUST HAVE BEEN MY IMAGINA-TION...

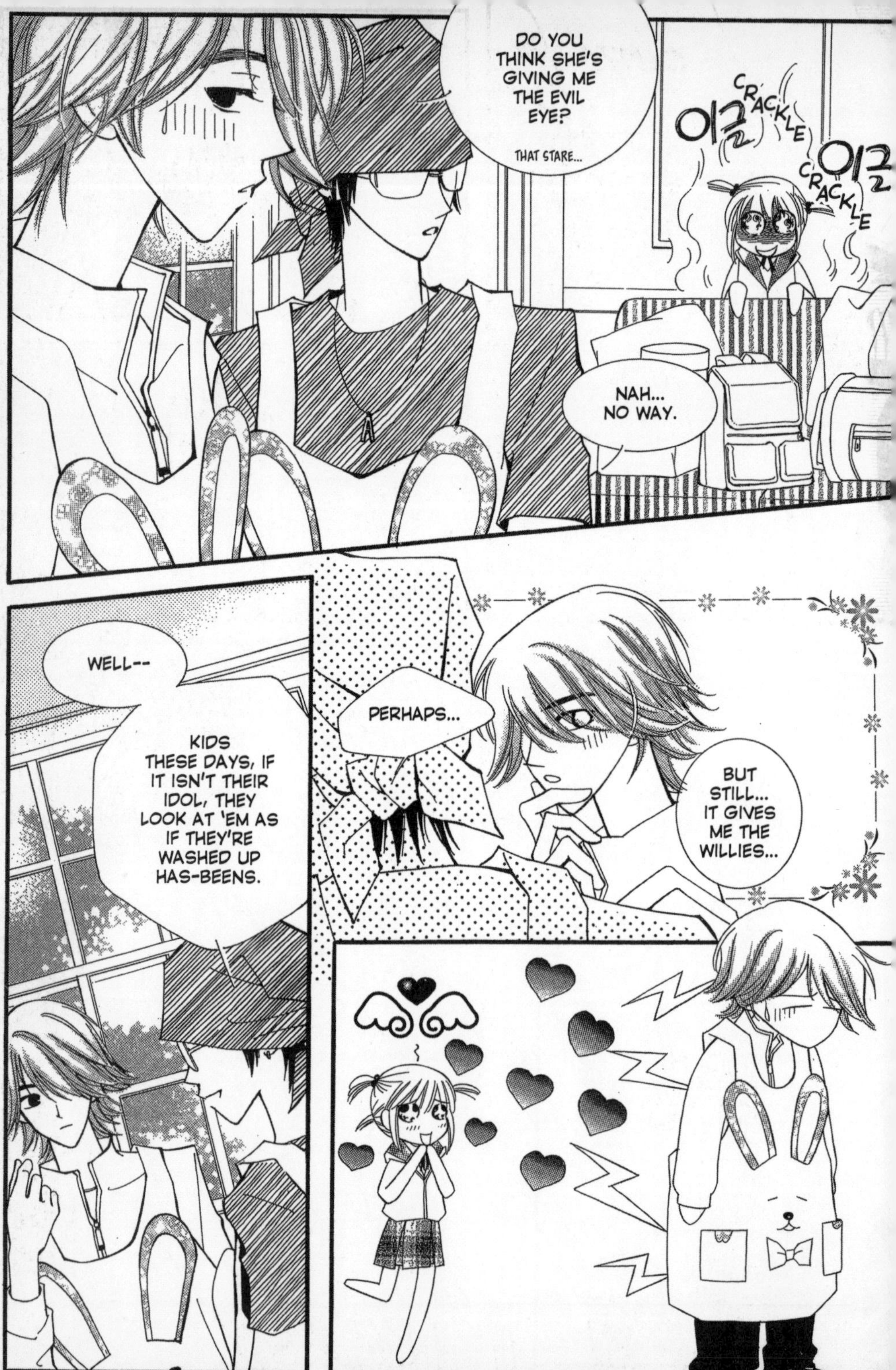
DO YOU THINK SHE'S GIVING ME THE EVIL EYE?
THAT STARE...
이글 CRACKLE
이글 CRACKLE
NAH... NO WAY.
WELL--
KIDS THESE DAYS, IF IT ISN'T THEIR IDOL, THEY LOOK AT 'EM AS IF THEY'RE WASHED UP HAS-BEENS.
PERHAPS...
BUT STILL... IT GIVES ME THE WILLIES...

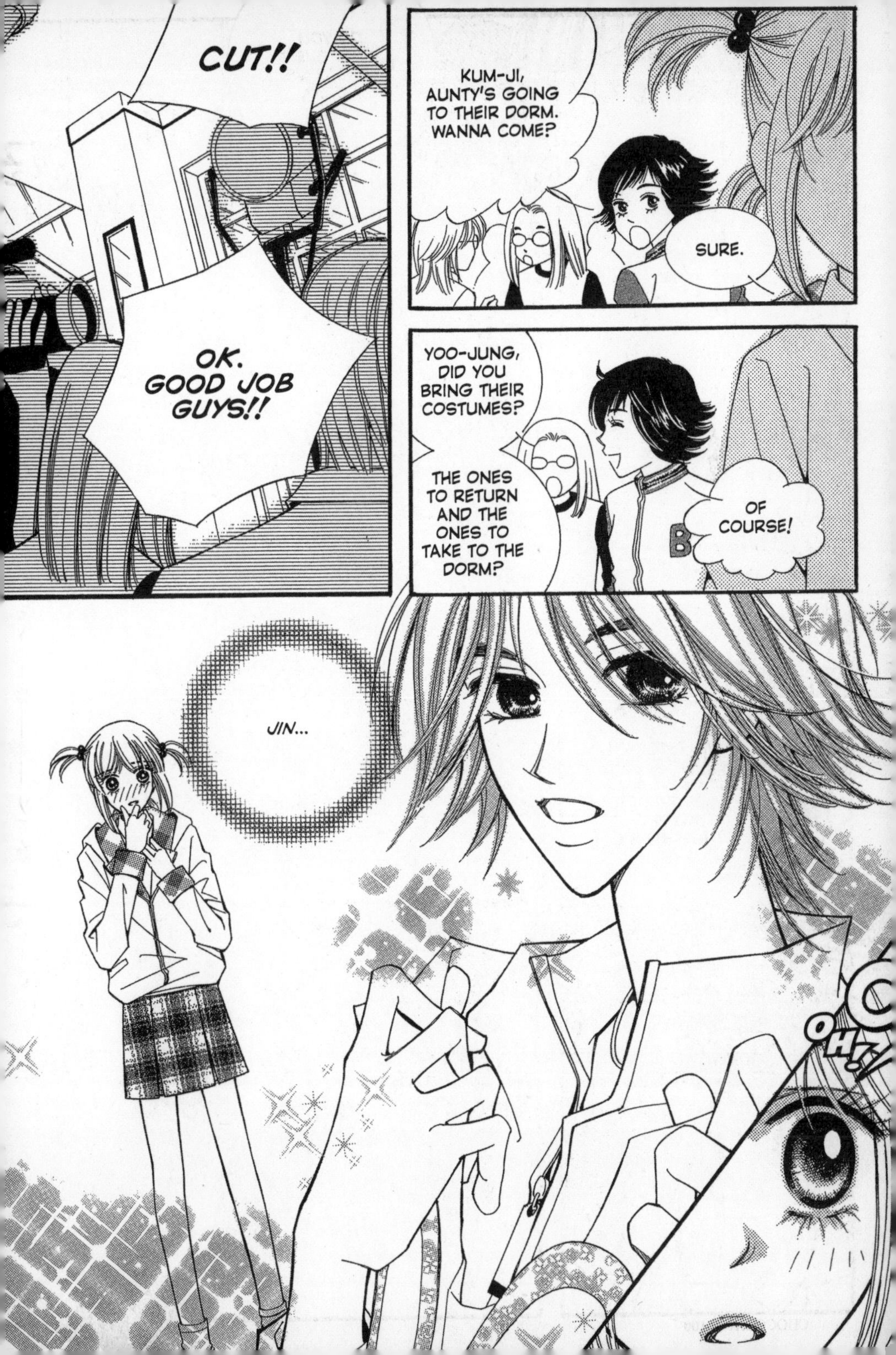
CUT!!
OK. GOOD JOB GUYS!!
KUM-JI, AUNTY'S GOING TO THEIR DORM. WANNA COME?
SURE.
YOO-JUNG, DID YOU BRING THEIR COSTUMES?
THE ONES TO RETURN AND THE ONES TO TAKE TO THE DORM?
OF COURSE!
JIN...
OH!?

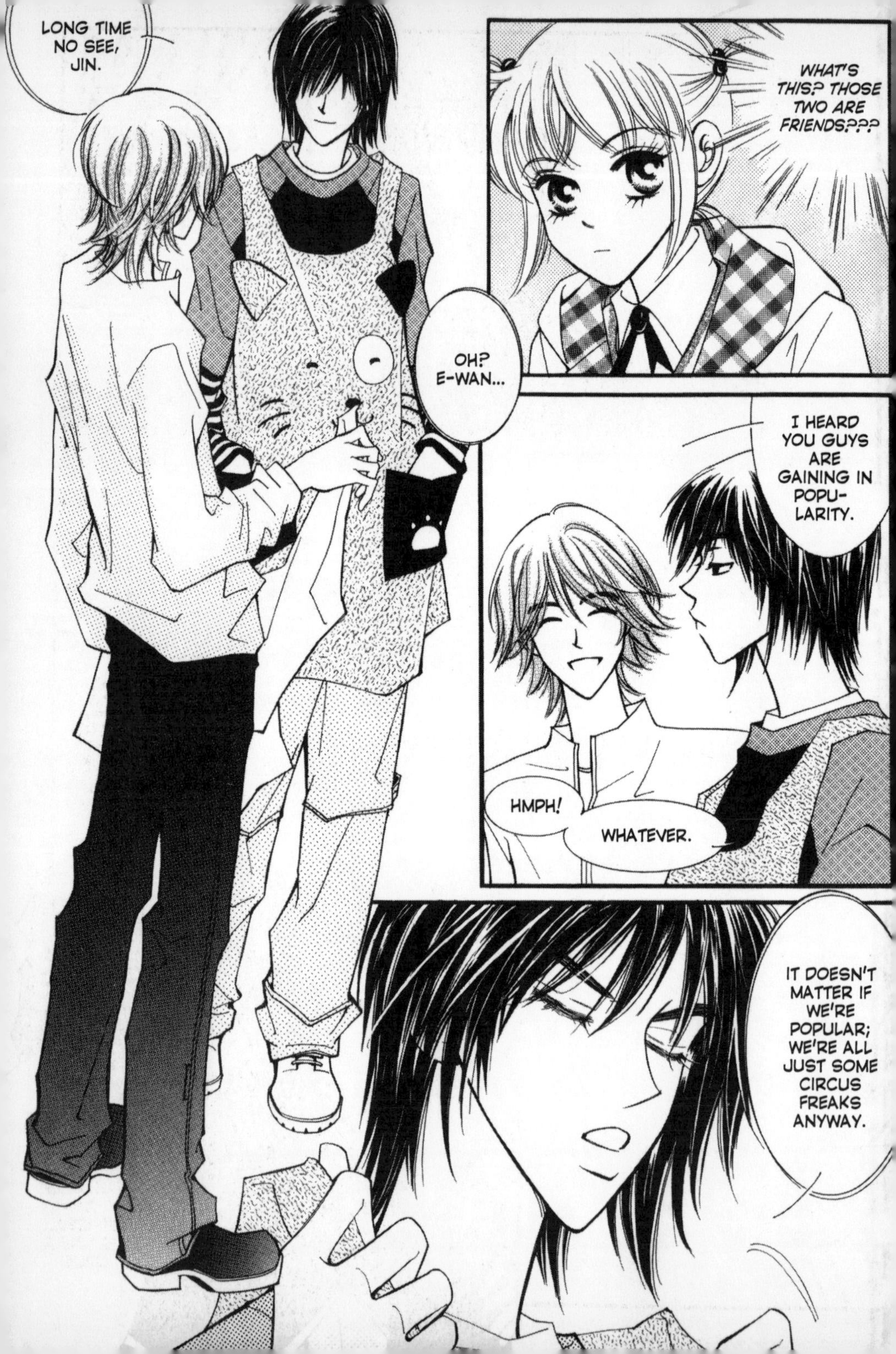
LONG TIME NO SEE, JIN.
OH? E-WAN...
WHAT'S THIS? THOSE TWO ARE FRIENDS???
I HEARD YOU GUYS ARE GAINING IN POPU-LARITY.
HMPH!
WHATEVER.
IT DOESN'T MATTER IF WE'RE POPULAR; WE'RE ALL JUST SOME CIRCUS FREAKS ANYWAY.

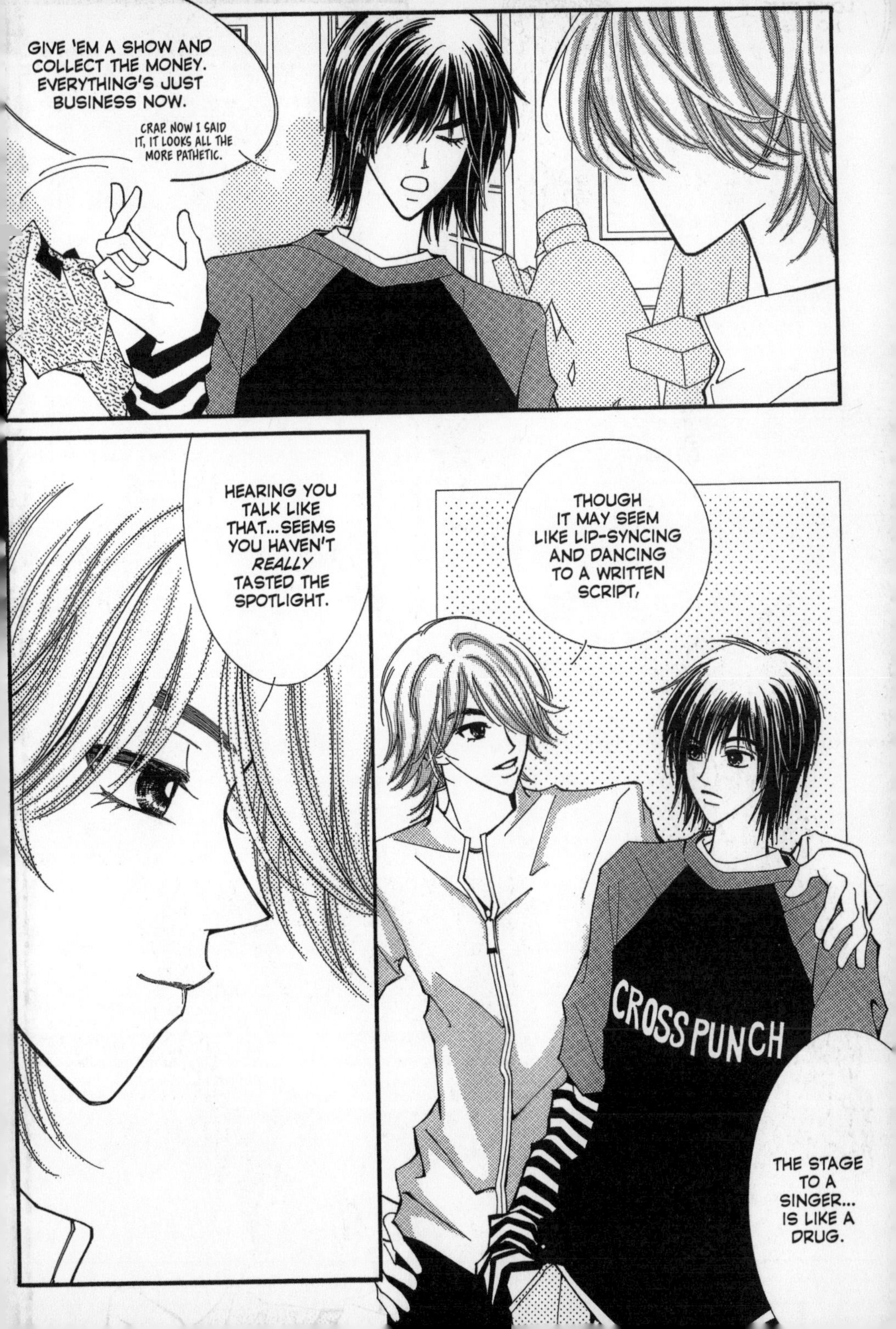
GIVE 'EM A SHOW AND COLLECT THE MONEY. EVERYTHING'S JUST BUSINESS NOW.
CRAP. NOW I SAID IT, IT LOOKS ALL THE MORE PATHETIC.
HEARING YOU TALK LIKE THAT...SEEMS YOU HAVEN'T *REALLY* TASTED THE SPOTLIGHT.
THOUGH IT MAY SEEM LIKE LIP-SYNCING AND DANCING TO A WRITTEN SCRIPT,
CROSS PUNCH
THE STAGE TO A SINGER... IS LIKE A DRUG.

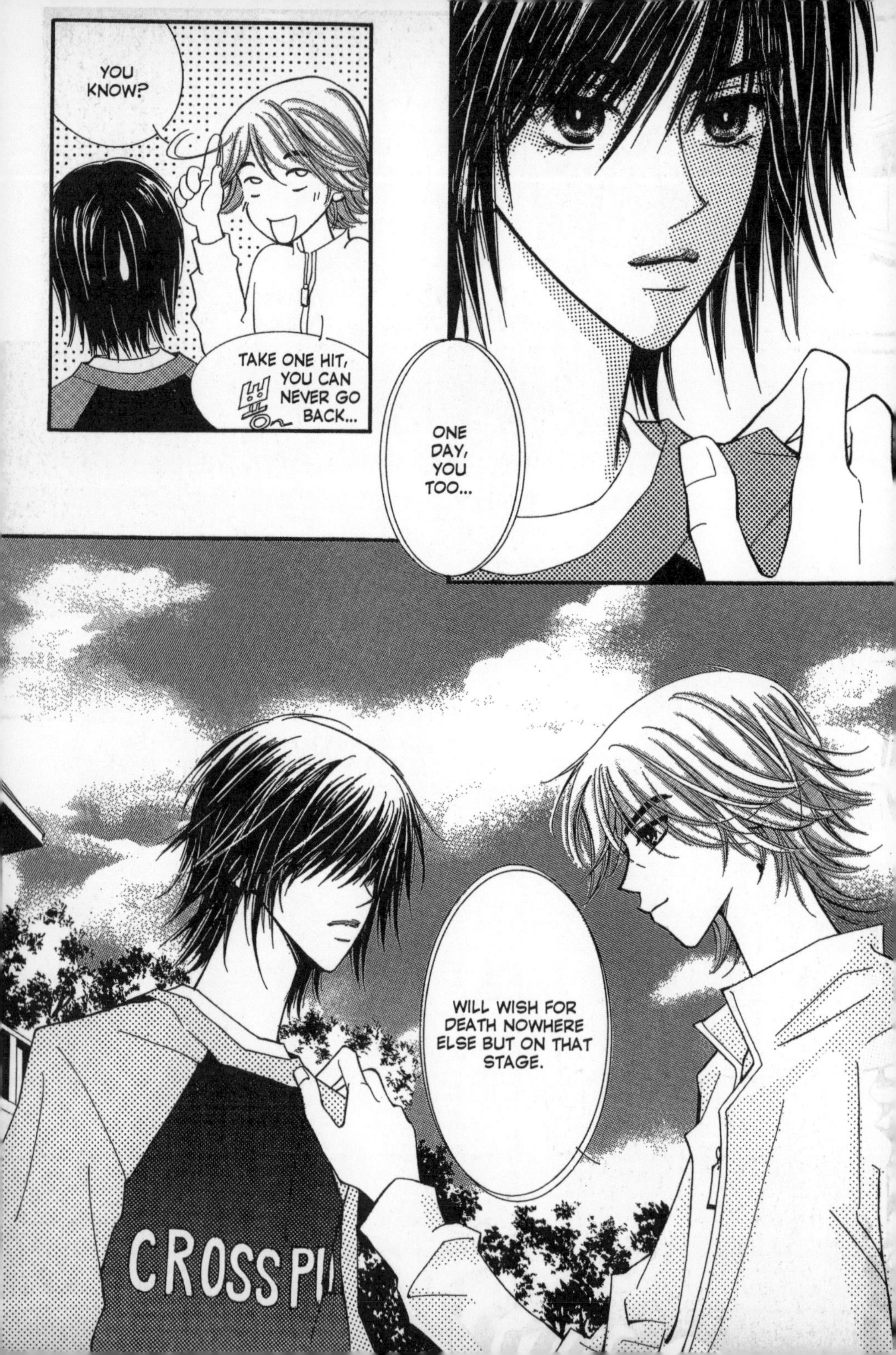
YOU KNOW?
TAKE ONE HIT, YOU CAN NEVER GO BACK...
뿅
ONE DAY, YOU TOO...
WILL WISH FOR DEATH NOWHERE ELSE BUT ON THAT STAGE.
CROSSPI

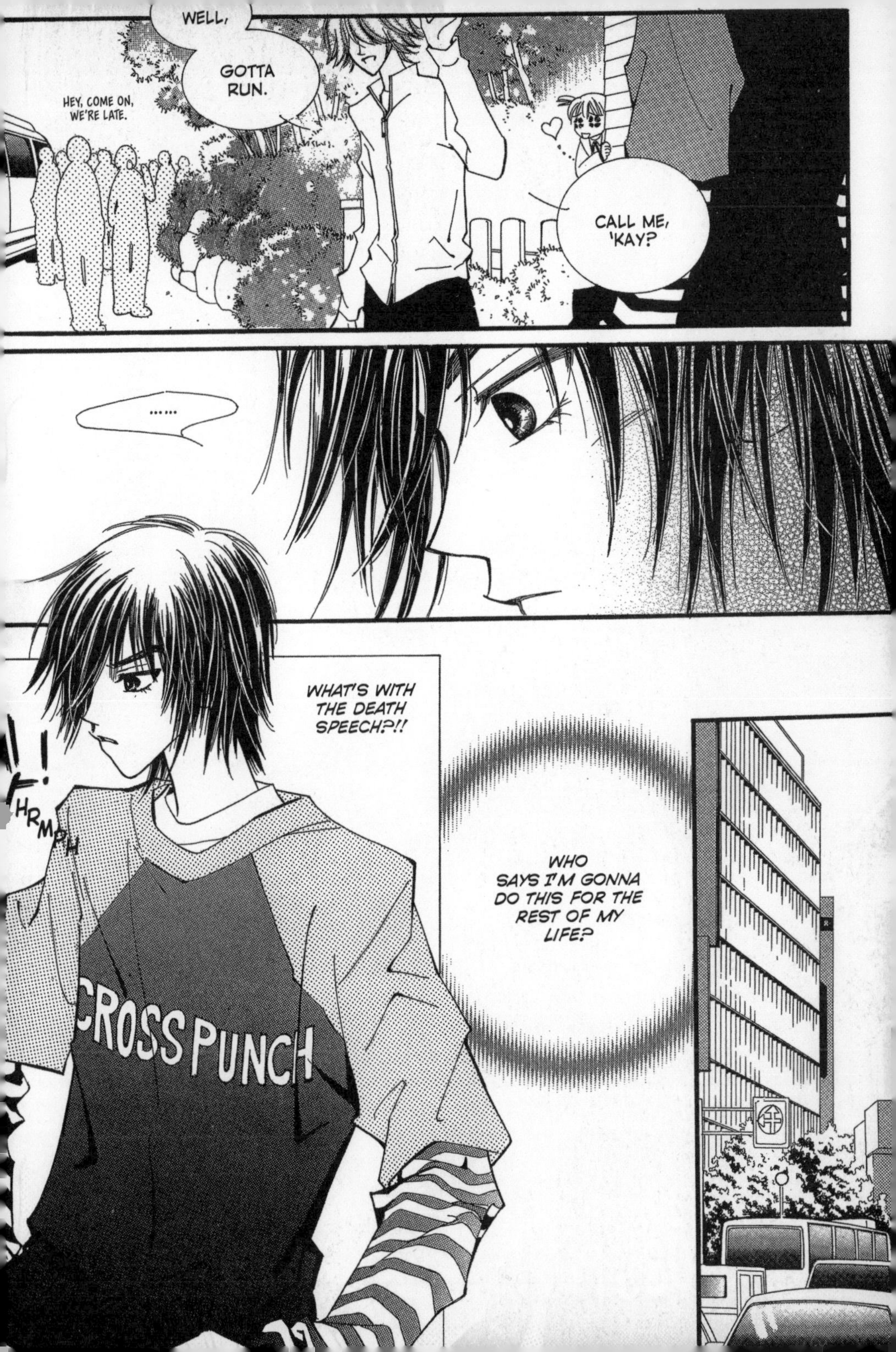
WELL,
GOTTA RUN.
HEY, COME ON, WE'RE LATE.
CALL ME, 'KAY?
……
HRMPH
WHAT'S WITH THE DEATH SPEECH?!!
CROSS PUNCH
WHO SAYS I'M GONNA DO THIS FOR THE REST OF MY LIFE?

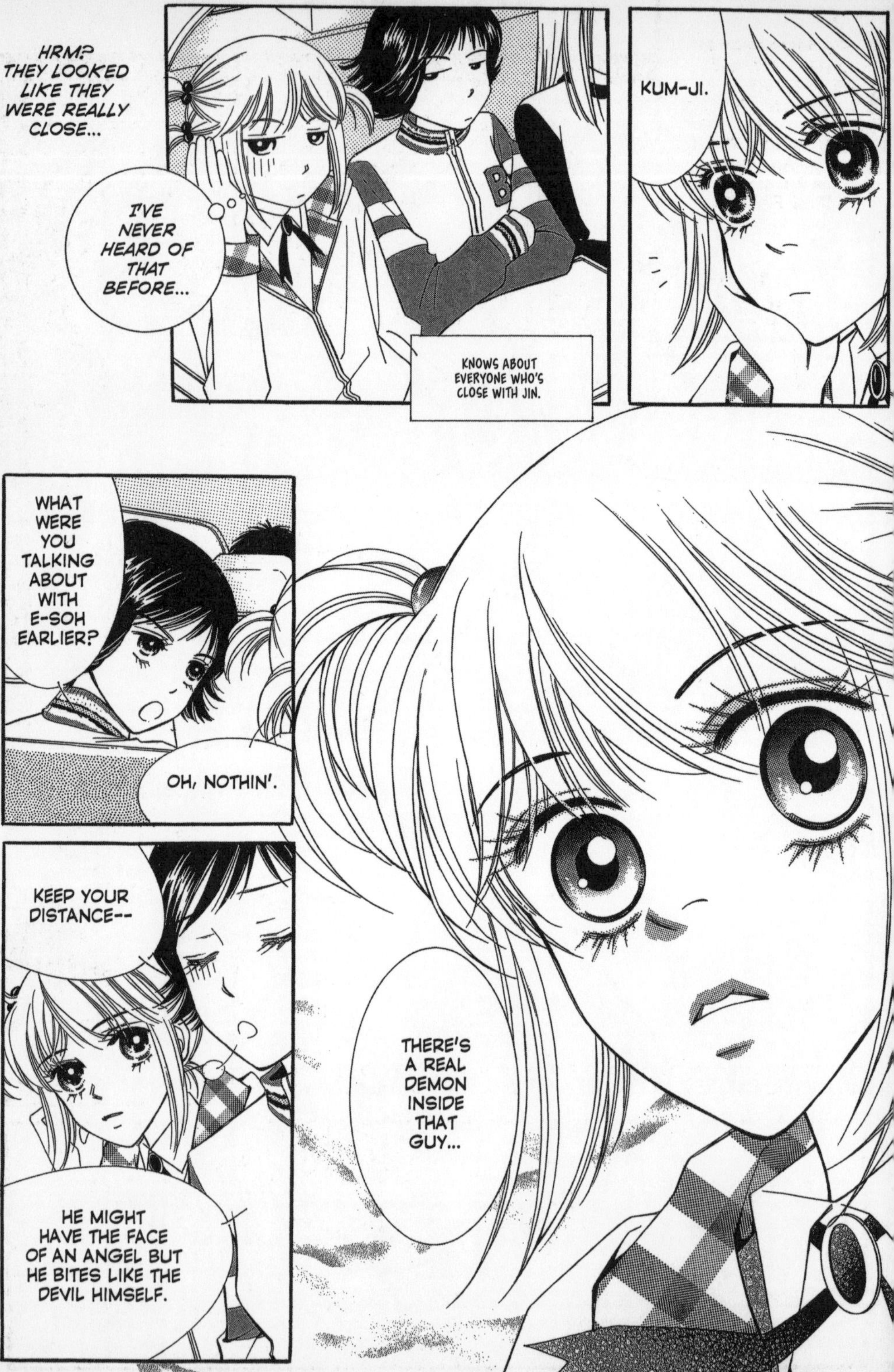
HRM? THEY LOOKED LIKE THEY WERE REALLY CLOSE...
I'VE NEVER HEARD OF THAT BEFORE...
KUM-JI.
KNOWS ABOUT EVERYONE WHO'S CLOSE WITH JIN.
WHAT WERE YOU TALKING ABOUT WITH E-SOH EARLIER?
OH, NOTHIN'.
KEEP YOUR DISTANCE--
HE MIGHT HAVE THE FACE OF AN ANGEL BUT HE BITES LIKE THE DEVIL HIMSELF.
THERE'S A REAL DEMON INSIDE THAT GUY...

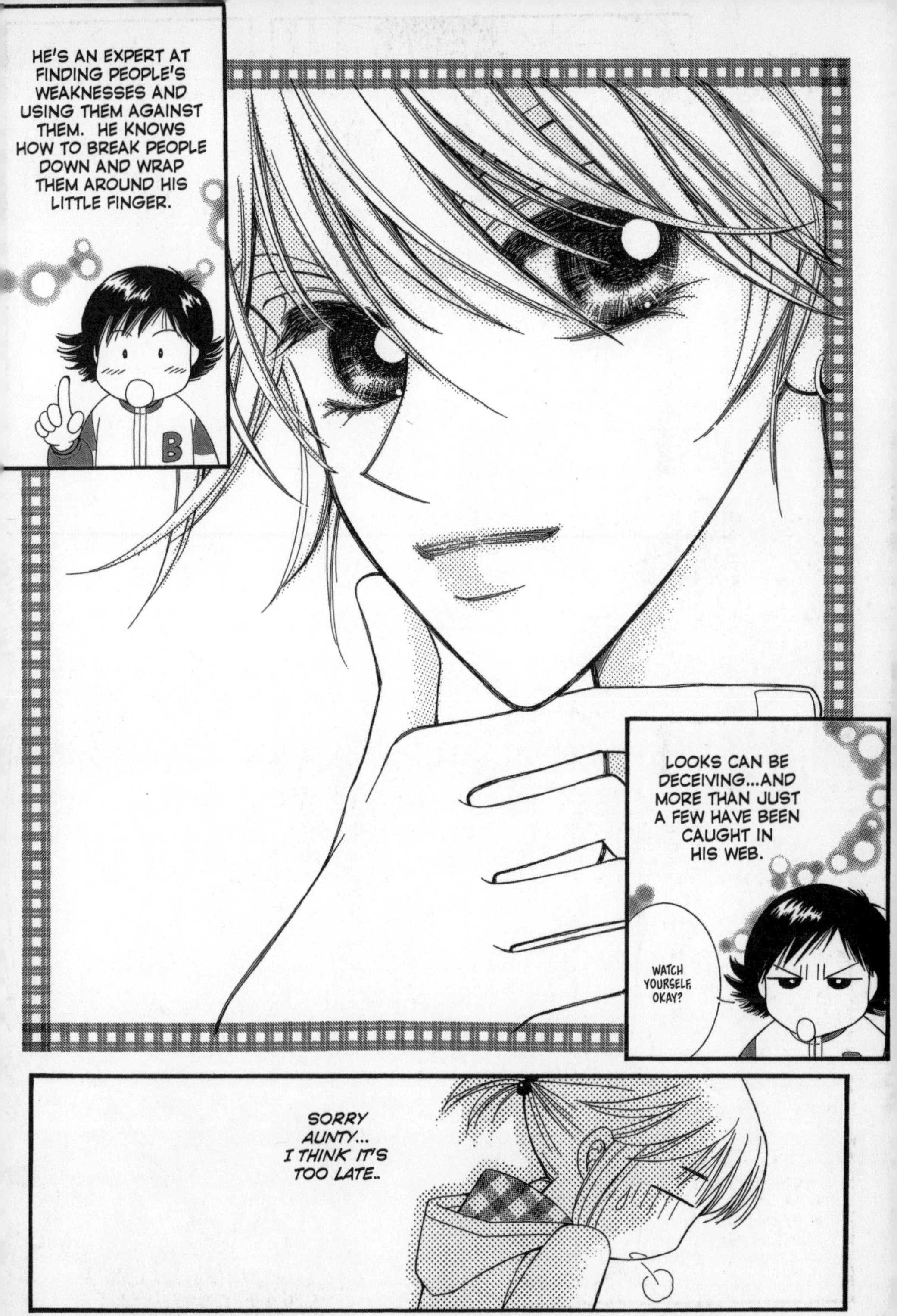
HE'S AN EXPERT AT FINDING PEOPLE'S WEAKNESSES AND USING THEM AGAINST THEM. HE KNOWS HOW TO BREAK PEOPLE DOWN AND WRAP THEM AROUND HIS LITTLE FINGER.
LOOKS CAN BE DECEIVING...AND MORE THAN JUST A FEW HAVE BEEN CAUGHT IN HIS WEB.
WATCH YOURSELF, OKAY?
SORRY AUNTY... I THINK IT'S TOO LATE..

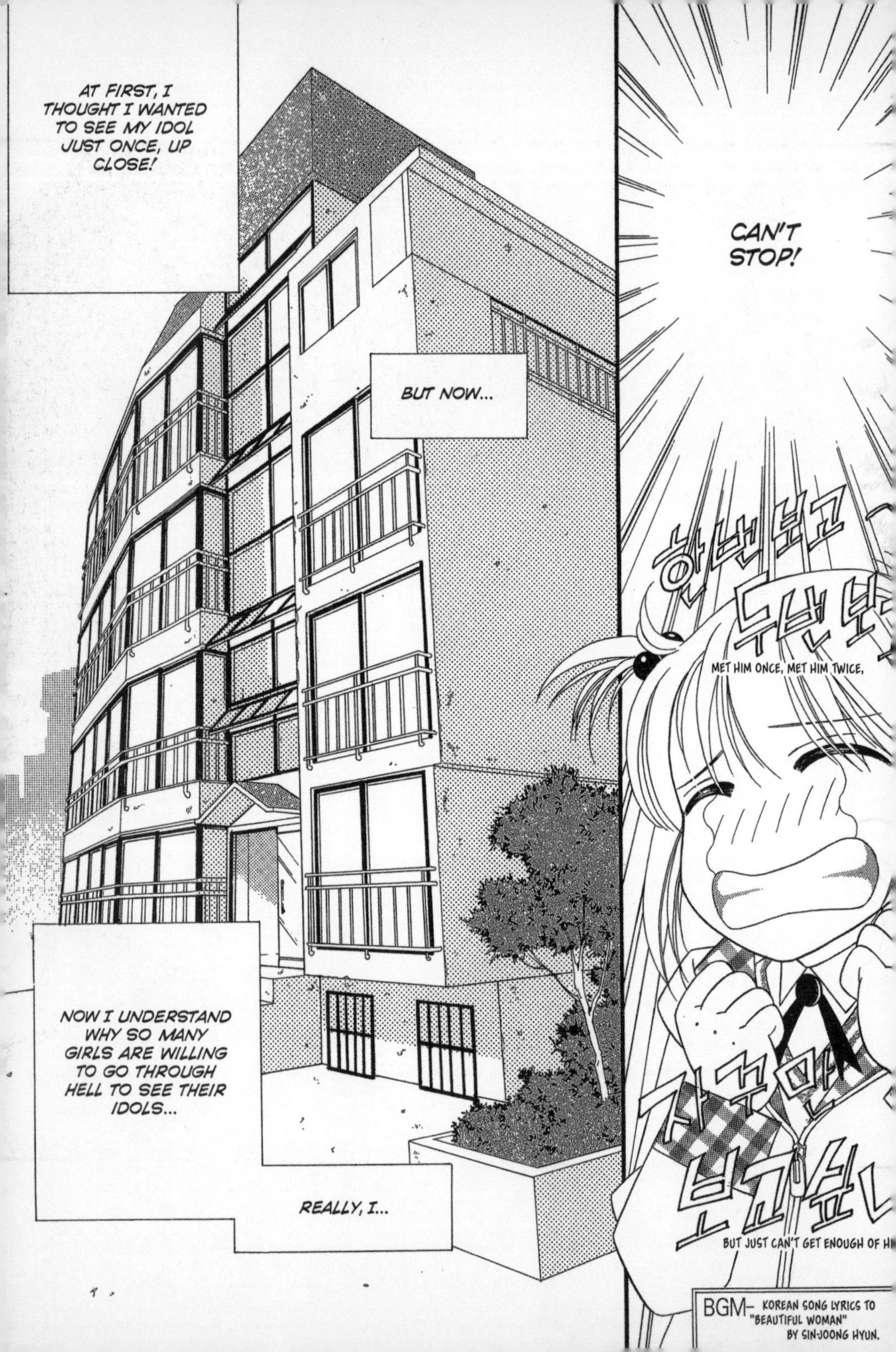
AT FIRST, I THOUGHT I WANTED TO SEE MY IDOL JUST ONCE, UP CLOSE!
BUT NOW...
NOW I UNDERSTAND WHY SO MANY GIRLS ARE WILLING TO GO THROUGH HELL TO SEE THEIR IDOLS...
REALLY, I...
CAN'T STOP!
한번보고
MET HIM ONCE, MET HIM TWICE,
자꾸만
BUT JUST CAN'T GET ENOUGH OF H
BGM– KOREAN SONG LYRICS TO "BEAUTIFUL WOMAN" BY SIN-JOONG HYUN.

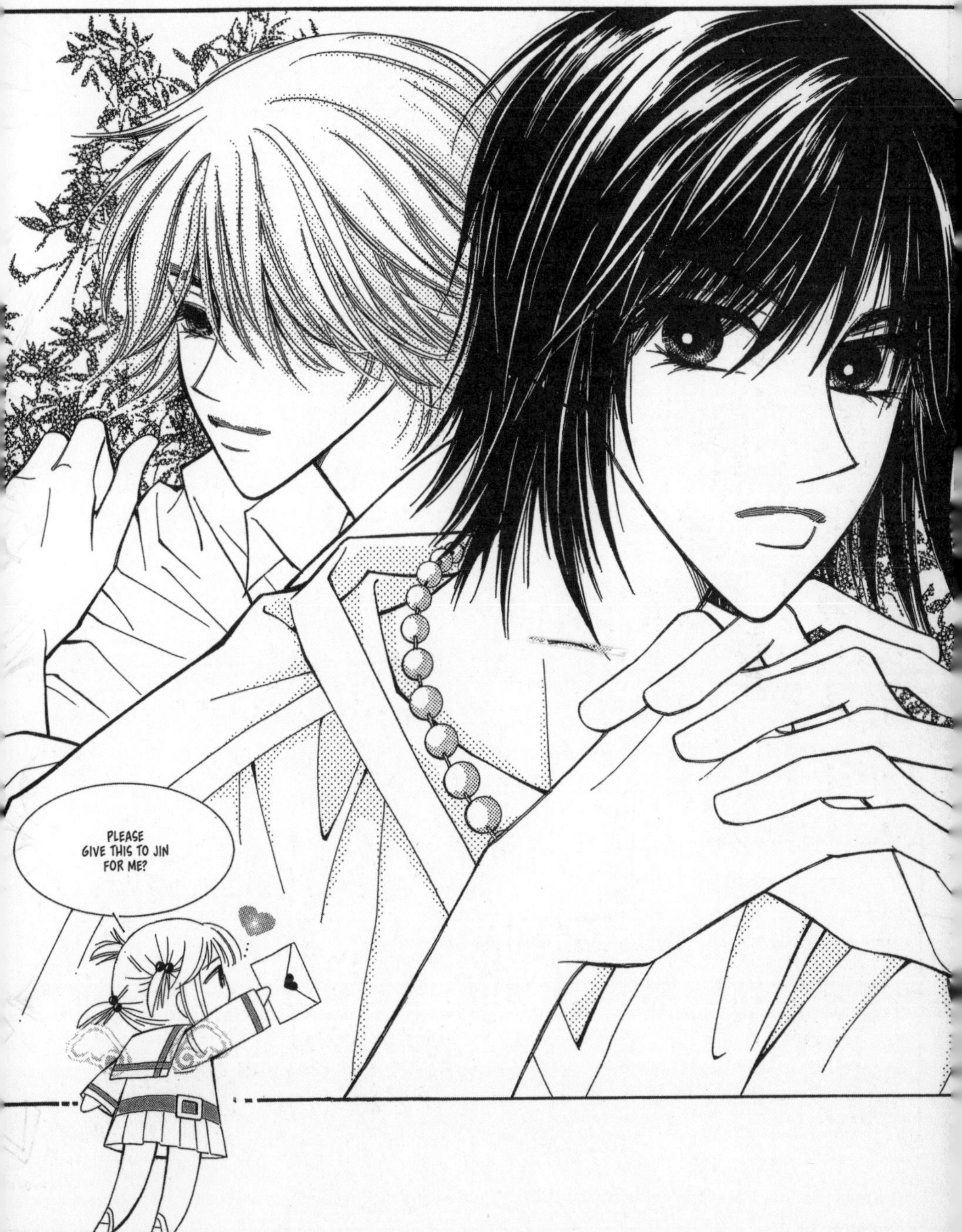
PLEASE GIVE THIS TO JIN FOR ME?

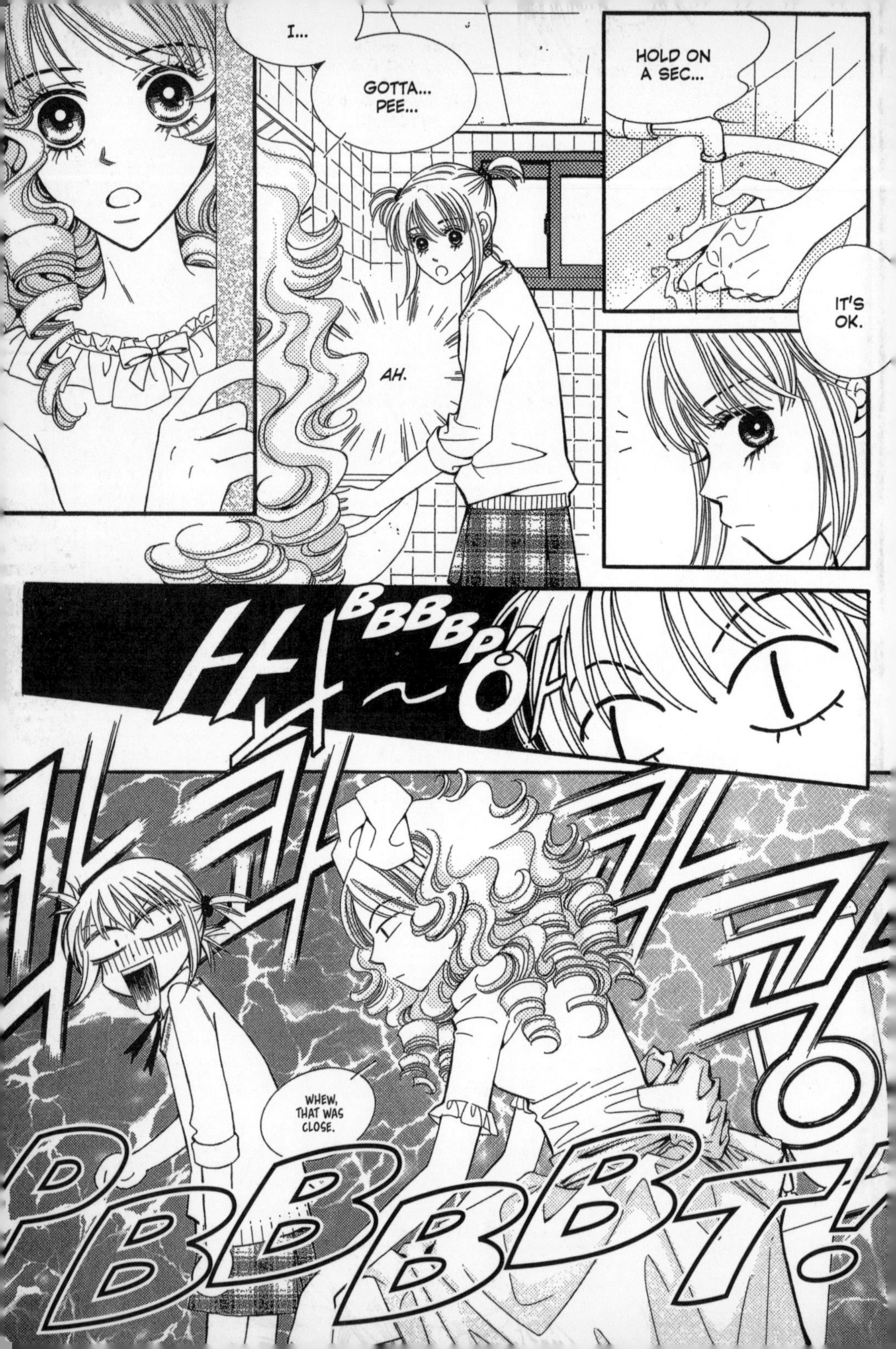

I...
GOTTA... PEE...
AH.
HOLD ON A SEC...
IT'S OK.
BBBBP!
WHEW, THAT WAS CLOSE.
PBBBT!

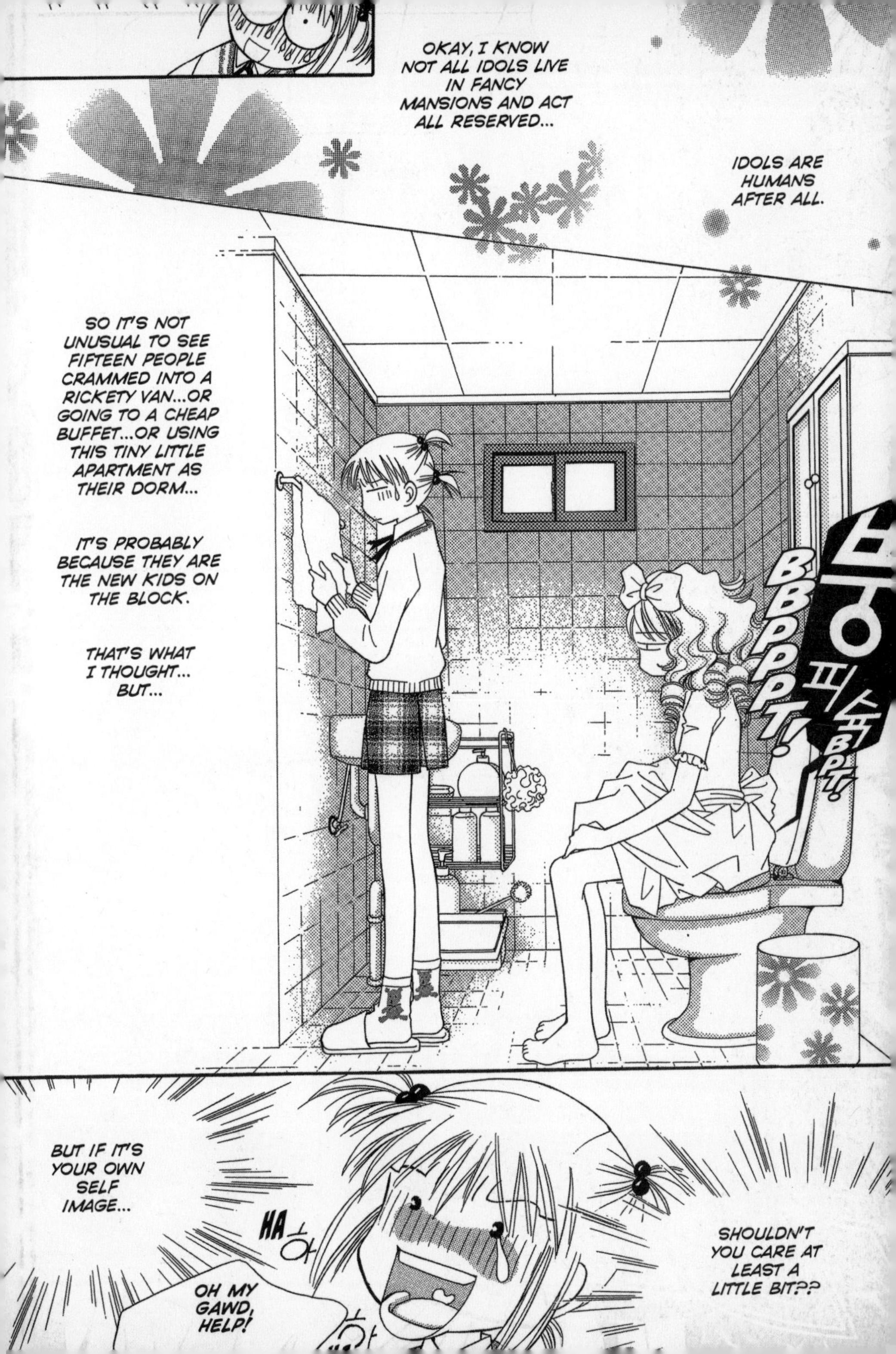
OKAY, I KNOW NOT ALL IDOLS LIVE IN FANCY MANSIONS AND ACT ALL RESERVED...
IDOLS ARE HUMANS AFTER ALL.
SO IT'S NOT UNUSUAL TO SEE FIFTEEN PEOPLE CRAMMED INTO A RICKETY VAN...OR GOING TO A CHEAP BUFFET...OR USING THIS TINY LITTLE APARTMENT AS THEIR DORM...
IT'S PROBABLY BECAUSE THEY ARE THE NEW KIDS ON THE BLOCK.
THAT'S WHAT I THOUGHT... BUT...
BBPPPT!
BPPT!
BUT IF IT'S YOUR OWN SELF IMAGE...
HA
OH MY GAWD, HELP!
SHOULDN'T YOU CARE AT LEAST A LITTLE BIT??

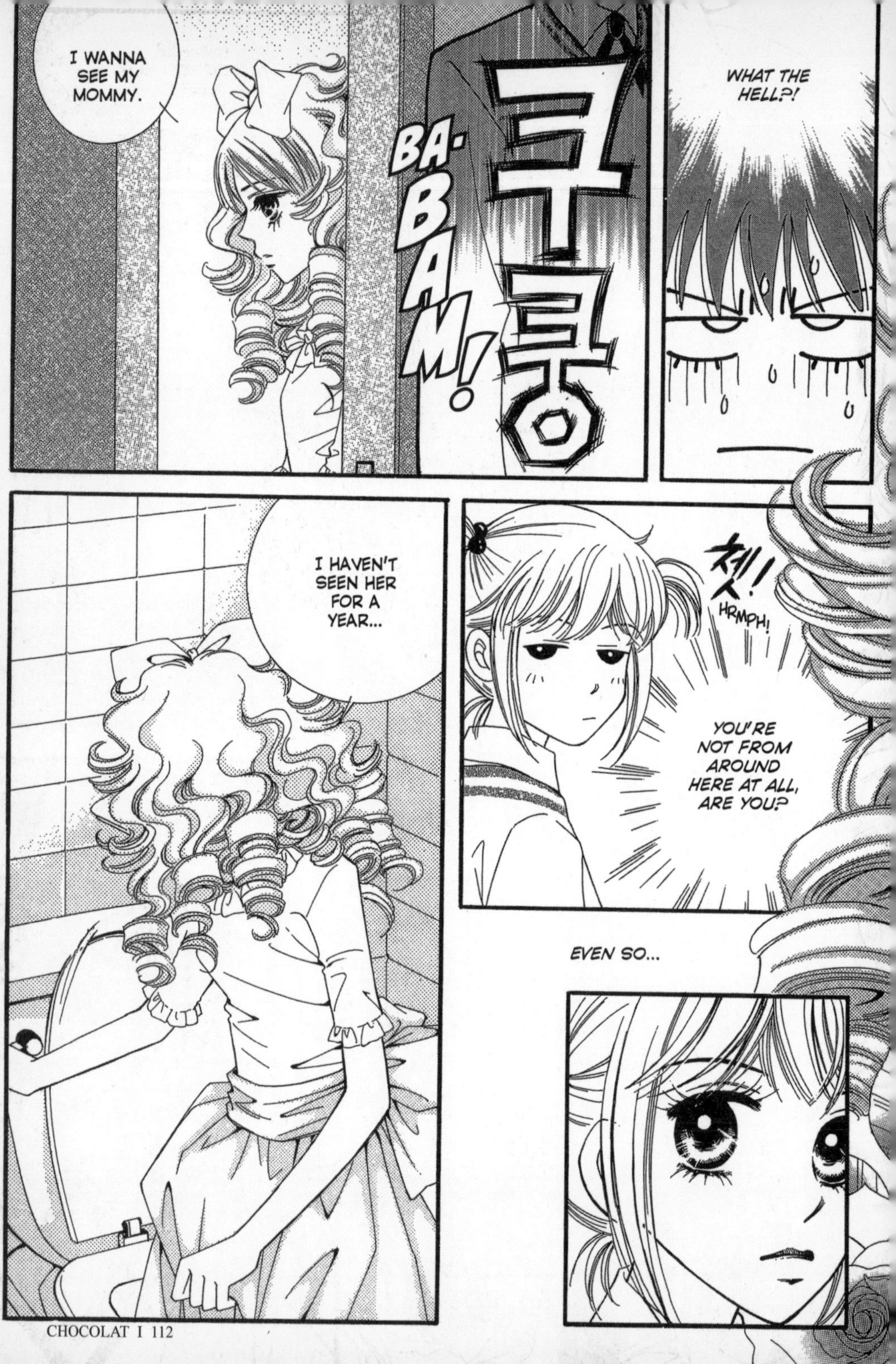
I WANNA SEE MY MOMMY.
쿠쿵
BA-BAM!
WHAT THE HELL?!
I HAVEN'T SEEN HER FOR A YEAR...
쳇!
HRMPH!
YOU'RE NOT FROM AROUND HERE AT ALL, ARE YOU?
EVEN SO...

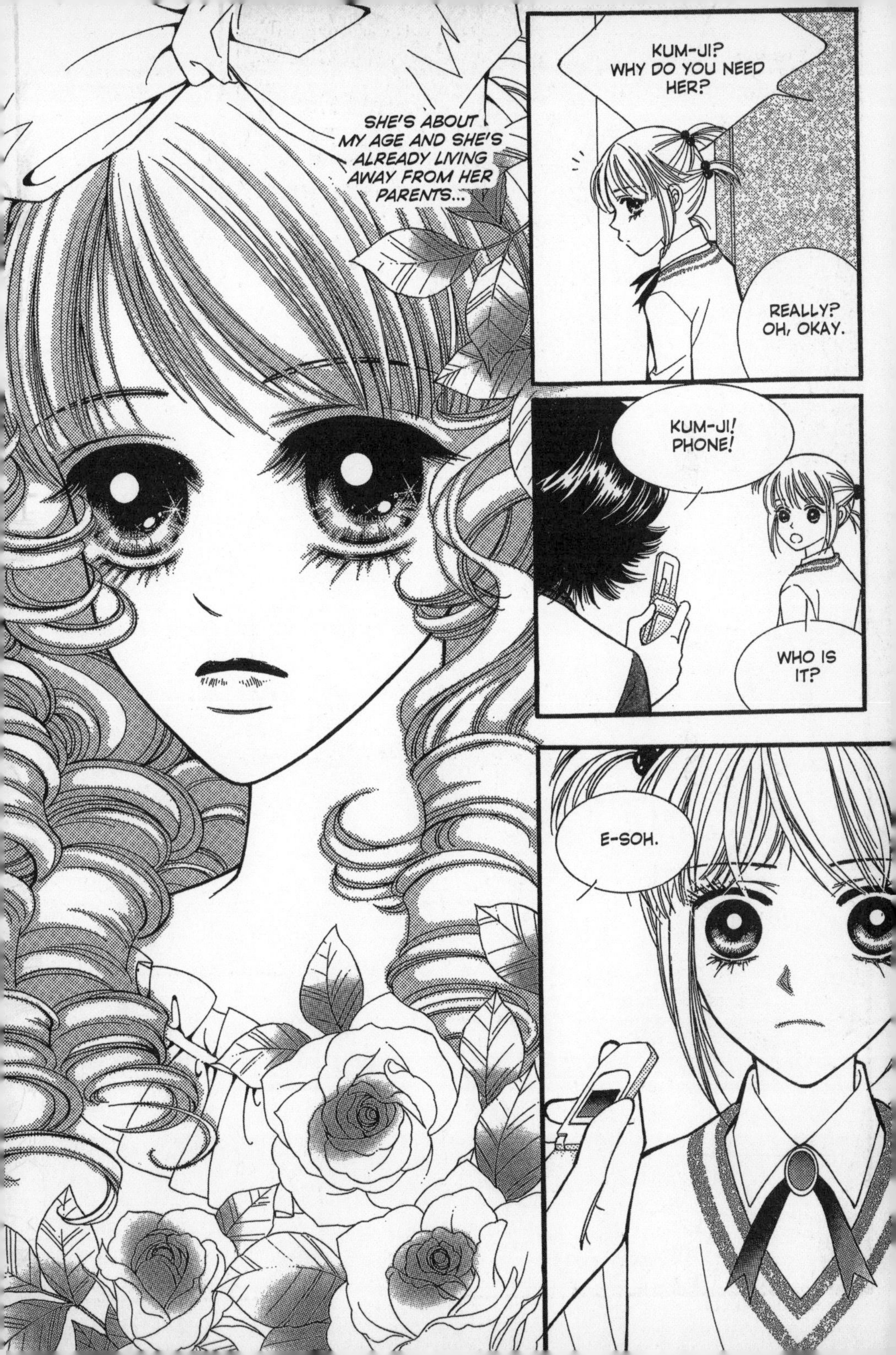
SHE'S ABOUT MY AGE AND SHE'S ALREADY LIVING AWAY FROM HER PARENTS...
KUM-JI? WHY DO YOU NEED HER?
REALLY? OH, OKAY.
KUM-JI! PHONE!
WHO IS IT?
E-SOH.

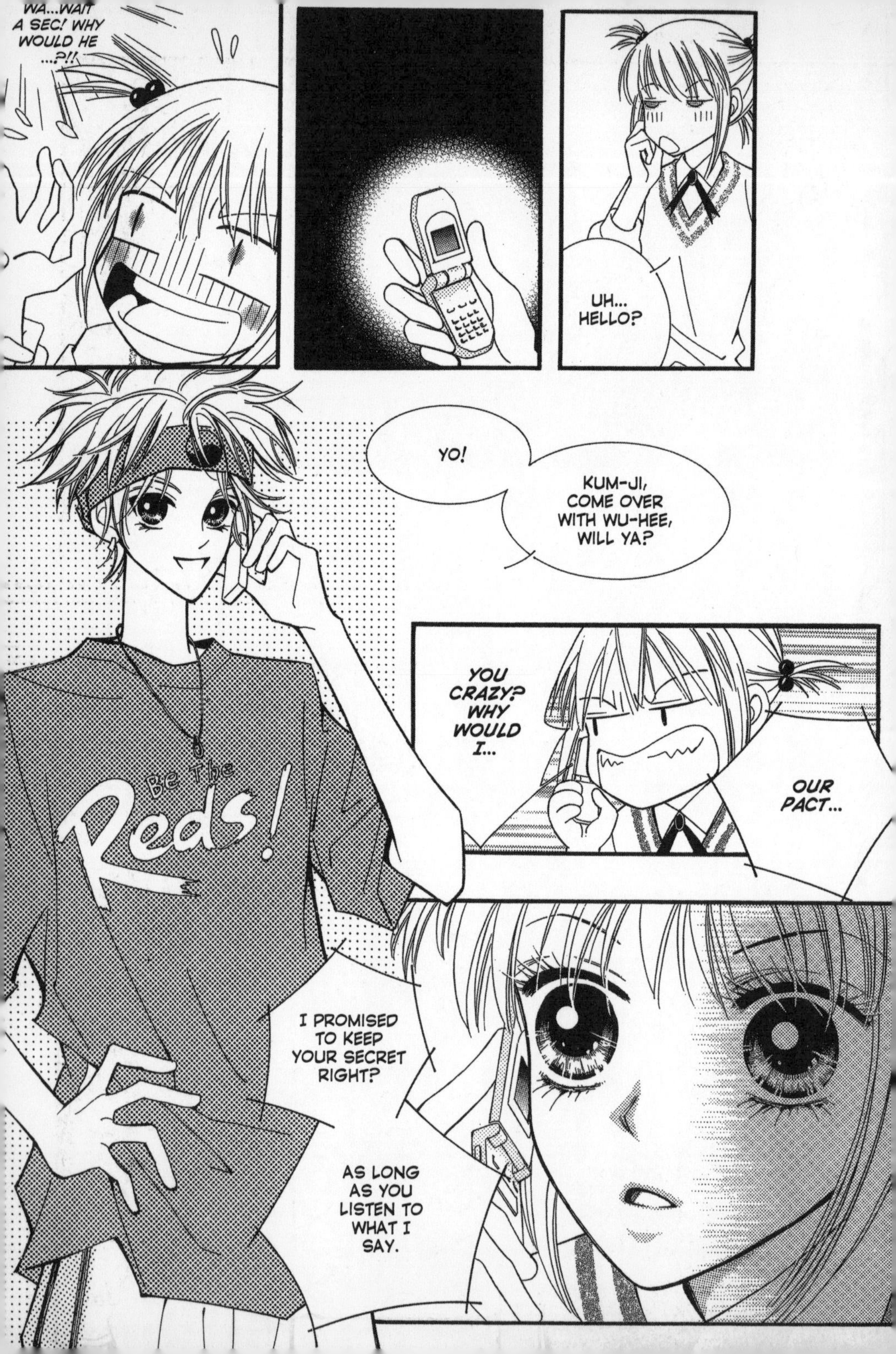
WA...WAIT A SEC! WHY WOULD HE ...?!!
UH... HELLO?
YO!
KUM-JI, COME OVER WITH WU-HEE, WILL YA?
Be The Reds!
YOU CRAZY? WHY WOULD I...
OUR PACT...
I PROMISED TO KEEP YOUR SECRET RIGHT?
AS LONG AS YOU LISTEN TO WHAT I SAY.

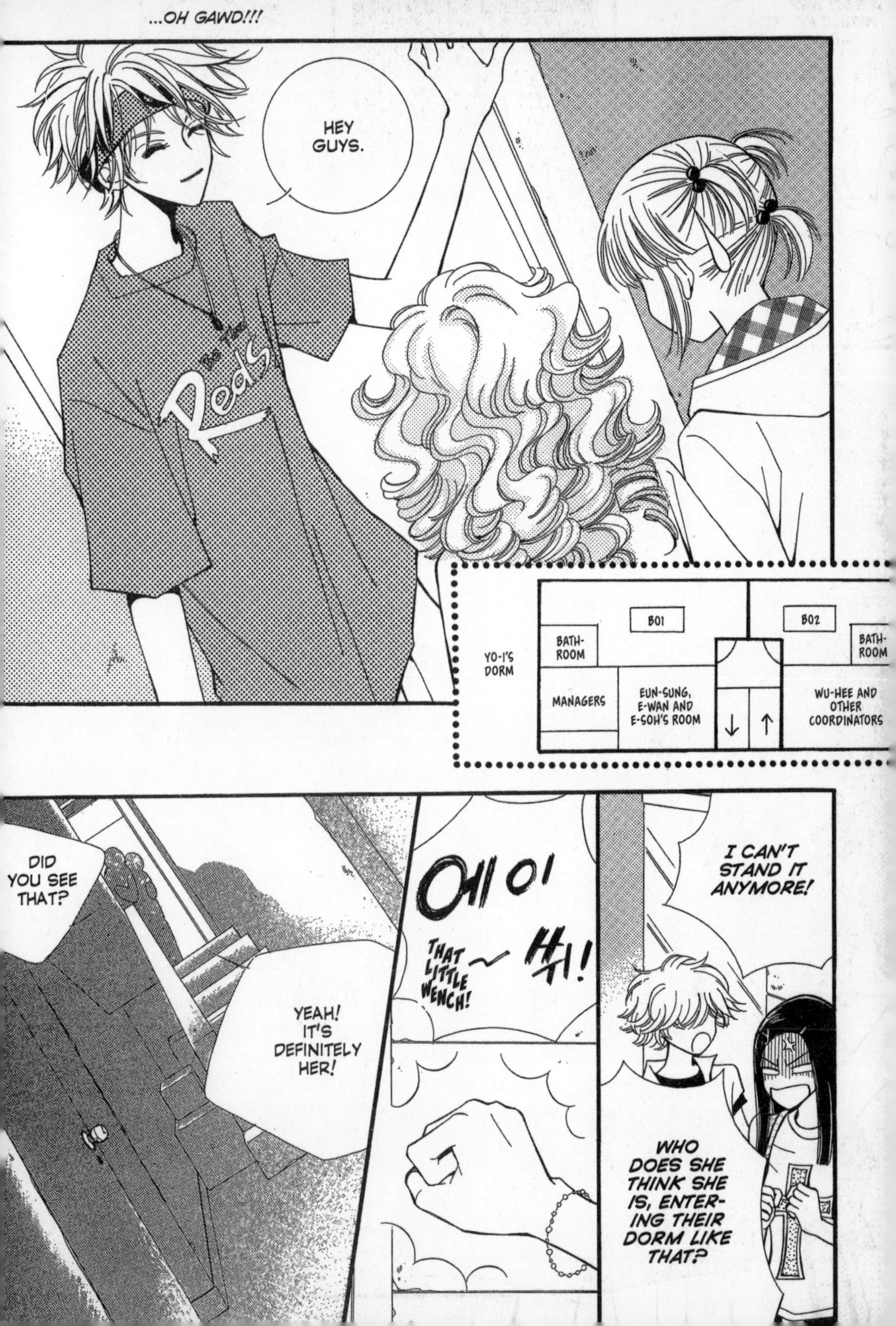
...OH GAWD!!!
HEY GUYS.
Be The Reds
YO-I'S DORM
B01
B02
BATH-ROOM
BATH-ROOM
MANAGERS
EUN-SUNG, E-WAN AND E-SOH'S ROOM
WU-HEE AND OTHER COORDINATORS
DID YOU SEE THAT?
YEAH! IT'S DEFINITELY HER!
THAT LITTLE WENCH!
I CAN'T STAND IT ANYMORE!
WHO DOES SHE THINK SHE IS, ENTER-ING THEIR DORM LIKE THAT?

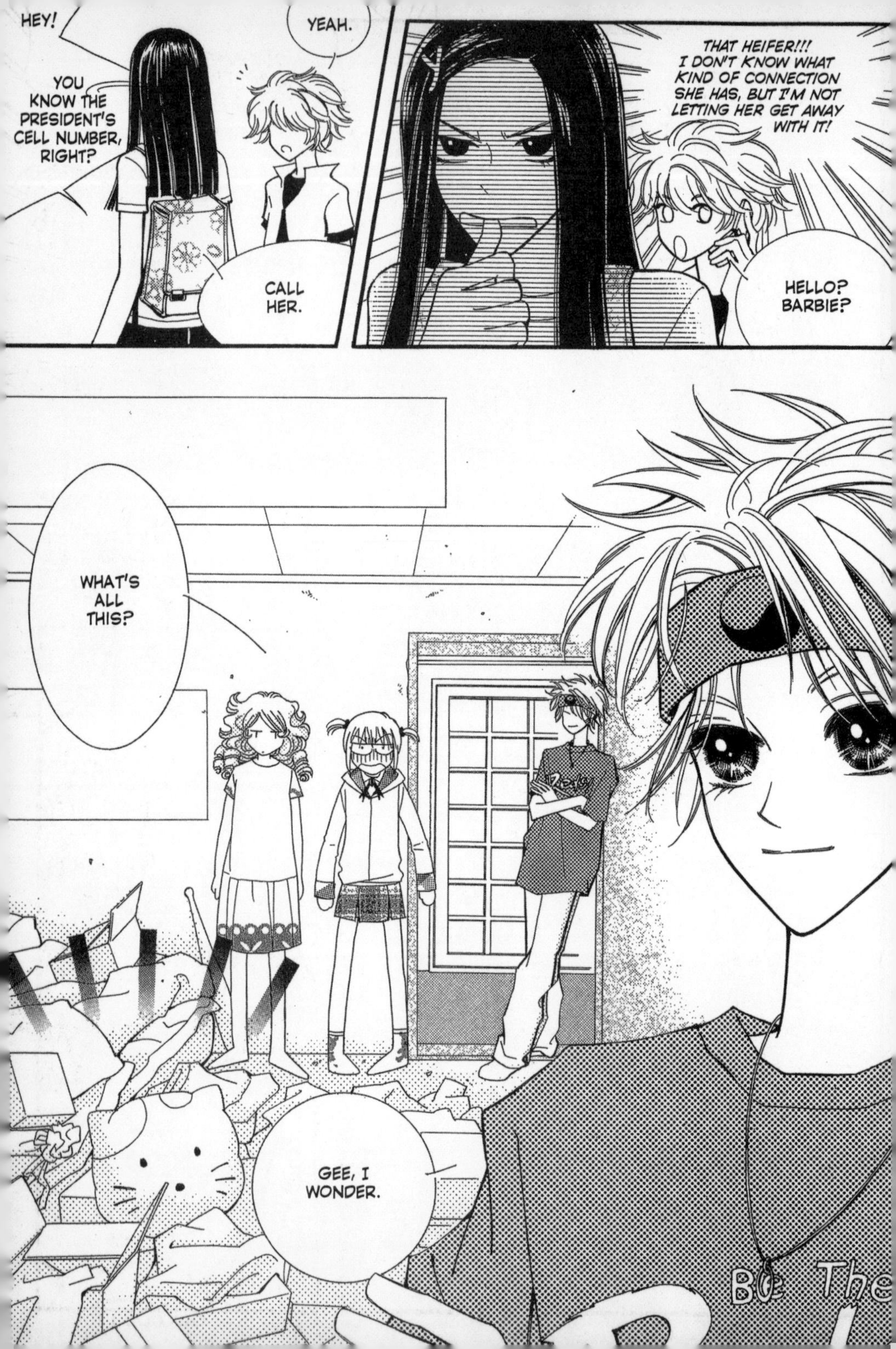
HEY!
YOU KNOW THE PRESIDENT'S CELL NUMBER, RIGHT?
YEAH.
CALL HER.
THAT HEIFER!!! I DON'T KNOW WHAT KIND OF CONNECTION SHE HAS, BUT I'M NOT LETTING HER GET AWAY WITH IT!
HELLO? BARBIE?
WHAT'S ALL THIS?
GEE, I WONDER.
Be The

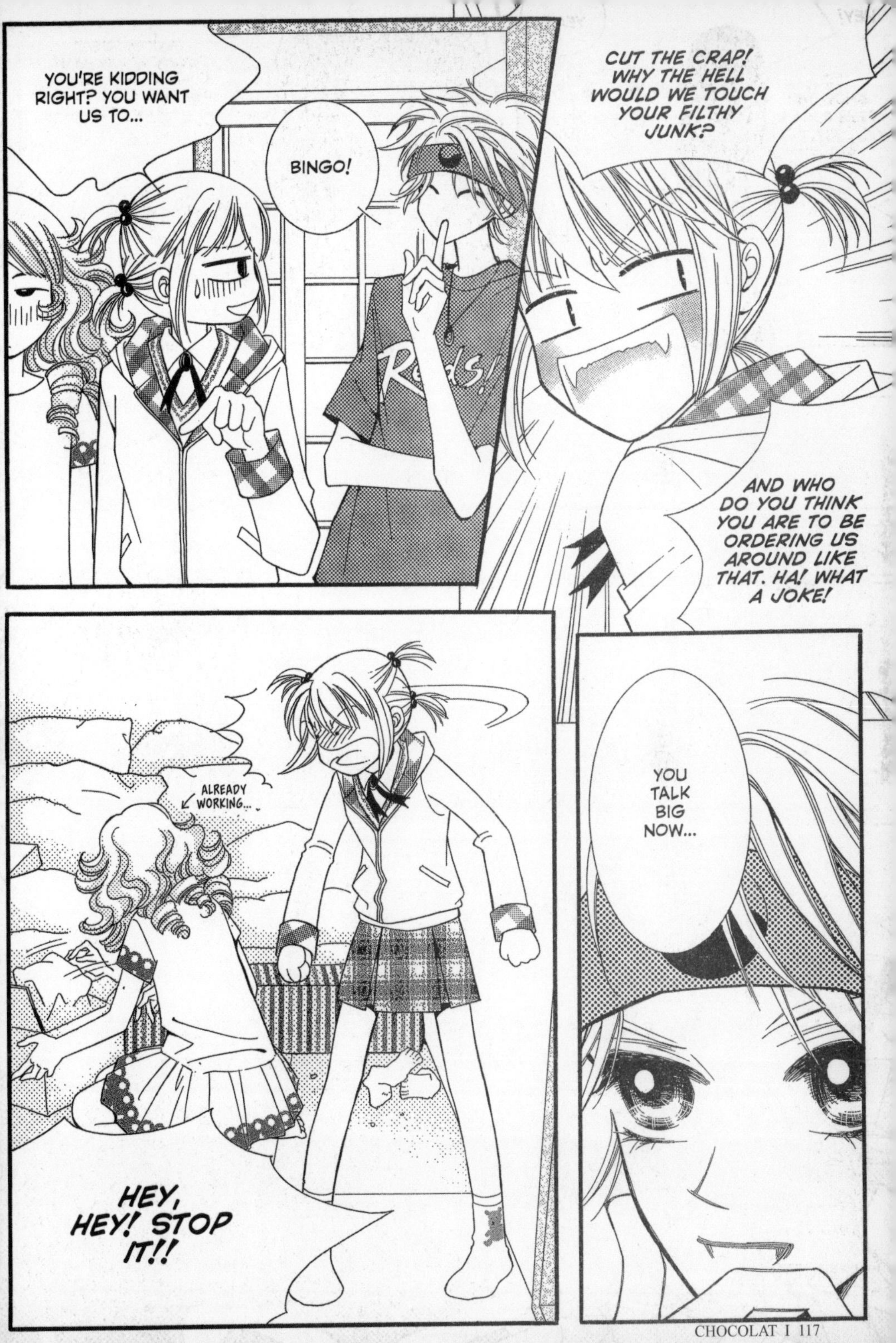
YOU'RE KIDDING RIGHT? YOU WANT US TO...
BINGO!
CUT THE CRAP! WHY THE HELL WOULD WE TOUCH YOUR FILTHY JUNK?
AND WHO DO YOU THINK YOU ARE TO BE ORDERING US AROUND LIKE THAT. HA! WHAT A JOKE!
ALREADY WORKING...
HEY, HEY! STOP IT!!
YOU TALK BIG NOW...

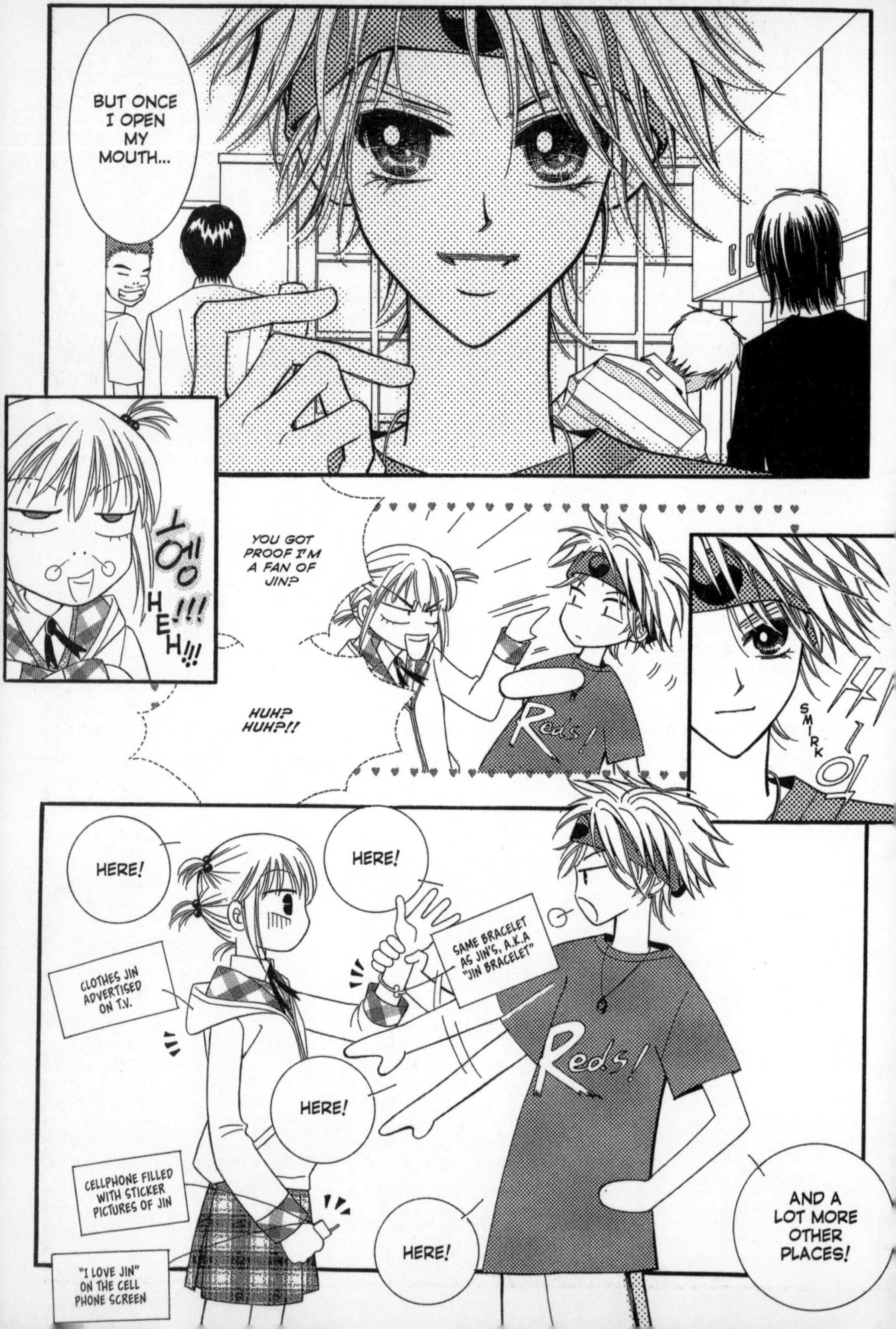
BUT ONCE I OPEN MY MOUTH...
HEH!!! HEH!!!
YOU GOT PROOF I'M A FAN OF JIN?
HUH? HUH?!!
SMIRK
HERE!
HERE!
CLOTHES JIN ADVERTISED ON T.V.
SAME BRACELET AS JIN'S, A.K.A "JIN BRACELET"
HERE!
CELLPHONE FILLED WITH STICKER PICTURES OF JIN
"I LOVE JIN" ON THE CELL PHONE SCREEN
HERE!
AND A LOT MORE OTHER PLACES!

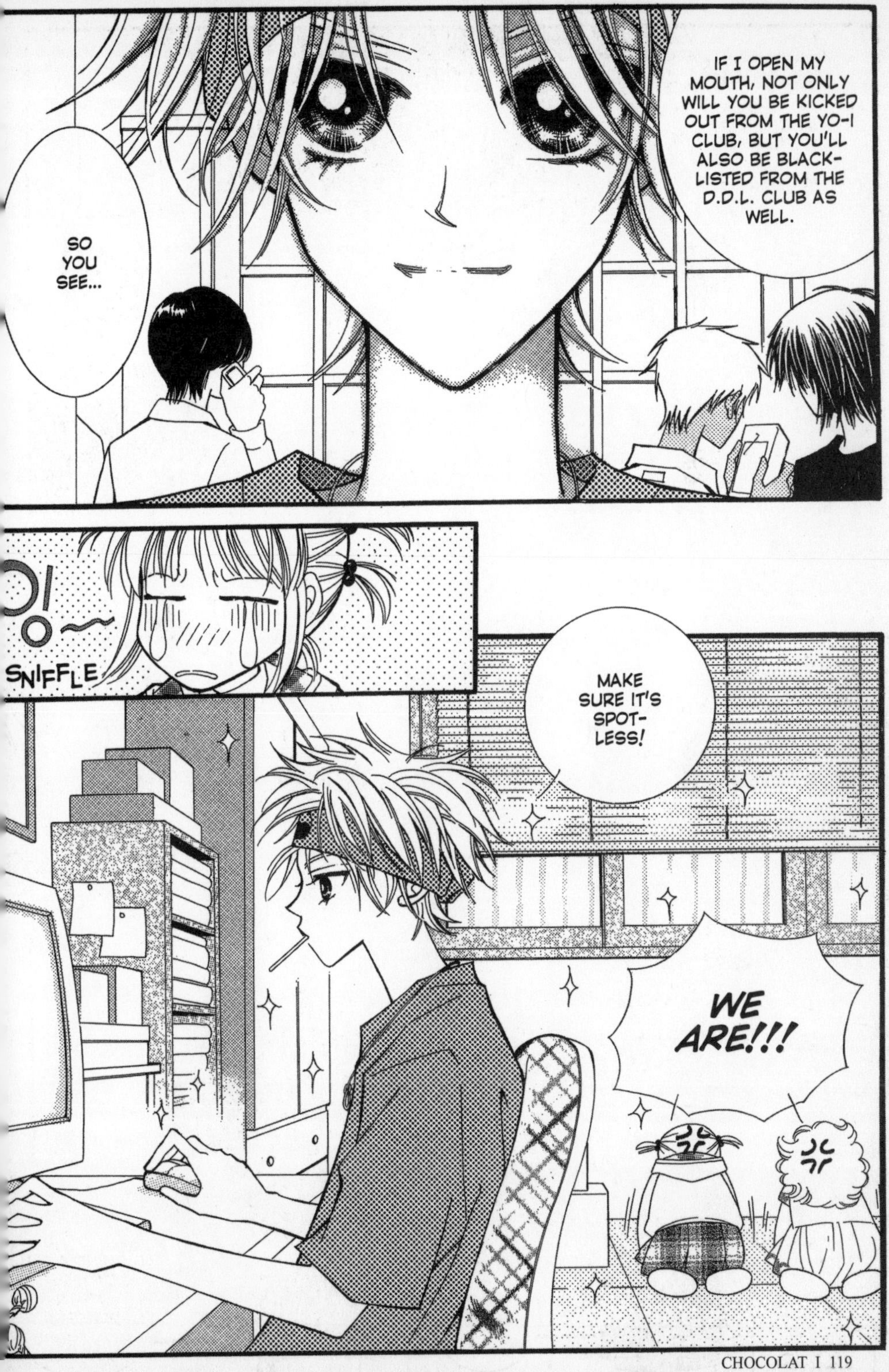
SO YOU SEE...
IF I OPEN MY MOUTH, NOT ONLY WILL YOU BE KICKED OUT FROM THE YO-I CLUB, BUT YOU'LL ALSO BE BLACK-LISTED FROM THE D.D.L. CLUB AS WELL.
O! O~~
SNIFFLE
MAKE SURE IT'S SPOT-LESS!
WE ARE!!!

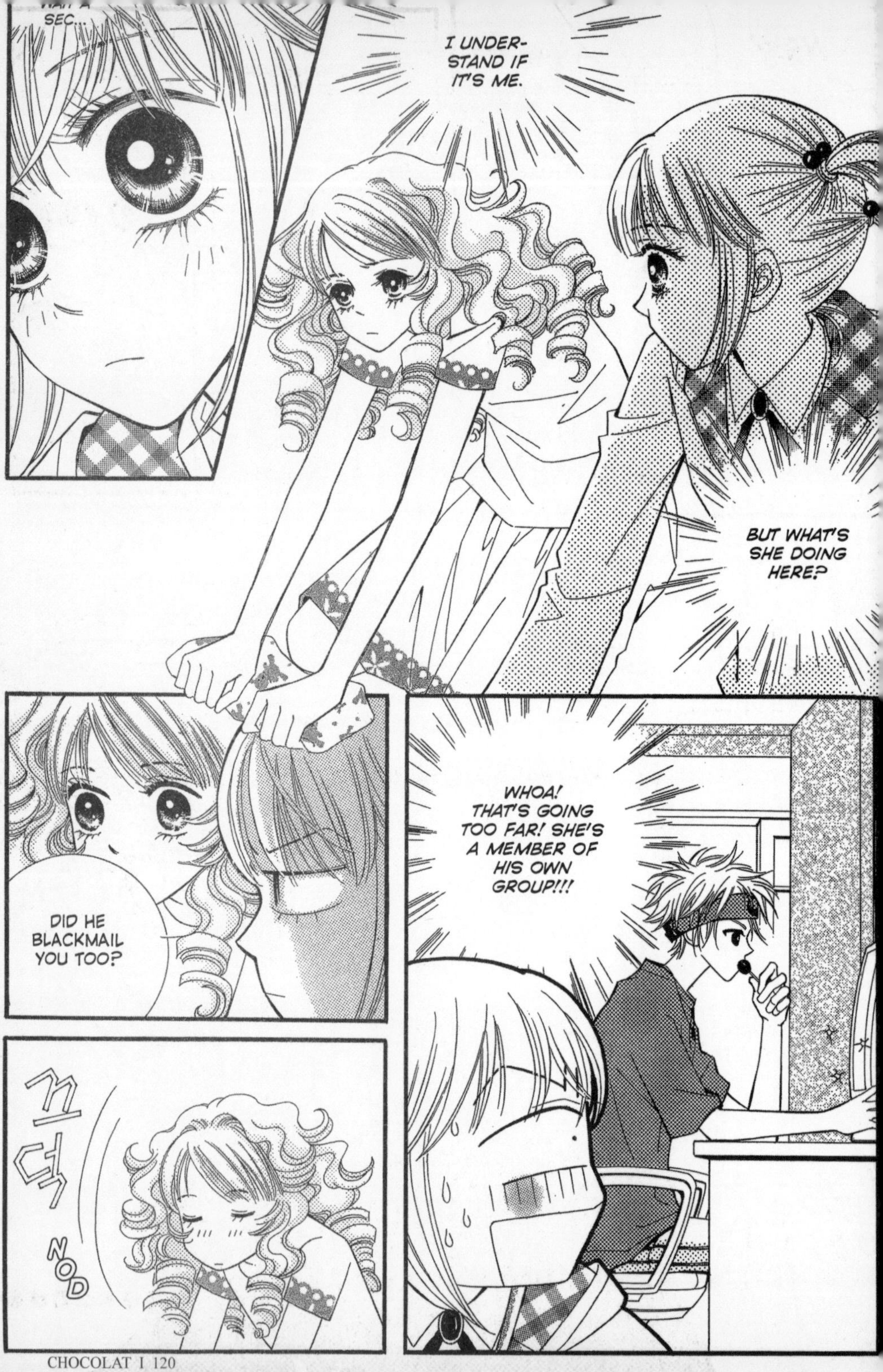
SEC...
I UNDER-STAND IF IT'S ME.
BUT WHAT'S SHE DOING HERE?
DID HE BLACKMAIL YOU TOO?
WHOA! THAT'S GOING TOO FAR! SHE'S A MEMBER OF HIS OWN GROUP!!!
끄덕
NOD

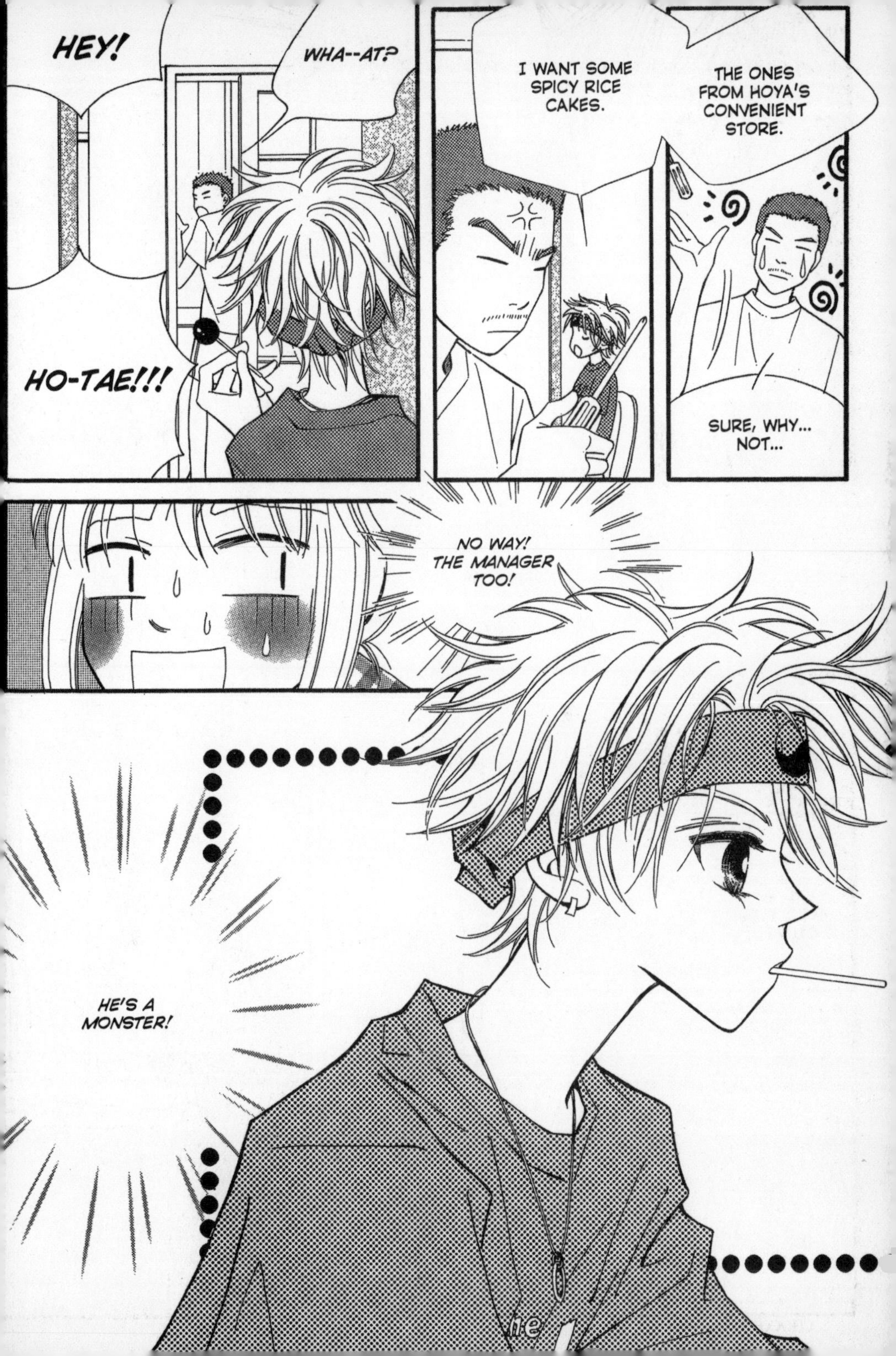
HEY!
HO-TAE!!!
WHA--AT?
I WANT SOME SPICY RICE CAKES.
THE ONES FROM HOYA'S CONVENIENT STORE.
SURE, WHY... NOT...
NO WAY! THE MANAGER TOO!
HE'S A MONSTER!

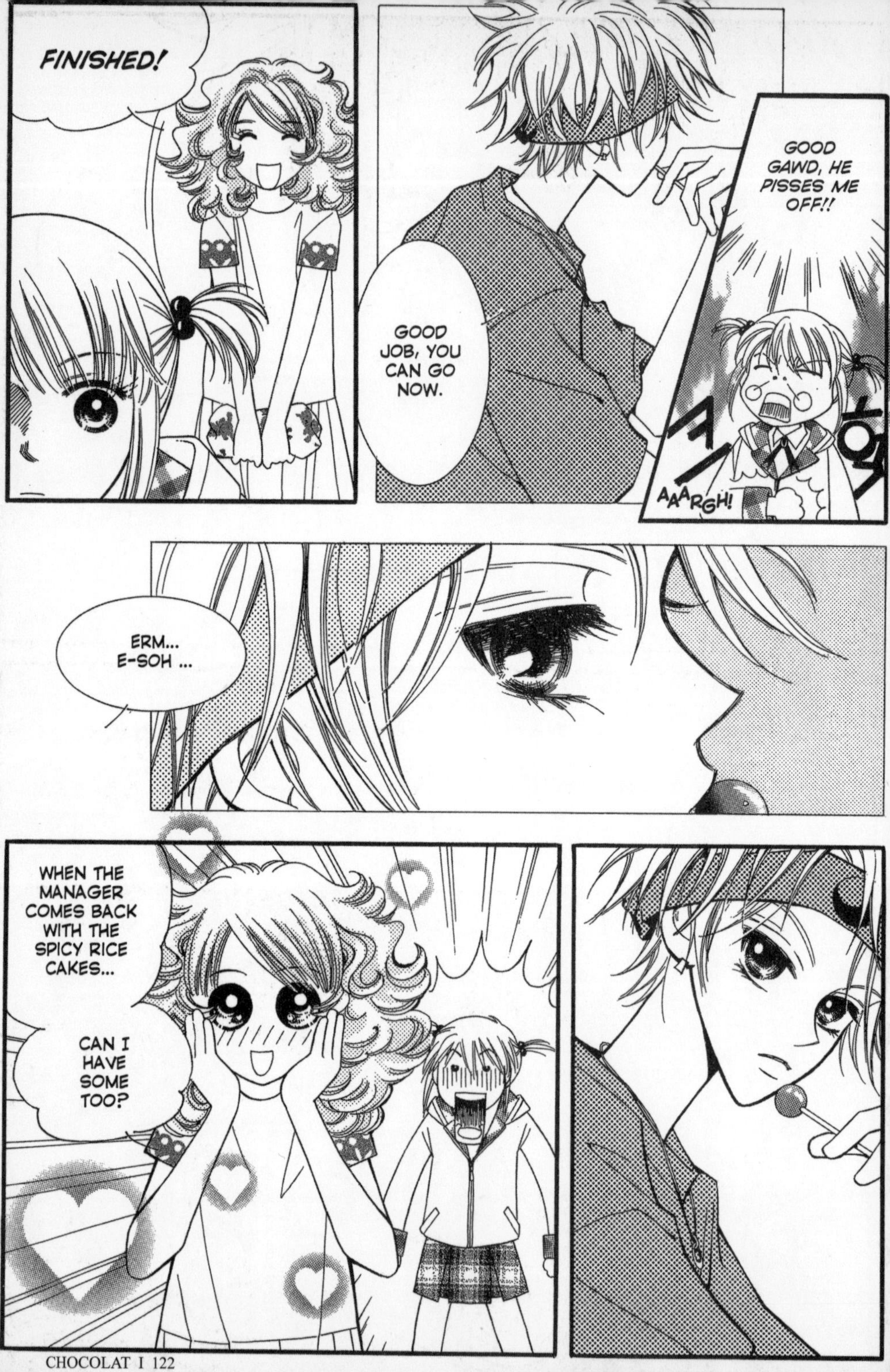
FINISHED!
GOOD JOB, YOU CAN GO NOW.
GOOD GAWD, HE PISSES ME OFF!!
AAARGH!
ERM... E-SOH ...
WHEN THE MANAGER COMES BACK WITH THE SPICY RICE CAKES...
CAN I HAVE SOME TOO?

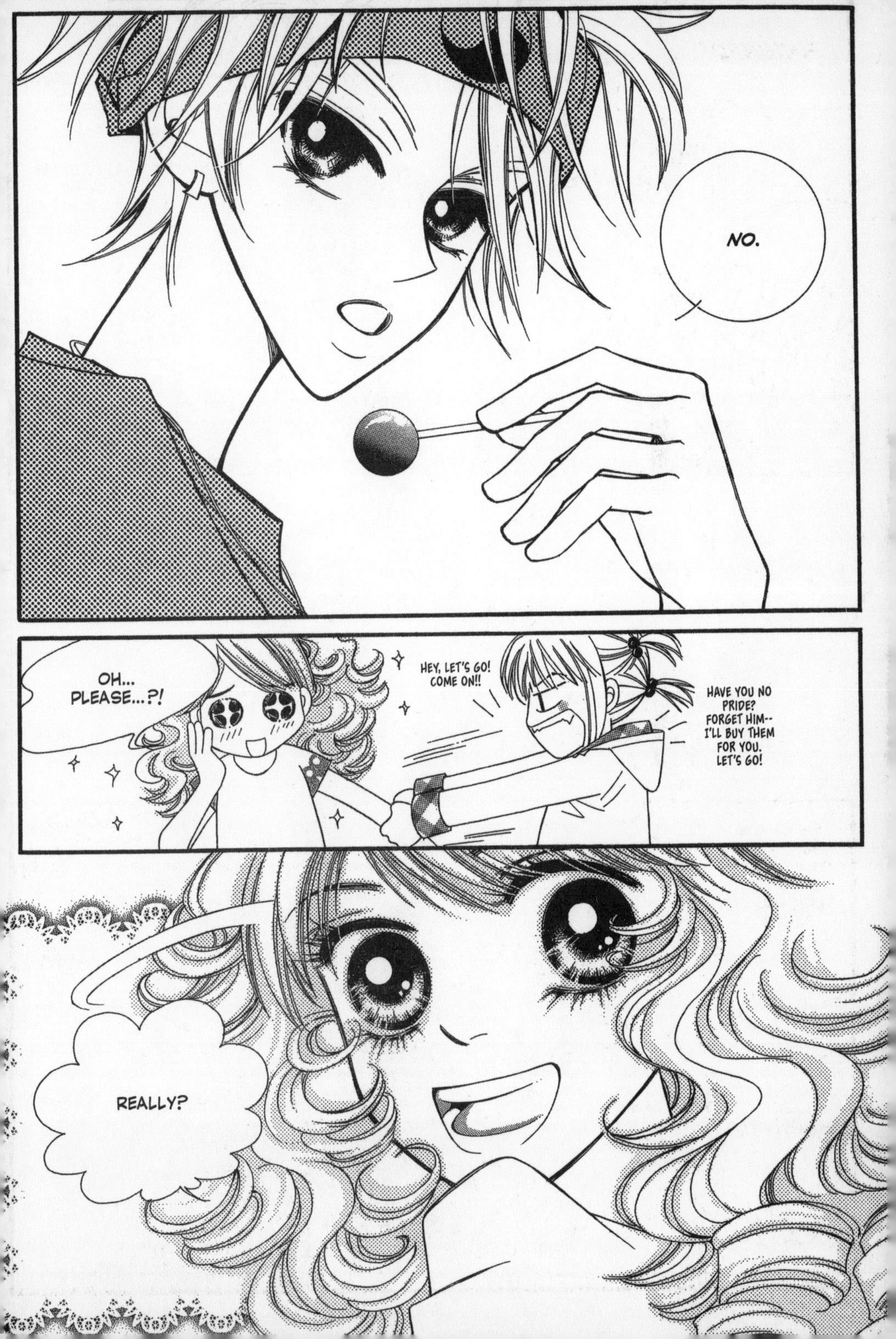
NO.
OH... PLEASE...?!
HEY, LET'S GO! COME ON!!
HAVE YOU NO PRIDE? FORGET HIM-- I'LL BUY THEM FOR YOU. LET'S GO!
REALLY?

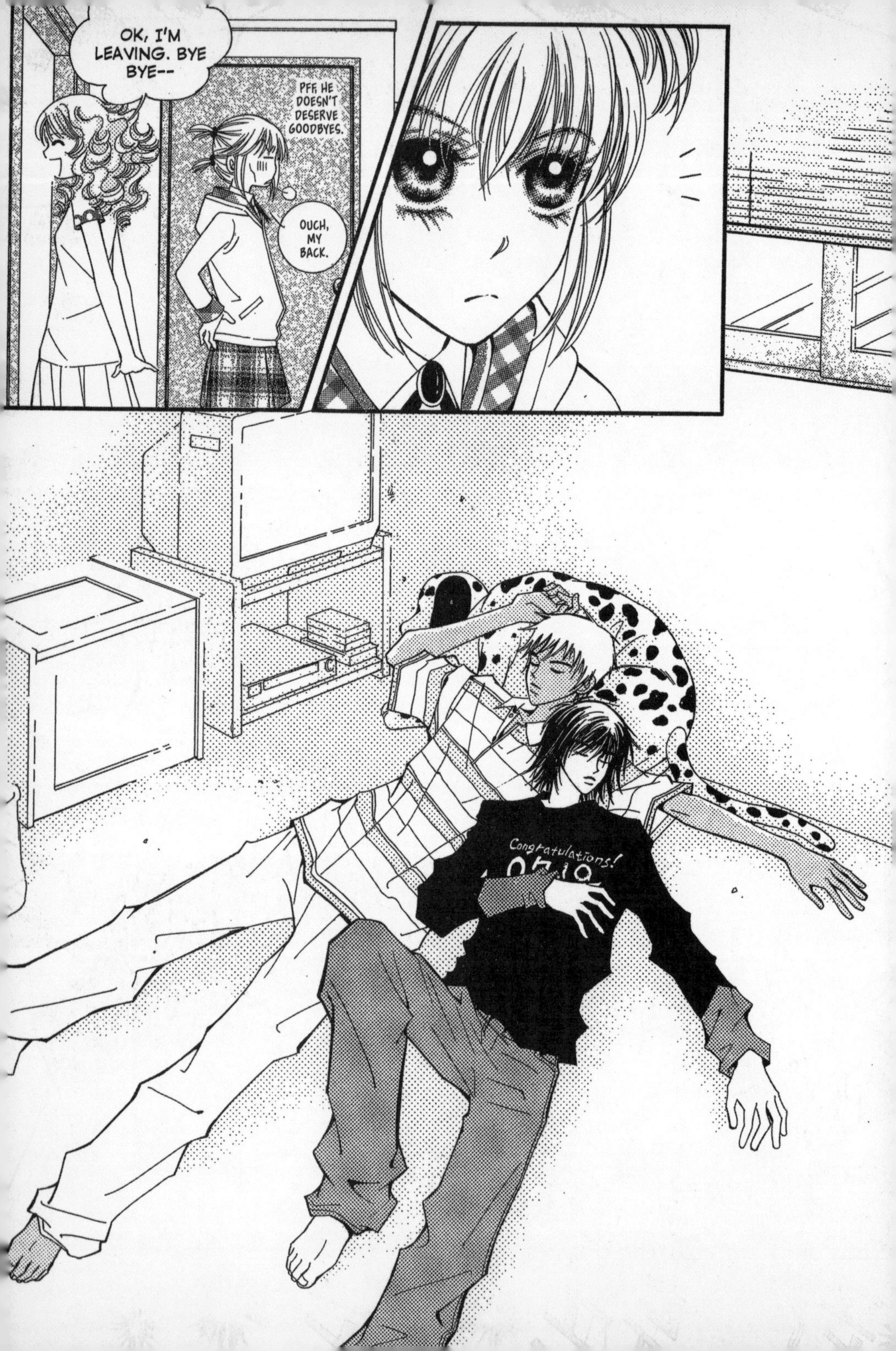

OK, I'M LEAVING. BYE BYE--
PFF, HE DOESN'T DESERVE GOODBYES.
OUCH, MY BACK.
Congratulations!

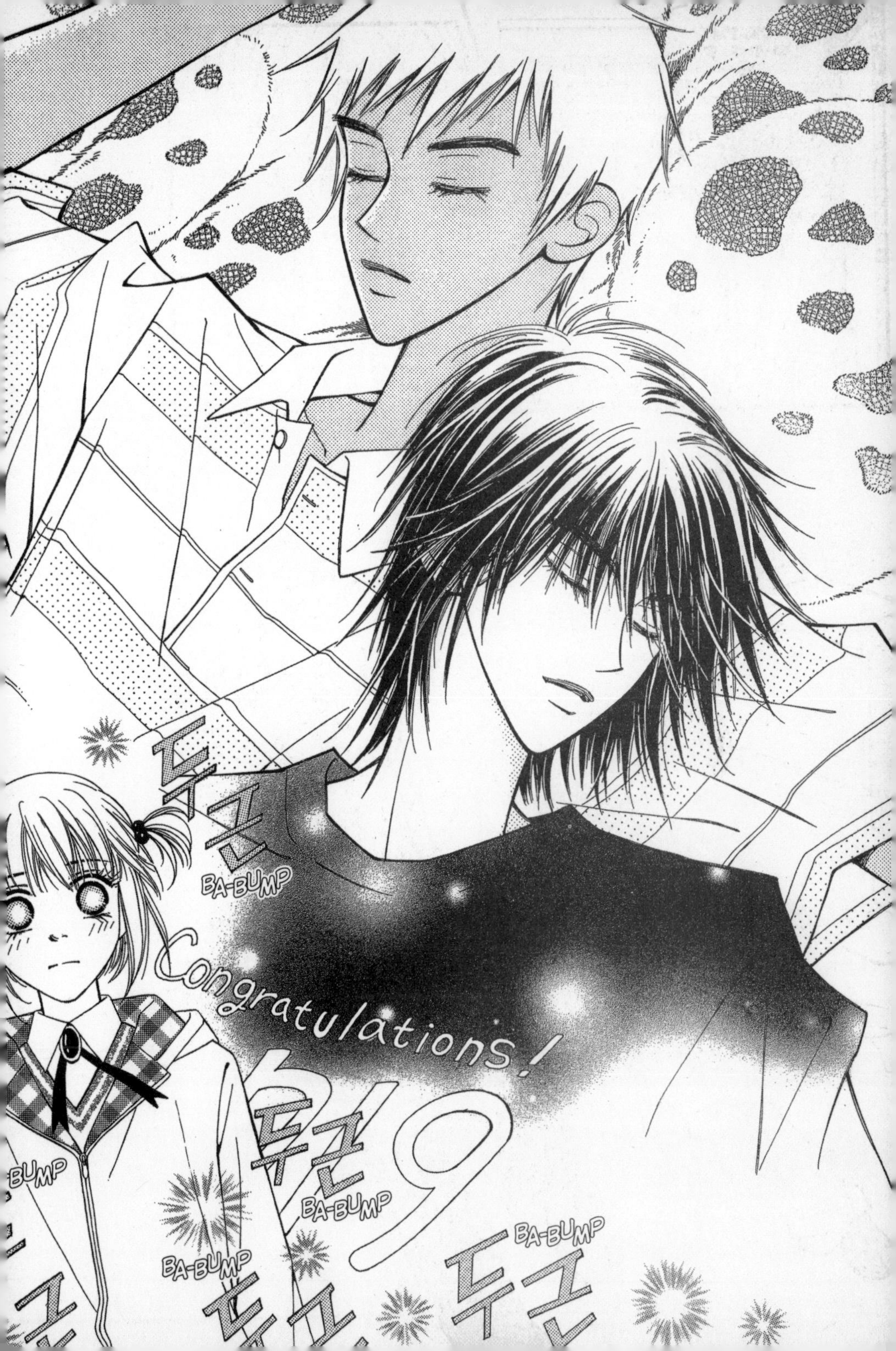
BA-BUMP
Congratulations!
BUMP
BA-BUMP
BA-BUMP
BA-BUMP

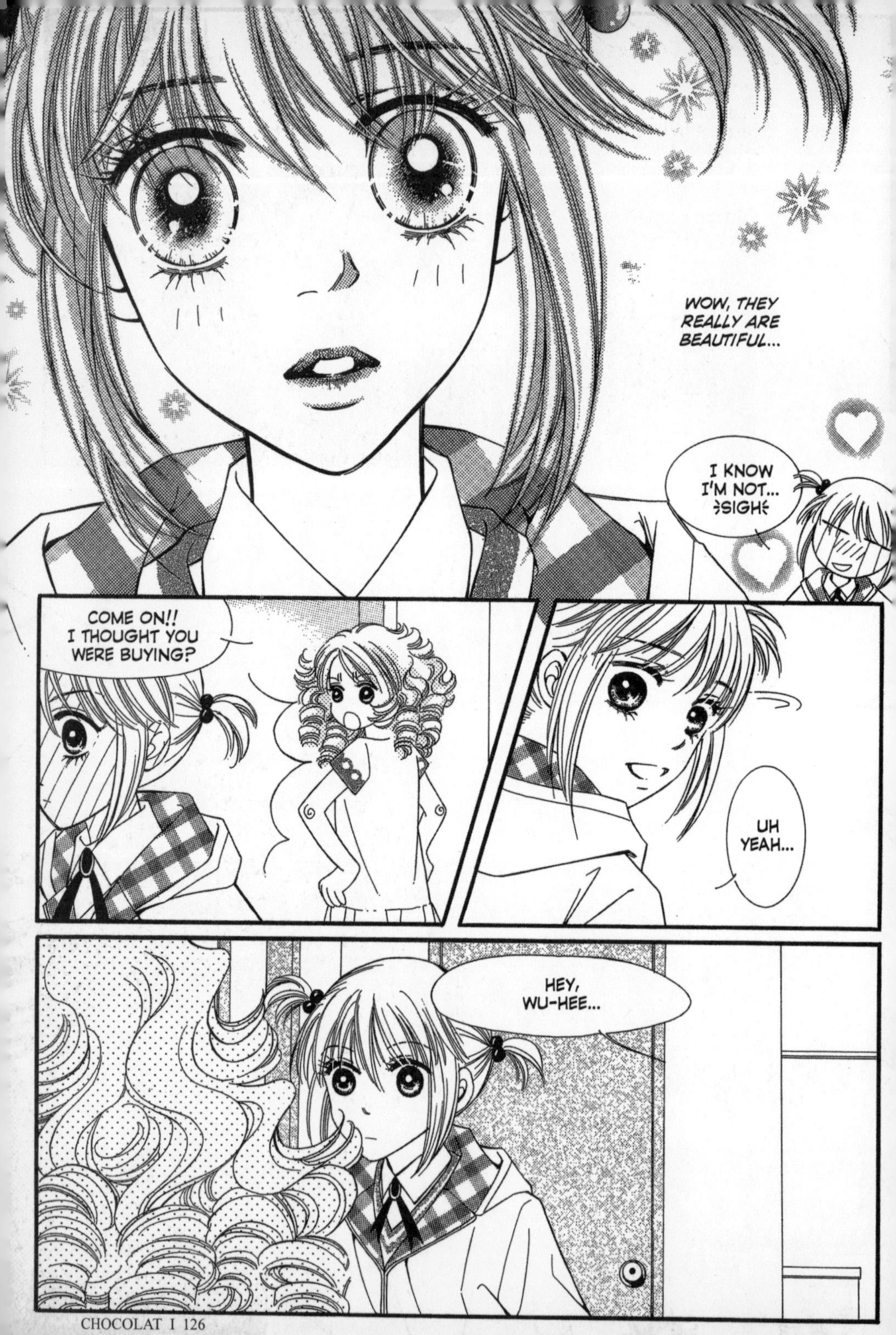
WOW, THEY REALLY ARE BEAUTIFUL...
I KNOW I'M NOT... ⊰SIGH⊱
COME ON!! I THOUGHT YOU WERE BUYING?
UH YEAH...
HEY, WU-HEE...

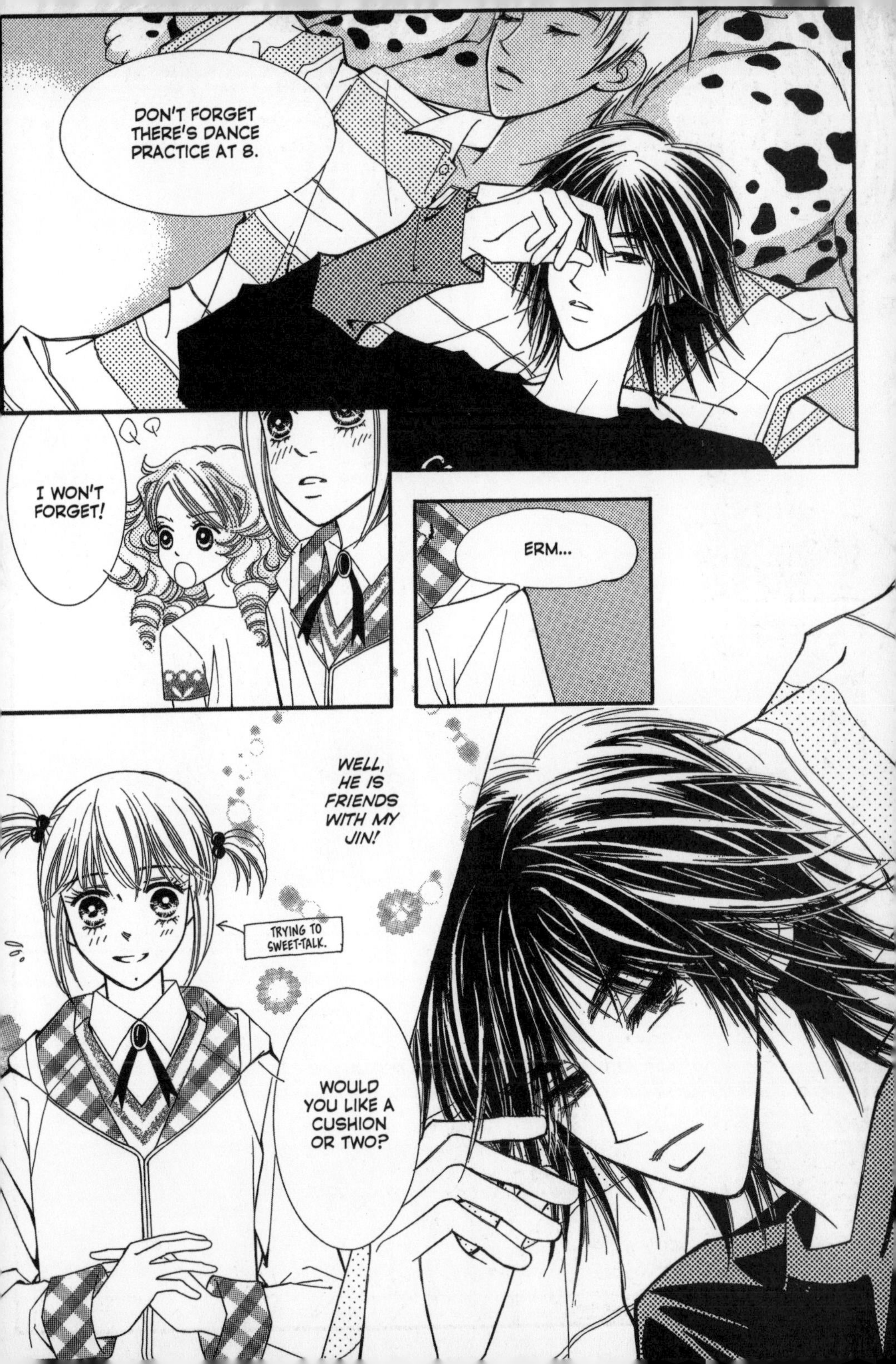
DON'T FORGET THERE'S DANCE PRACTICE AT 8.
I WON'T FORGET!
ERM...
WELL, HE IS FRIENDS WITH MY JIN!
TRYING TO SWEET-TALK.
WOULD YOU LIKE A CUSHION OR TWO?

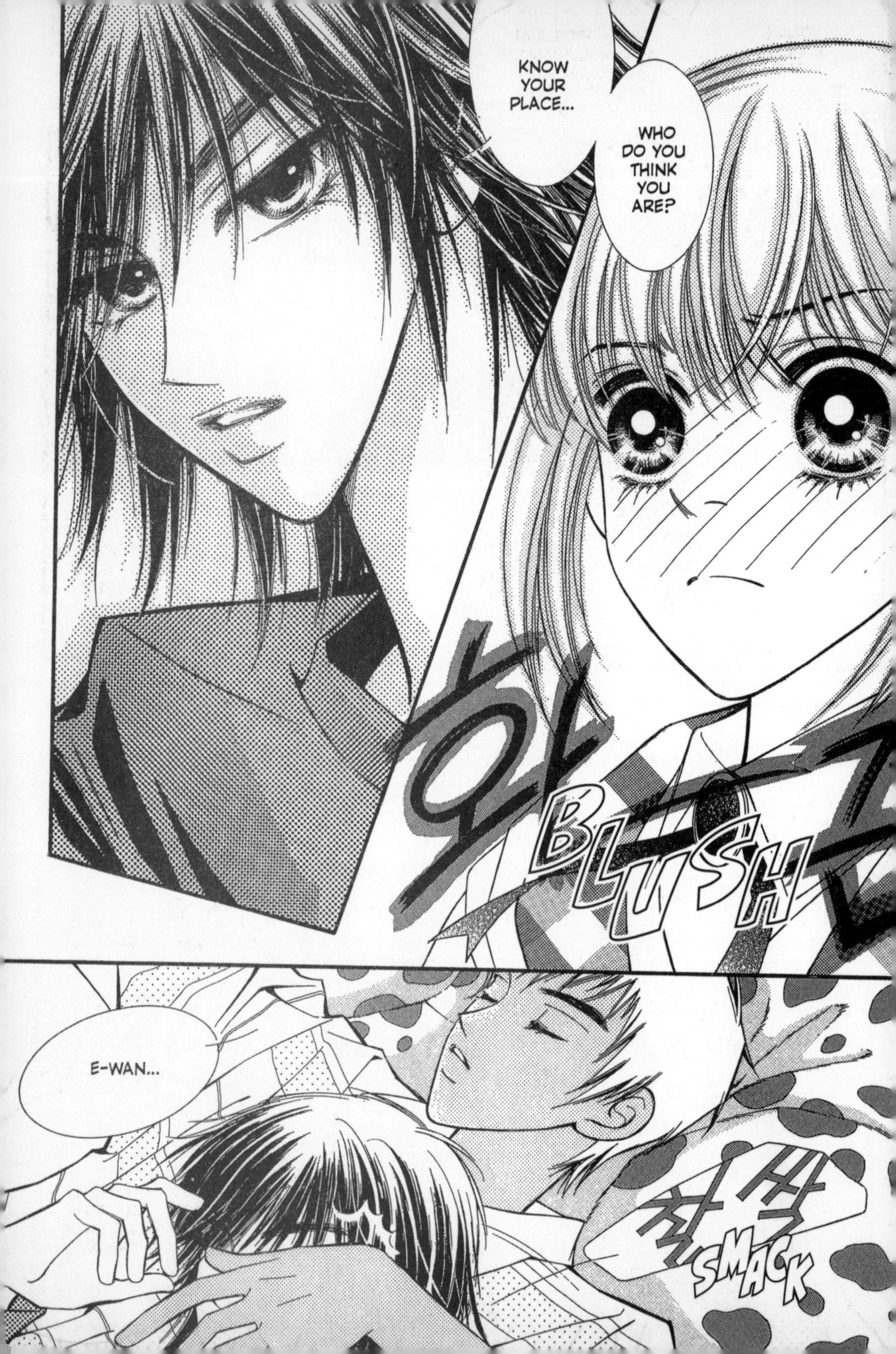
KNOW YOUR PLACE...
WHO DO YOU THINK YOU ARE?
BLUSH
E-WAN...
SMACK

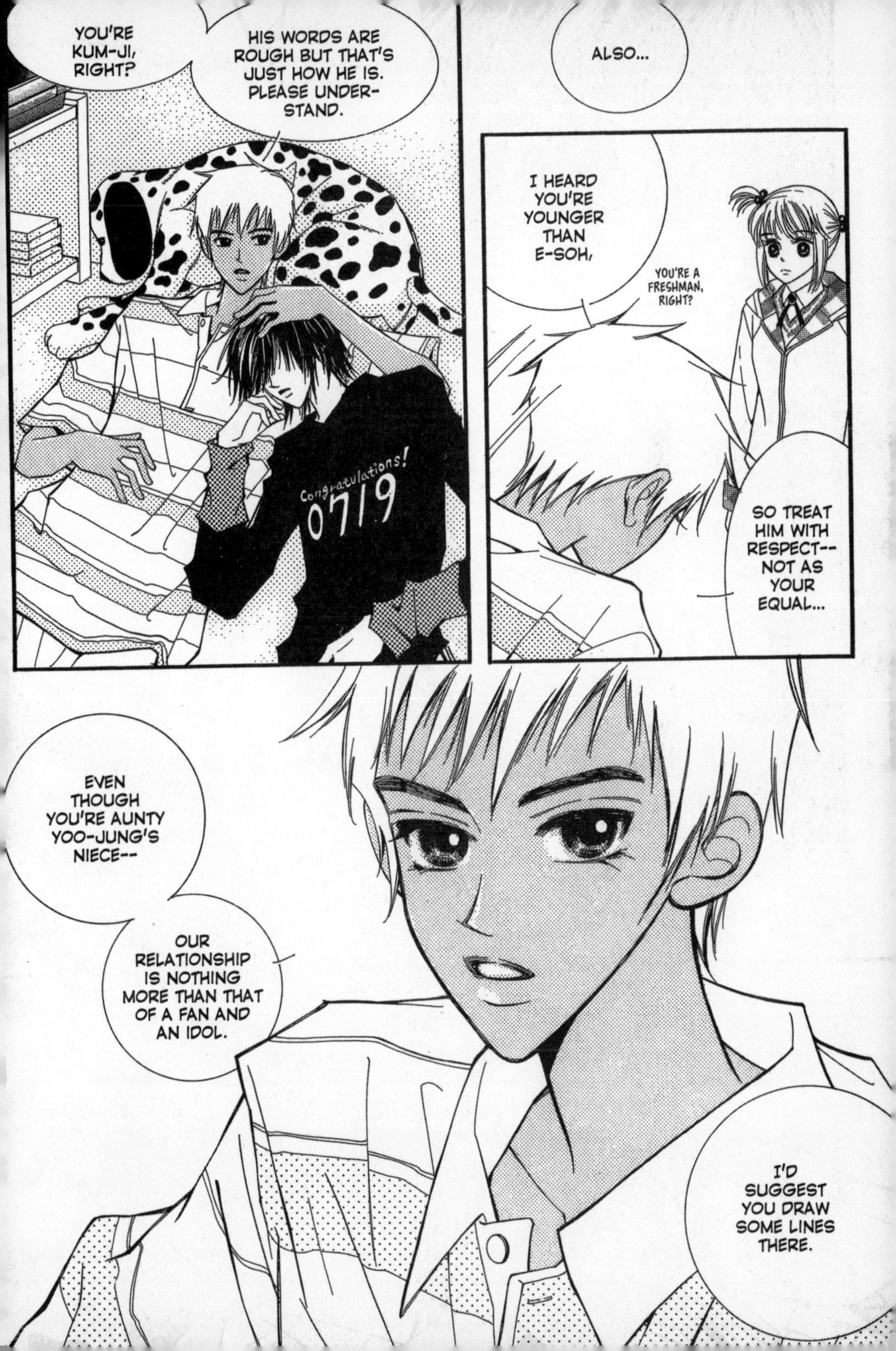
YOU'RE KUM-JI, RIGHT?
HIS WORDS ARE ROUGH BUT THAT'S JUST HOW HE IS. PLEASE UNDER-STAND.
Congratulations! 0719
ALSO...
I HEARD YOU'RE YOUNGER THAN E-SOH,
YOU'RE A FRESHMAN, RIGHT?
SO TREAT HIM WITH RESPECT-- NOT AS YOUR EQUAL...
EVEN THOUGH YOU'RE AUNTY YOO-JUNG'S NIECE--
OUR RELATIONSHIP IS NOTHING MORE THAN THAT OF A FAN AND AN IDOL.
I'D SUGGEST YOU DRAW SOME LINES THERE.

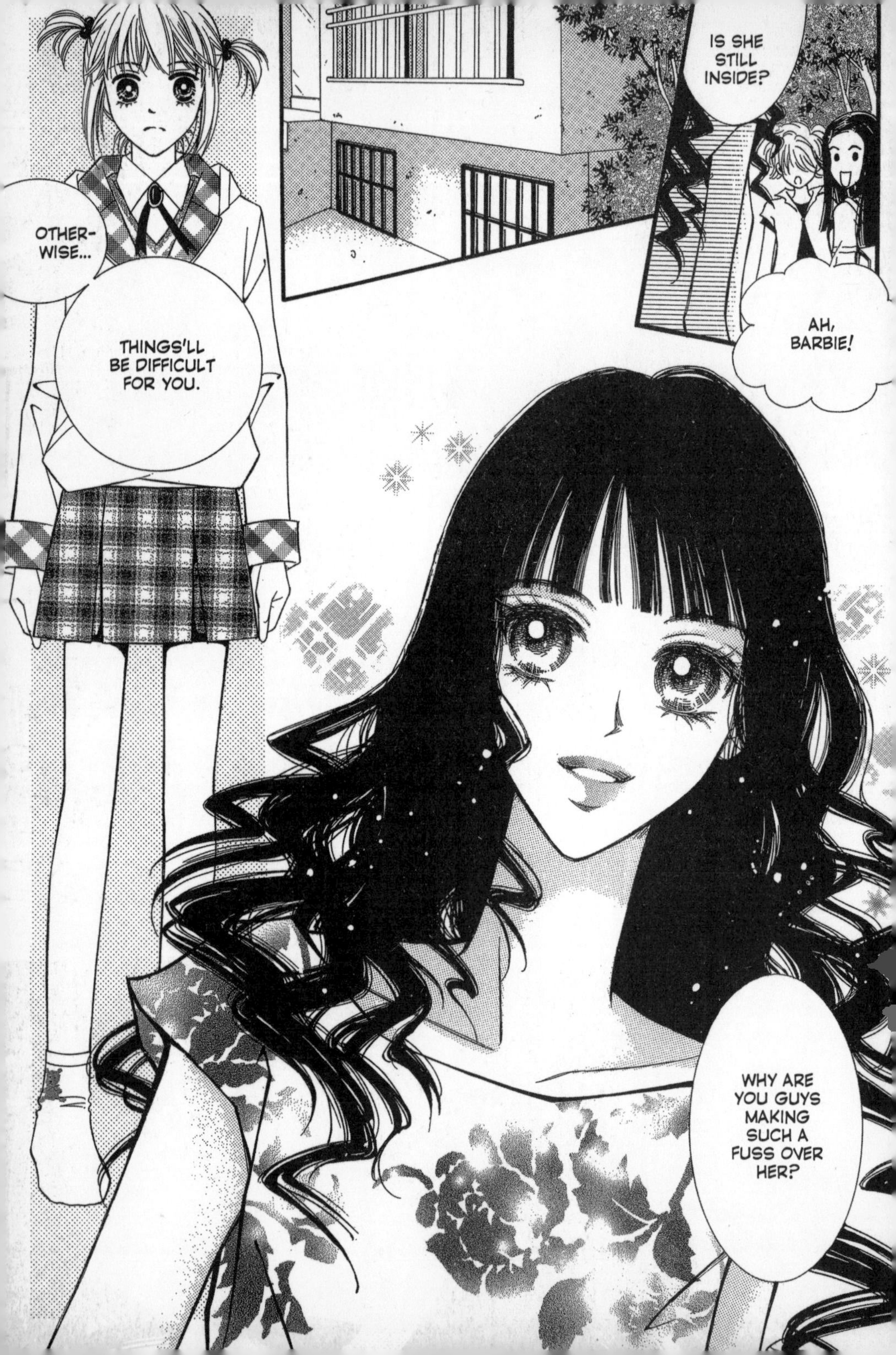
OTHER-WISE...
THINGS'LL BE DIFFICULT FOR YOU.
IS SHE STILL INSIDE?
AH, BARBIE!
WHY ARE YOU GUYS MAKING SUCH A FUSS OVER HER?

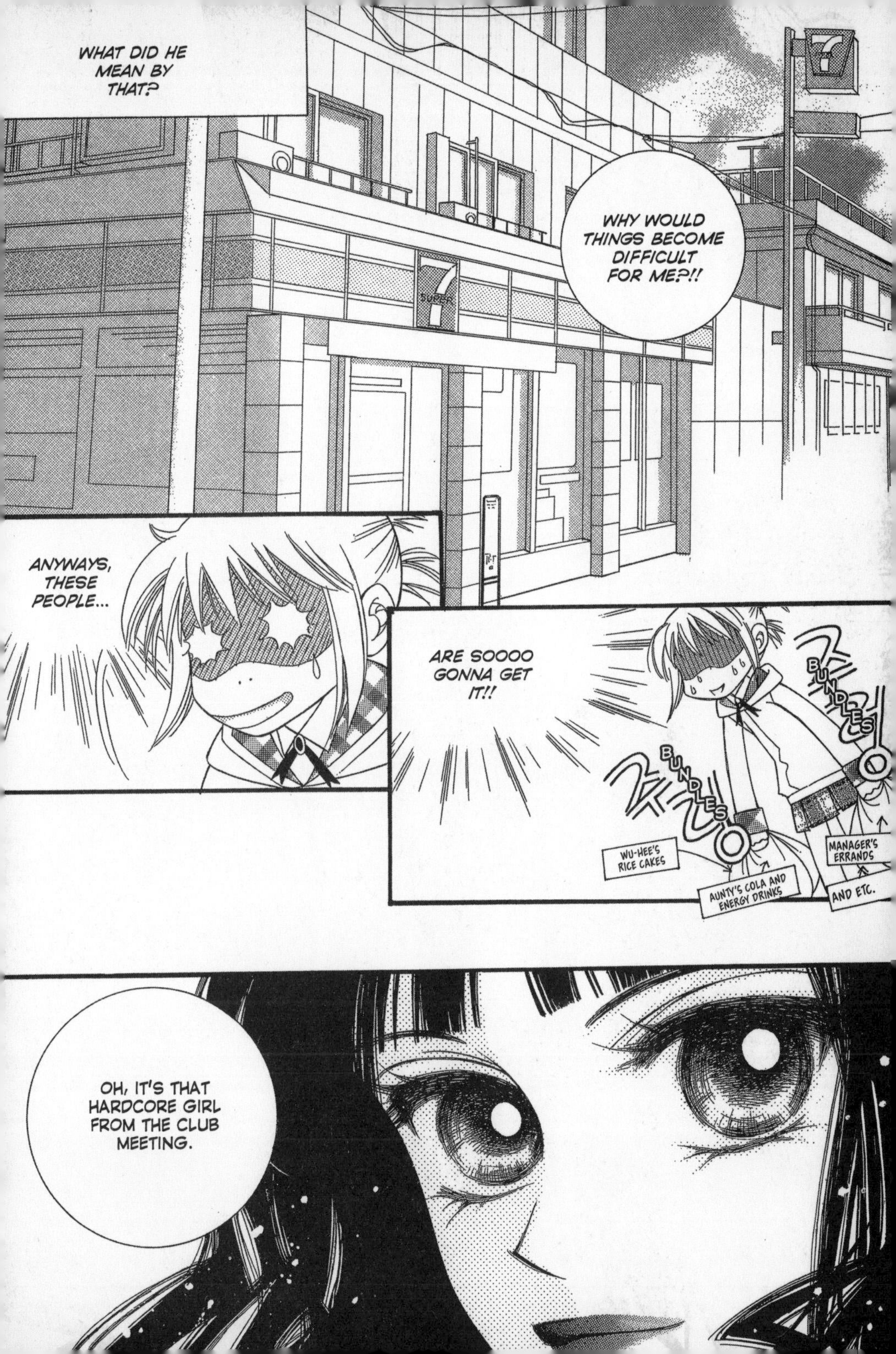
WHAT DID HE MEAN BY THAT?
WHY WOULD THINGS BECOME DIFFICULT FOR ME?!!
ANYWAYS, THESE PEOPLE...
ARE SOOOO GONNA GET IT!!
BUNDLES
BUNDLES
WU-HEE'S RICE CAKES
AUNTY'S COLA AND ENERGY DRINKS
MANAGER'S ERRANDS
AND ETC.
OH, IT'S THAT HARDCORE GIRL FROM THE CLUB MEETING.

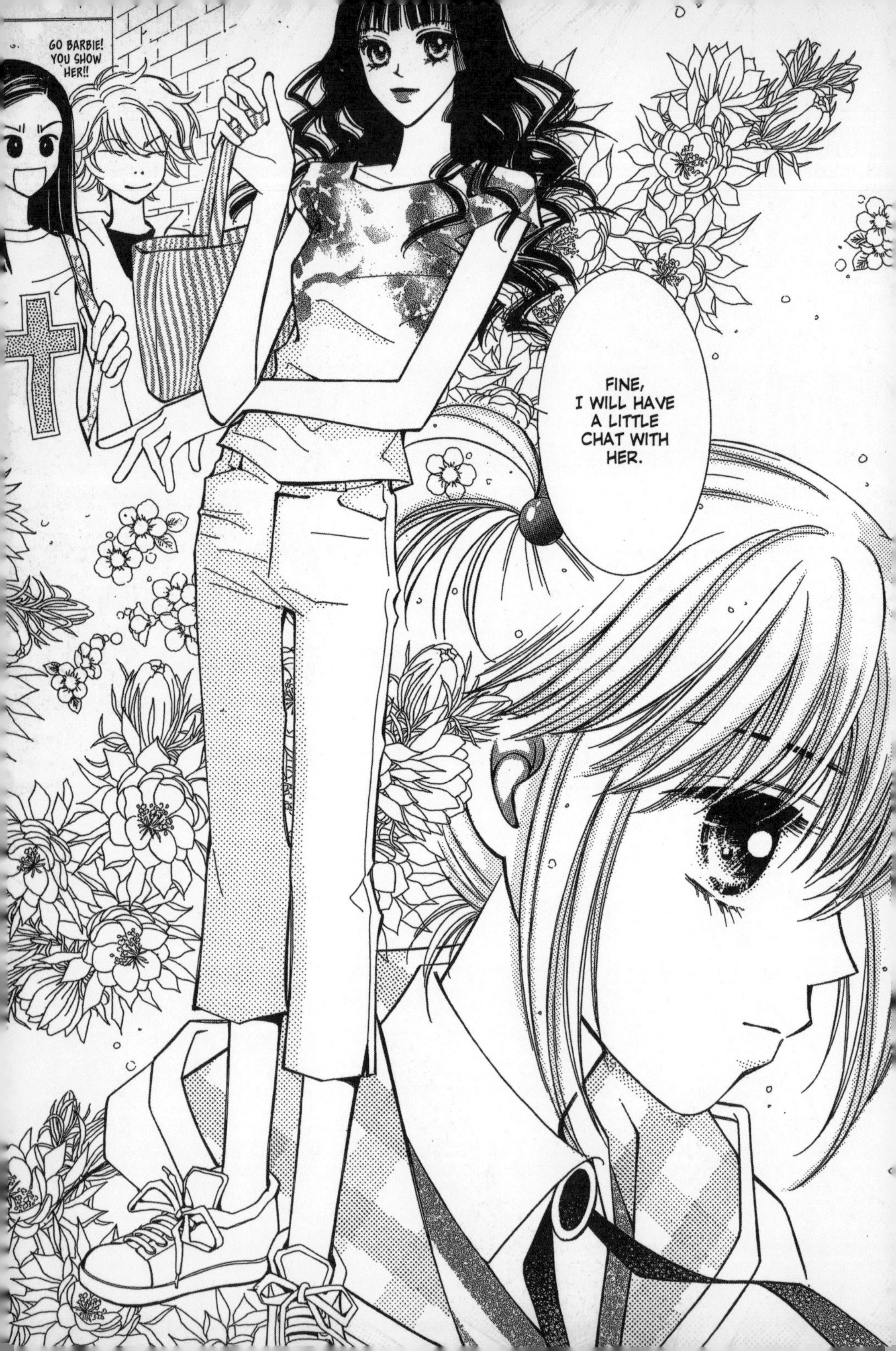
GO BARBIE! YOU SHOW HER!!
FINE, I WILL HAVE A LITTLE CHAT WITH HER.

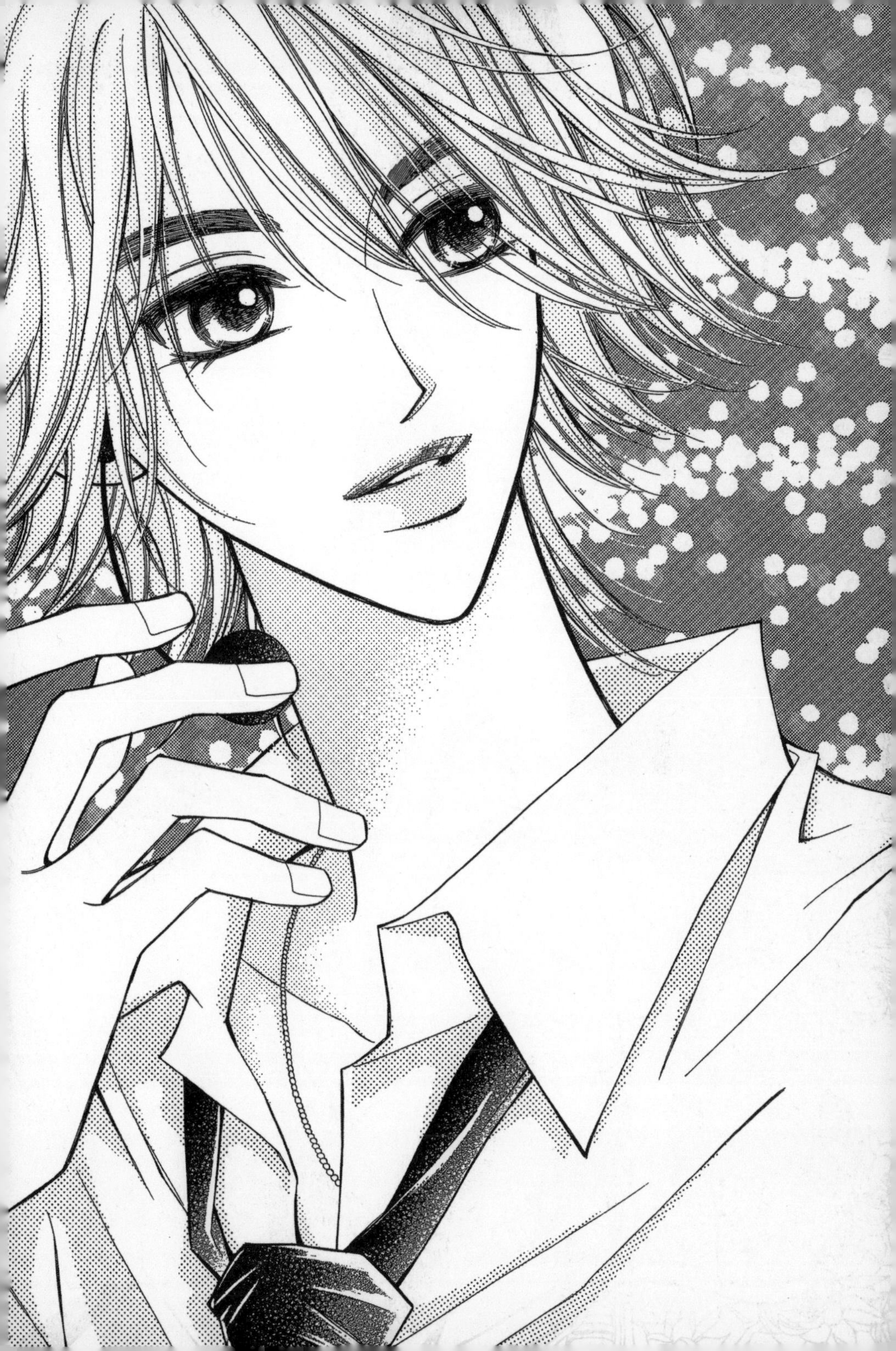

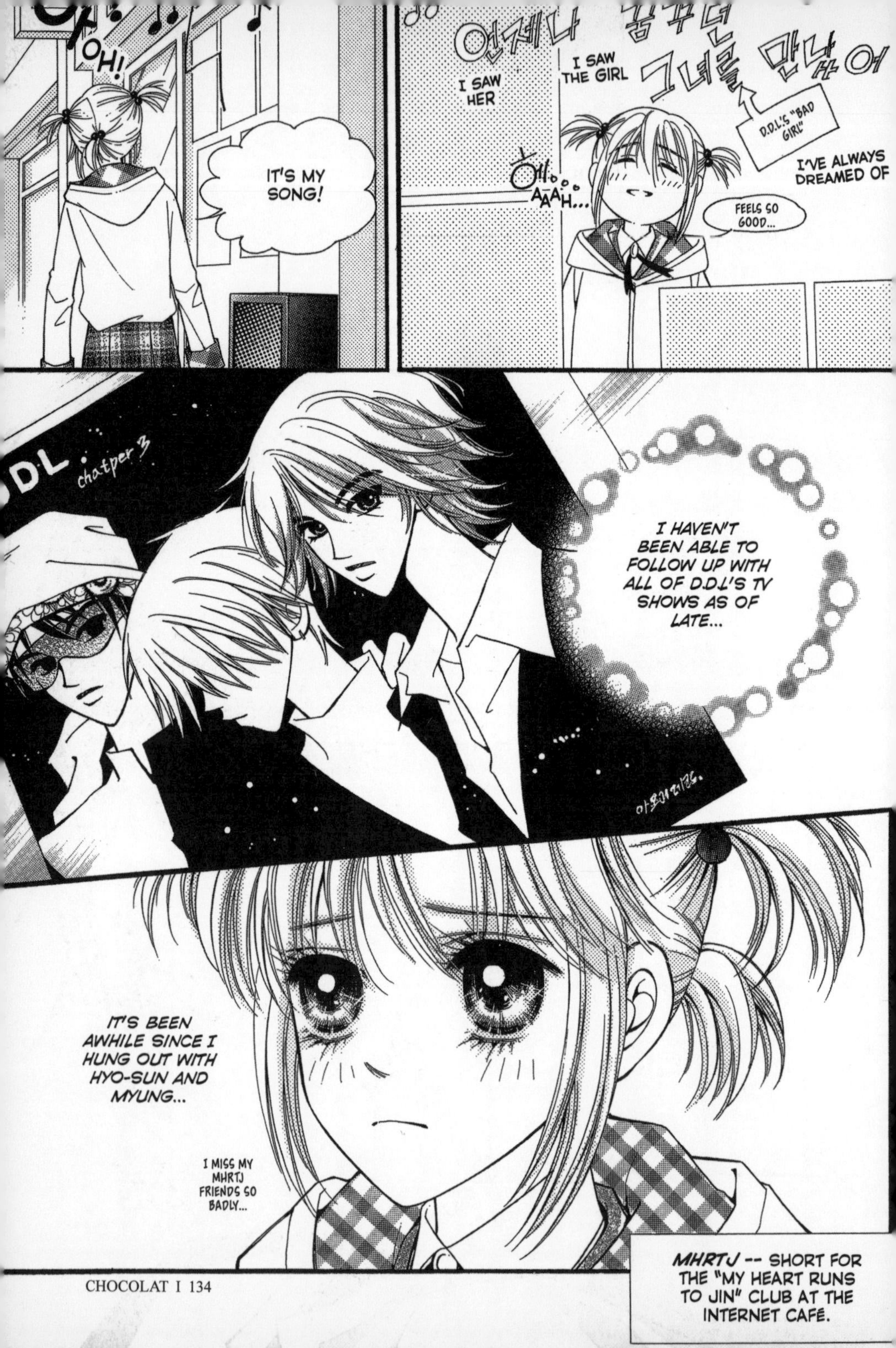
OH!
IT'S MY SONG!
언제나 꿈꾸던 그녀를 만났어
I SAW HER
I SAW THE GIRL
D.D.L'S "BAD GIRL"
I'VE ALWAYS DREAMED OF
AAAH...
FEELS SO GOOD...
D·L
chatper 3
I HAVEN'T BEEN ABLE TO FOLLOW UP WITH ALL OF D.D.L'S TV SHOWS AS OF LATE...
IT'S BEEN AWHILE SINCE I HUNG OUT WITH HYO-SUN AND MYUNG...
I MISS MY MHRTJ FRIENDS SO BADLY...
MHRTJ -- SHORT FOR THE "MY HEART RUNS TO JIN" CLUB AT THE INTERNET CAFÉ.

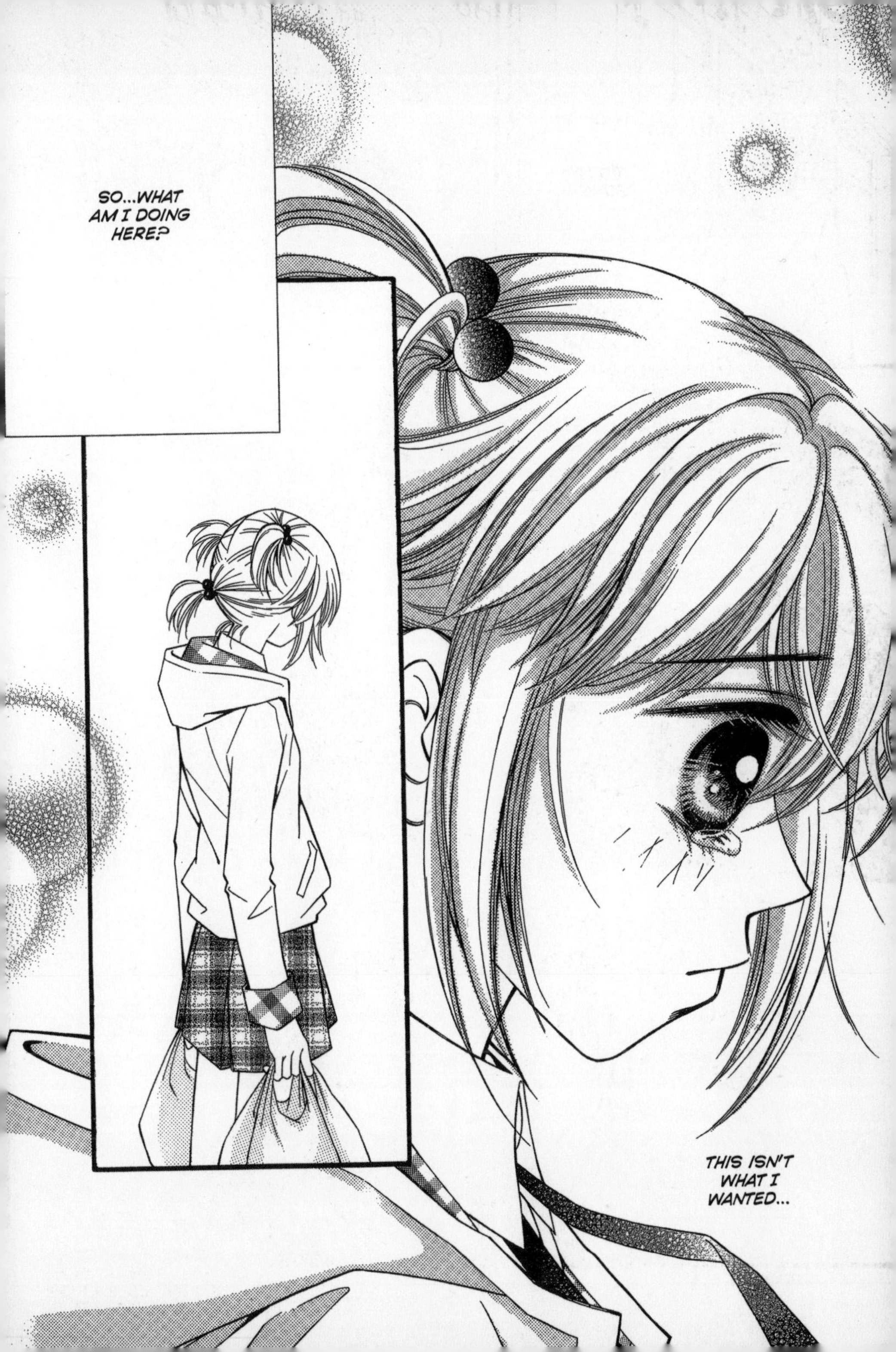
SO...WHAT AM I DOING HERE?
THIS ISN'T WHAT I WANTED...

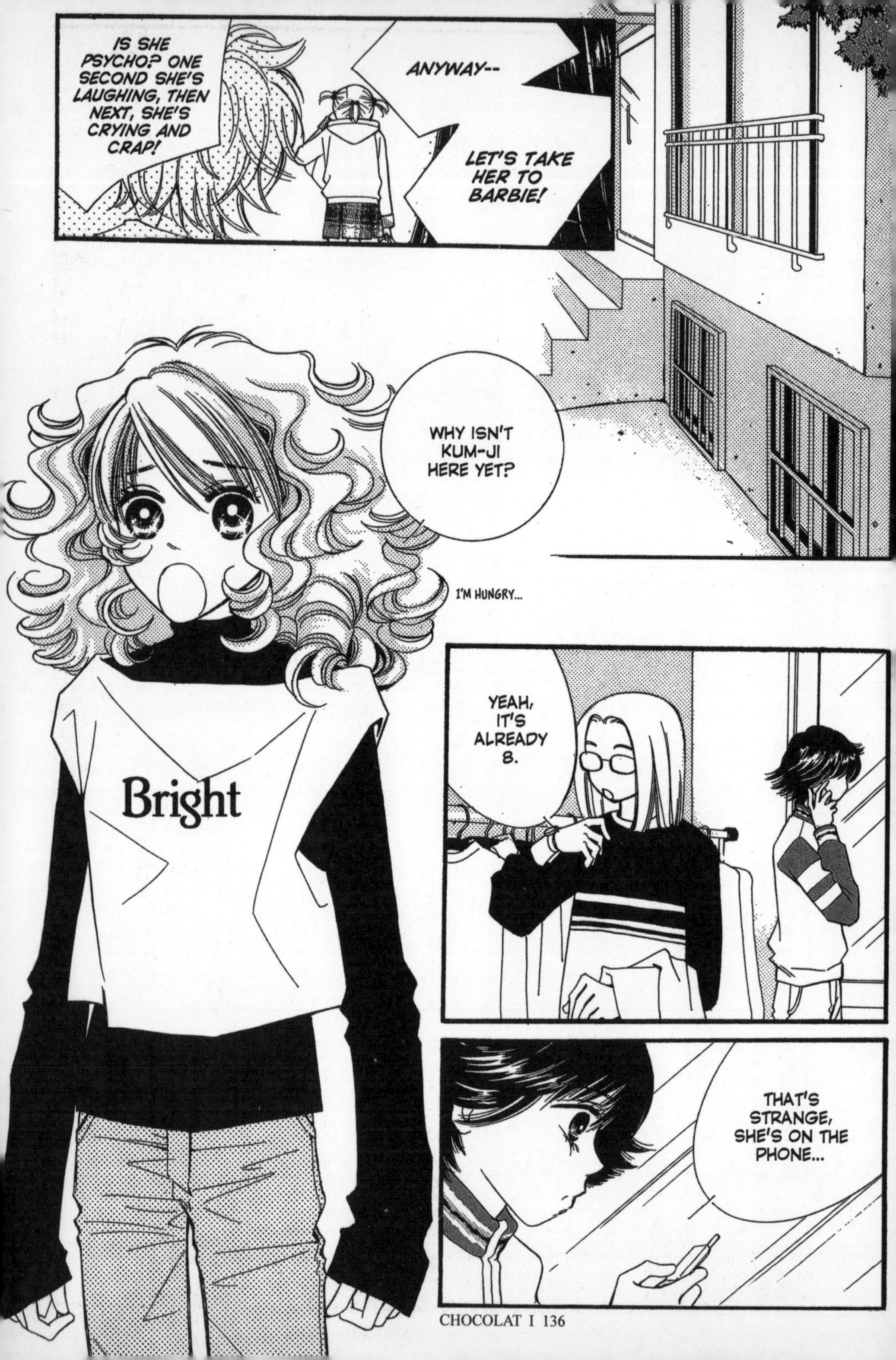
IS SHE PSYCHO? ONE SECOND SHE'S LAUGHING, THEN NEXT, SHE'S CRYING AND CRAP!
ANYWAY--
LET'S TAKE HER TO BARBIE!
WHY ISN'T KUM-JI HERE YET?
I'M HUNGRY...
Bright
YEAH, IT'S ALREADY 8.
THAT'S STRANGE, SHE'S ON THE PHONE...

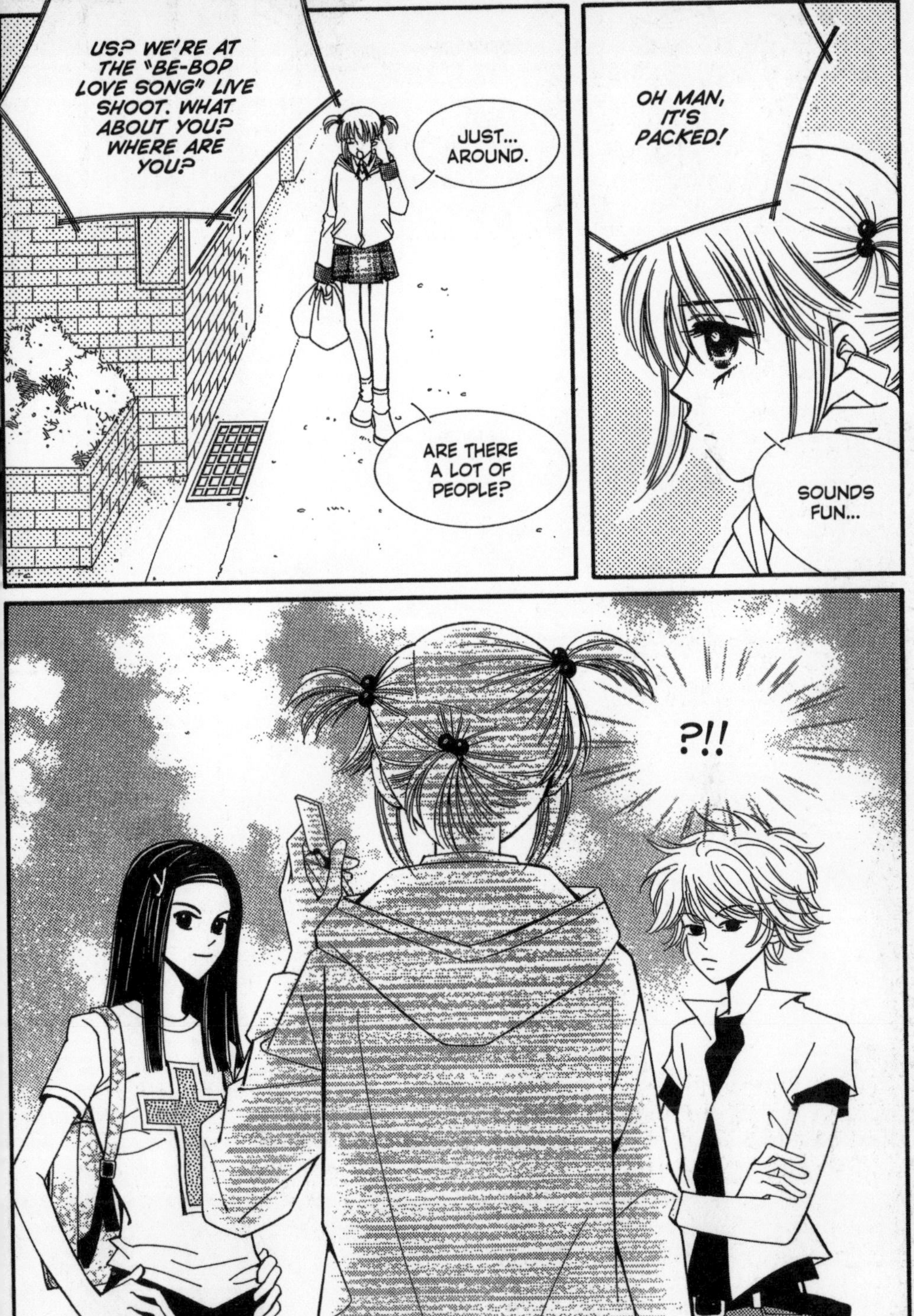
US? WE'RE AT THE "BE-BOP LOVE SONG" LIVE SHOOT. WHAT ABOUT YOU? WHERE ARE YOU?
JUST... AROUND.
ARE THERE A LOT OF PEOPLE?
OH MAN, IT'S PACKED!
SOUNDS FUN...
?!!

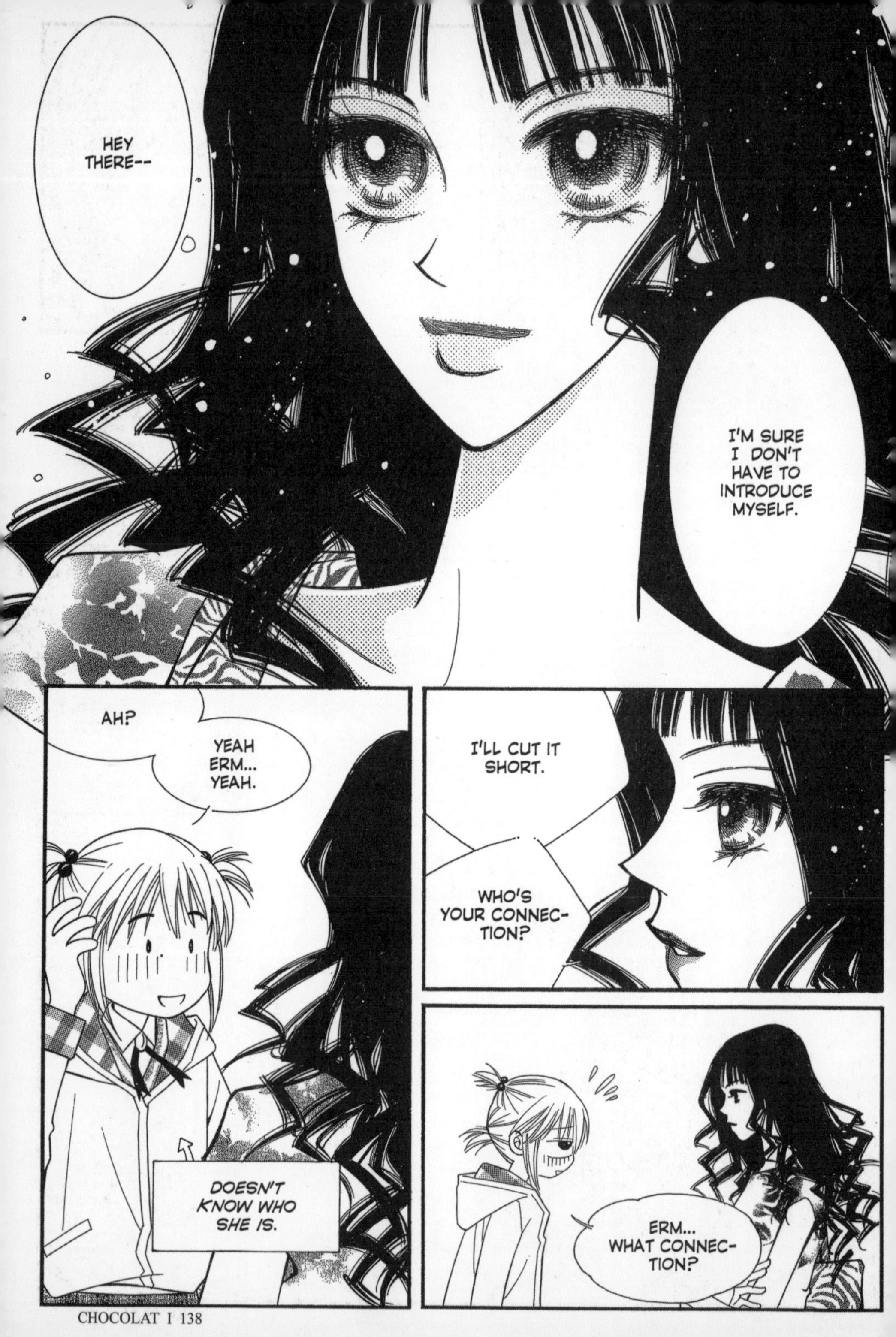
HEY THERE--
I'M SURE I DON'T HAVE TO INTRODUCE MYSELF.
AH?
YEAH ERM... YEAH.
DOESN'T KNOW WHO SHE IS.
I'LL CUT IT SHORT.
WHO'S YOUR CONNEC-TION?
ERM... WHAT CONNEC-TION?

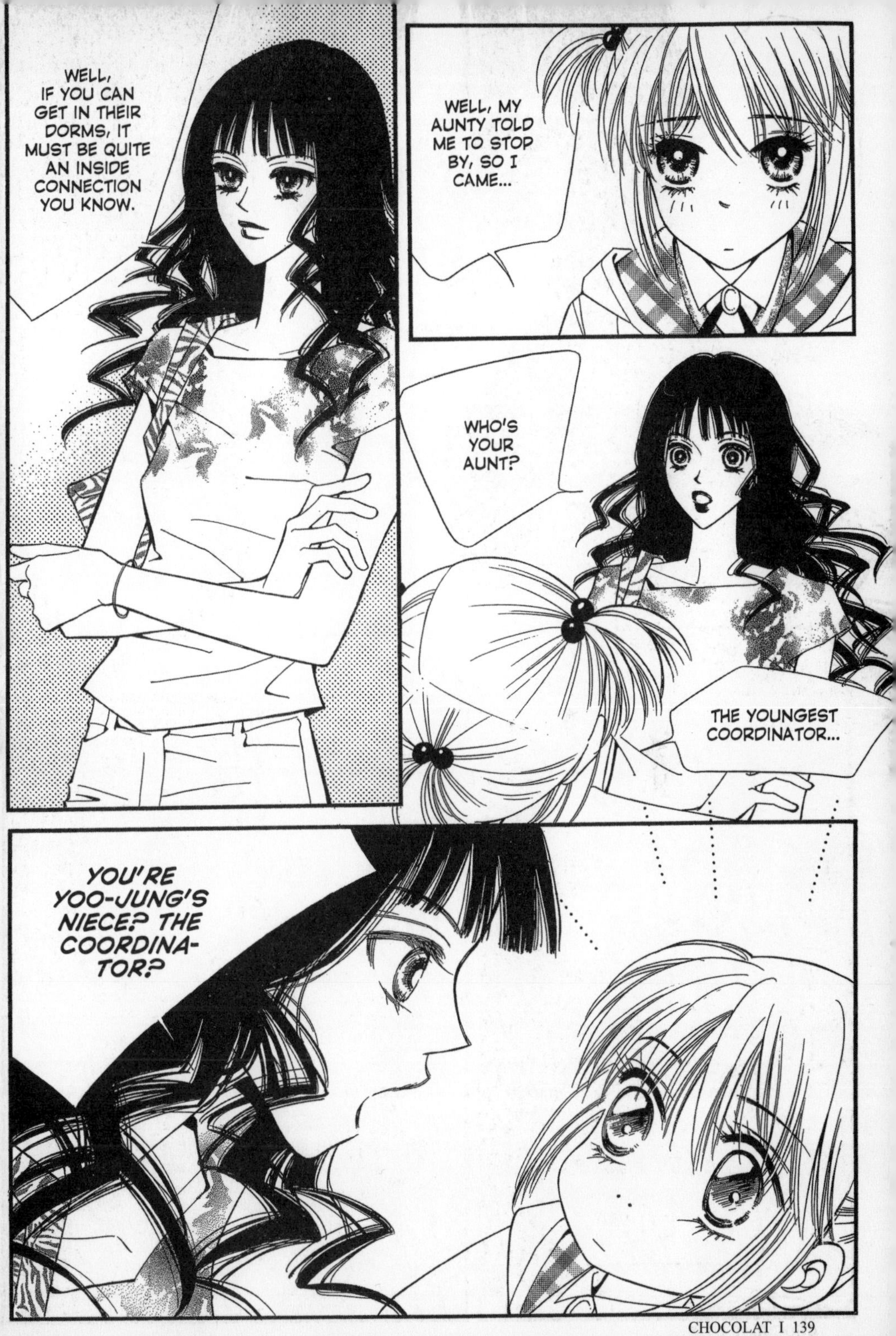
WELL, IF YOU CAN GET IN THEIR DORMS, IT MUST BE QUITE AN INSIDE CONNECTION YOU KNOW.
WELL, MY AUNTY TOLD ME TO STOP BY, SO I CAME...
WHO'S YOUR AUNT?
THE YOUNGEST COORDINATOR...
YOU'RE YOO-JUNG'S NIECE? THE COORDINATOR?

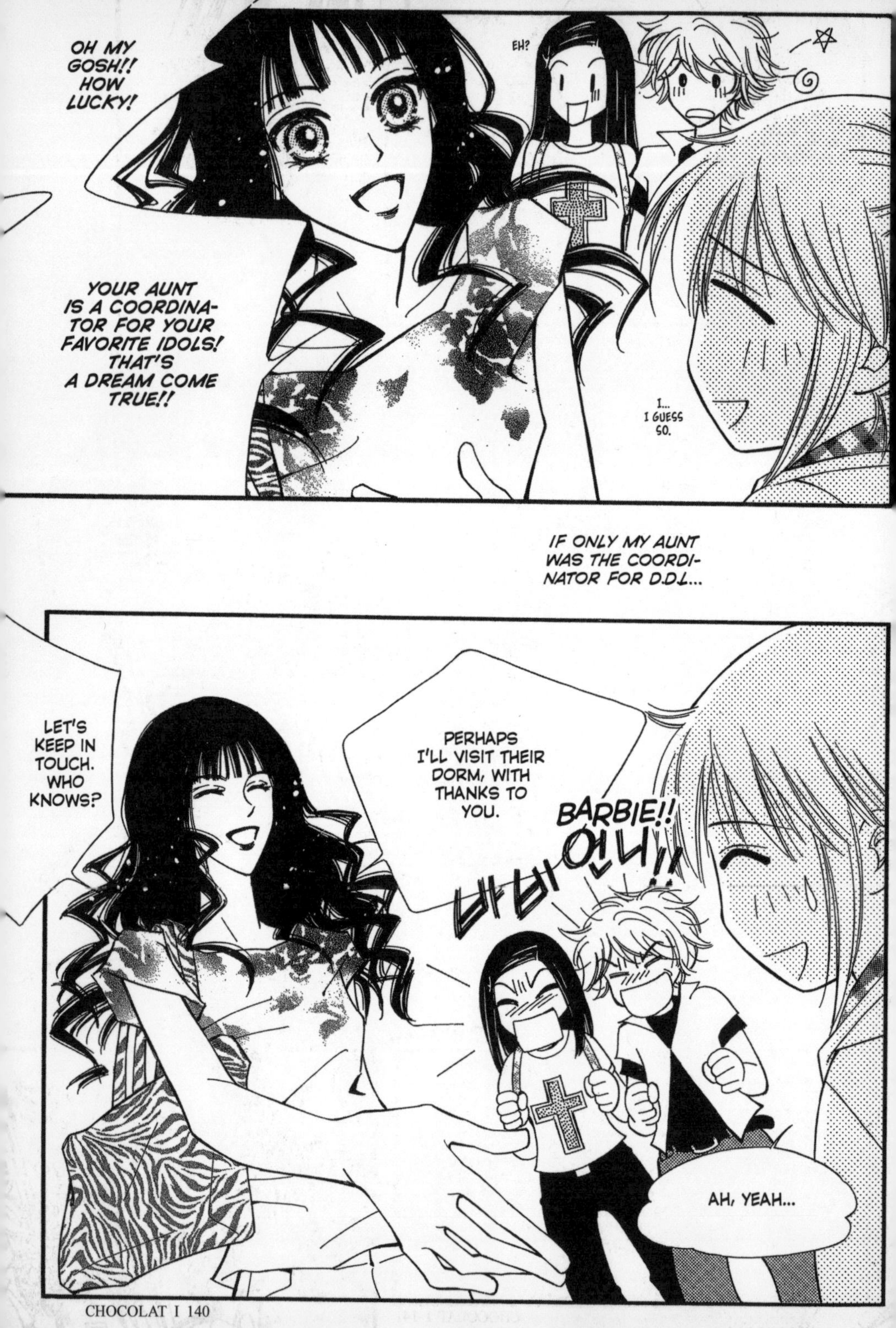
OH MY GOSH!! HOW LUCKY!
EH?
YOUR AUNT IS A COORDINATOR FOR YOUR FAVORITE IDOLS! THAT'S A DREAM COME TRUE!!
I... I GUESS SO.
IF ONLY MY AUNT WAS THE COORDINATOR FOR D.D.L...
LET'S KEEP IN TOUCH. WHO KNOWS?
PERHAPS I'LL VISIT THEIR DORM, WITH THANKS TO YOU.
BARBIE!!
바비 언니!!
AH, YEAH...

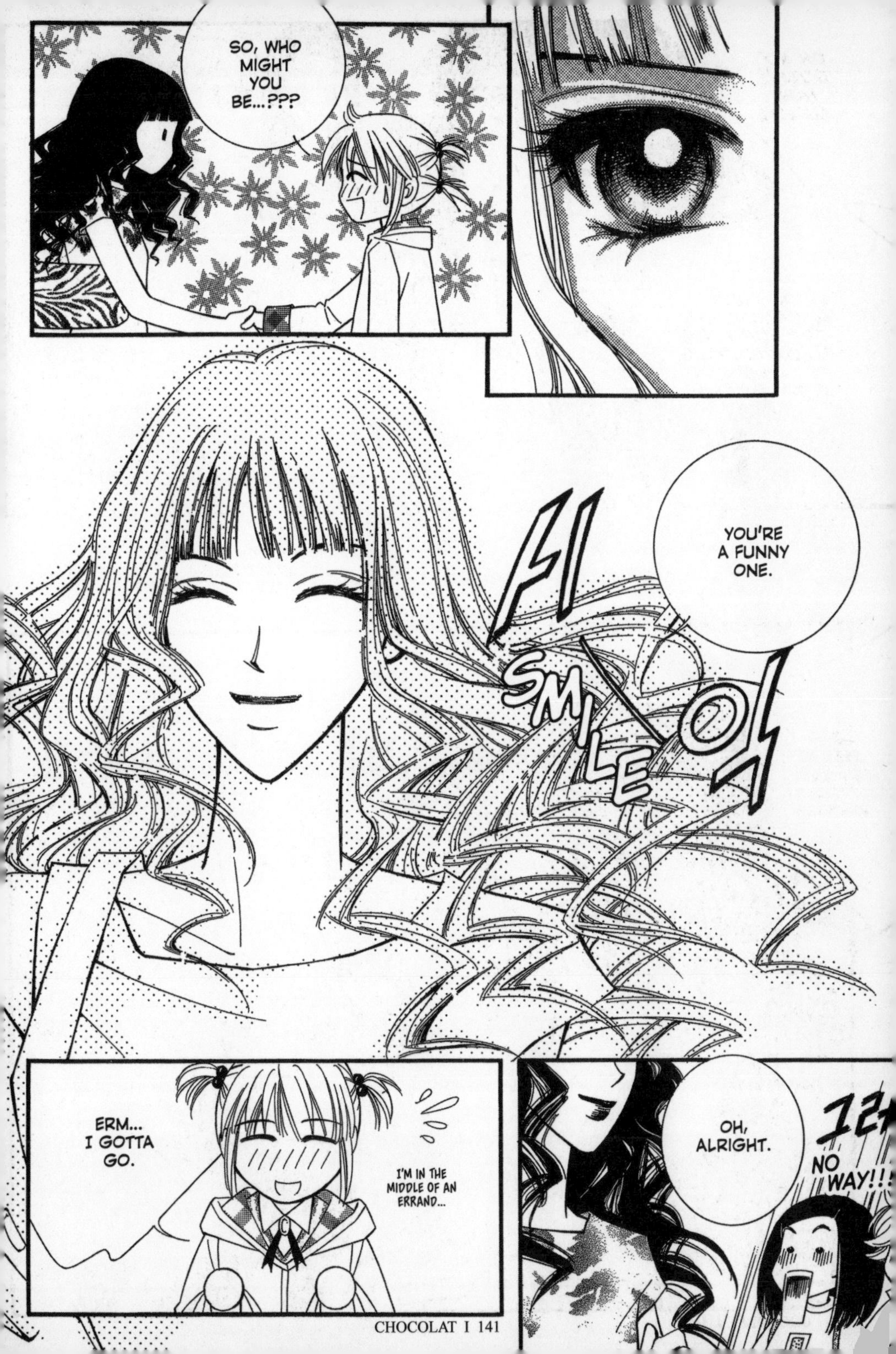
SO, WHO MIGHT YOU BE...???
YOU'RE A FUNNY ONE.
SMILE
ERM... I GOTTA GO.
I'M IN THE MIDDLE OF AN ERRAND...
OH, ALRIGHT.
NO WAY!!!

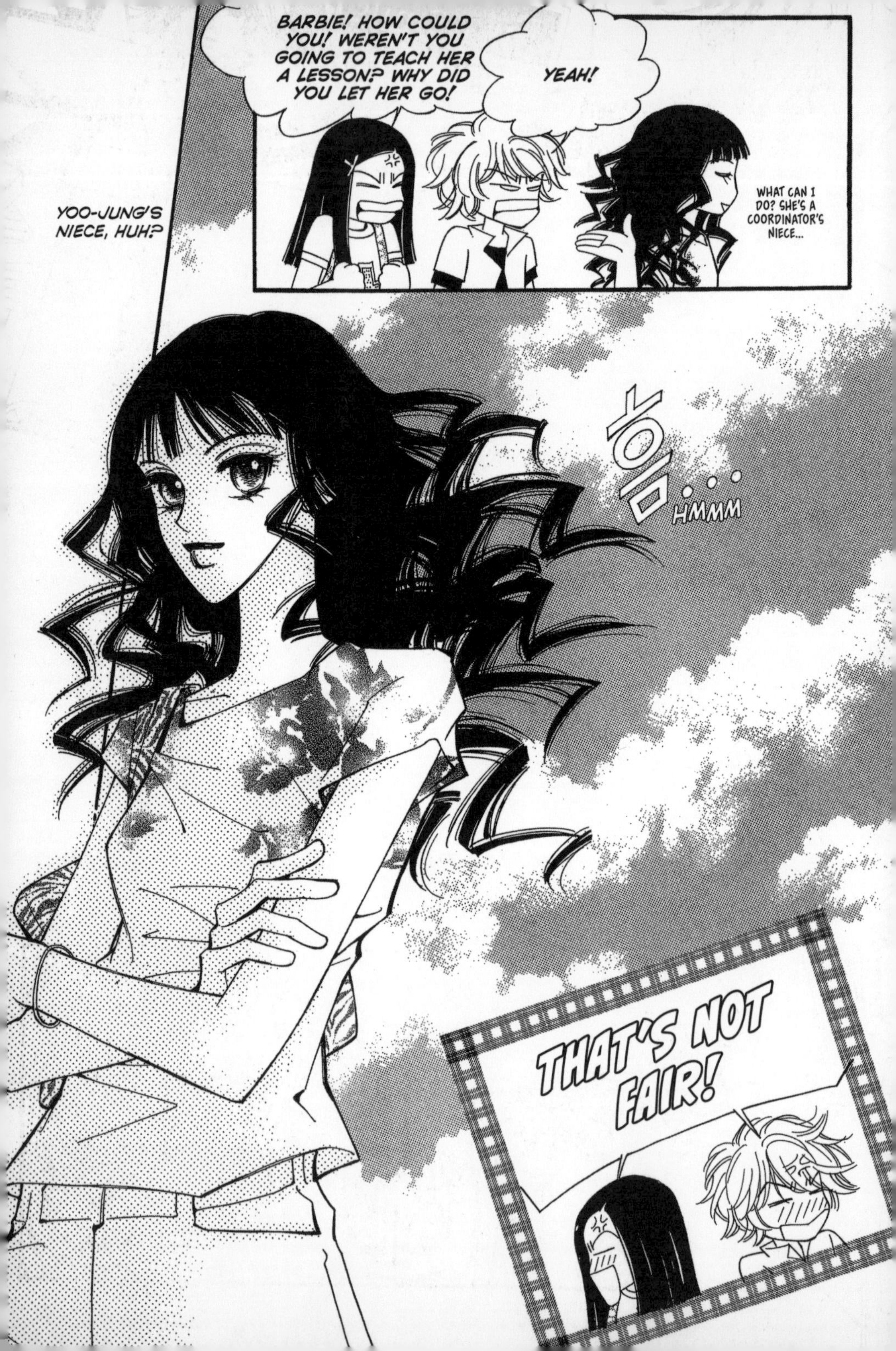
BARBIE! HOW COULD YOU! WEREN'T YOU GOING TO TEACH HER A LESSON? WHY DID YOU LET HER GO!
YEAH!
WHAT CAN I DO? SHE'S A COORDINATOR'S NIECE...
YOO-JUNG'S NIECE, HUH?
...HMMM
THAT'S NOT FAIR!

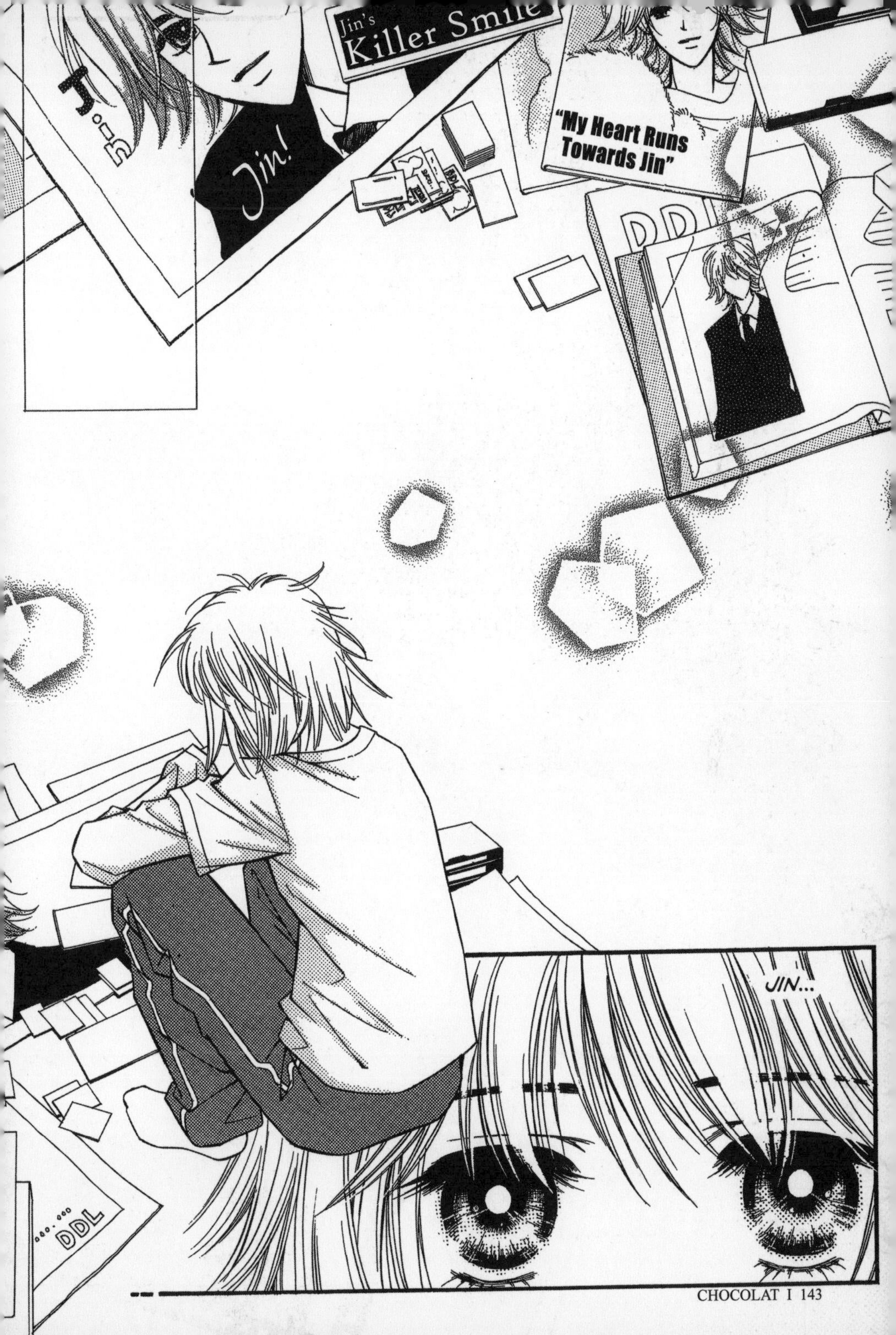
Jin's
Killer Smile
Jin!
"My Heart Runs Towards Jin"
DDL
JIN...

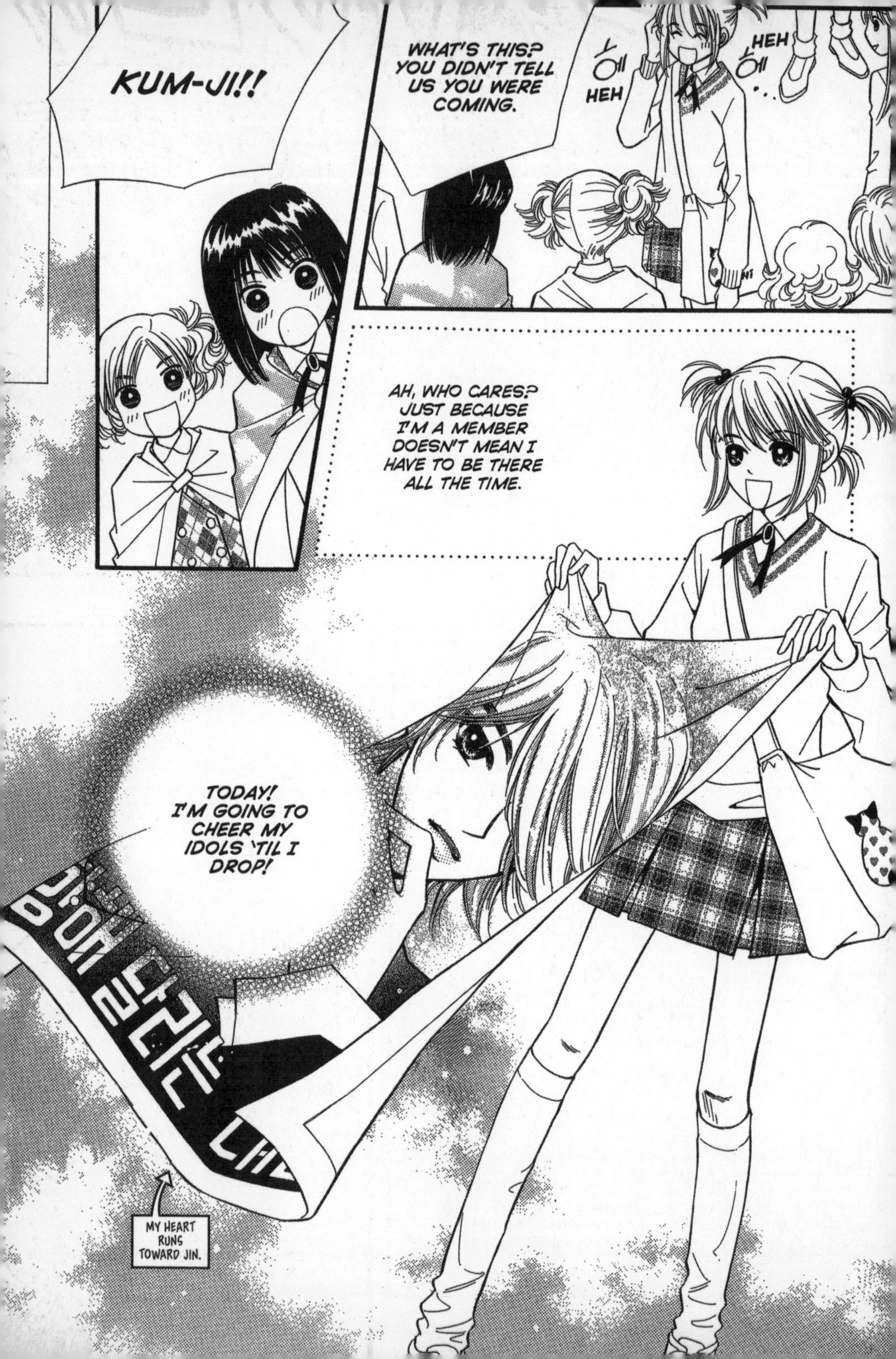
KUM-JI!!
WHAT'S THIS? YOU DIDN'T TELL US YOU WERE COMING.
HEH
HEH...
AH, WHO CARES? JUST BECAUSE I'M A MEMBER DOESN'T MEAN I HAVE TO BE THERE ALL THE TIME.
TODAY! I'M GOING TO CHEER MY IDOLS 'TIL I DROP!
MY HEART RUNS TOWARD JIN.

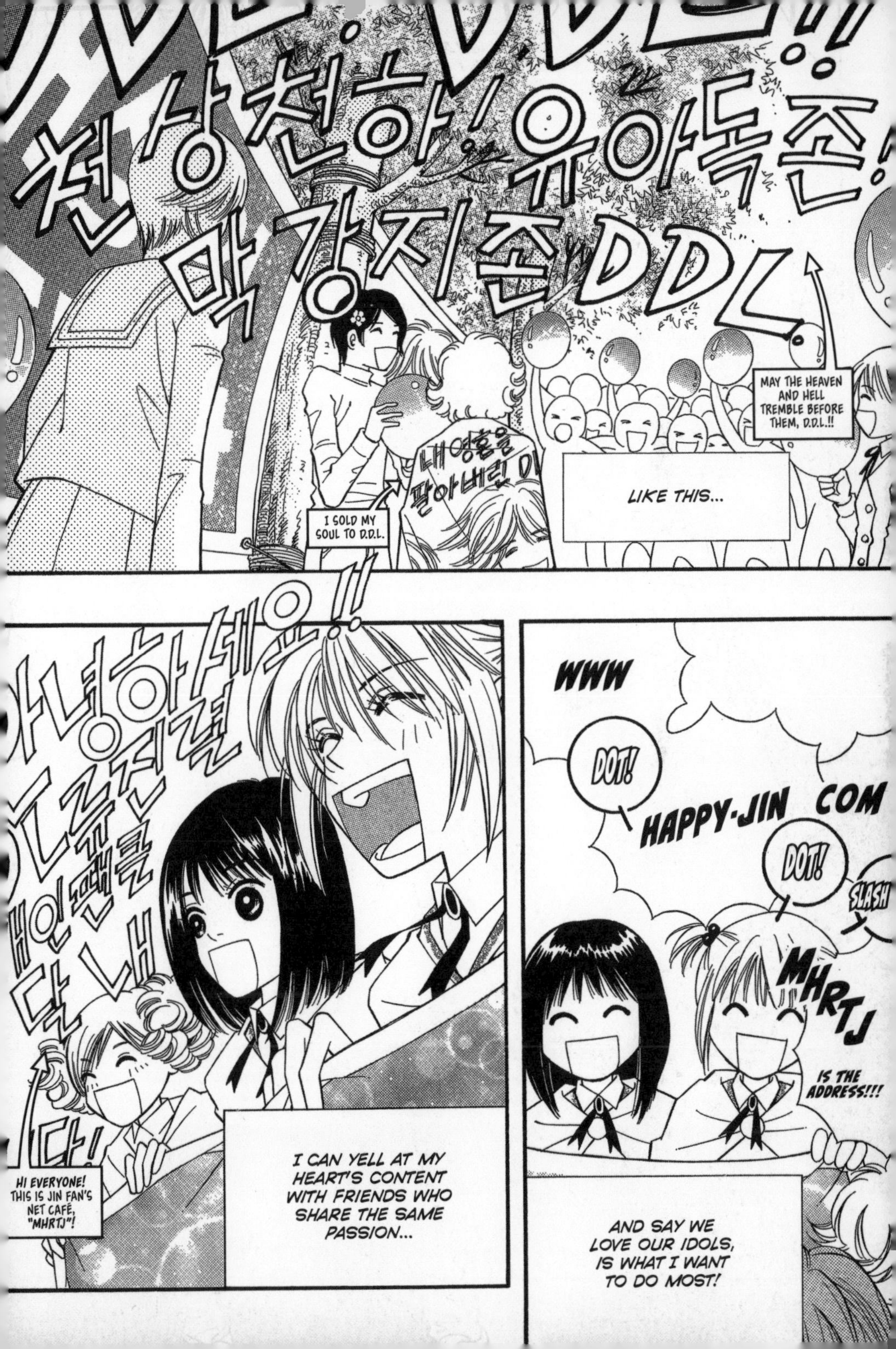

천상천하! 유아독존!
막강지존 DDL
MAY THE HEAVEN AND HELL TREMBLE BEFORE THEM, D.D.L.!!
I SOLD MY SOUL TO D.D.L.
LIKE THIS...
안녕하세요!!
HI EVERYONE! THIS IS JIN FAN'S NET CAFÉ, "MHRTJ"!
I CAN YELL AT MY HEART'S CONTENT WITH FRIENDS WHO SHARE THE SAME PASSION...
WWW
DOT!
HAPPY-JIN
DOT!
COM
SLASH
MHRTJ
IS THE ADDRESS!!!
AND SAY WE LOVE OUR IDOLS, IS WHAT I WANT TO DO MOST!

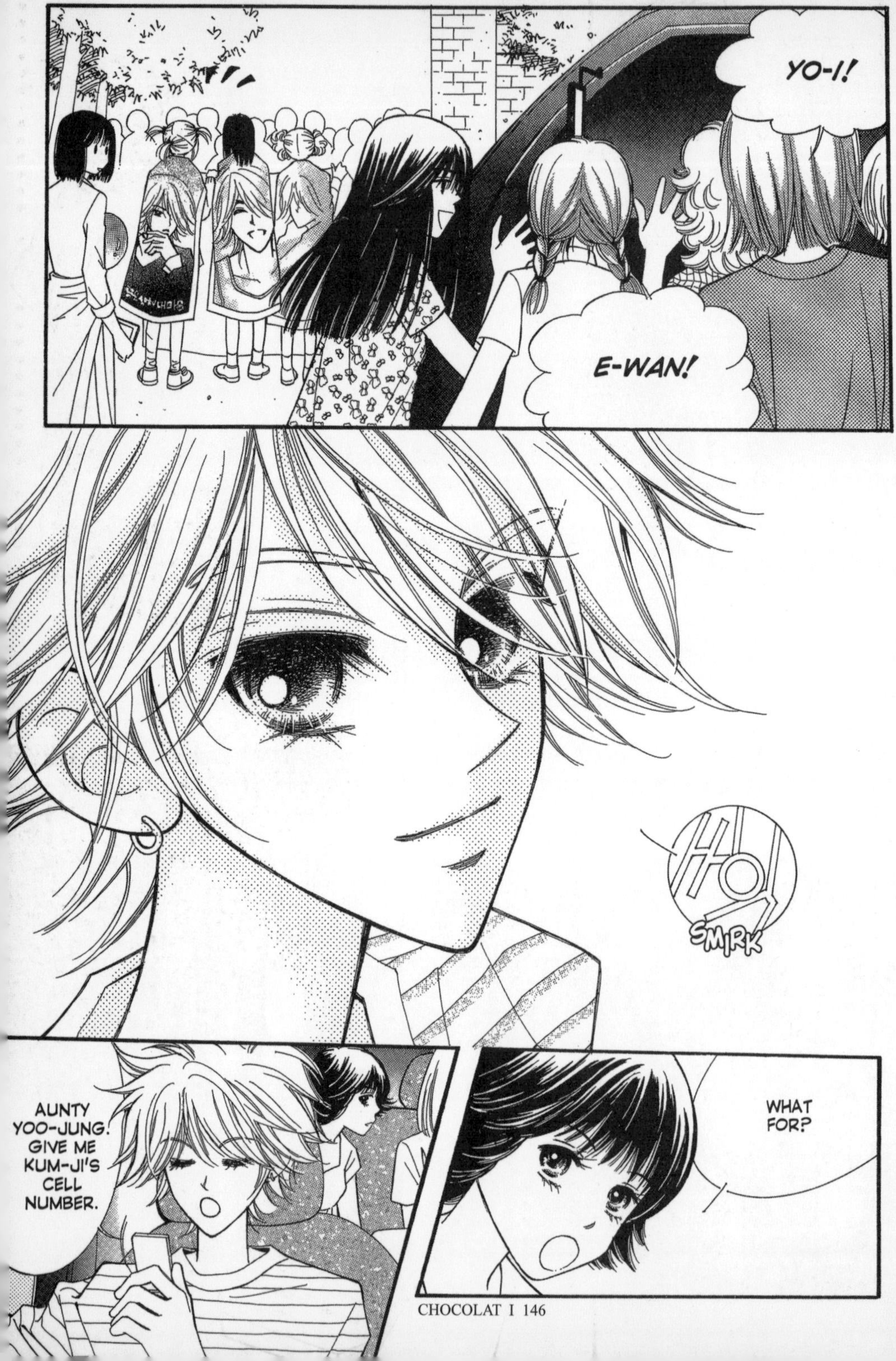
YO-I!
E-WAN!
SMIRK
AUNTY YOO-JUNG. GIVE ME KUM-JI'S CELL NUMBER.
WHAT FOR?

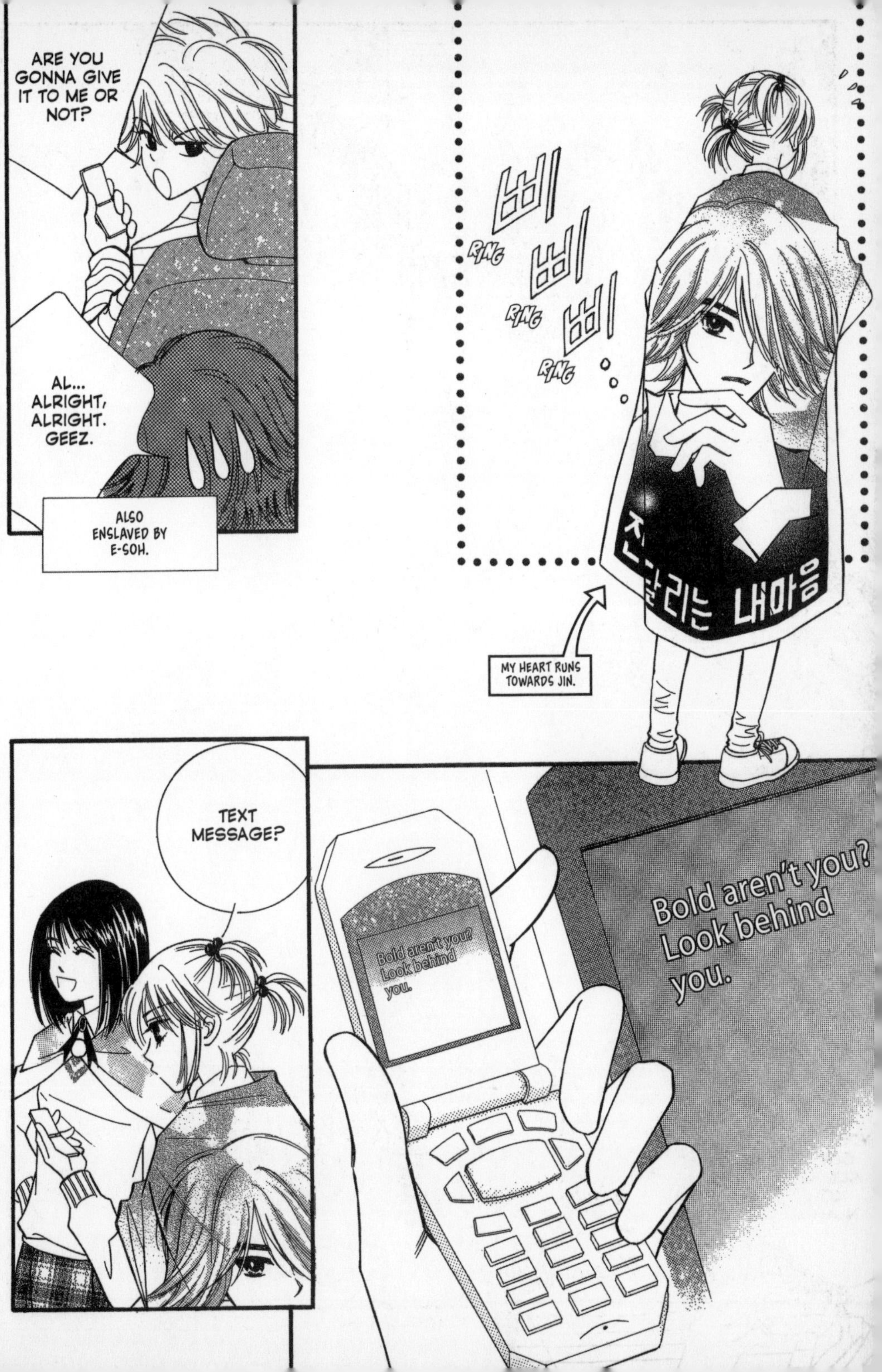
ARE YOU GONNA GIVE IT TO ME OR NOT?
AL... ALRIGHT, ALRIGHT. GEEZ.
ALSO ENSLAVED BY E-SOH.
삐
RING
삐
RING
삐
RING
진
리는 내마음
MY HEART RUNS TOWARDS JIN.
TEXT MESSAGE?
Bold aren't you? Look behind you.
Bold aren't you? Look behind you.

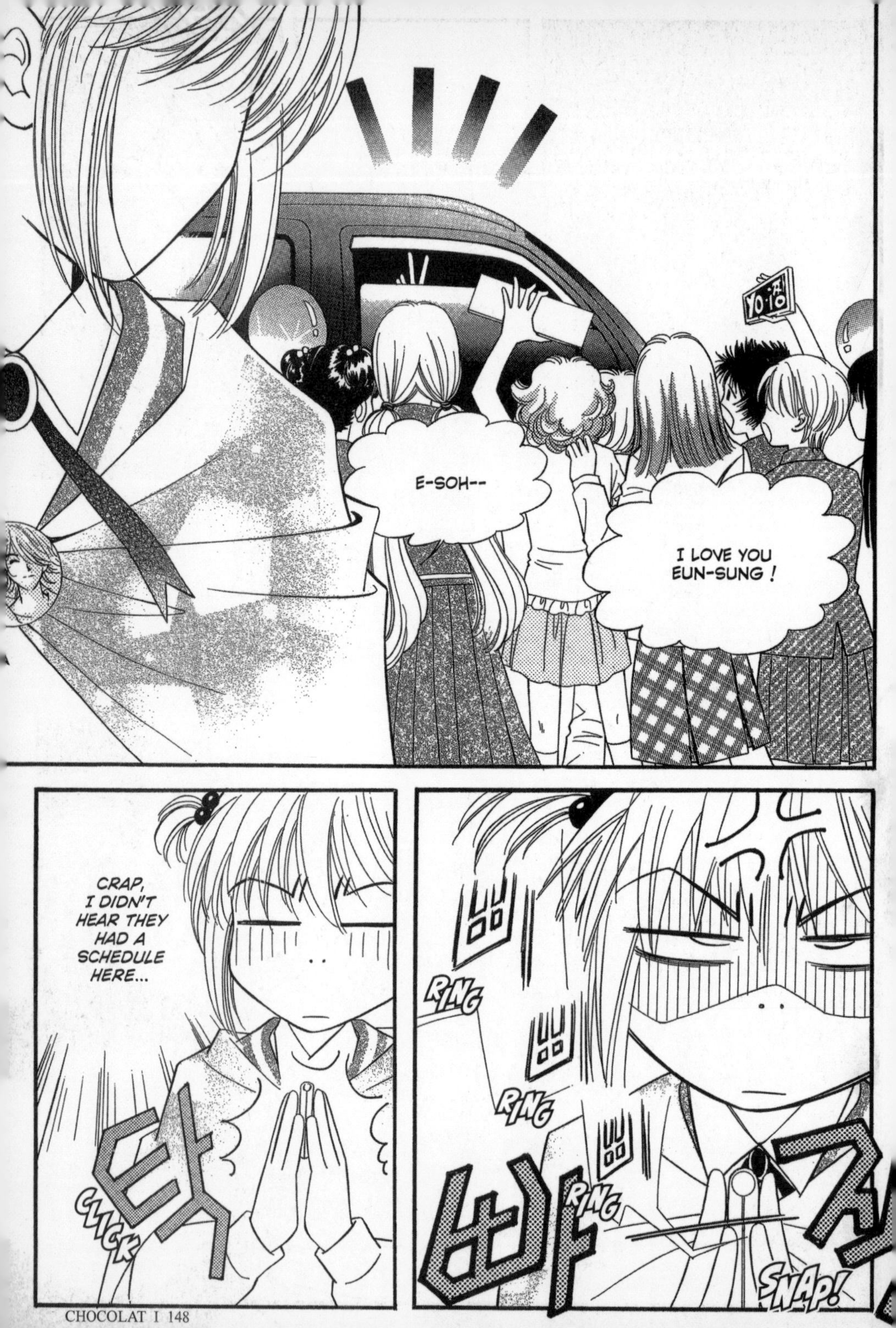
E-SOH--
I LOVE YOU EUN-SUNG !
CRAP, I DIDN'T HEAR THEY HAD A SCHEDULE HERE...
CLICK
RING
RING
RING
SNAP!

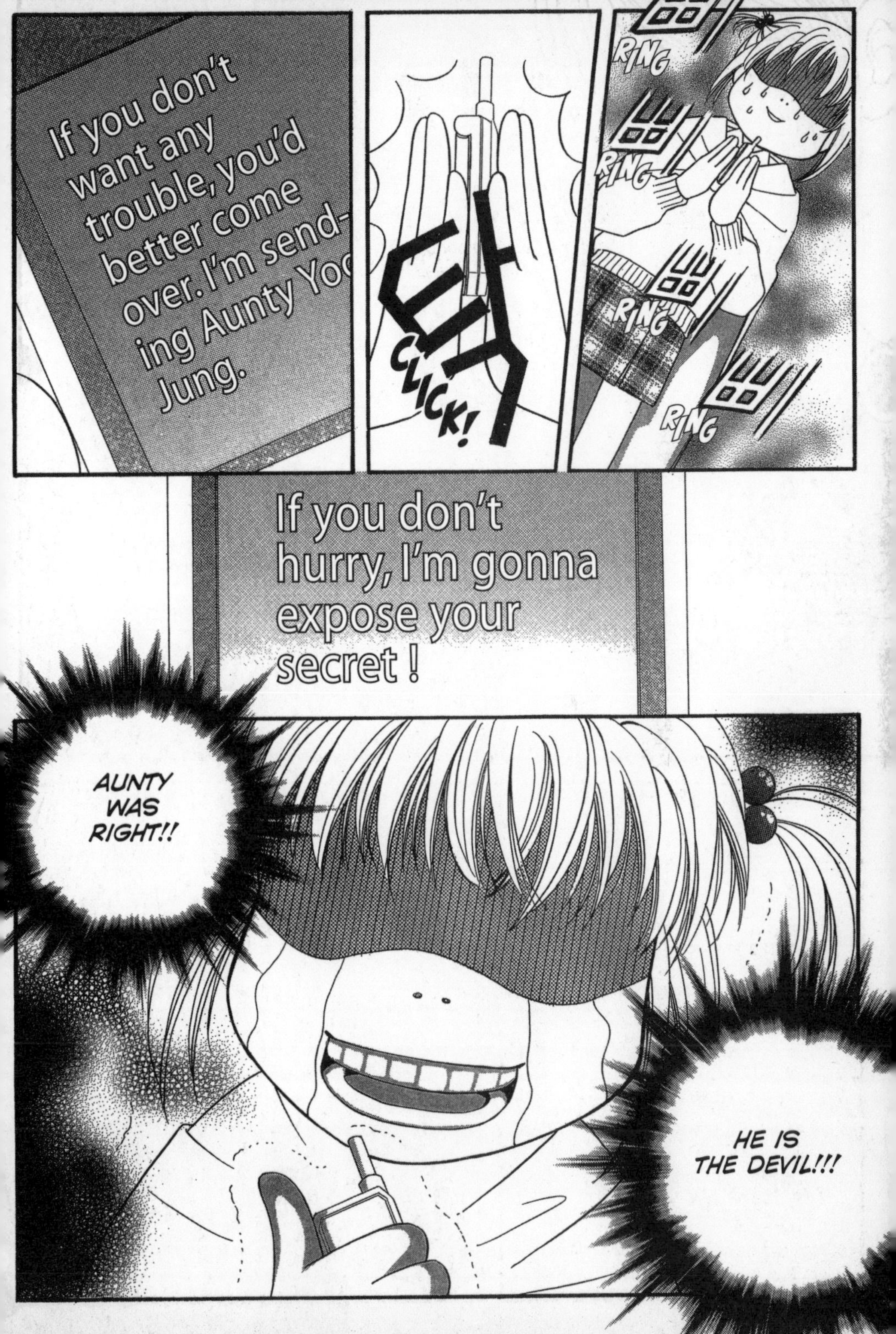
If you don't want any trouble, you'd better come over. I'm send-ing Aunty Yoo Jung.
CLICK!
RING
RING
RING
RING
If you don't hurry, I'm gonna expose your secret !
AUNTY WAS RIGHT!!
HE IS THE DEVIL!!!

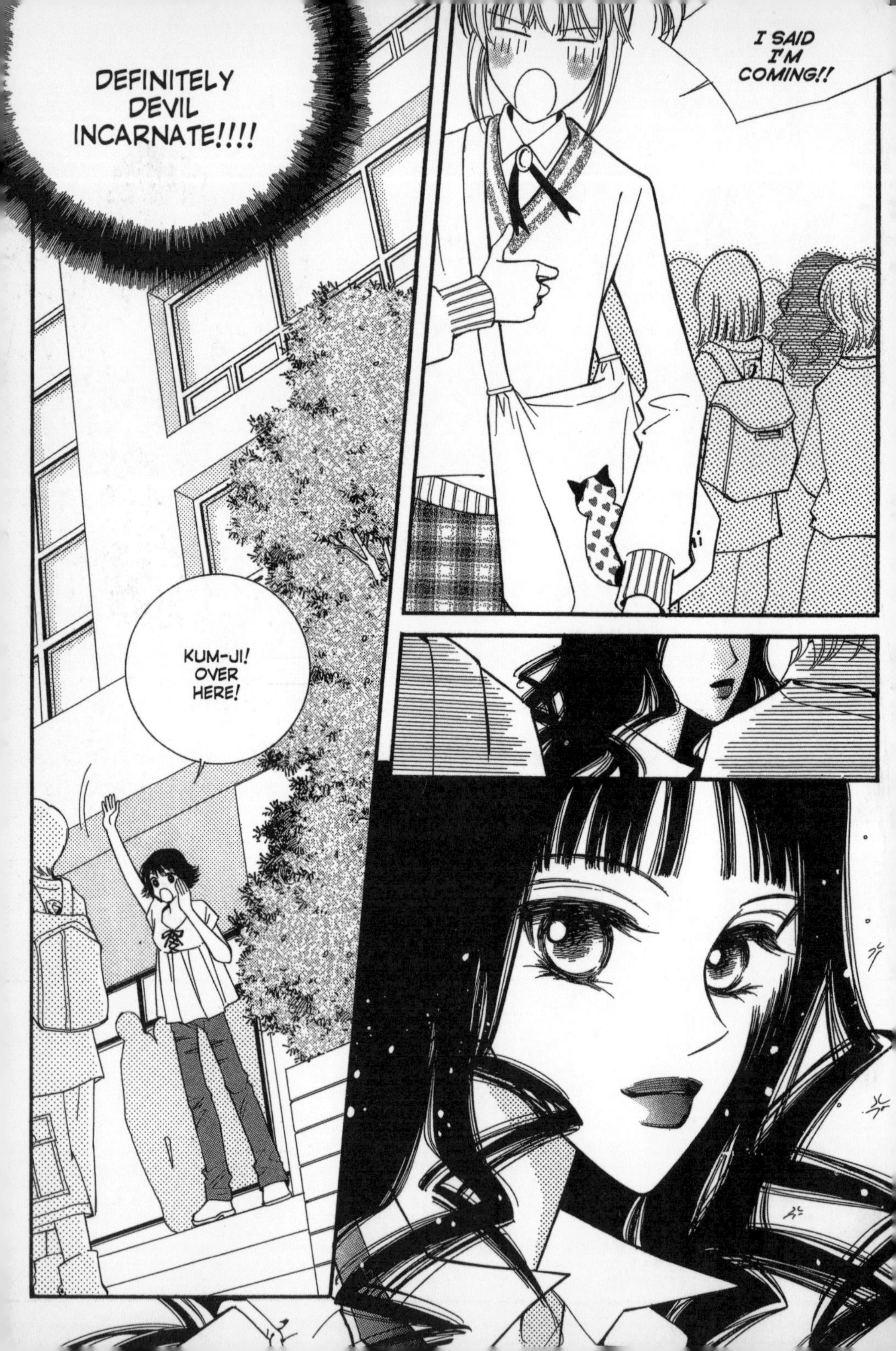
DEFINITELY DEVIL INCARNATE!!!!
KUM-JI! OVER HERE!
I SAID I'M COMING!!

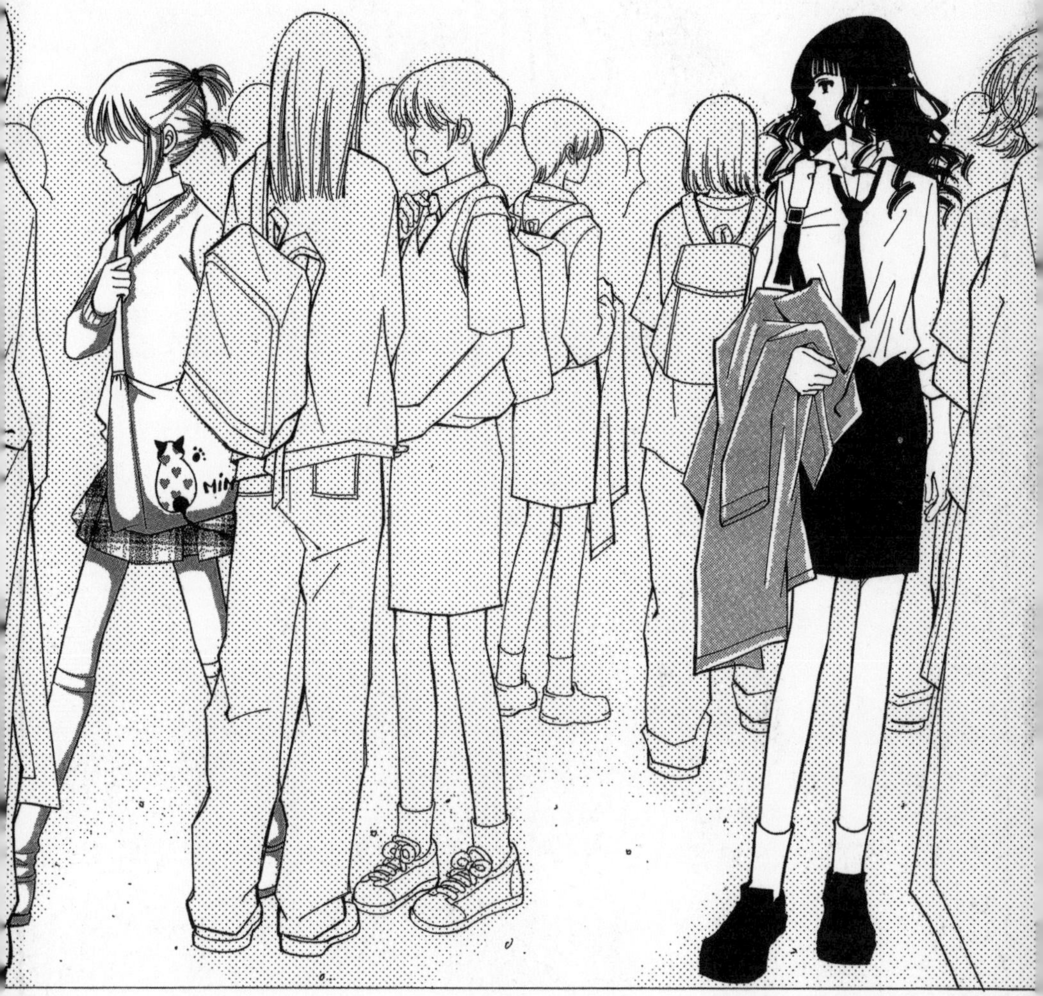

YOU REALLY ARE
A SHOW-OFF,
AREN'T YOU?

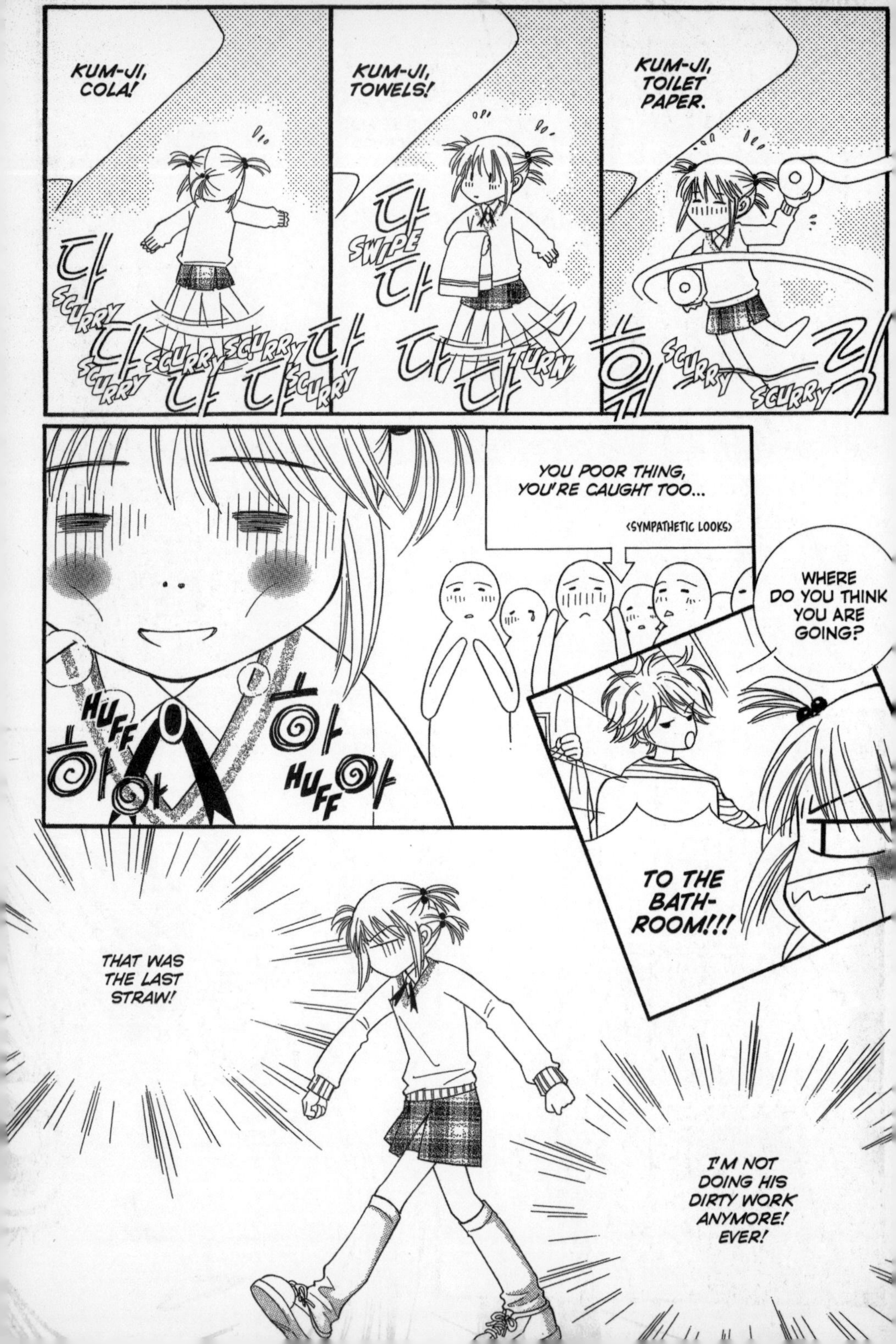

KUM-JI, COLA!
SCURRY
SCURRY
SCURRY
SCURRY
SCURRY
KUM-JI, TOWELS!
SWIPE
TURN
KUM-JI, TOILET PAPER.
SCURRY
SCURRY
HUFF
HUFF
YOU POOR THING, YOU'RE CAUGHT TOO...
‹SYMPATHETIC LOOKS›
WHERE DO YOU THINK YOU ARE GOING?
TO THE BATH-ROOM!!!
THAT WAS THE LAST STRAW!
I'M NOT DOING HIS DIRTY WORK ANYMORE! EVER!

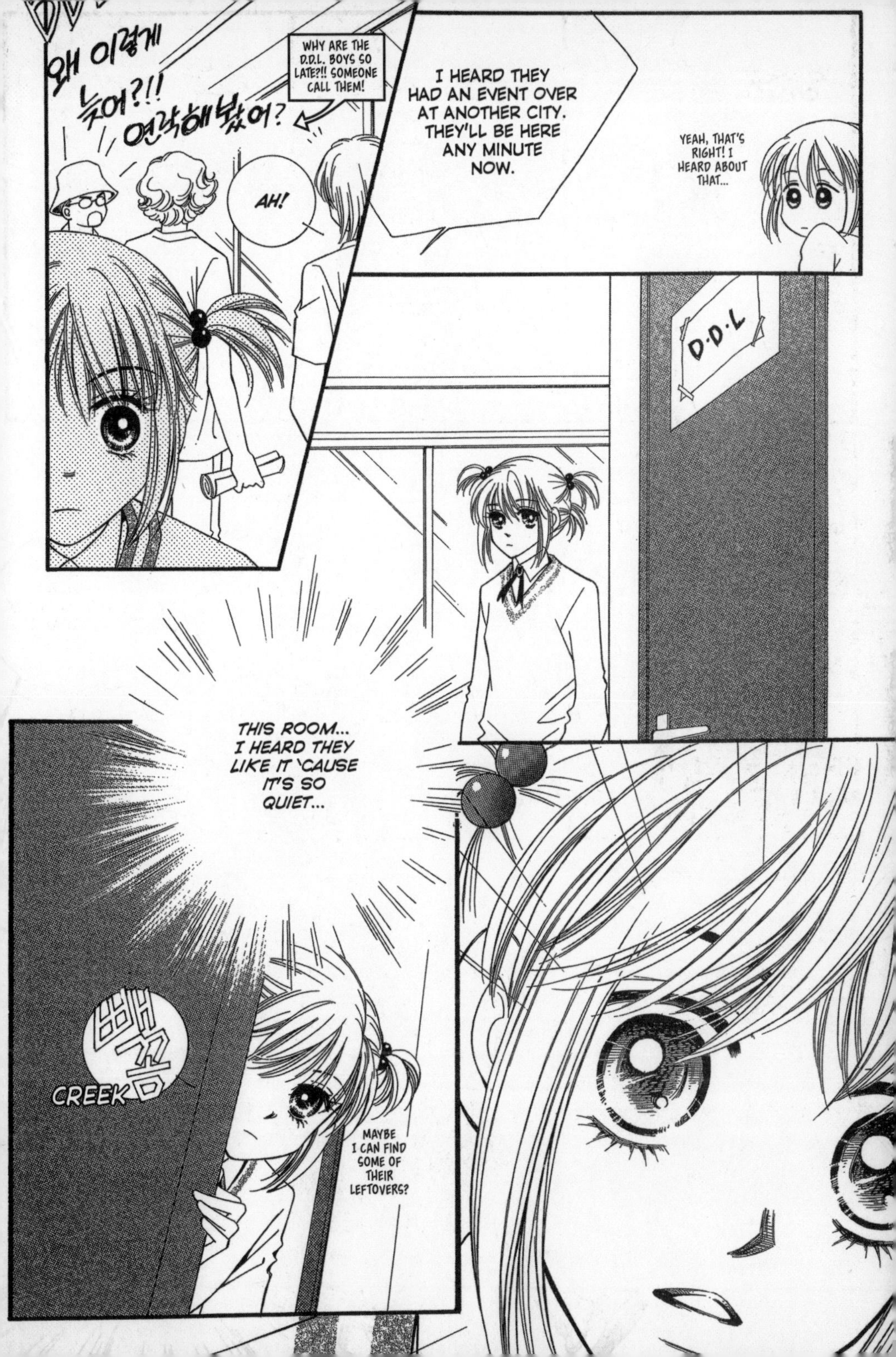
왜 이렇게 늦어?!! 연락해봤어?
WHY ARE THE D.D.L. BOYS SO LATE?!! SOMEONE CALL THEM!
AH!
I HEARD THEY HAD AN EVENT OVER AT ANOTHER CITY. THEY'LL BE HERE ANY MINUTE NOW.
YEAH, THAT'S RIGHT! I HEARD ABOUT THAT...
D·D·L
THIS ROOM... I HEARD THEY LIKE IT 'CAUSE IT'S SO QUIET...
빼꼼
CREEK
MAYBE I CAN FIND SOME OF THEIR LEFTOVERS?

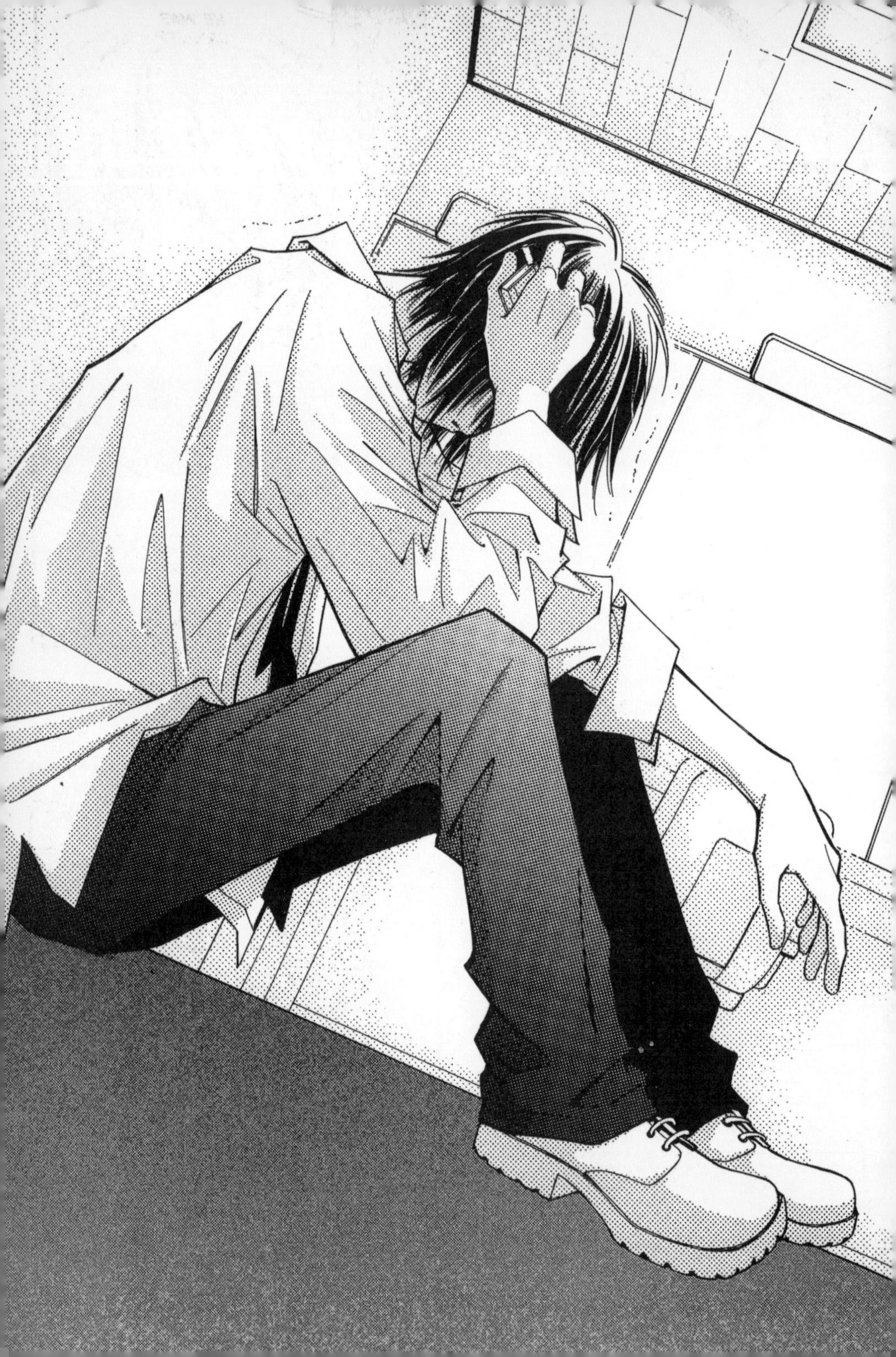

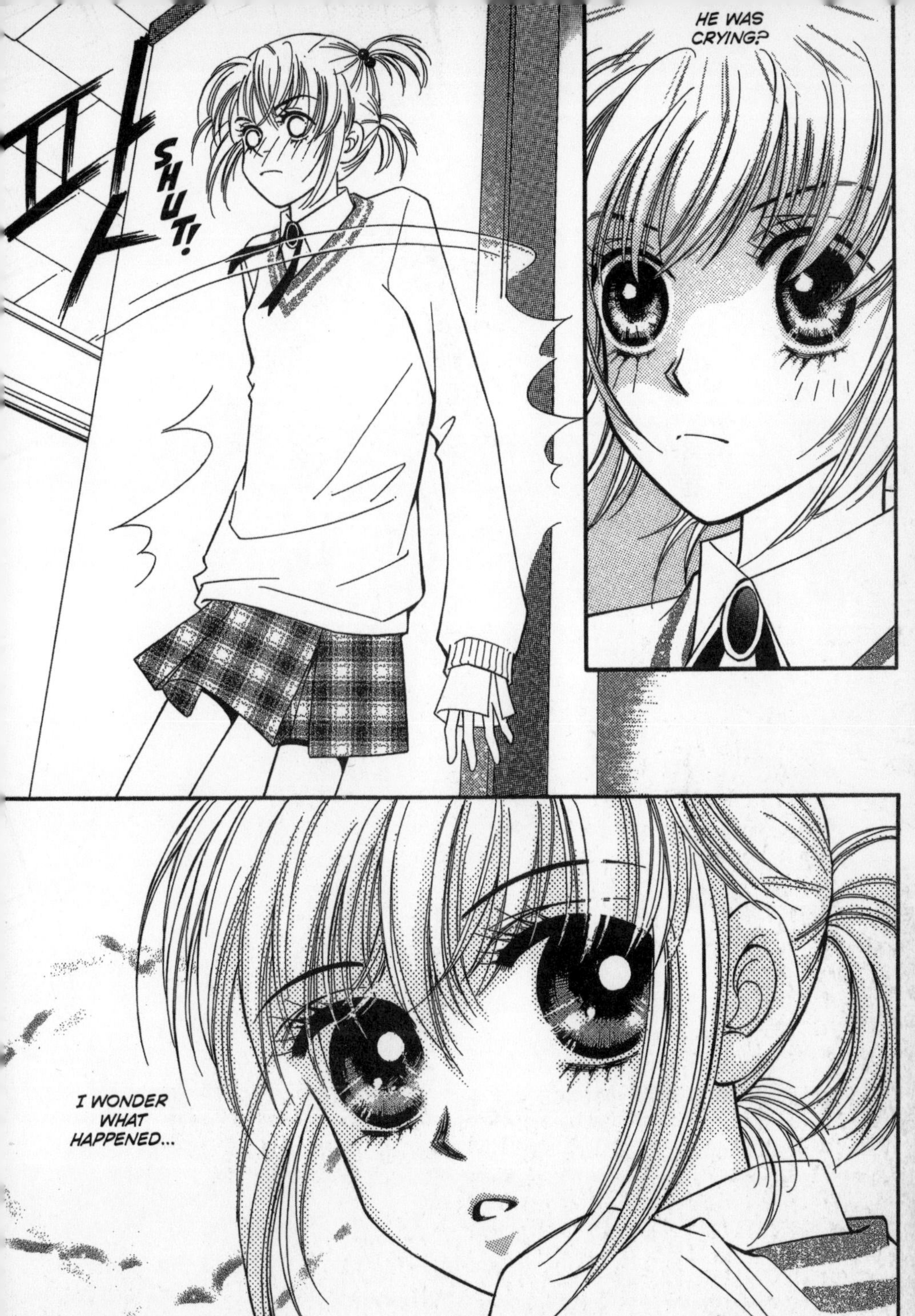
SHUT!
HE WAS CRYING?
I WONDER WHAT HAPPENED...

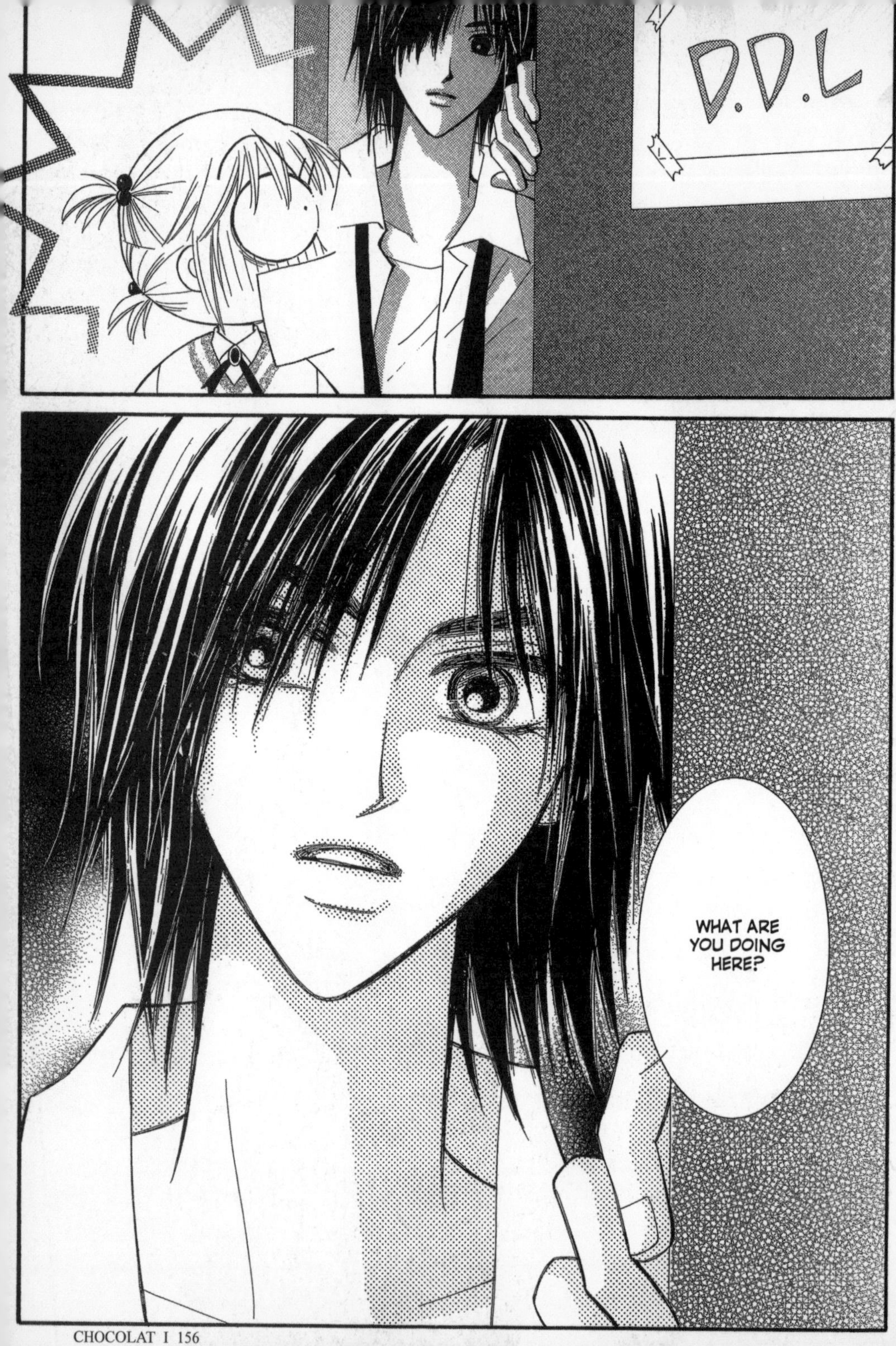
D.D.L
WHAT ARE YOU DOING HERE?

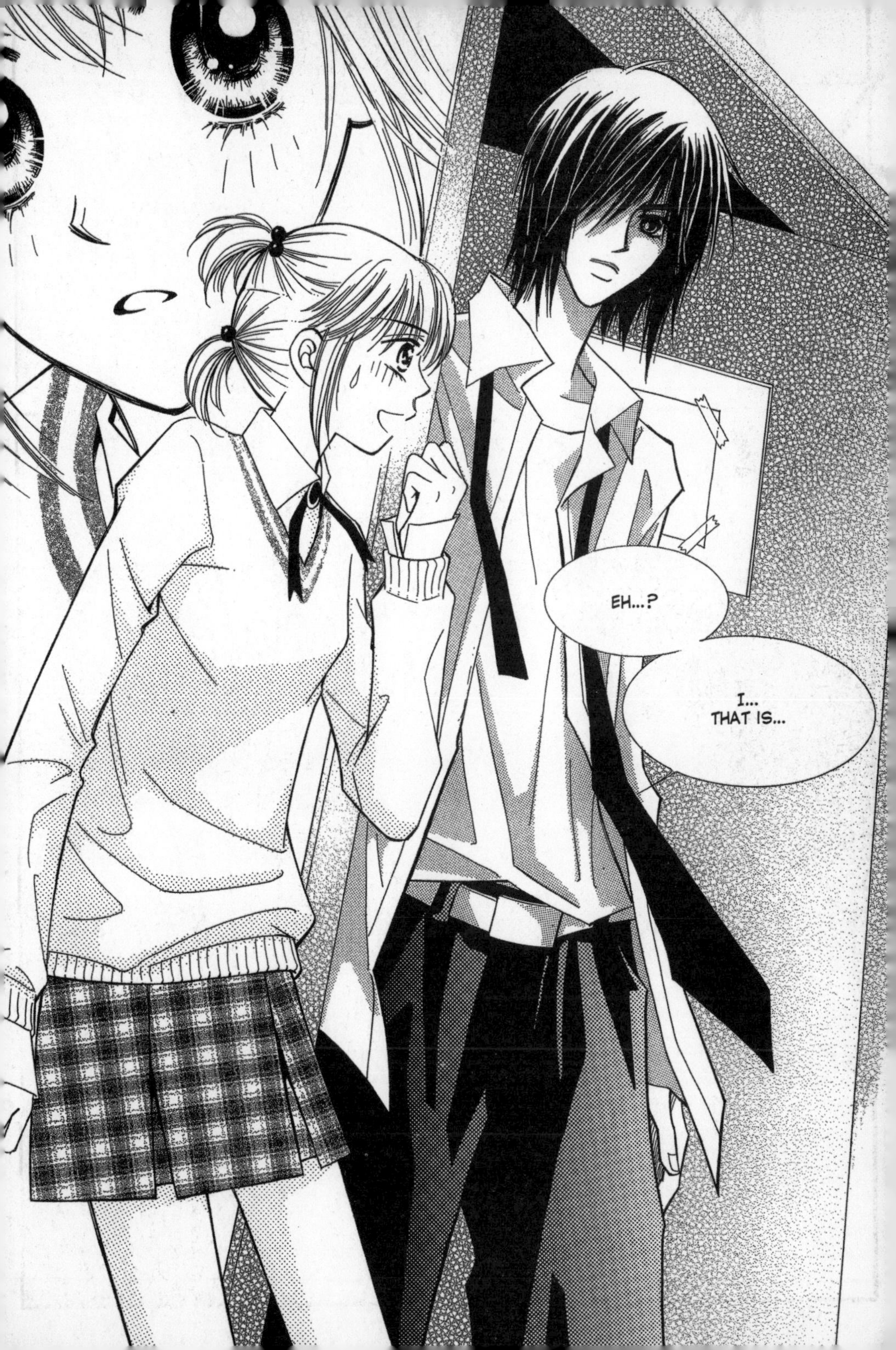
EH...?
I...
THAT IS...

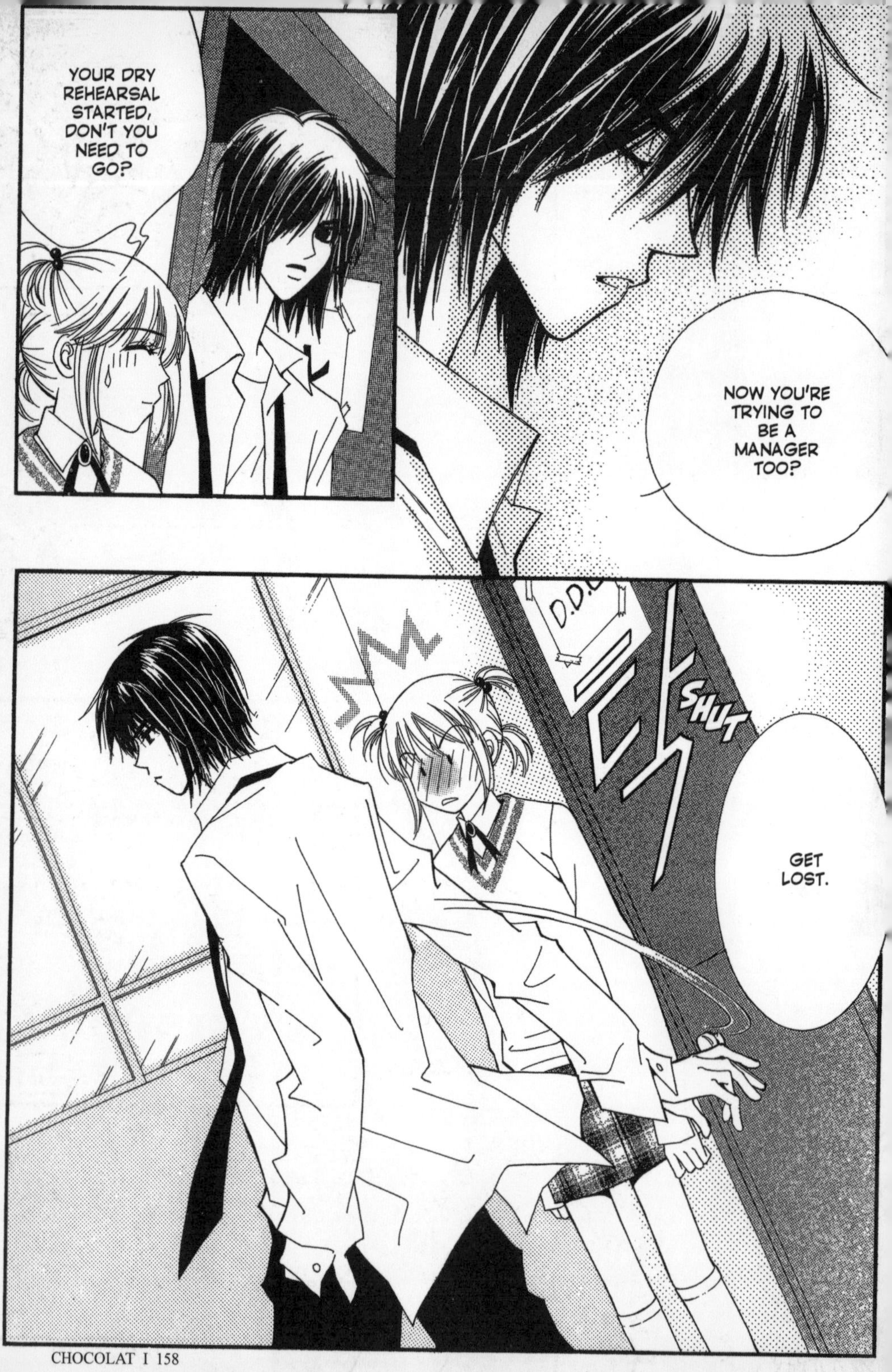
YOUR DRY REHEARSAL STARTED, DON'T YOU NEED TO GO?
NOW YOU'RE TRYING TO BE A MANAGER TOO?
SHUT
GET LOST.

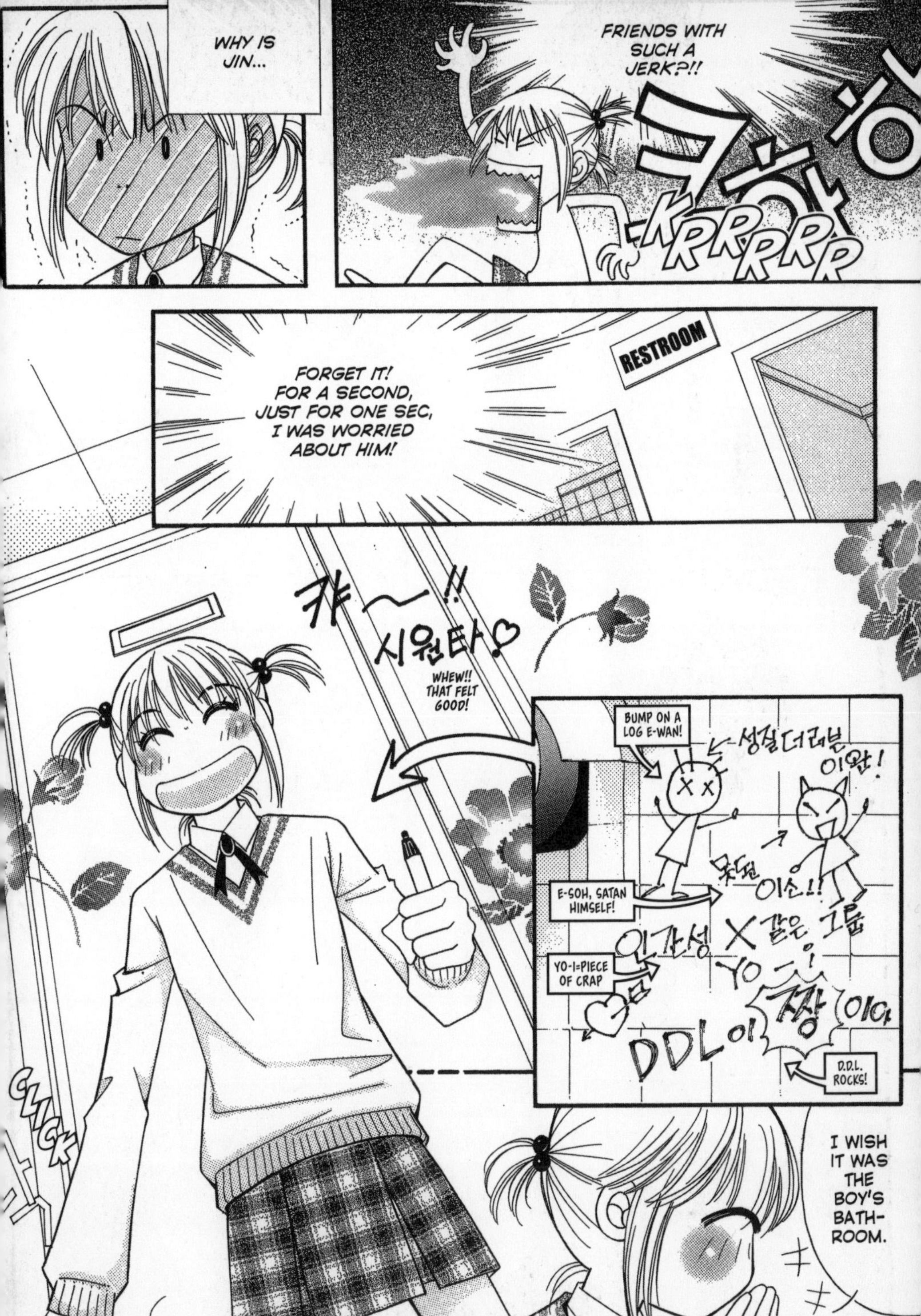

WHY IS JIN...
FRIENDS WITH SUCH A JERK?!!
크하
KRRRRRRR
RESTROOM
FORGET IT! FOR A SECOND, JUST FOR ONE SEC, I WAS WORRIED ABOUT HIM!
캬~!!
시원타♡
WHEW!! THAT FELT GOOD!
BUMP ON A LOG E-WAN!
성질더러븐 이완!
E-SOH, SATAN HIMSELF!
못된 이손!!
YO-I=PIECE OF CRAP
인간성 X같은 그룹
YO-I
DDL이 짱이다
D.D.L. ROCKS!
CLICK
I WISH IT WAS THE BOY'S BATH-ROOM.

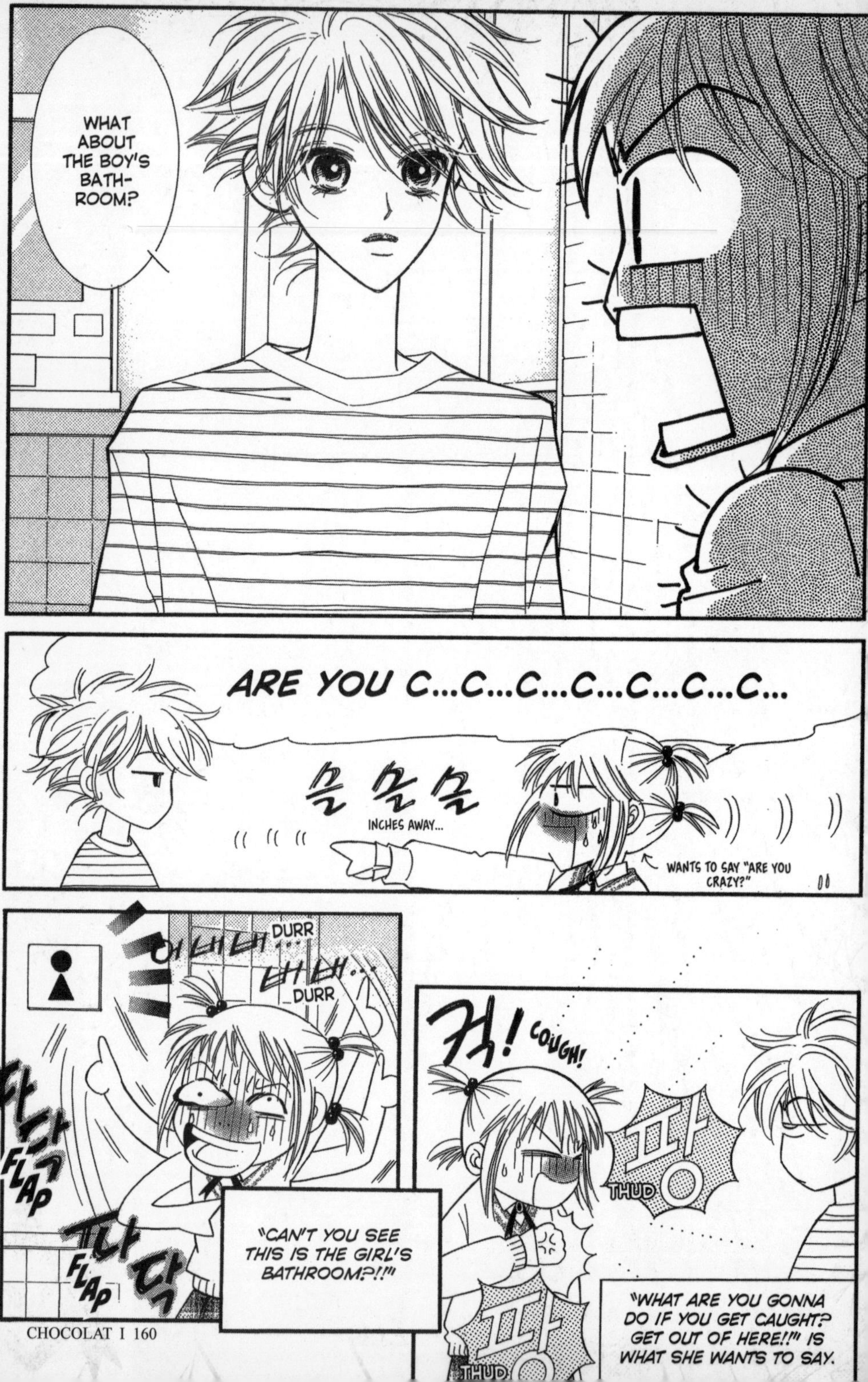
WHAT ABOUT THE BOY'S BATH-ROOM?
ARE YOU C...C...C...C...C...C...C...
INCHES AWAY...
WANTS TO SAY "ARE YOU CRAZY?"
DURR
DURR
FLAP
FLAP
"CAN'T YOU SEE THIS IS THE GIRL'S BATHROOM?!"
컥!
COUGH!
THUD
THUD
"WHAT ARE YOU GONNA DO IF YOU GET CAUGHT? GET OUT OF HERE!!" IS WHAT SHE WANTS TO SAY.

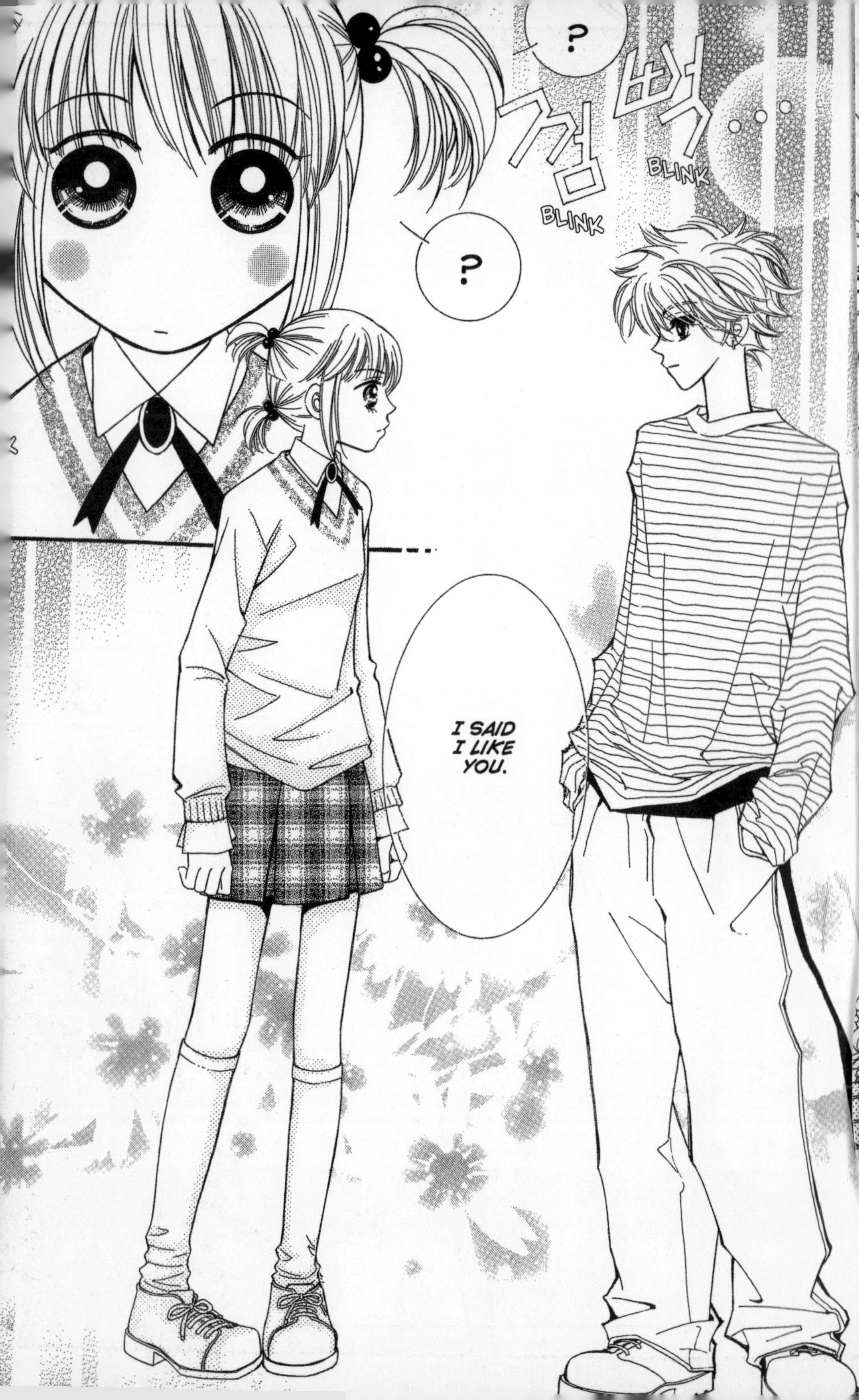
?
BLINK
BLINK
?
I SAID I LIKE YOU.

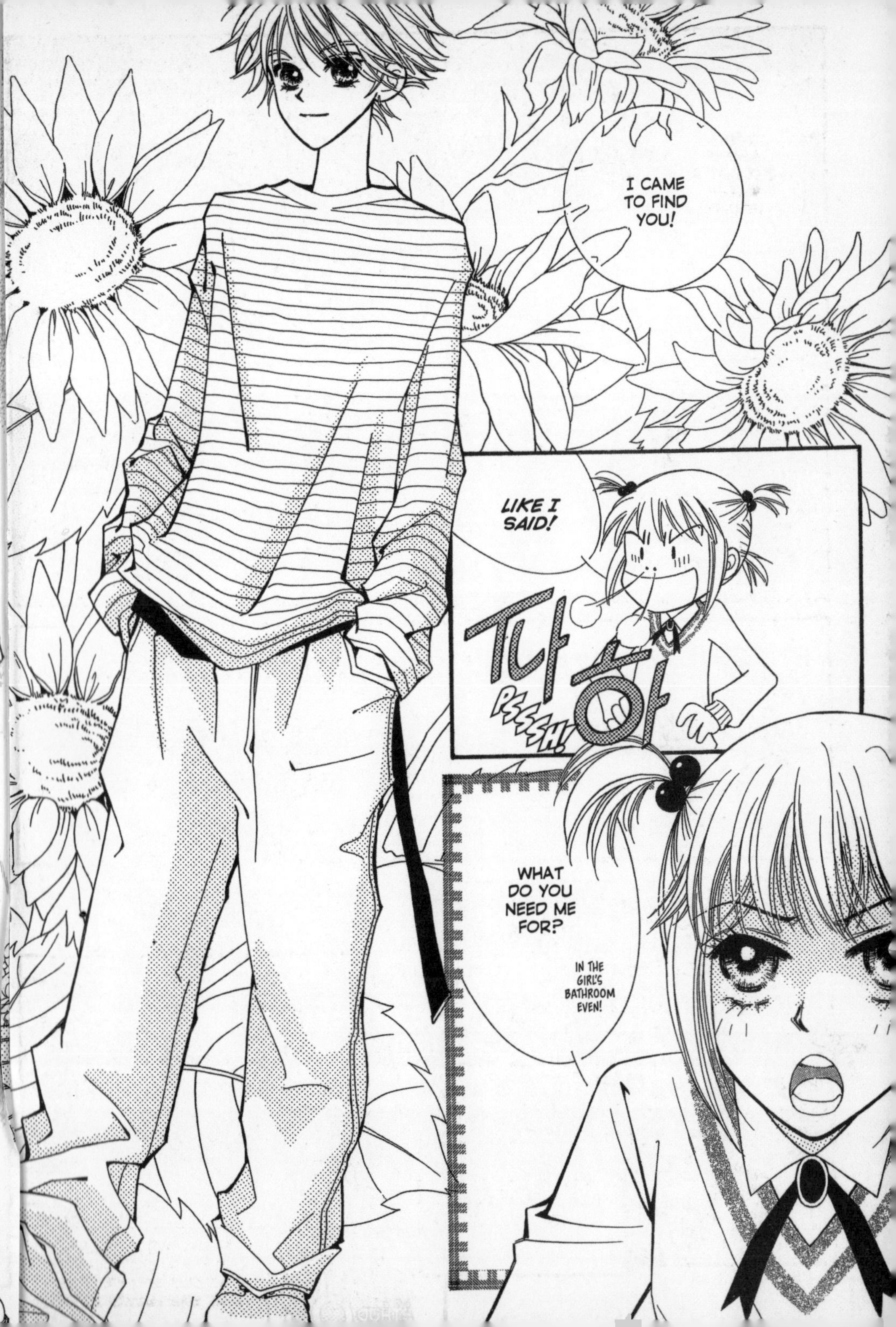
I CAME TO FIND YOU!
LIKE I SAID!
PSSSH!
WHAT DO YOU NEED ME FOR?
IN THE GIRL'S BATHROOM EVEN!

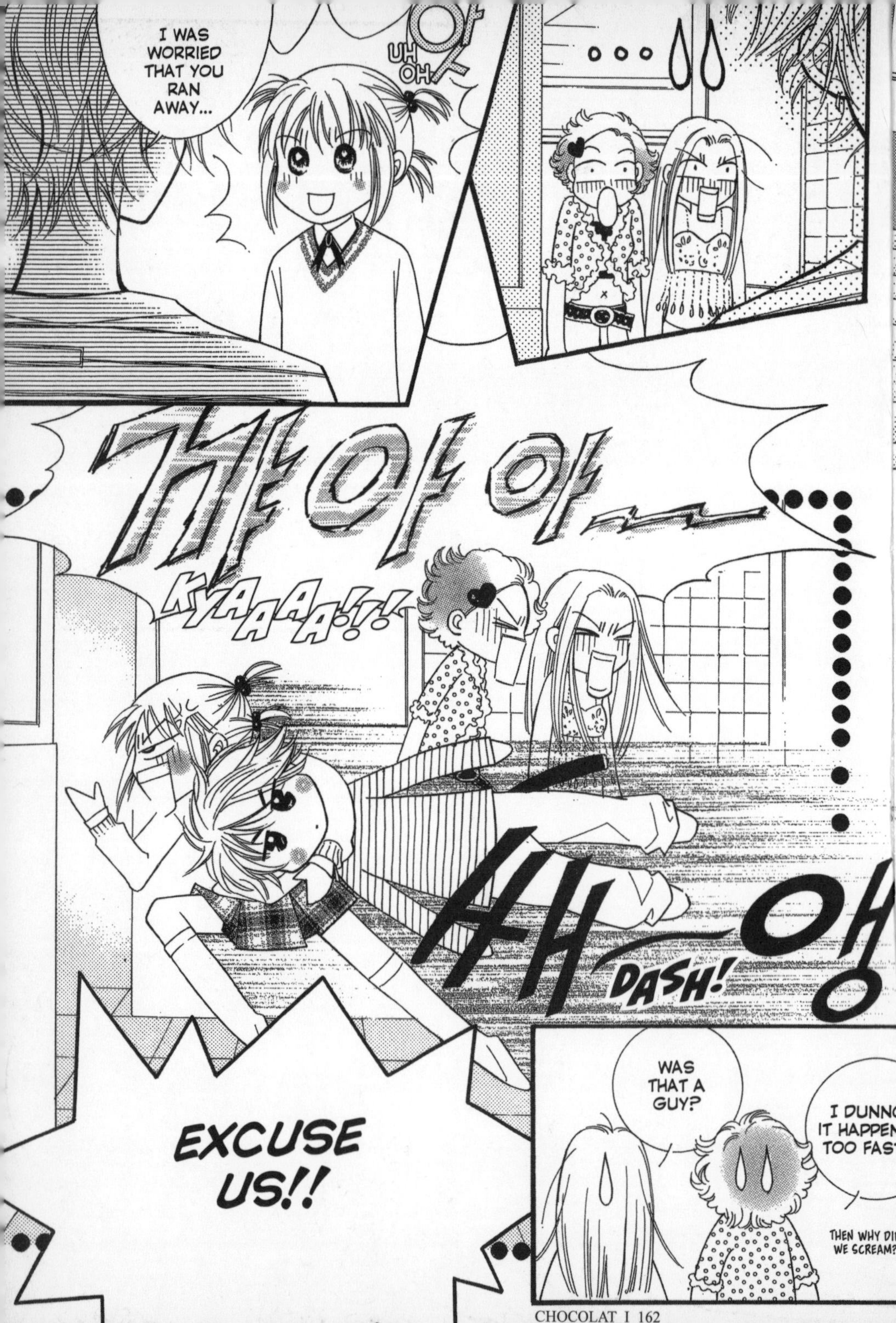
I WAS WORRIED THAT YOU RAN AWAY...
UH OH
꺄아아~
KYAAAA!!!
쌔~앵
DASH!
EXCUSE US!!
WAS THAT A GUY?
I DUNNO IT HAPPEN TOO FAST
THEN WHY DID WE SCREAM?

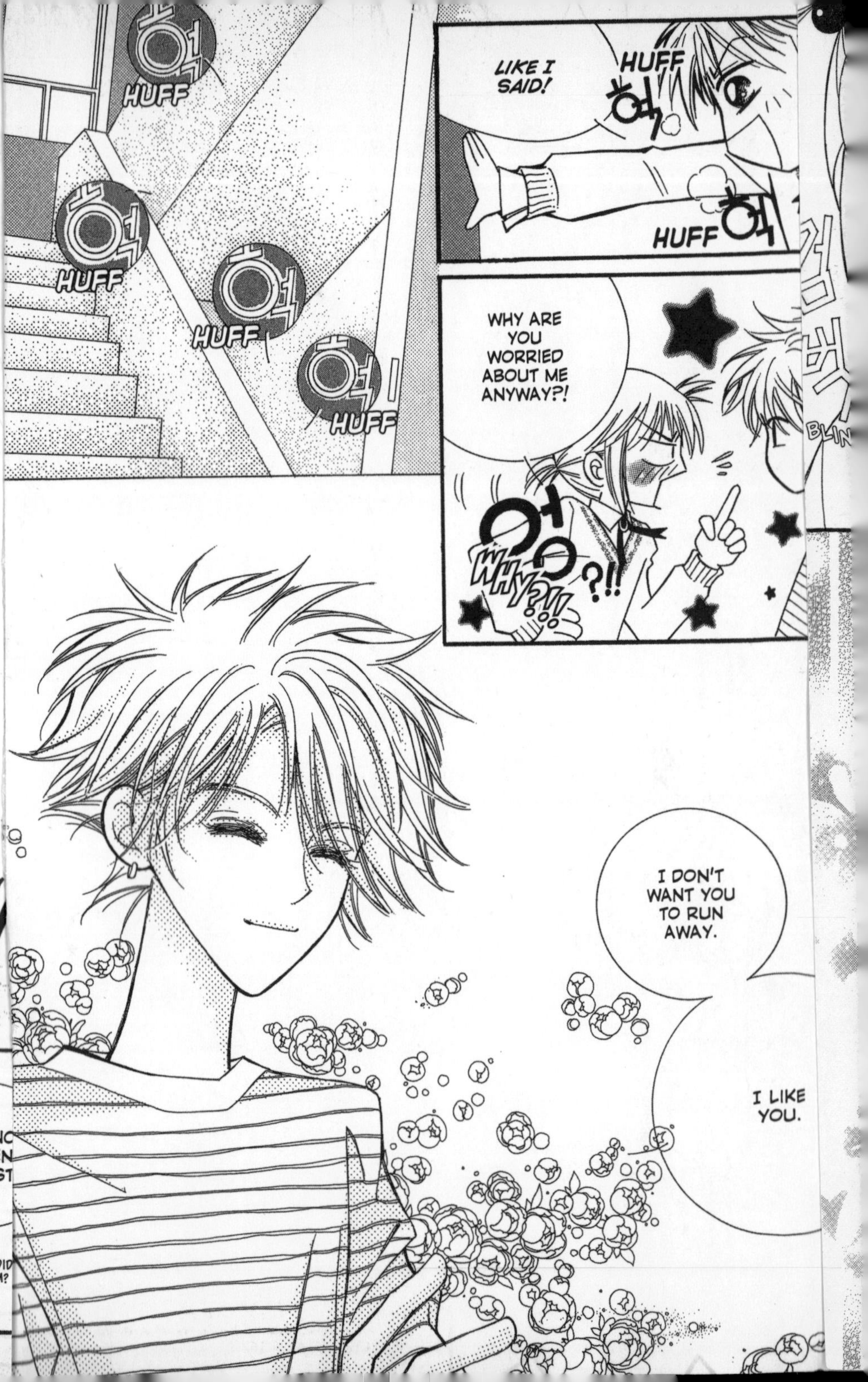
헉
HUFF
헉
HUFF
헉
HUFF
헉
HUFF
LIKE I SAID!
HUFF
HUFF
WHY ARE YOU WORRIED ABOUT ME ANYWAY?!
엉
WHY?!!
?!!
I DON'T WANT YOU TO RUN AWAY.
I LIKE YOU.

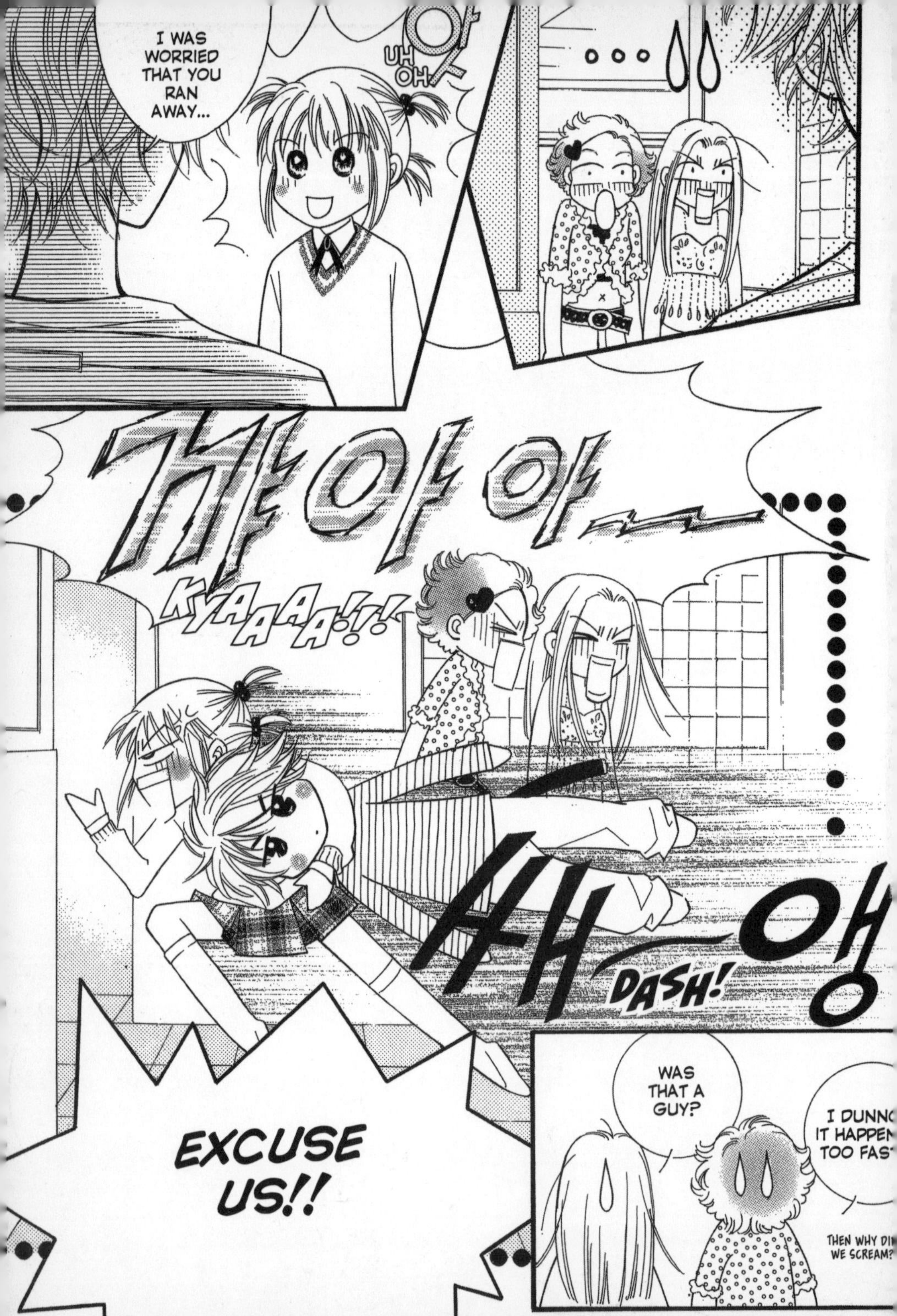
I WAS WORRIED THAT YOU RAN AWAY...
UH OH
KYAAAA!!!
DASH!
EXCUSE US!!
WAS THAT A GUY?
I DUNN IT HAPPEN TOO FAS
THEN WHY DI WE SCREAM?

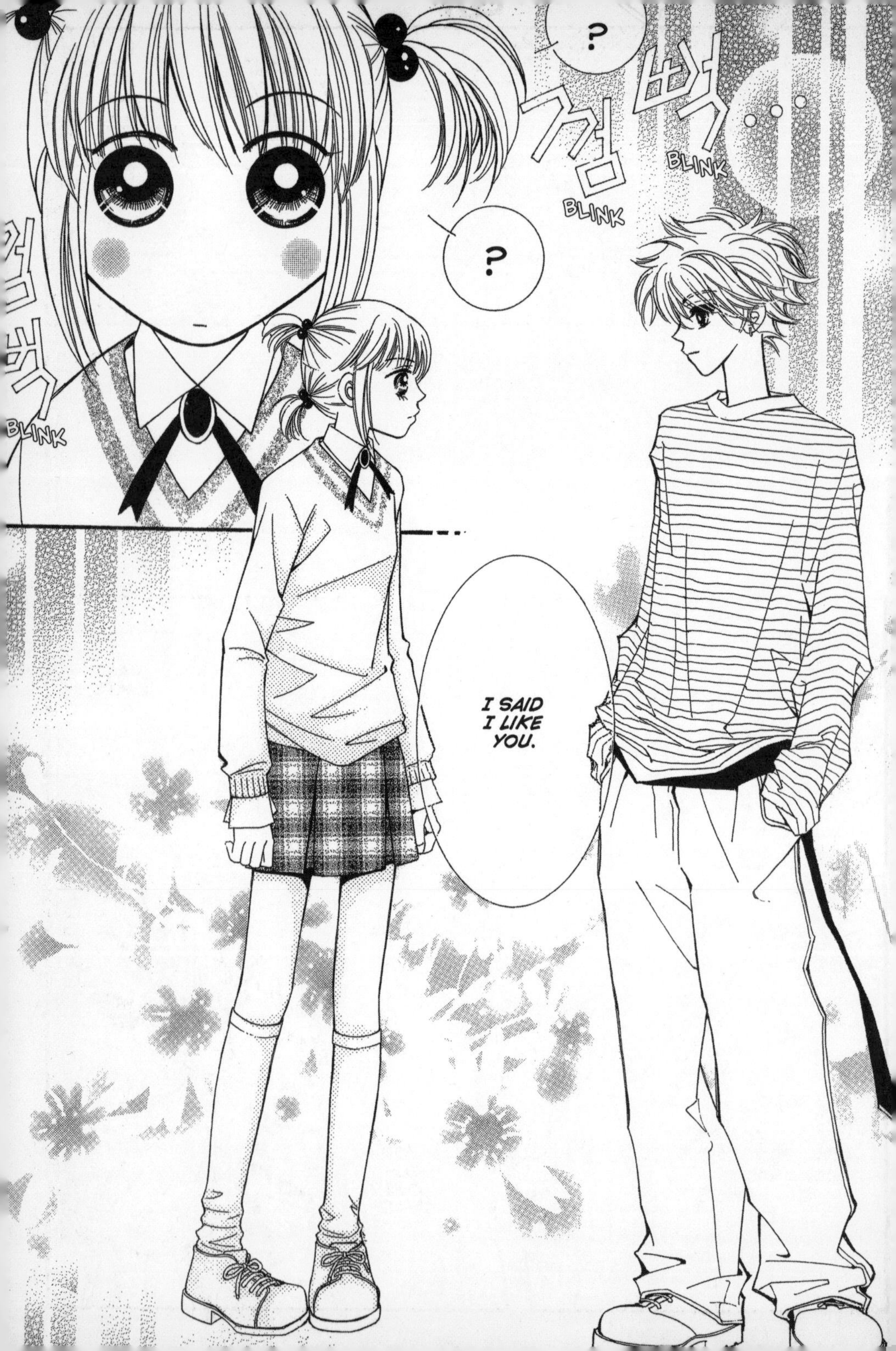
BLINK
?
?
BLINK
...
BLINK
I SAID I LIKE YOU.

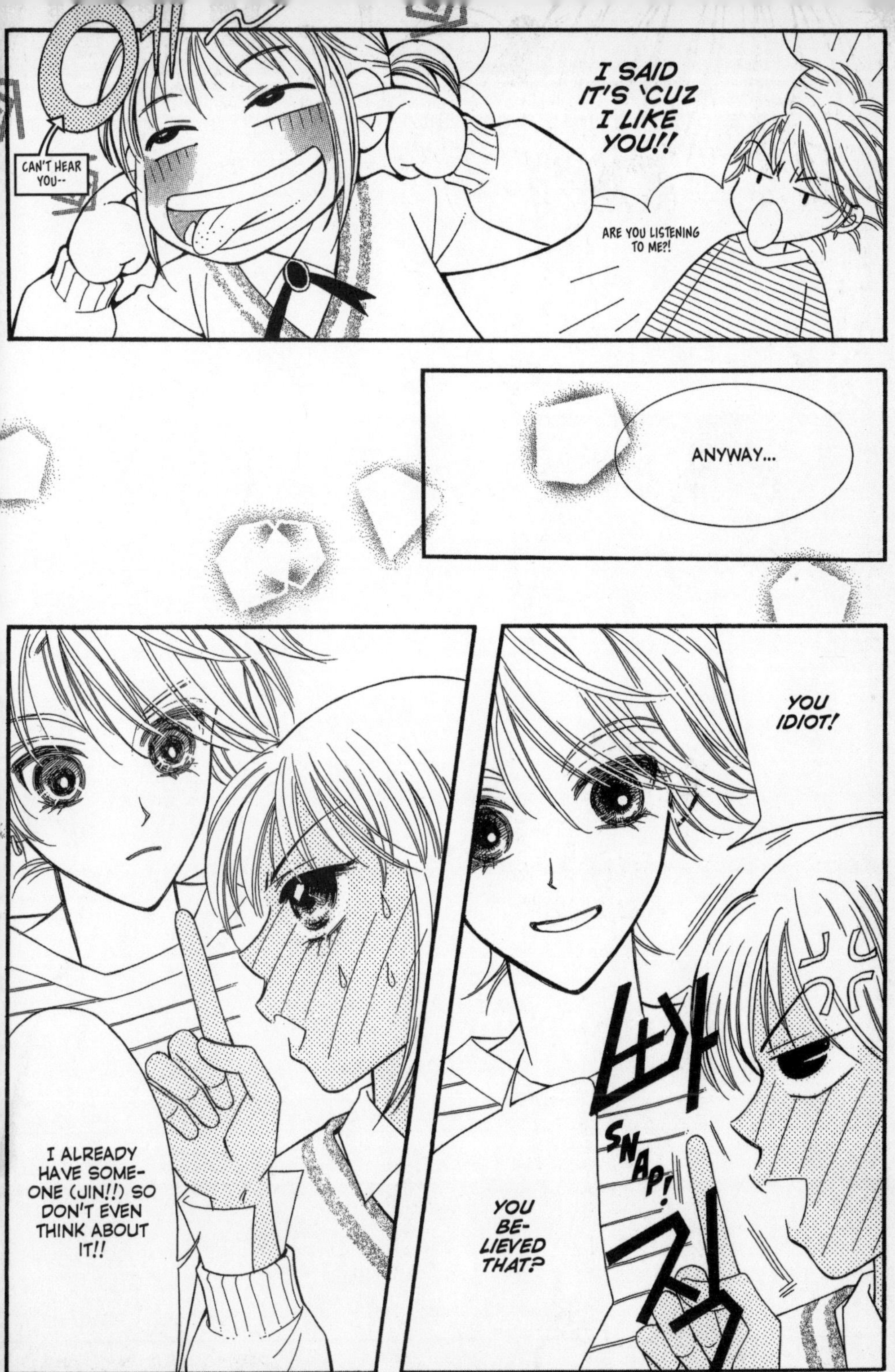
CAN'T HEAR YOU--
I SAID IT'S 'CUZ I LIKE YOU!!
ARE YOU LISTENING TO ME?!
ANYWAY...
I ALREADY HAVE SOME-ONE (JIN!!) SO DON'T EVEN THINK ABOUT IT!!
YOU IDIOT!
SNAP!
YOU BE-LIEVED THAT?

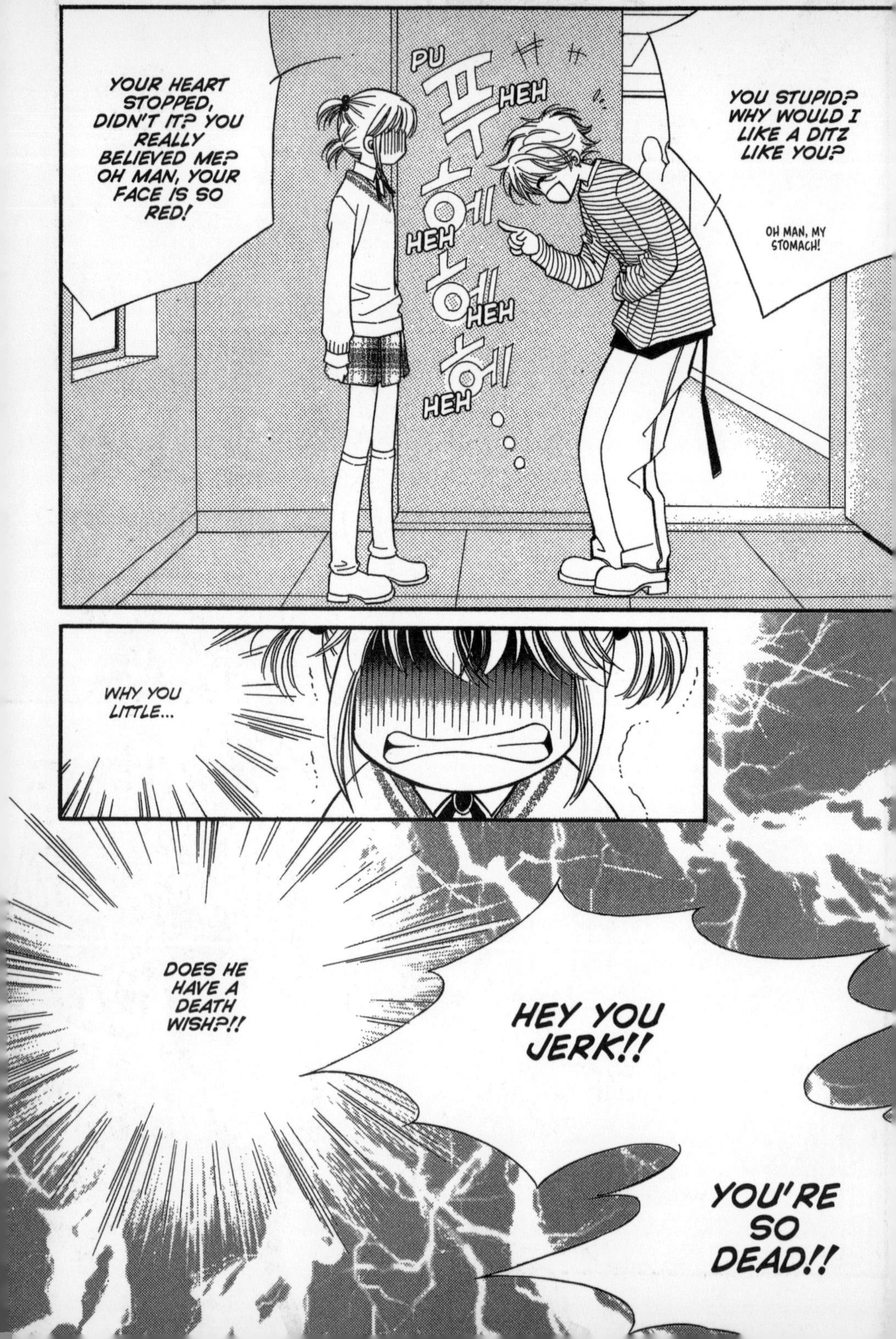

YOUR HEART STOPPED, DIDN'T IT? YOU REALLY BELIEVED ME? OH MAN, YOUR FACE IS SO RED!
PU
HEH
HEH
HEH
HEH
YOU STUPID? WHY WOULD I LIKE A DITZ LIKE YOU?
OH MAN, MY STOMACH!
WHY YOU LITTLE...
DOES HE HAVE A DEATH WISH?!!
HEY YOU JERK!!
YOU'RE SO DEAD!!

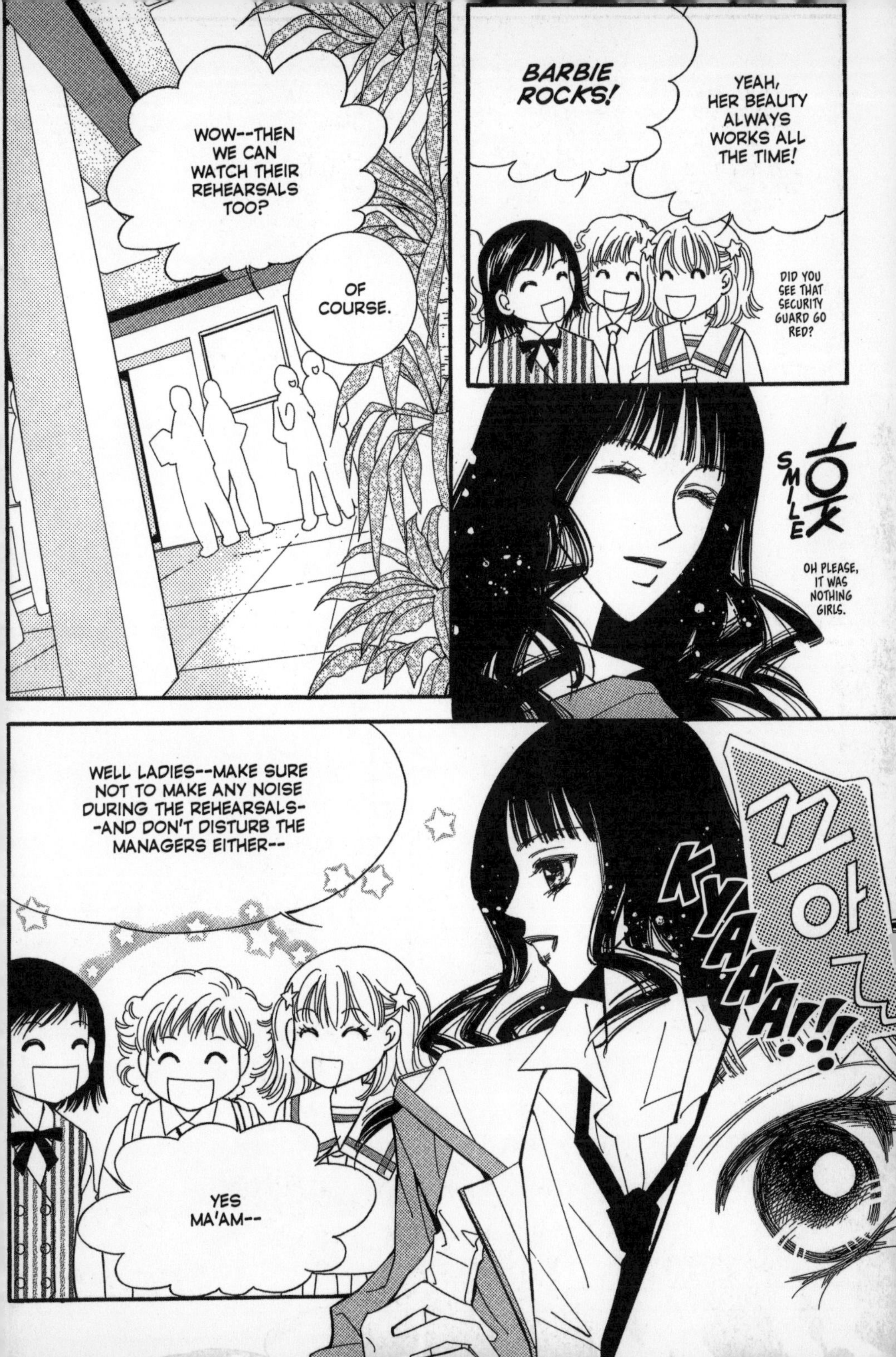
WOW--THEN WE CAN WATCH THEIR REHEARSALS TOO?
OF COURSE.
BARBIE ROCKS!
YEAH, HER BEAUTY ALWAYS WORKS ALL THE TIME!
DID YOU SEE THAT SECURITY GUARD GO RED?
SMILE
OH PLEASE, IT WAS NOTHING GIRLS.
WELL LADIES--MAKE SURE NOT TO MAKE ANY NOISE DURING THE REHEARSALS- -AND DON'T DISTURB THE MANAGERS EITHER--
YES MA'AM--
KYAAAA!!!

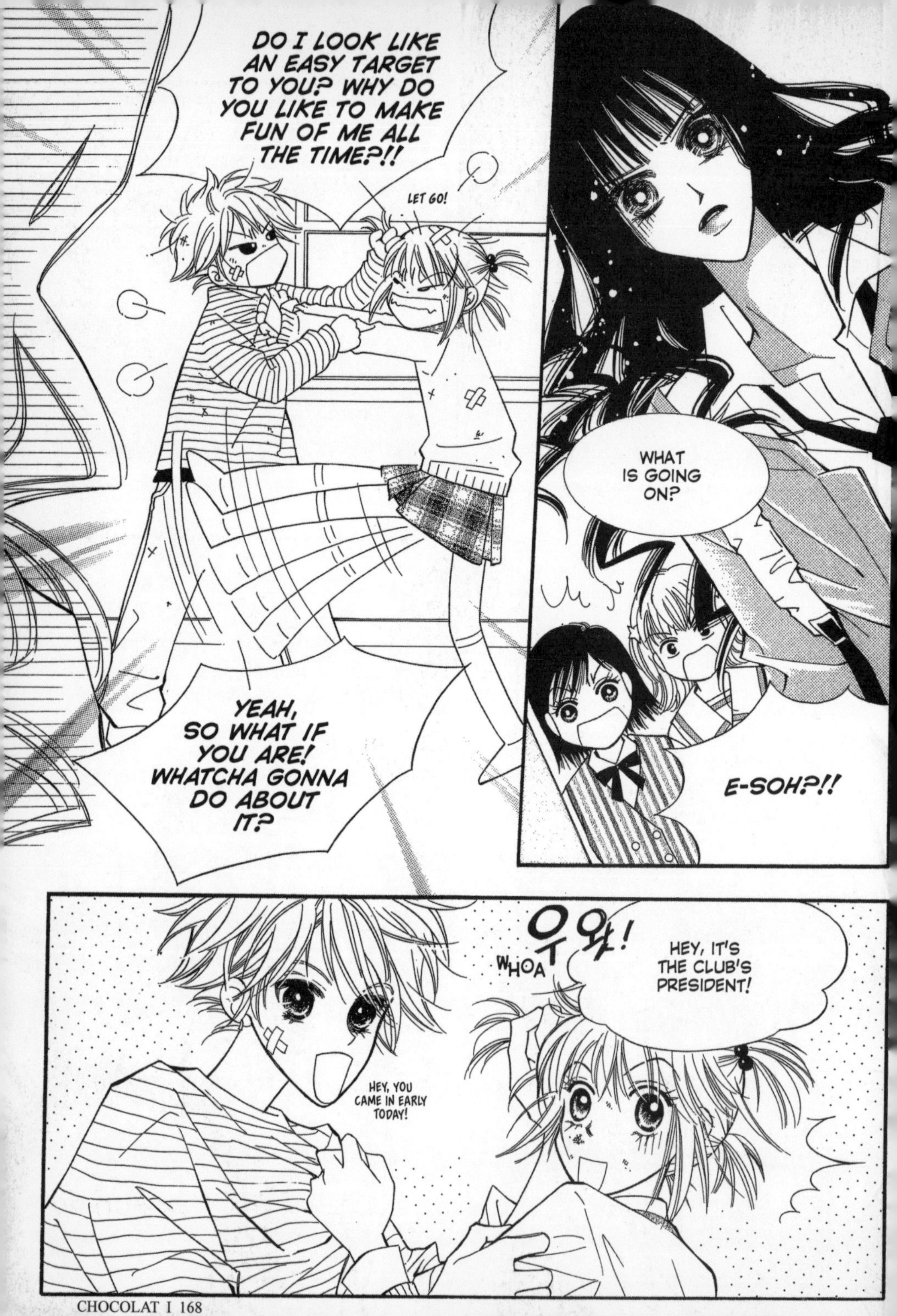
DO I LOOK LIKE AN EASY TARGET TO YOU? WHY DO YOU LIKE TO MAKE FUN OF ME ALL THE TIME?!!
LET GO!
YEAH, SO WHAT IF YOU ARE! WHATCHA GONNA DO ABOUT IT?
WHAT IS GOING ON?
E-SOH?!!
HEY, YOU CAME IN EARLY TODAY!
우와!
WHOA
HEY, IT'S THE CLUB'S PRESIDENT!

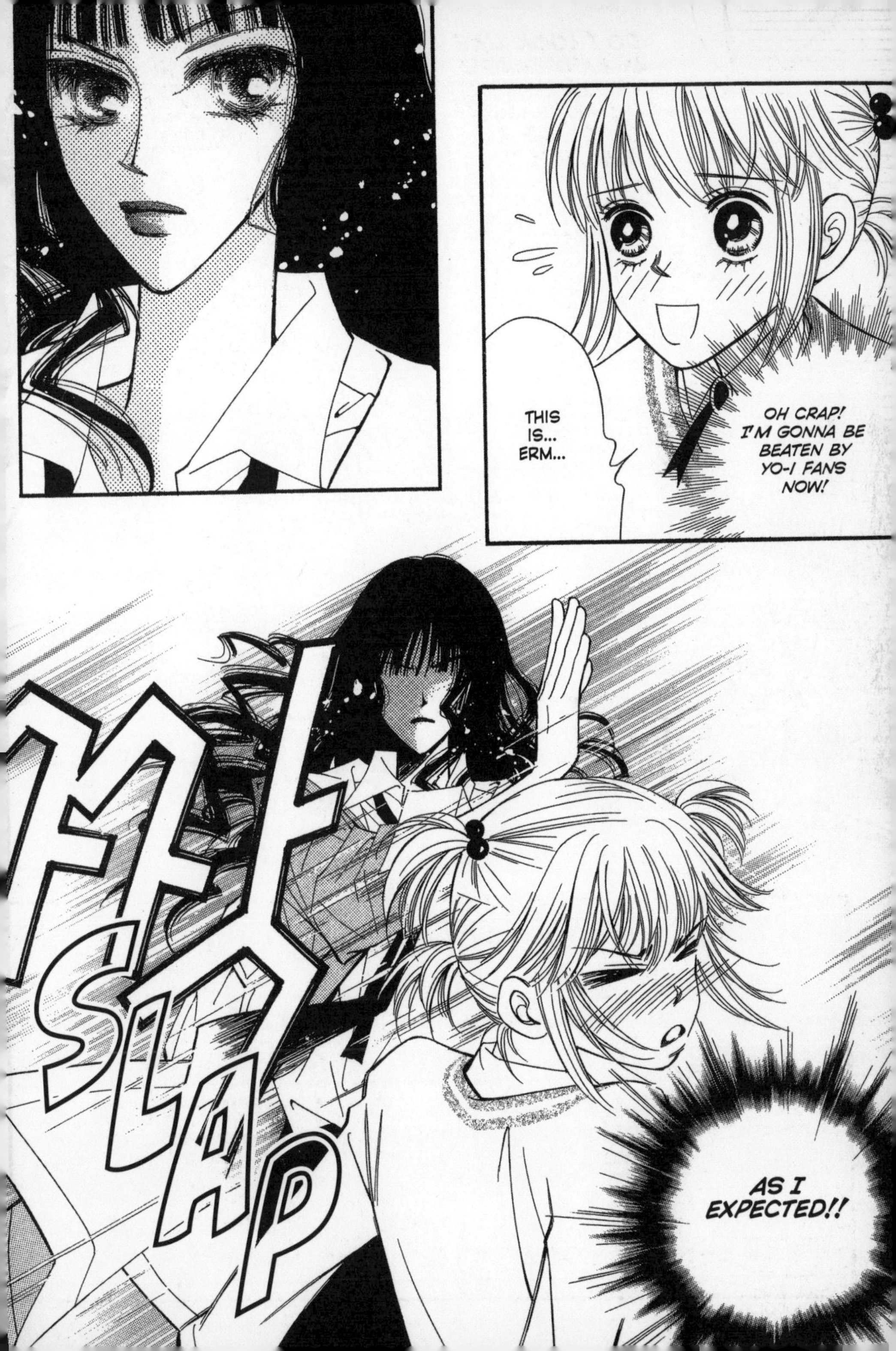
THIS IS... ERM...
OH CRAP! I'M GONNA BE BEATEN BY YO-I FANS NOW!
SLAP
AS I EXPECTED!!

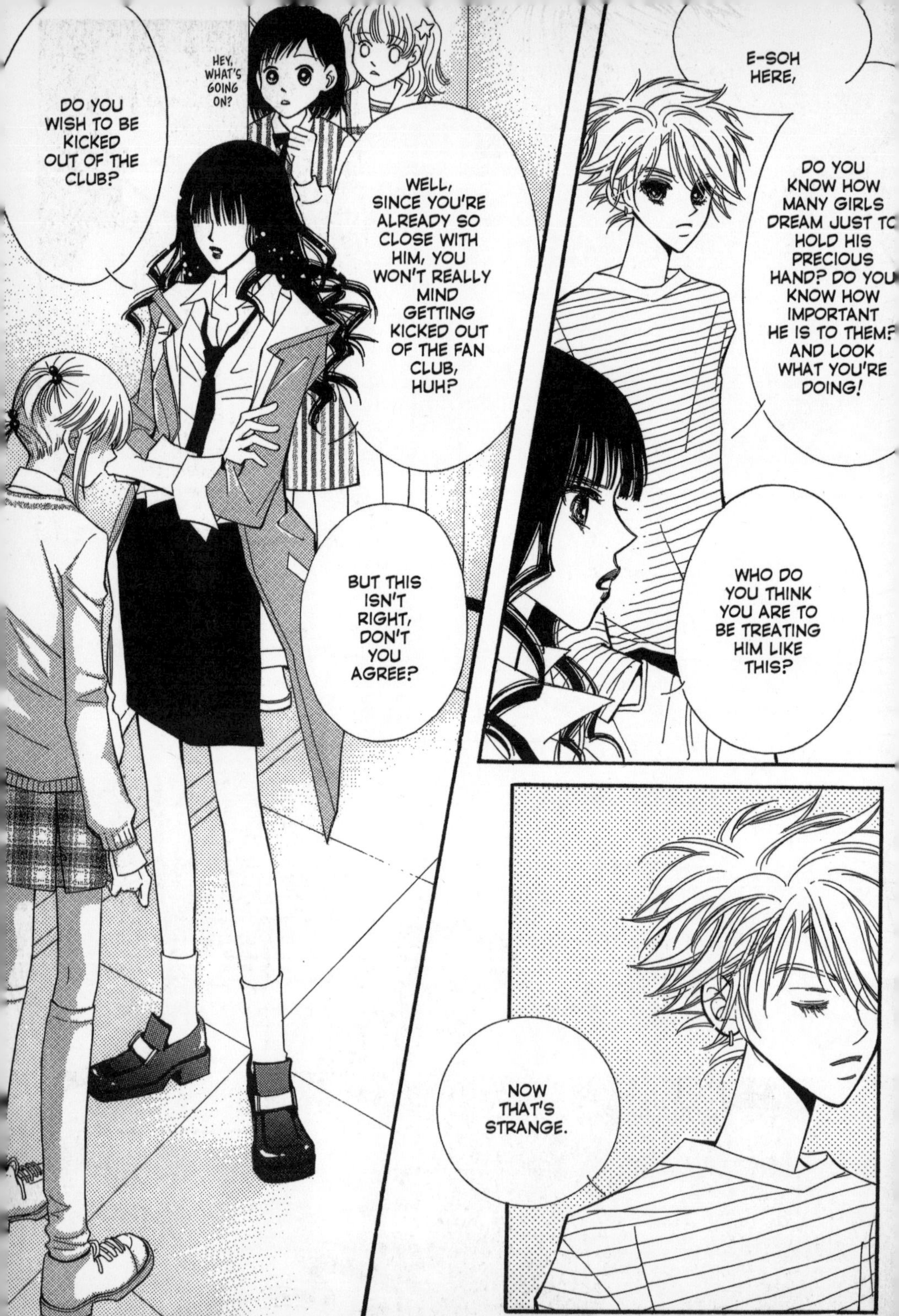
DO YOU WISH TO BE KICKED OUT OF THE CLUB?
HEY, WHAT'S GOING ON?
WELL, SINCE YOU'RE ALREADY SO CLOSE WITH HIM, YOU WON'T REALLY MIND GETTING KICKED OUT OF THE FAN CLUB, HUH?
BUT THIS ISN'T RIGHT, DON'T YOU AGREE?
E-SOH HERE,
DO YOU KNOW HOW MANY GIRLS DREAM JUST TO HOLD HIS PRECIOUS HAND? DO YOU KNOW HOW IMPORTANT HE IS TO THEM? AND LOOK WHAT YOU'RE DOING!
WHO DO YOU THINK YOU ARE TO BE TREATING HIM LIKE THIS?
NOW THAT'S STRANGE.

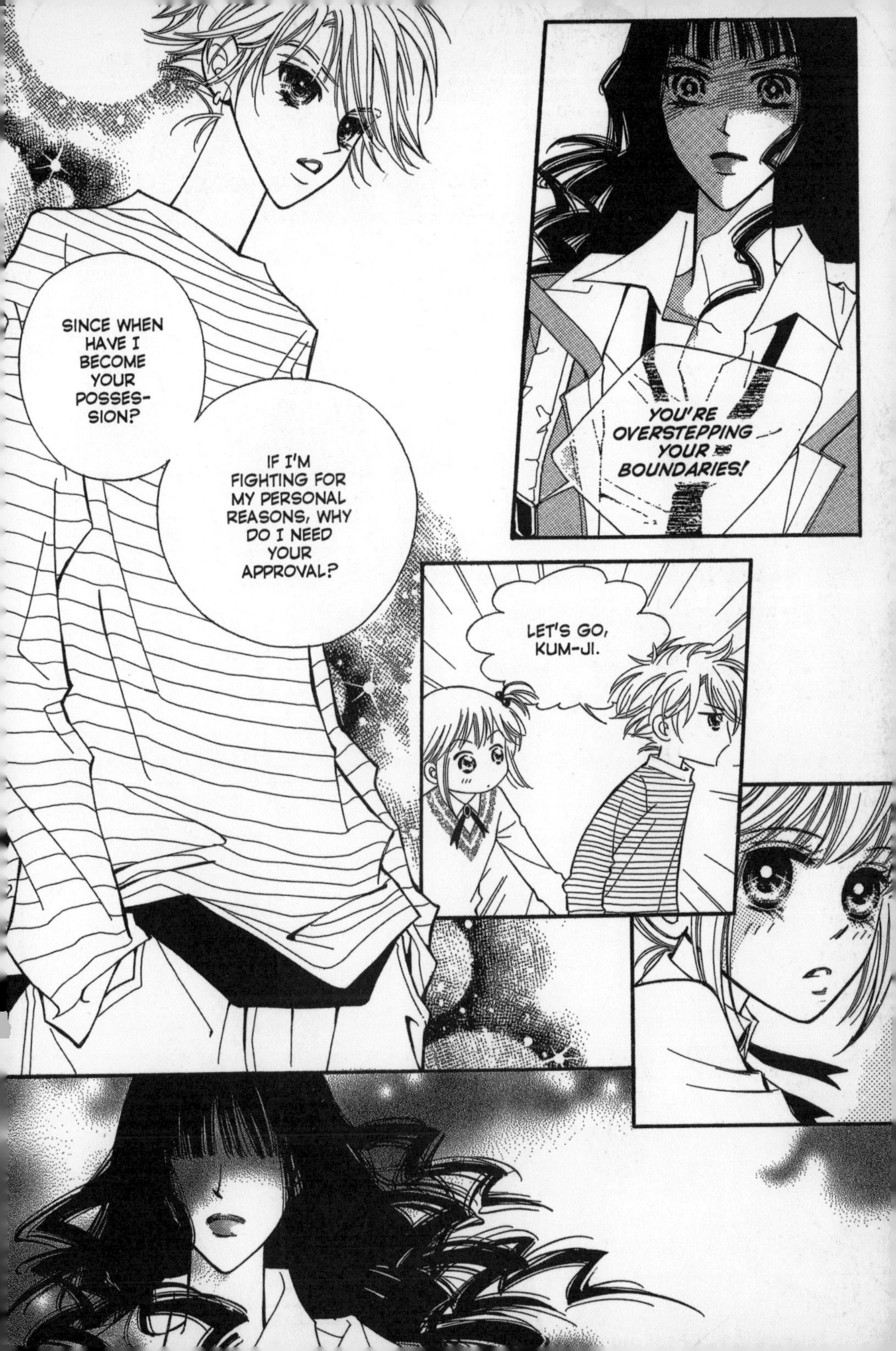
SINCE WHEN HAVE I BECOME YOUR POSSESSION?
IF I'M FIGHTING FOR MY PERSONAL REASONS, WHY DO I NEED YOUR APPROVAL?
YOU'RE OVERSTEPPING YOUR BOUNDARIES!
LET'S GO, KUM-JI.

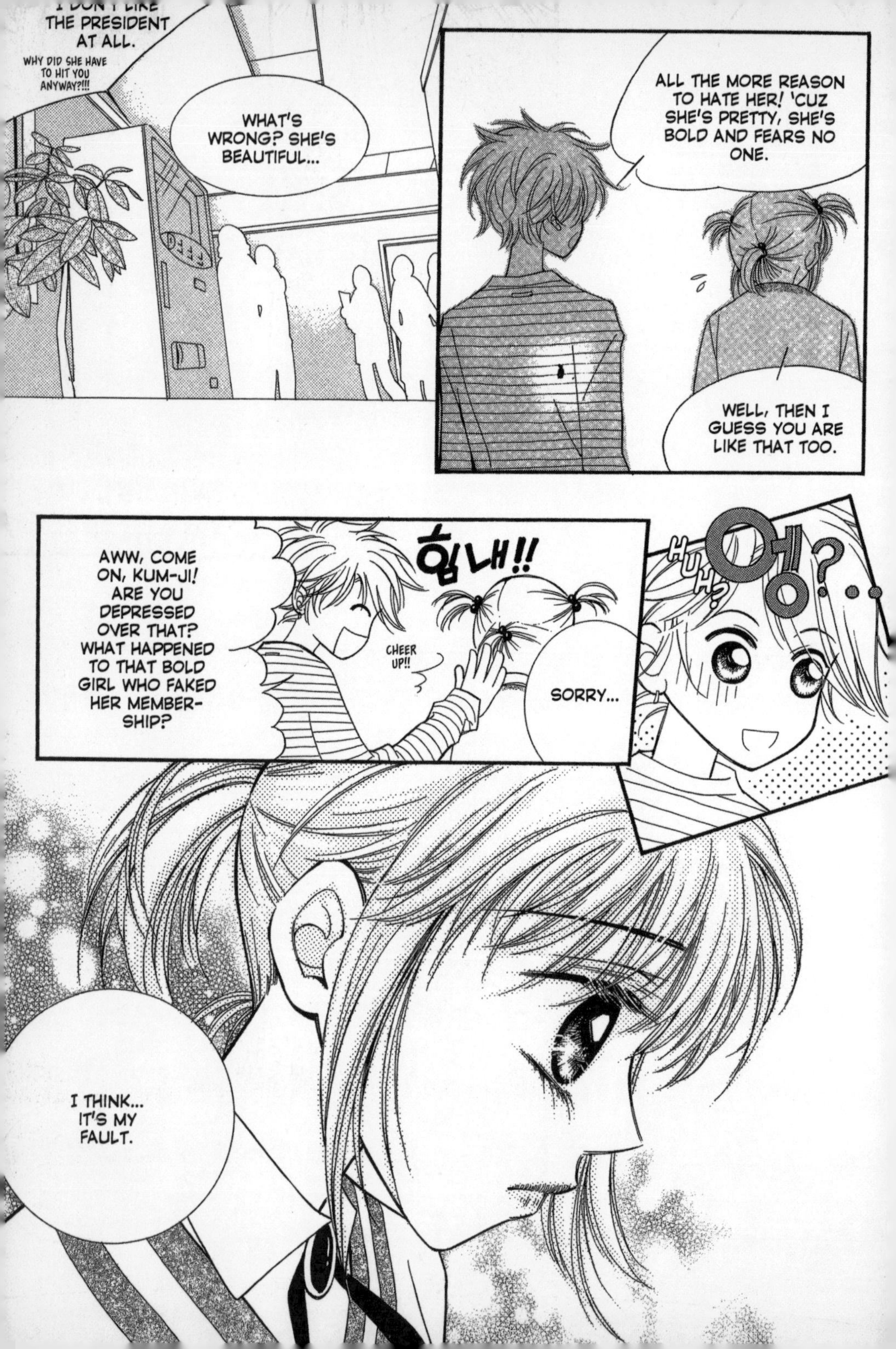
THE PRESIDENT AT ALL.
WHY DID SHE HAVE TO HIT YOU ANYWAY?!!!
WHAT'S WRONG? SHE'S BEAUTIFUL...
ALL THE MORE REASON TO HATE HER! 'CUZ SHE'S PRETTY, SHE'S BOLD AND FEARS NO ONE.
WELL, THEN I GUESS YOU ARE LIKE THAT TOO.
AWW, COME ON, KUM-JI! ARE YOU DEPRESSED OVER THAT? WHAT HAPPENED TO THAT BOLD GIRL WHO FAKED HER MEMBER-SHIP?
힘내!!
CHEER UP!!
SORRY...
HUH?
엉?..
I THINK... IT'S MY FAULT.

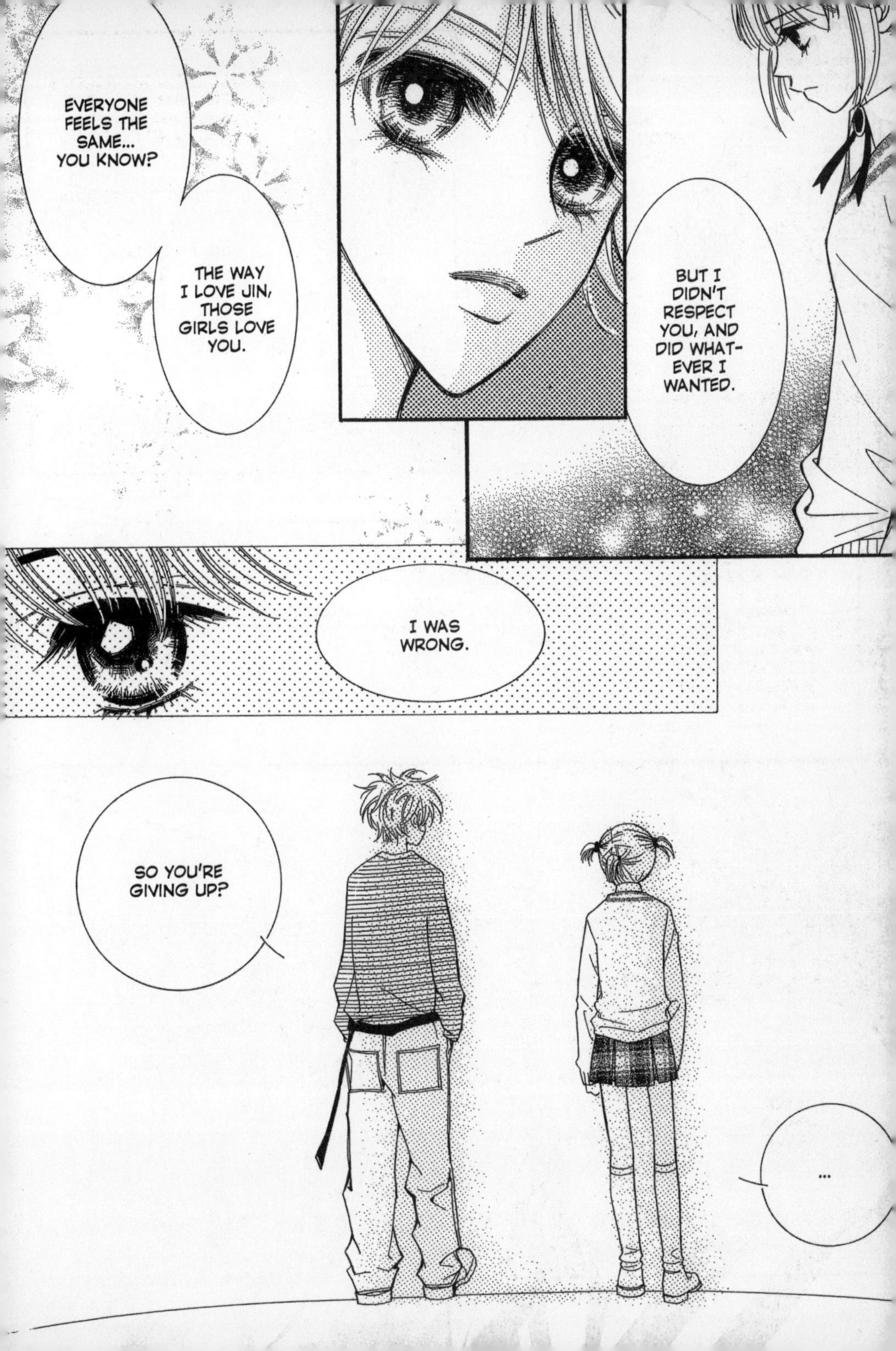
EVERYONE FEELS THE SAME... YOU KNOW?
THE WAY I LOVE JIN, THOSE GIRLS LOVE YOU.
BUT I DIDN'T RESPECT YOU, AND DID WHAT-EVER I WANTED.
I WAS WRONG.
SO YOU'RE GIVING UP?
...

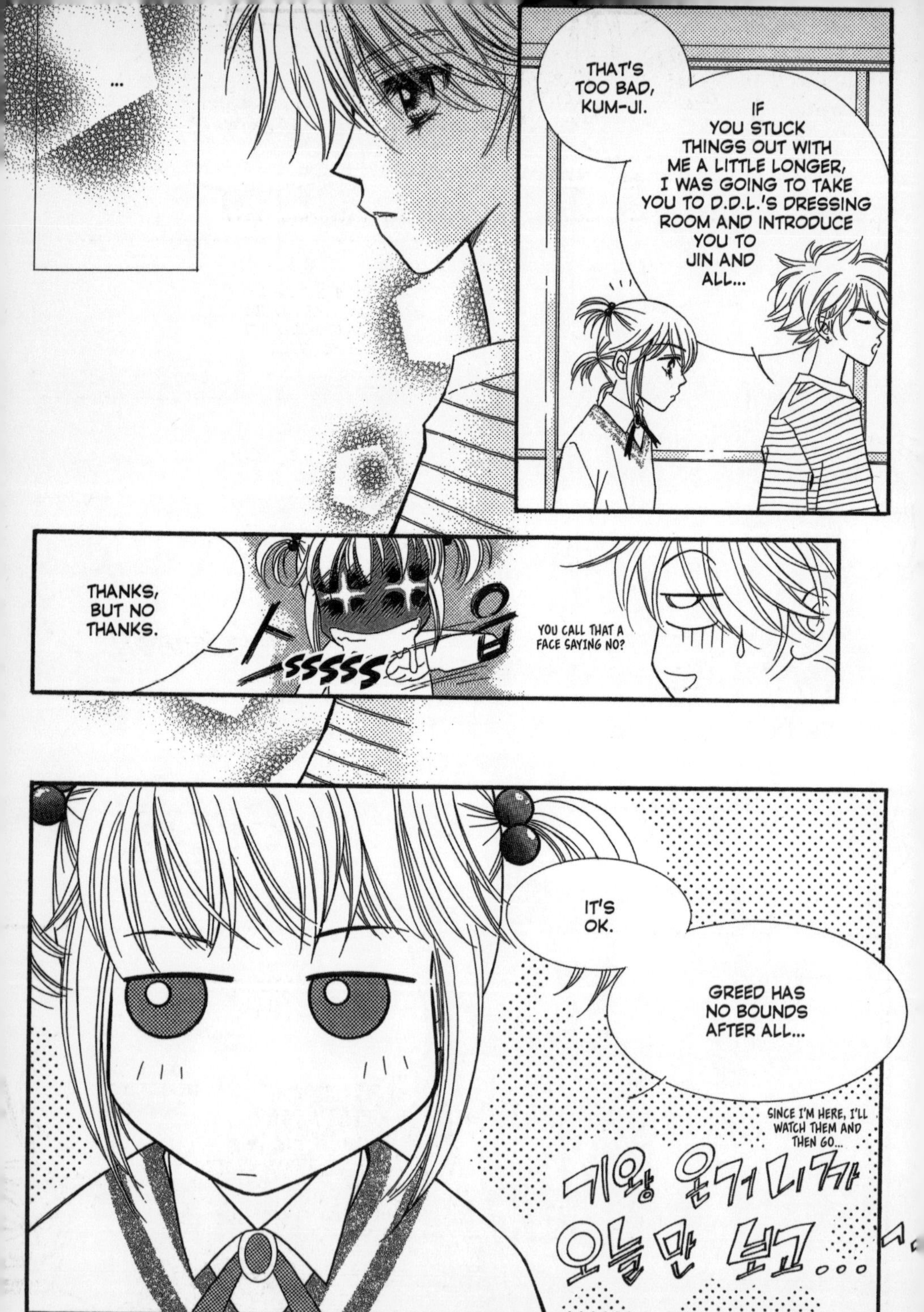
...
THAT'S TOO BAD, KUM-JI.
IF YOU STUCK THINGS OUT WITH ME A LITTLE LONGER, I WAS GOING TO TAKE YOU TO D.D.L.'S DRESSING ROOM AND INTRODUCE YOU TO JIN AND ALL...
THANKS, BUT NO THANKS.
SSSSS
YOU CALL THAT A FACE SAYING NO?
IT'S OK.
GREED HAS NO BOUNDS AFTER ALL...
SINCE I'M HERE, I'LL WATCH THEM AND THEN GO...
기왕 온거니까 오늘만 보고...

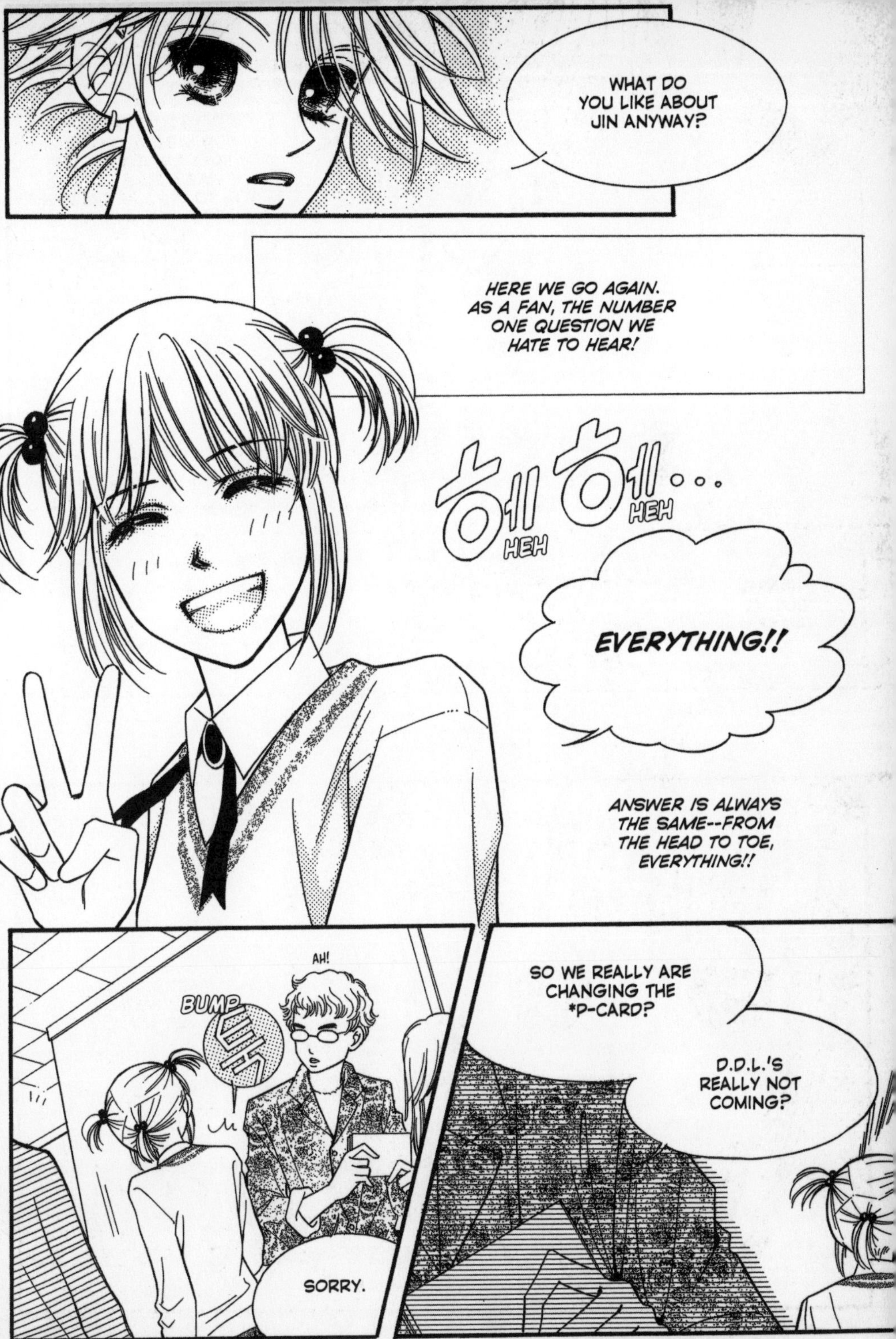
WHAT DO YOU LIKE ABOUT JIN ANYWAY?
HERE WE GO AGAIN. AS A FAN, THE NUMBER ONE QUESTION WE HATE TO HEAR!
헤헤...
HEH
HEH
EVERYTHING!!
ANSWER IS ALWAYS THE SAME--FROM THE HEAD TO TOE, EVERYTHING!!
AH!
BUMP
SORRY.
SO WE REALLY ARE CHANGING THE *P-CARD?
D.D.L.'S REALLY NOT COMING?

*P-CARD : SCRIPT WITH THE LIST OF CONTESTANTS FOR THE ANNOUNCER.

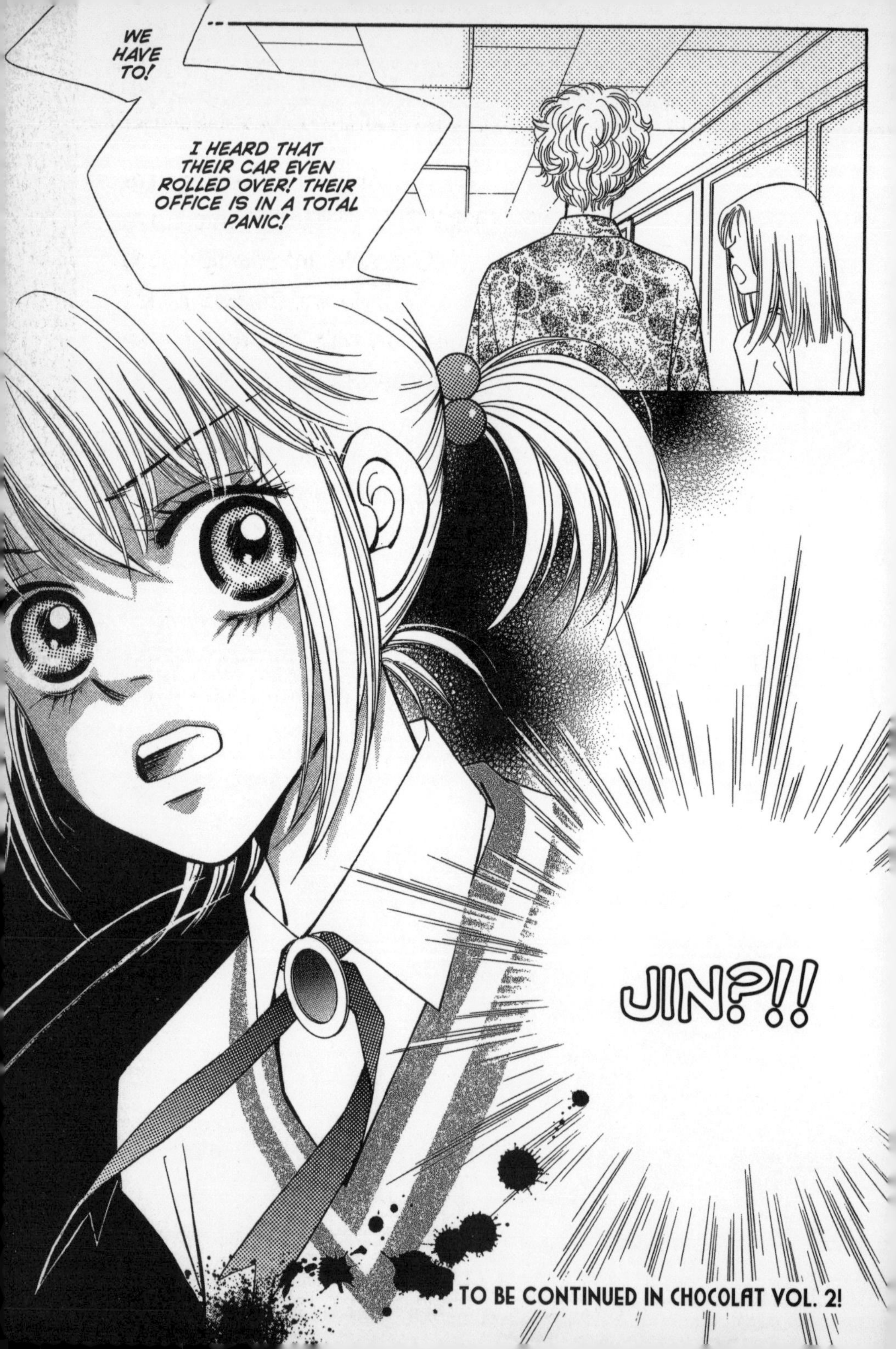

WE HAVE TO!
I HEARD THAT THEIR CAR EVEN ROLLED OVER! THEIR OFFICE IS IN A TOTAL PANIC!
JIN?!!
TO BE CONTINUED IN CHOCOLAT VOL. 2!

APPENDIX

About the creator

● ● ● ● ● ● ● ● ● ●

Chocolat
Ji-Sang Shin/Geo

In 1991, Manhwa artist Ji-Sang
Shin debuted with <Potato Plot of
Meme and Gushiki>, and Geo
with <The City of Gray>. Over
time, they each developed their
own colorful stories and style. As
they became closer
acquaintances, the two formed a
working partnership in 1996,
collaborating on <2x8 SONG!>.
Now, they are working together on
<Chocolat>, while also preparing
other new titles, creating a brand
new world for the readers to enjoy.
One of their recent titles is <The
Sad Love Story> - Based on the
famous drama that made a huge
hit in Korea, and also in Japan.
<The Sad Love Story> is also
published in Japan.

Other Major works
<2x8 SONG!>, <Sandwich>,
<Triangle>, <The Sad Love Story>

Quick Chat with the Creator

Two g.o.d. worshippers from Busan

Ji-Sang Shin/Geo

CHOCOLAT

Manhwa artist Ji-Sang Shin and Geo live in Busan, Korea. Not only are they close friends, they are both HUGE fans of g.o.d. (K-pop boy band) They may draw "cool" characters but in reality are more like your typical girls-next-door. They also both love animals. *^^*

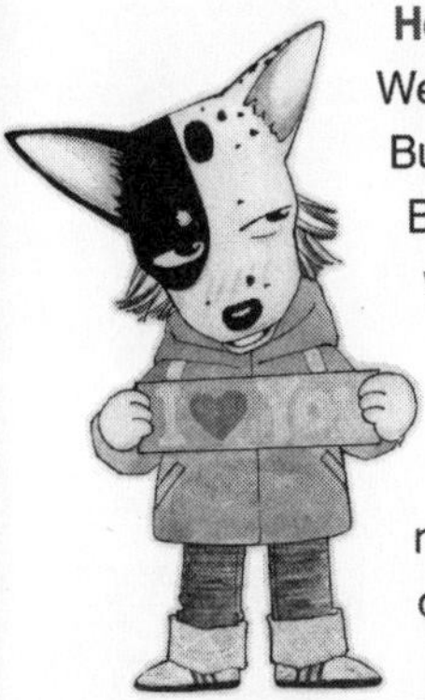

How did you meet?
Well, we first met at a Busan Manhwa club. Back then, Poopyhead was a junior in high school, and Lil' Cheapskate was 20 years old. (Our nicknames are based on our pet dogs' names.) What's most interesting is we both remember the first impressions of each other very well.

Poopyhead : Big sis? I didn't know what her problem was but she had this mean glare all that day!!
Lil' Cheapskate : Geo? She was a prissy know-it-all. The way she looked down on people - made me want to smack her... -_-+ Later, while working under Jin Kim, our teacher, we realized we were more alike. To this day we still stick together, through thick and thin.

How do you distribute the work?
Lil' Cheapskate takes care of the story while Poopyhead lays out the panels. Inking and other tasks depend on the characters we draw. We both work on the finishing touches.

What do you dislike about the other? ^^;
Geo : Big sis... She's lazy, messy, mean, weak-willed, forgetful and a complete klutz! And the amount of food she eats... (foams at the mouth)
Ji-Sang : Oh yeah?! Geo is... cheap, stubborn, selfish, complains too much... and dumb...! (Point for Ji-Sang!!)

What are the pros and cons of working together?
Pros : We can cover each other's weaknesses. We also finish our work faster than if worked separately.
Cons: (Both sigh deeply)

Are there any memorable moments to tell from the g.o.d. fan club?
Well, we only joined the club recently and Busan is pretty quiet when it comes to events. But at one of their concerts, we went nuts - our throats were sore for a month.

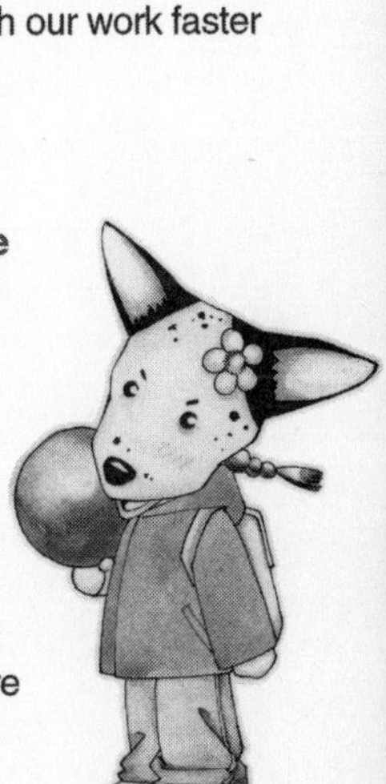

Character Introduction

Chocolat

Ji-Sang Shin&Geo

What would you do if an idol confesses their love to you?

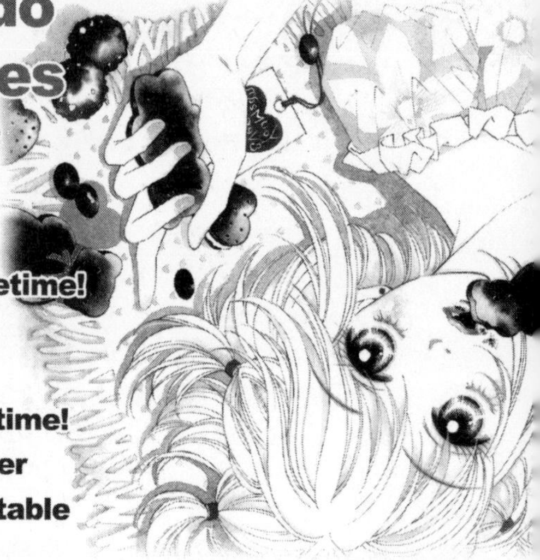

The main character Kum-Ji of <Chocolat>▲

It's a fantasy that most everyone dreams of at least once in their lifetime! What would you do if a hot star confesses his love for you... In fact, two of them - at the same time! You'll never be able to go back after just one bite of this dreamy, delectable <Chocolat>!

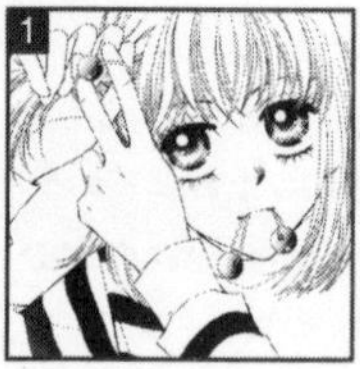
1
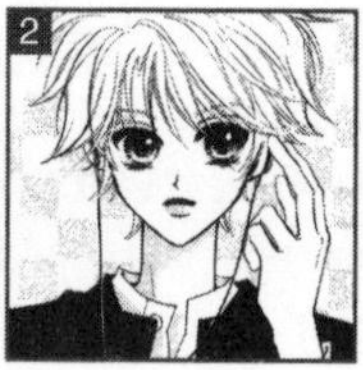
2
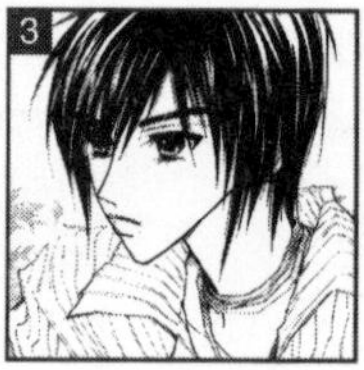
3
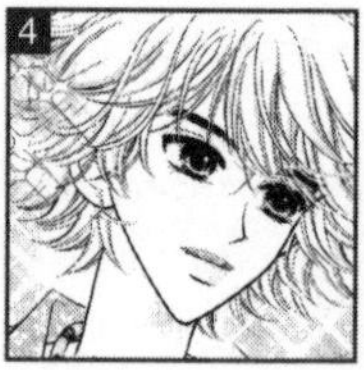
4
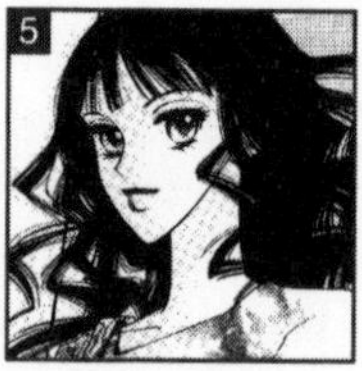
5

1. Kum-Ji Hwang : A hardcore fan of Jin Ryu of D.D.L. Unfortunately, membership to the fan club is closed. So, in hopes of catching a glimpse of him, Kum-Ji joins the Yo-I fan club. Pretending to be a fan of Yo-I, all the while secretly cheering on Jin, is far more difficult than she anticipated - her secret is soon discovered - by E-Soh!

2. E-Soh: A member of a new idol group, Yo-I. He discovers Kum-Ji's secret and blackmails her.

3. E-Wan : A member of Yo-I - typically cold and distant. He also seems to be very close to Jin Ryu, which peaks Kum-Ji's interest.

4. Jin Ryu : Member of the popular idol group, D.D.L. Known for his good looks and killer smile, he is the object of Kum-Ji's affection.

5. Che-Ryun Yang : A.K.A Barbie. The beautiful president of the Yo-I fan club. She doesn't like the development of Kum-Ji and E-Soh's rapidly growing relationship.

Behind the Story : Ji-Sang Shin/Geo's Idol Love Story

At the very first planning meeting for <Chocolat>, the two artists were extremely confident about writing a comic based on fan club stories. Perhaps that is why, in <Chocolat>, the fan club stories feel so real. Don't you get a bit envious of how they can model these characters from themselves and their favorite idols? Let's give it up for these two who trek from BuSan to Seoul to show their love and devotion for g.o.d.!

"I have five perfect gods; the g.o.d.!" -Ji-Sang Shin/Geo-

The five men we love the more than anything in the whole world, g.o.d.! We knew from the beginning there was something very special about these five men.
Jjuni bro, who knows the meaning of kindness and gentleness, ***Denji***, who is cute but deep, ***Kae-Jang***, whose sense of humor makes us laugh, ***Hoi***, who has a gorgeous killer smile that takes our breath away, and last but not least, the youngest, ***Tae-Soo***, who has the cutest disposition.
Until our dying day, we will love g.o.d. with all our hearts. <Chocolat> is about loving that special someone from afar. At the concert finales, when the entire audience waves farewell with blue balloons, Danny shouts, "Don't cheat on us while we're away!" and we all cry out, "We wouldn't! We'll wait only for you!!!". There are times when Tae-Soo greets us with an energetic "Hey everyone! How've y'all been?!", and we reply in unison "Hi, we've been well!!"
That feeling of unity between a pop star and their fans... We hope you will experience those feelings while reading <Chocolat>...

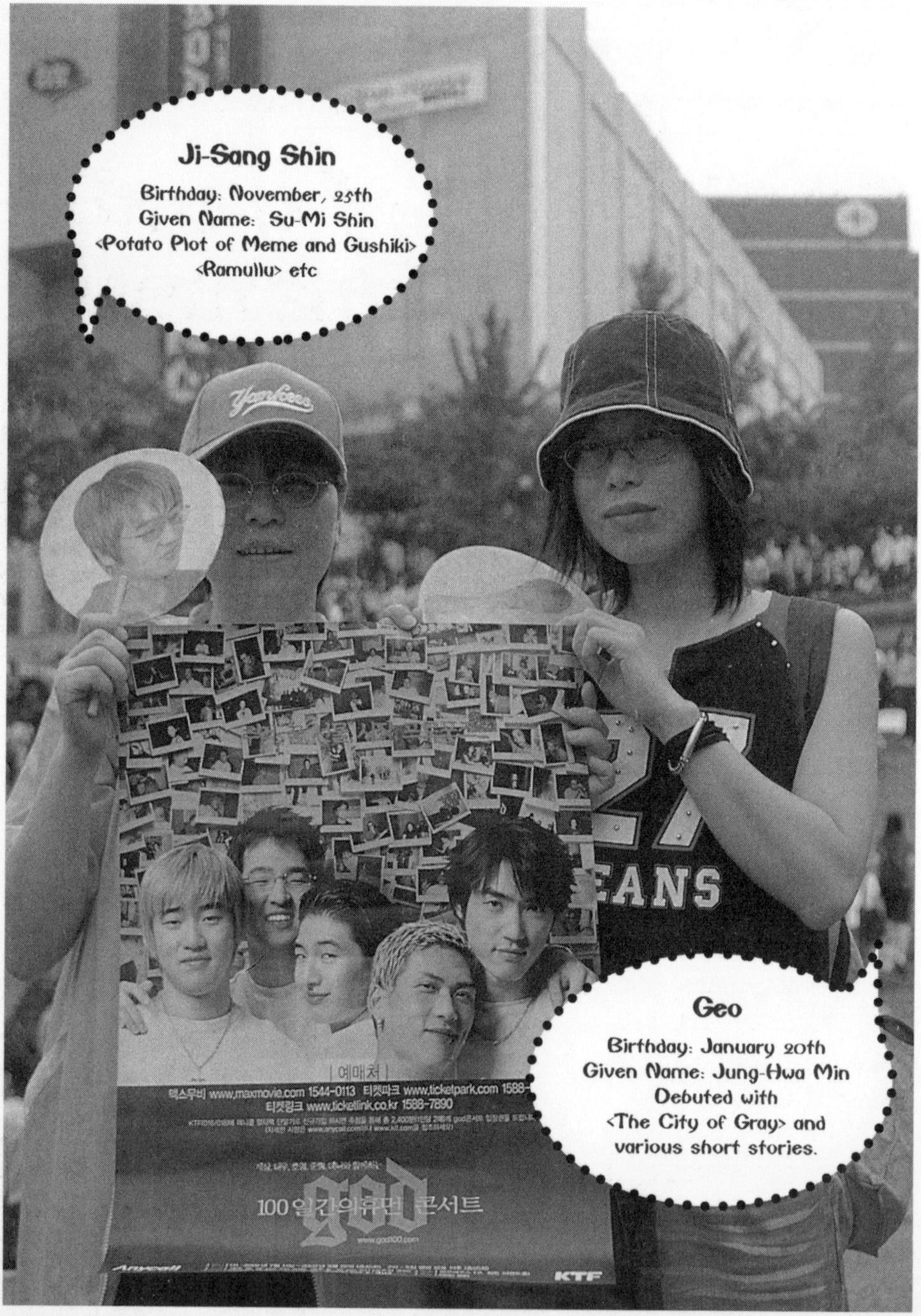
Ji-Sang Shin
Birthday: November, 25th
Given Name: Su-Mi Shin
<Potato Plot of Meme and Gushiki>
<Ramullu> etc
Geo
Birthday: January 20th
Given Name: Jung-Hwa Min
Debuted with
<The City of Gray> and
various short stories.
예매처
맥스무비 www.maxmovie.com 1544-0113 티켓파크 www.ticketpark.com
티켓링크 www.ticketlink.co.kr 1588-7890
KTF

CHOCOLAT Ji-Sang Shin · Geo : Stories from Hardcore Fangirls

For the love of g.o.d., love of manhwa

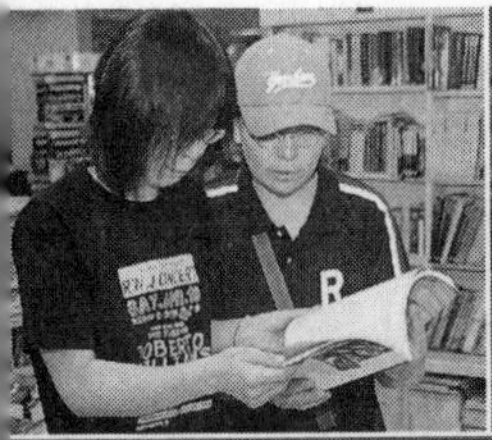
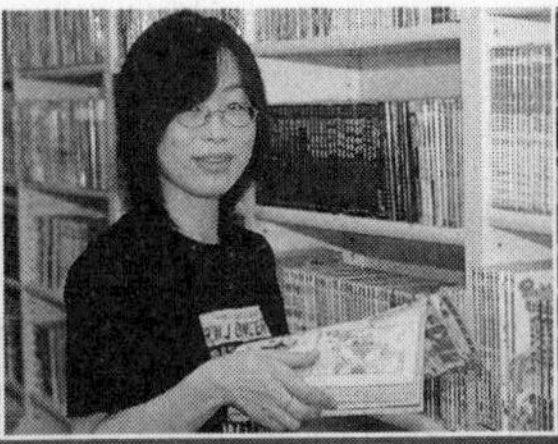
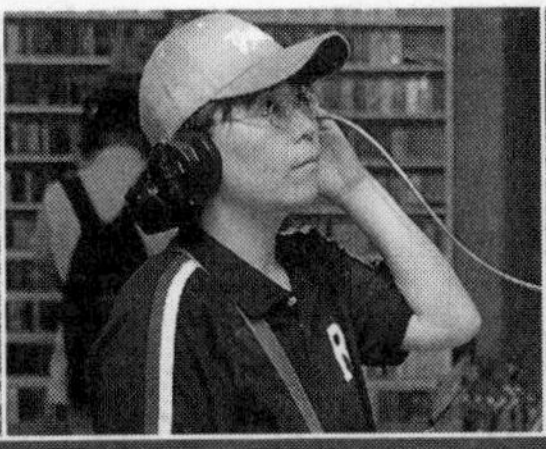
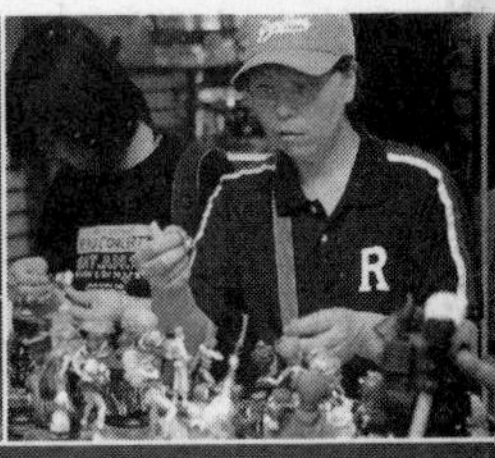

Endless Love for "g.o.d."

If you have been following any of Ji-Sang Shin and Geo's work, you would instantly realize that they are hardcore fans of "g.o.d."(Note: g.o.d. is a five man performance group that's extremely popular in Korea. Most of their songs have a pop or R&B flavor.) So strong is their love of g.o.d., they not only joined the fan club, attended many of g.o.d.'s events, but dedicate a good portion of their free time to sharing this love with younger audiences. Although they both live in Busan (A southern port city), they are known to travel to Seoul for g.o.d. concerts and attending both weekend shows.

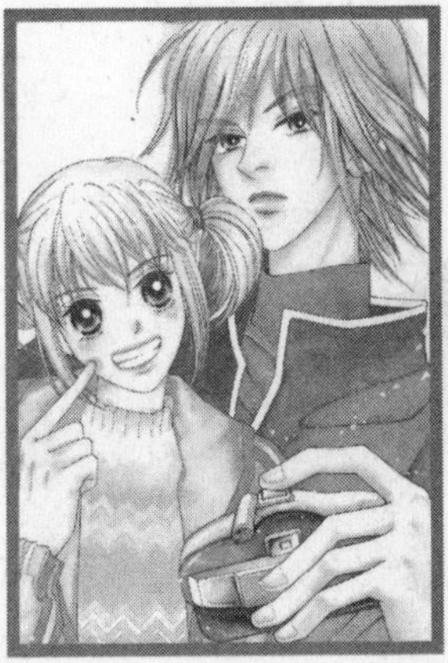

Ji-Sang: I didn't immediately fall in love with g.o.d. as I didn't have a television set when their first album came out. When I heard their first debut song on the radio, I just thought it was a nice song.

Exactly when their love began for the idol group, neither is quite sure. Despite being latecomers to the fan club, they work tirelessly with the younger fans and enjoy the energy of their innocent adoration. They love to read the teens' posts and relate to their youthful excitement and enthusiasm. However, depression lurks from time to time when they think their love for g.o.d may eventually extinguish. They hope the memories of their unconditional love and the happiness from these moments may never die.

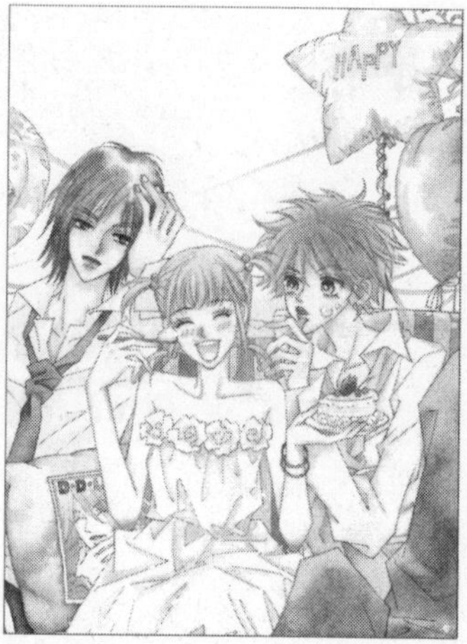
HAPPY

New Beginnings

The big sis, Ji-Sang Shin, and her juvenile partner in crime, Geo. For teens, they may have been unknown until recently, but in the world of manhwa, they are quite famous. Ji-Sang Shin's work, <Potato Plot of Meme and Gushiki> and Geo's <The City of Gray> are considered classics and well-known amongst "manwha-maniacs" (the equivalent of otaku/fangirls). In their first collaborative work, <2X8 SONG>, they stepped away from their known style and tapped into the teen audience with a heart-warming story.

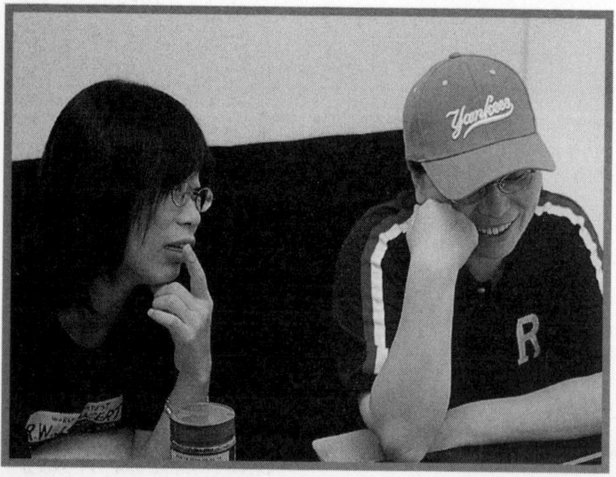
Yankees
R

Ji-Sang: Why did we change our style? Well one day I realized I liked teenagers. Perhaps it's a sign of old age. (lol) Kids are so cute - fresh-faced, without makeup. It made me want to draw them. Also, through my involvement with the g.o.d. fan club, I feel closer to their generation.

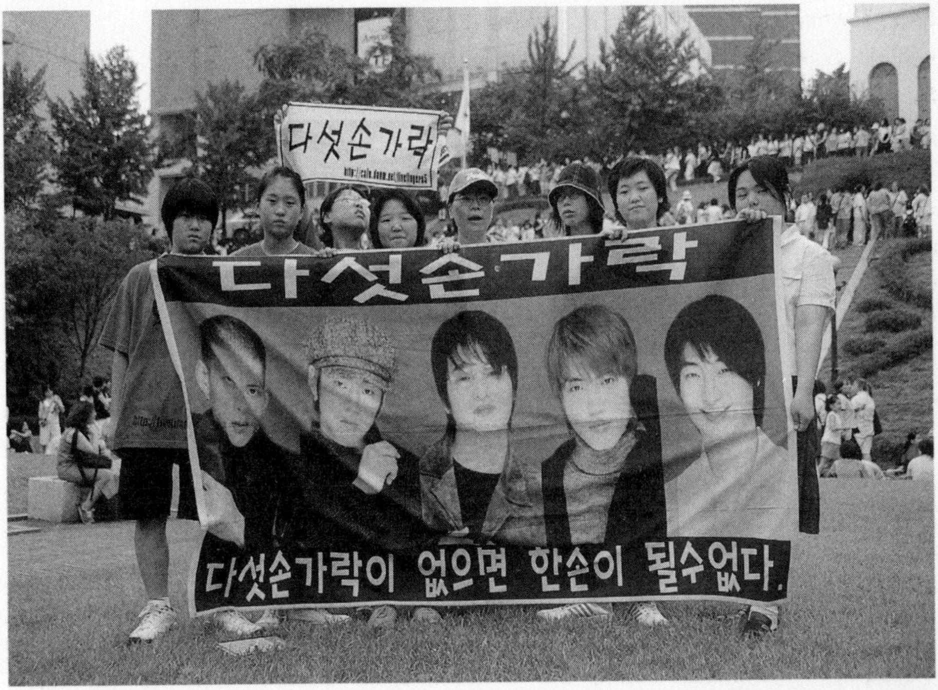
다섯손가락
다섯손가락
다섯손가락이 없으면 한손이 될수없다.

Geo: During a short part-time job we realized we work together well...

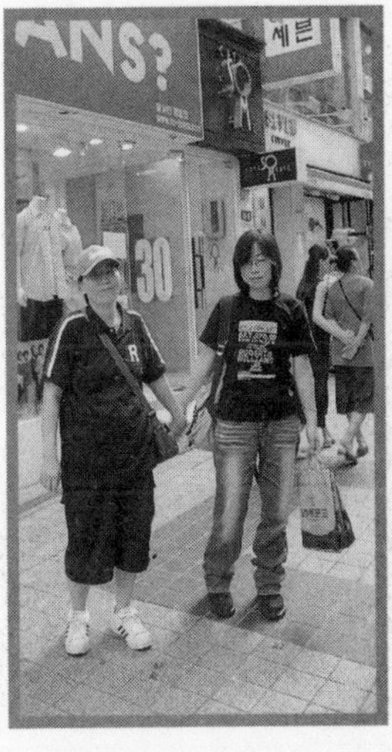

Different yet similar...

According to the artists, they developed a love-hate relationship working together. ^_^ As they are always together, they say they fight constantly. "It's because our personalities clash," or so they say. Yet it's because of their differences that they are able to work together to this day.

Geo: Big sis acts like a stereotypical old lady sometimes. When she's out, she wanders off and forgets to go to her meeting

places. There are times when we go out together, I just want to ignore her.

Ji-Sang: Geo acts like a spoiled brat. She pretends to be all neat and tidy, nagging about washing cups after they are

used. She acts so prissy when she's at the dinner table too. She's lucky she's ugly; otherwise people would say she's stuck-up. People tend to just accept her as "cute."

Like their personal lives, they divide their work according to their strengths. Ji-Sang Shin takes care of the story, female characters, and other extra characters. Geo draws E-Wan, E-Soh, Jin, Eun-Sung and other male characters. When rooming together, Ji-Sang prepares the food while Geo does the cleaning.

Ji-Sang: I've always sucked at drawing guy characters - to the point of possibly quitting. When I worked with Geo during our part-time job, I figured it wouldn't be bad to work together. You see, Geo's really good at drawing guy characters.

Ji-Sang often spoke for both of them during the interview while Geo added her opinions here and there. Seeing as how they are so different yet know each other well enough to get along was astonishing. Both say they are very happy that they can draw manhwa all day long. We hope that they'll continue to draw great manhwa for years to come!

**LET'S ASK THE AUTHORS OF <CHOCOLAT>,
WHAT THEY THINK OF THEIR WORK!!
IT'S TIME FOR SOME FUN AND HONEST TALK
WITH THE AUTHORS AND THEIR FANS!**

1. How was <Chocolat> created?

<Chocolat> was started all thanks to Lil' Cheapskate's fan club's uniform! At the first meeting we had with the editors to start a new series, we proudly showed Lil' Cheapskate's fan club uniform. After seeing her uniform the editor suggested we create a story about fan clubs and we agreed! And that's how <Chocolat> was created! Or so the legend goes...

2. Is there any character in <Chocolat> you feel best resembles you?

Poopyhead is sort of like E-Wan (with his mean streak).
Kum-Ji and coordinator Yoo-Jung are a bit like Lil' Cheapskate. ^^;;

3. Any memorable moments while drawing <Chocolat>?

It must be the letters from the fans. Such as, "Please get E-Soh and Kum-Ji together" or "E-Wan X Kum-Ji please T.T" etc... and the best suggestion of all, "Kill that $@!##$ Barbie please!!" @.@;;

4. What do you want the readers to learn from reading <Chocolat>?

Memories of love fade as the time passes, just like memories of hatred. We hope you all live your moments to the fullest and have no regrets later.

5. Lastly, to the fans of <Chocolat>!!

We would be grateful if you read <Chocolat> with love 'til the end.
And everyone : We *heart* you!!!

Bring it on!

vol.1

Baek HyeKyung

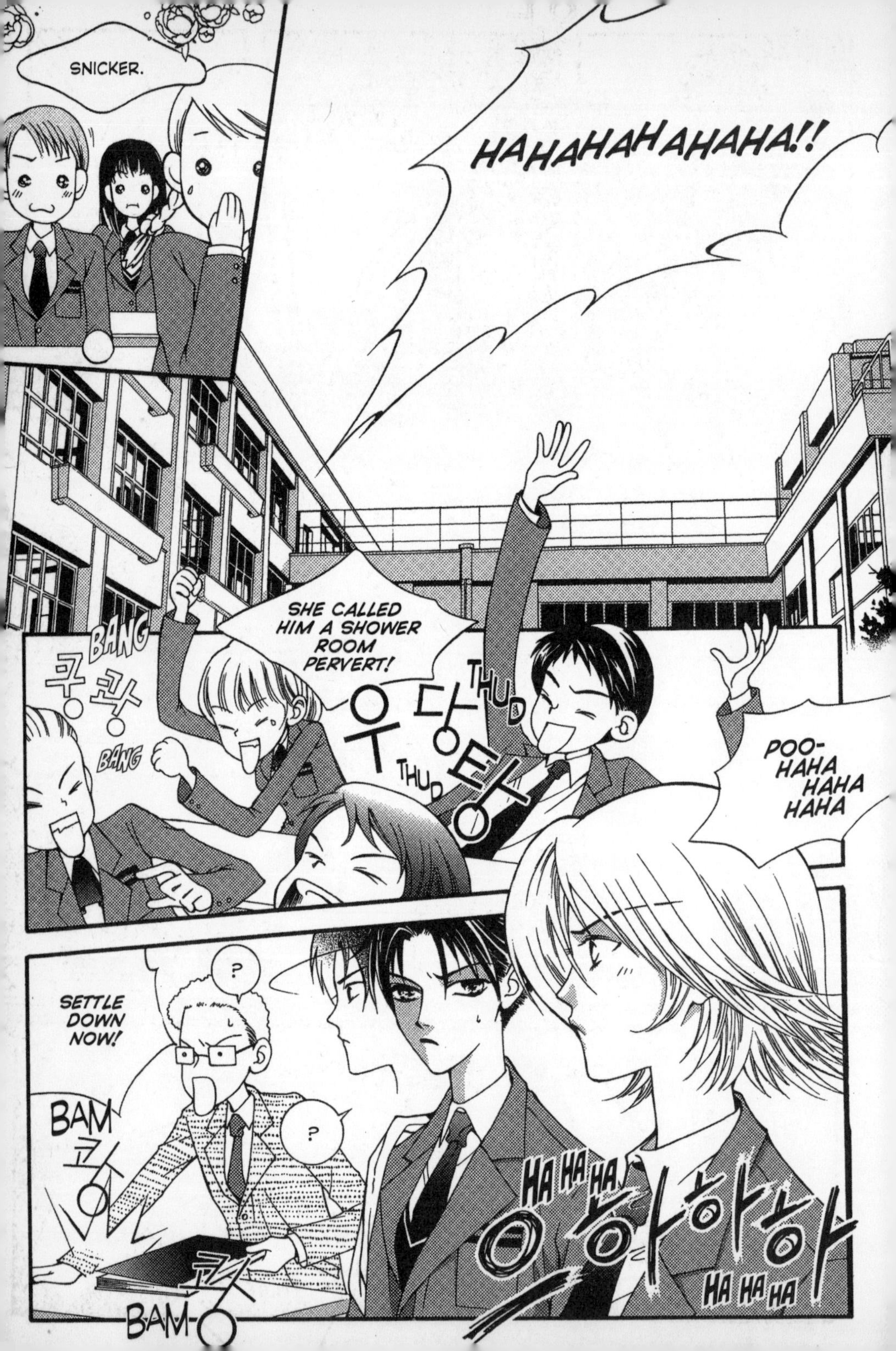
SNICKER.
HAHAHAHAHAHA!!
BANG
쿵쾅
BANG
SHE CALLED HIM A SHOWER ROOM PERVERT!
우당탕
THUD
THUD
POO-HAHA HAHA HAHA
?
SETTLE DOWN NOW!
?
BAM
쾅
BAM
쾅
HA HA HA
으하하하
HA HA HA

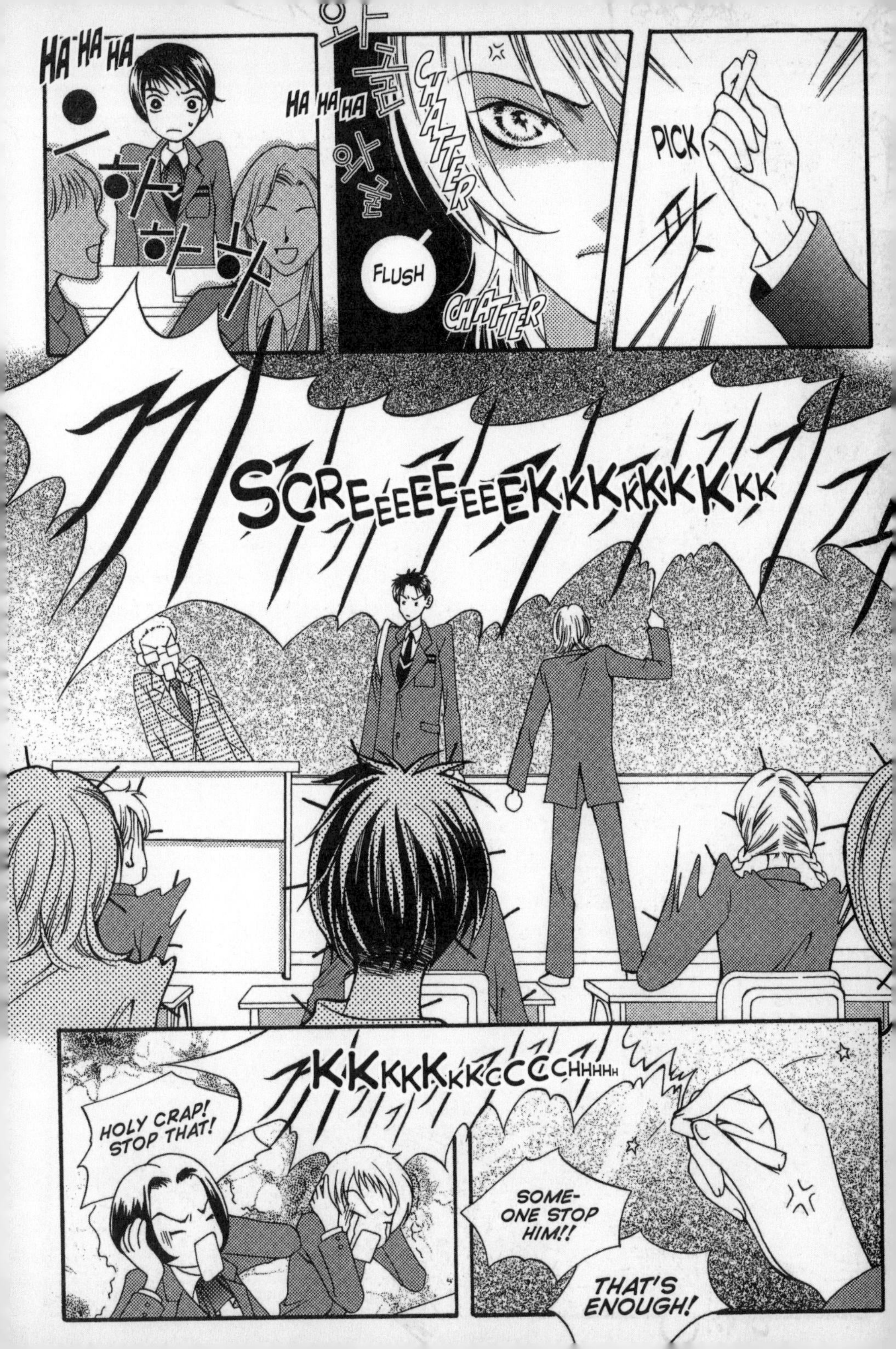
HA-HA-HA
하하핫
HA HA HA
와글와글
CHATTER
FLUSH
CHATTER
PICK
픽
SCREEEEEEEEEKKKKKKKKKK
KKKKKKKCCCCHHHHH
HOLY CRAP! STOP THAT!
SOME-ONE STOP HIM!!
THAT'S ENOUGH!

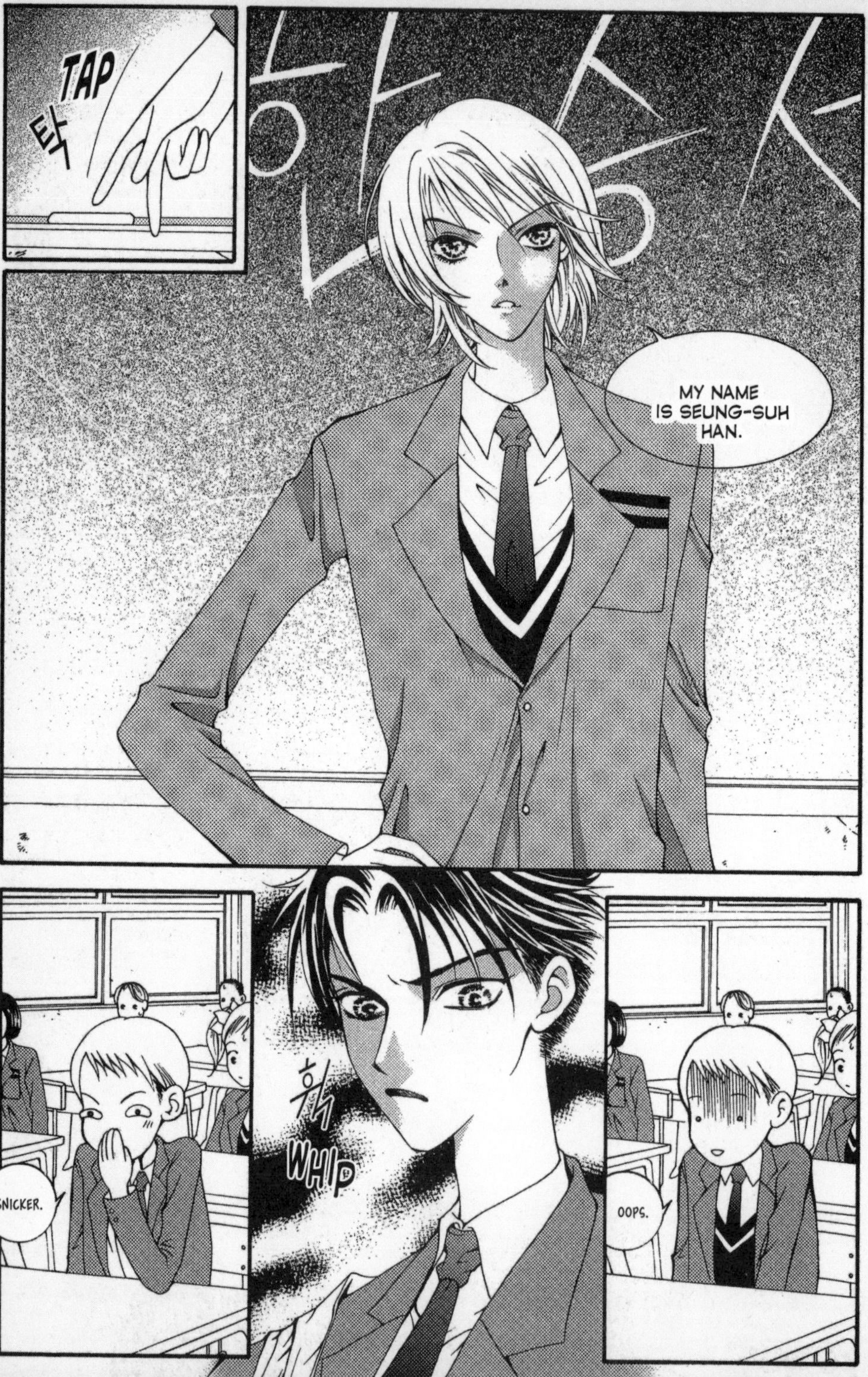
TAP
탁
MY NAME IS SEUNG-SUH HAN.
SNICKER.
휙
WHIP
OOPS.

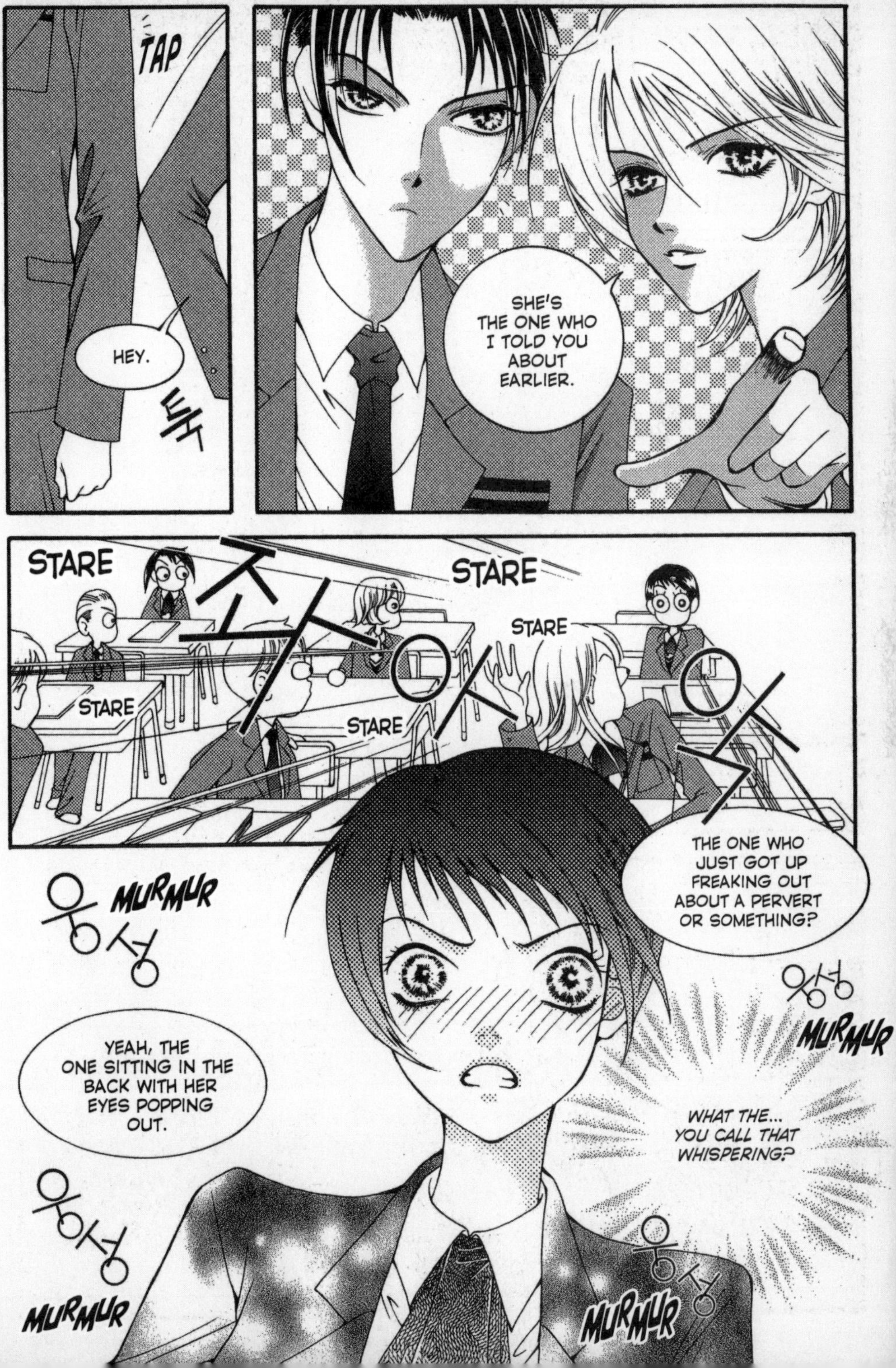
TAP
HEY.
SHE'S THE ONE WHO I TOLD YOU ABOUT EARLIER.
STARE
STARE
STARE
STARE
STARE
MURMUR
THE ONE WHO JUST GOT UP FREAKING OUT ABOUT A PERVERT OR SOMETHING?
MURMUR
YEAH, THE ONE SITTING IN THE BACK WITH HER EYES POPPING OUT.
WHAT THE... YOU CALL THAT WHISPERING?
MURMUR
MURMUR

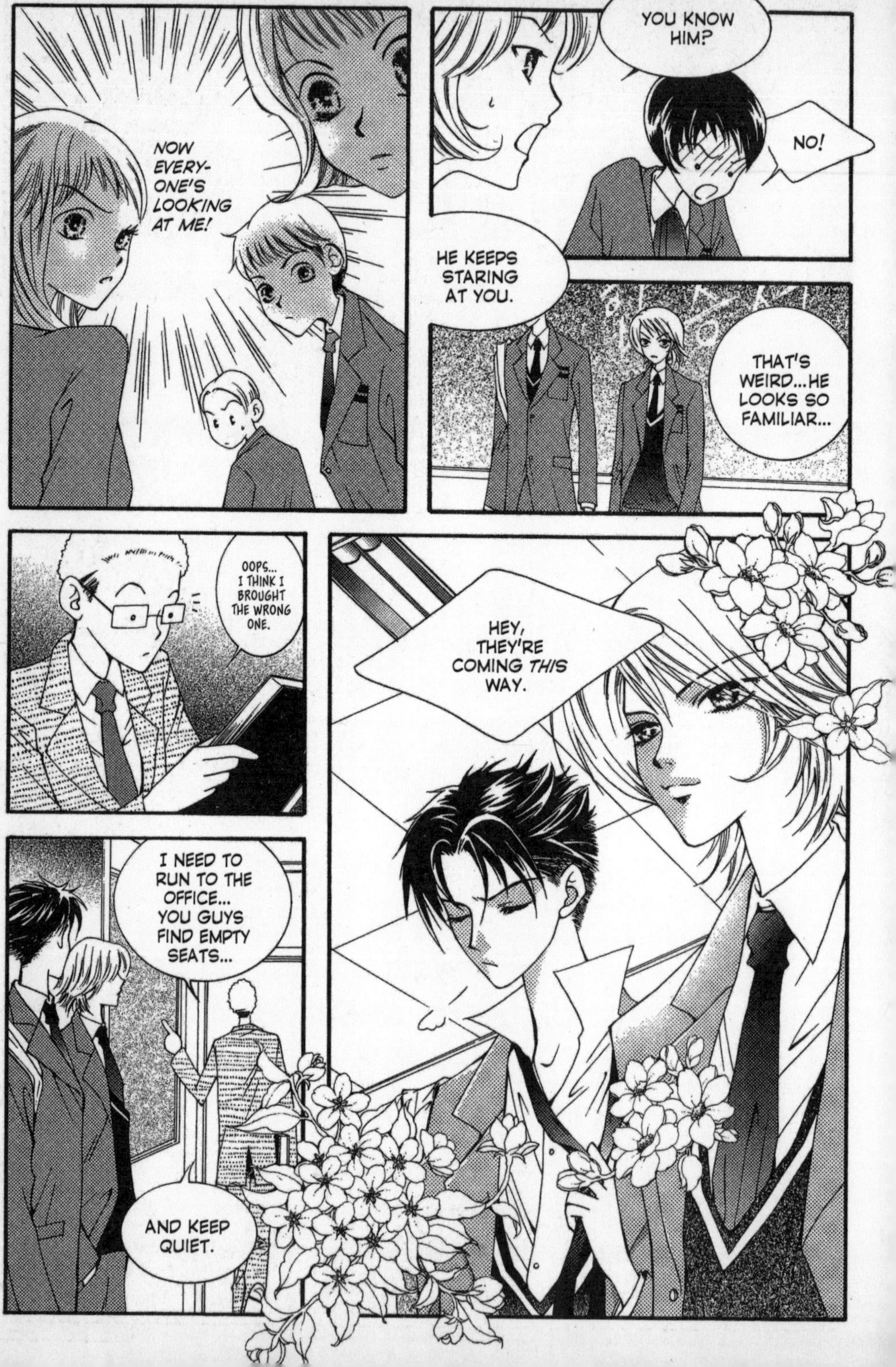
NOW EVERY-ONE'S LOOKING AT ME!
YOU KNOW HIM?
NO!
HE KEEPS STARING AT YOU.
THAT'S WEIRD...HE LOOKS SO FAMILIAR...
OOPS... I THINK I BROUGHT THE WRONG ONE.
I NEED TO RUN TO THE OFFICE... YOU GUYS FIND EMPTY SEATS...
AND KEEP QUIET.
HEY, THEY'RE COMING *THIS* WAY.

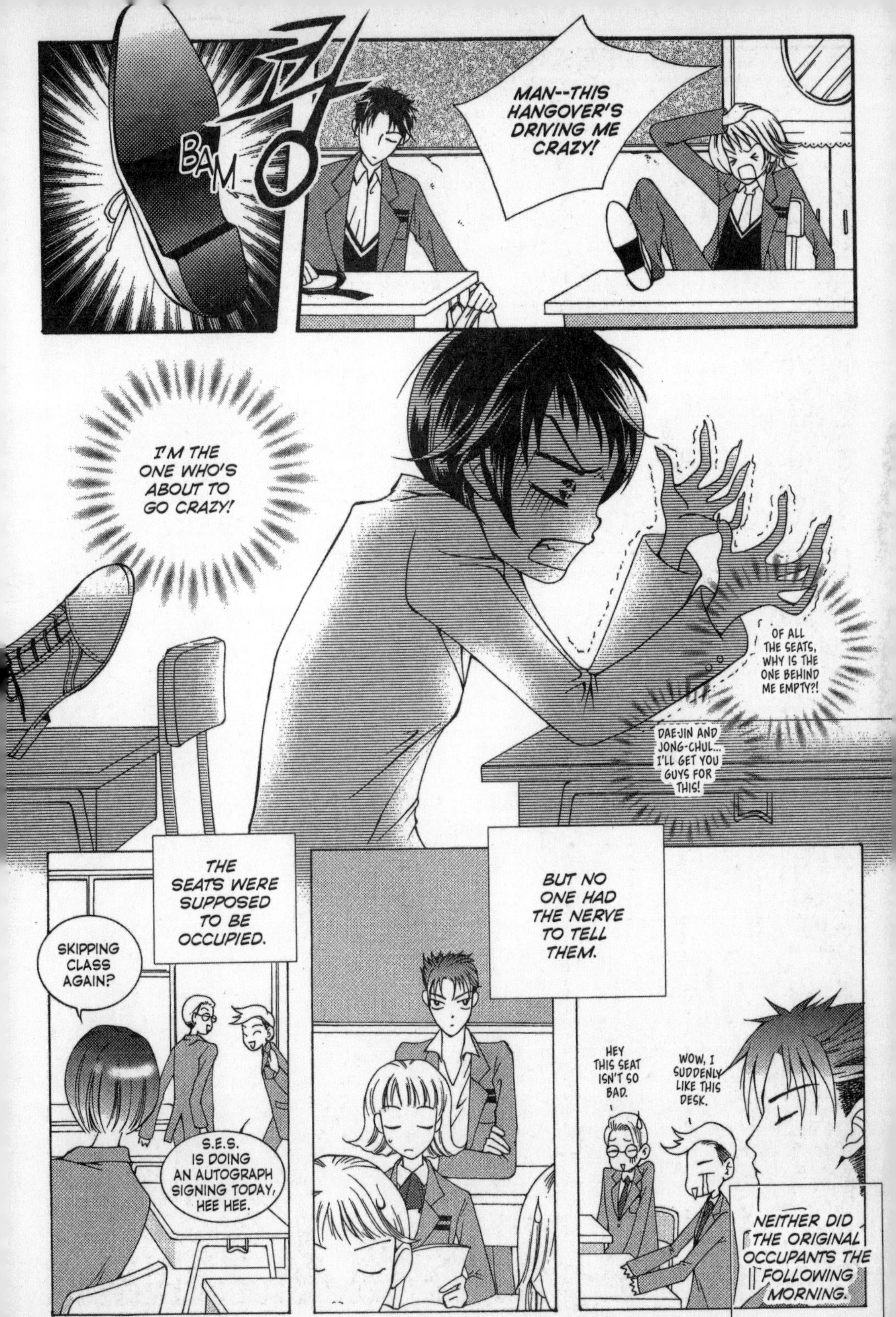
BAM
MAN--THIS HANGOVER'S DRIVING ME CRAZY!
I'M THE ONE WHO'S ABOUT TO GO CRAZY!
OF ALL THE SEATS, WHY IS THE ONE BEHIND ME EMPTY?!
DAE-JIN AND JONG-CHUL... I'LL GET YOU GUYS FOR THIS!
THE SEATS WERE SUPPOSED TO BE OCCUPIED.
SKIPPING CLASS AGAIN?
S.E.S. IS DOING AN AUTOGRAPH SIGNING TODAY, HEE HEE.
BUT NO ONE HAD THE NERVE TO TELL THEM.
HEY THIS SEAT ISN'T SO BAD.
WOW, I SUDDENLY LIKE THIS DESK.
NEITHER DID THE ORIGINAL OCCUPANTS THE FOLLOWING MORNING.

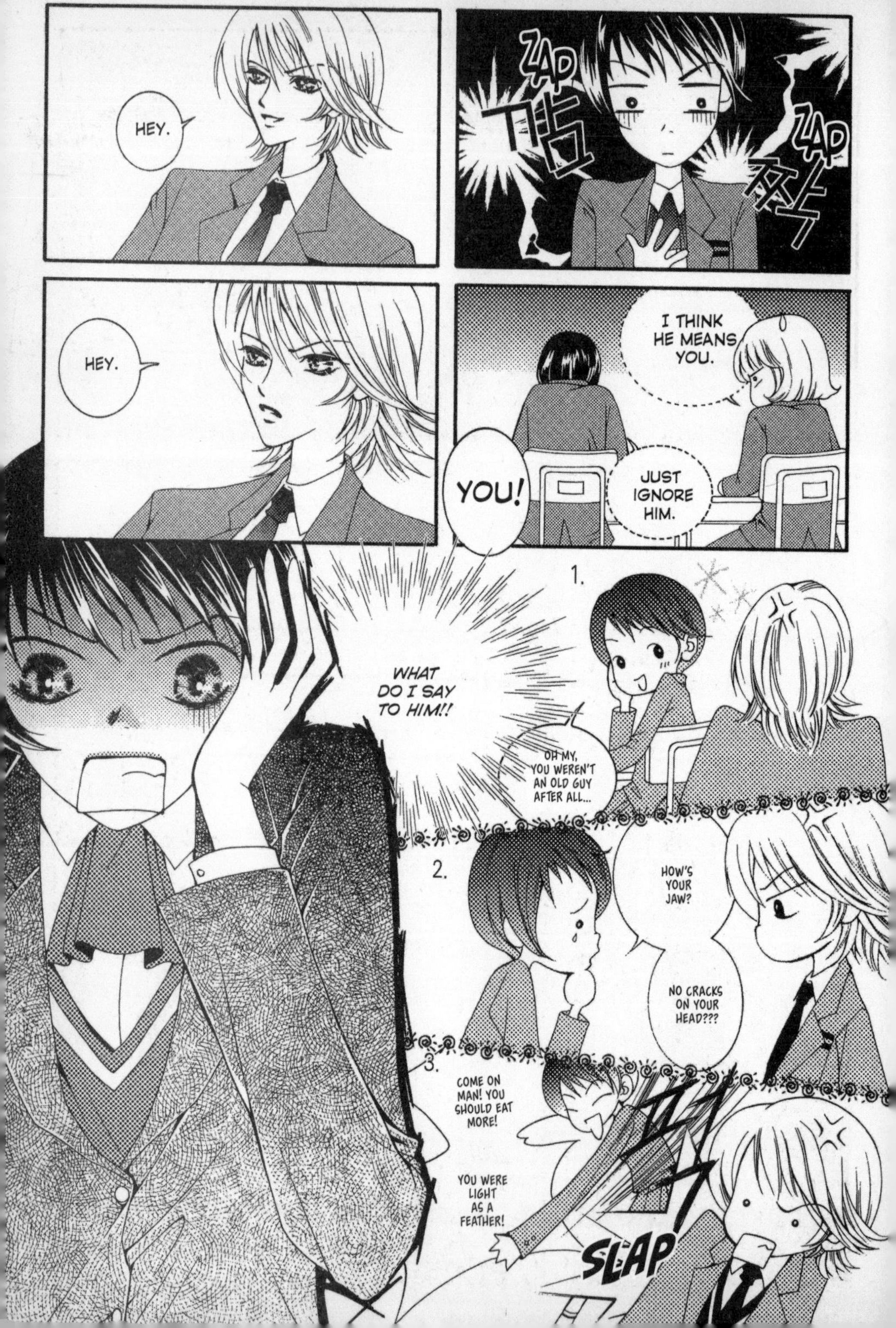
HEY.
ZAP
ZAP
HEY.
I THINK HE MEANS YOU.
YOU!
JUST IGNORE HIM.
WHAT DO I SAY TO HIM!!
1.
OH MY, YOU WEREN'T AN OLD GUY AFTER ALL...
2.
HOW'S YOUR JAW?
NO CRACKS ON YOUR HEAD???
3.
COME ON MAN! YOU SHOULD EAT MORE!
YOU WERE LIGHT AS A FEATHER!
SLAP

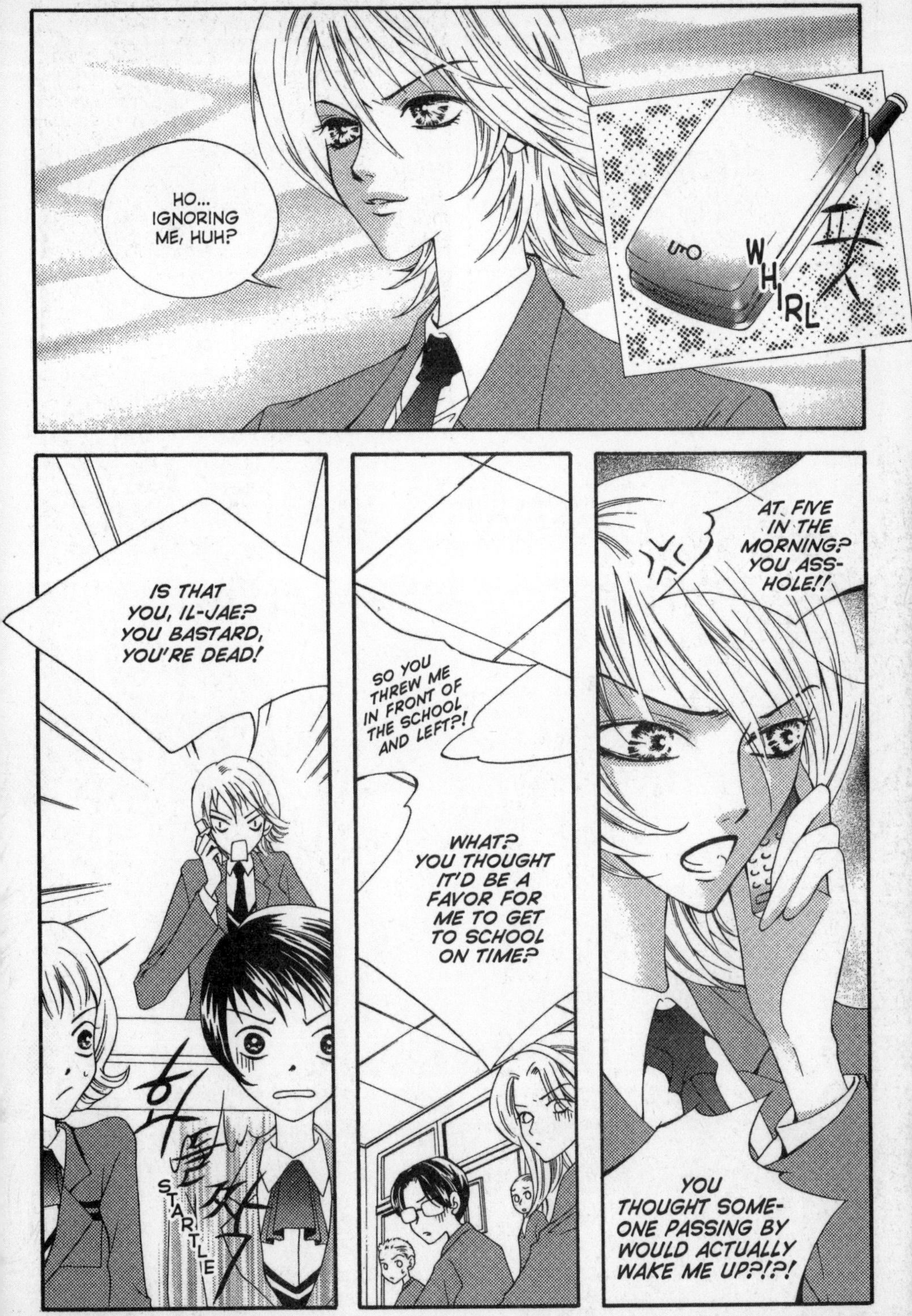
HO... IGNORING ME, HUH?
WHIRL
IS THAT YOU, IL-JAE? YOU BASTARD, YOU'RE DEAD!
STARTLE
SO YOU THREW ME IN FRONT OF THE SCHOOL AND LEFT?!
WHAT? YOU THOUGHT IT'D BE A FAVOR FOR ME TO GET TO SCHOOL ON TIME?
AT FIVE IN THE MORNING? YOU ASS-HOLE!!
YOU THOUGHT SOME-ONE PASSING BY WOULD ACTUALLY WAKE ME UP?!?!

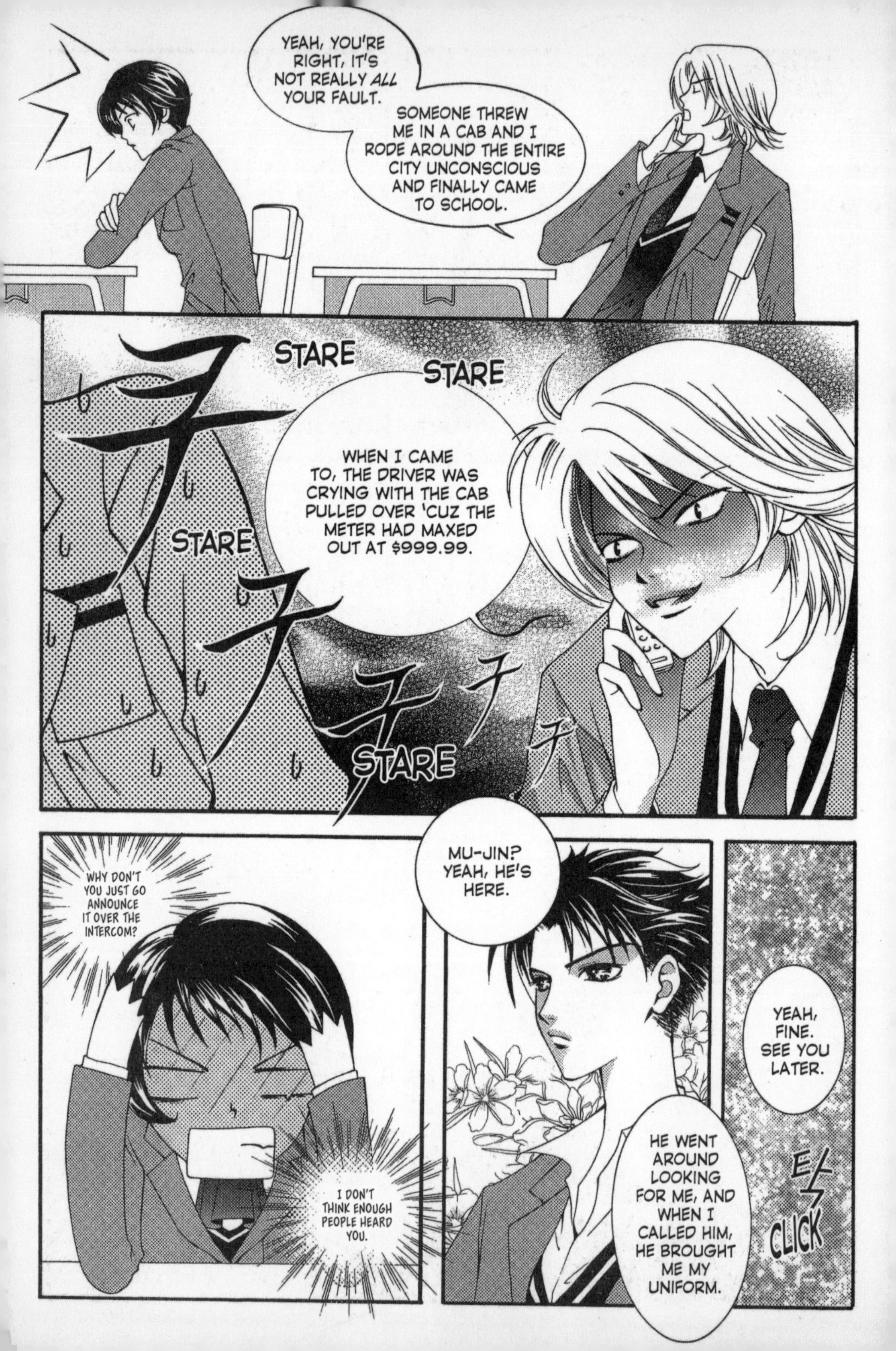
YEAH, YOU'RE RIGHT, IT'S NOT REALLY *ALL* YOUR FAULT.
SOMEONE THREW ME IN A CAB AND I RODE AROUND THE ENTIRE CITY UNCONSCIOUS AND FINALLY CAME TO SCHOOL.
STARE
STARE
STARE
WHEN I CAME TO, THE DRIVER WAS CRYING WITH THE CAB PULLED OVER 'CUZ THE METER HAD MAXED OUT AT $999.99.
STARE
WHY DON'T YOU JUST GO ANNOUNCE IT OVER THE INTERCOM?
I DON'T THINK ENOUGH PEOPLE HEARD YOU.
MU-JIN? YEAH, HE'S HERE.
HE WENT AROUND LOOKING FOR ME, AND WHEN I CALLED HIM, HE BROUGHT ME MY UNIFORM.
YEAH, FINE. SEE YOU LATER.
CLICK

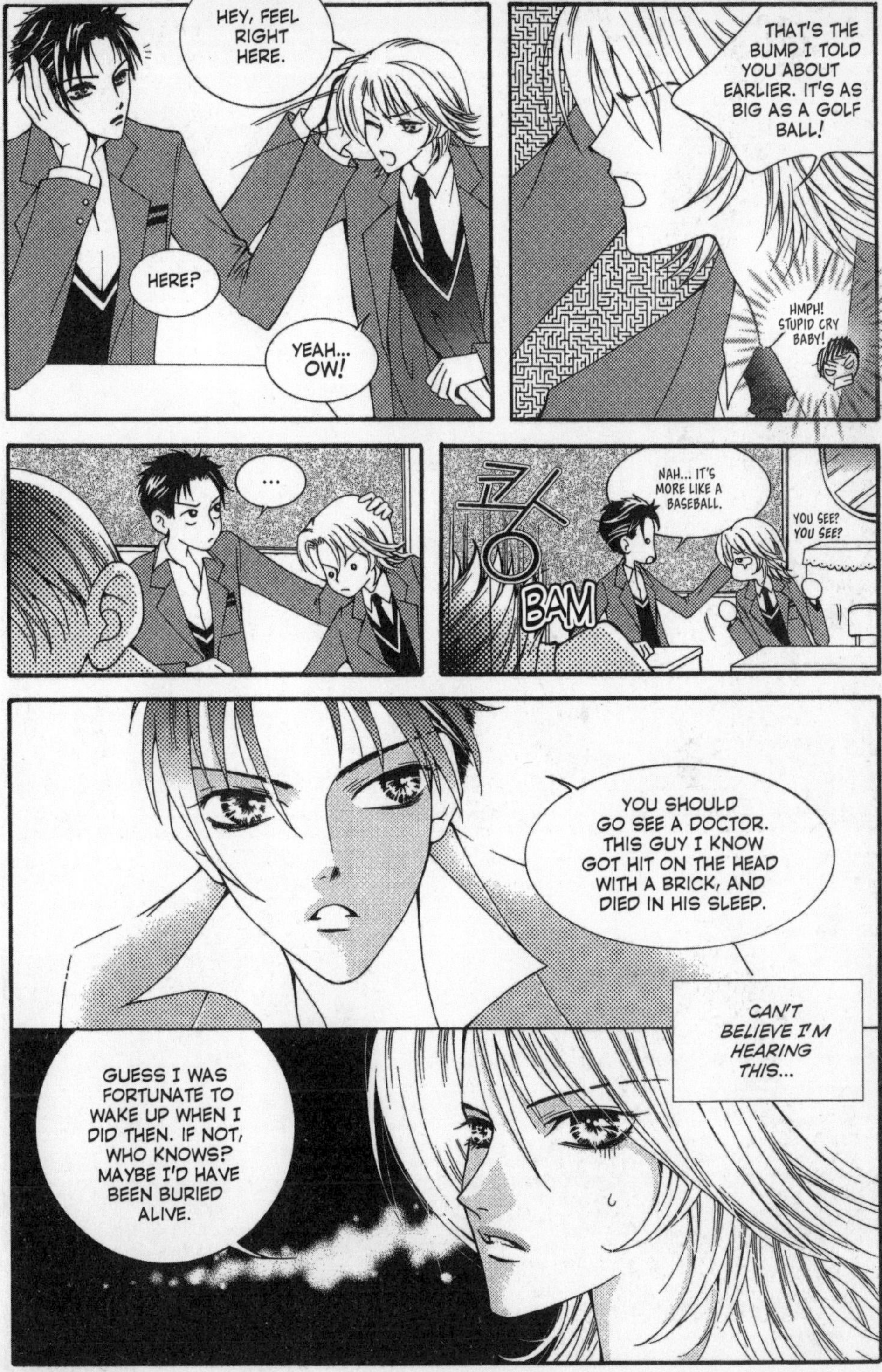
HEY, FEEL RIGHT HERE.
HERE?
YEAH... OW!
THAT'S THE BUMP I TOLD YOU ABOUT EARLIER. IT'S AS BIG AS A GOLF BALL!
HMPH! STUPID CRY BABY!
...
BAM
NAH... IT'S MORE LIKE A BASEBALL.
YOU SEE? YOU SEE?
YOU SHOULD GO SEE A DOCTOR. THIS GUY I KNOW GOT HIT ON THE HEAD WITH A BRICK, AND DIED IN HIS SLEEP.
GUESS I WAS FORTUNATE TO WAKE UP WHEN I DID THEN. IF NOT, WHO KNOWS? MAYBE I'D HAVE BEEN BURIED ALIVE.
CAN'T BELIEVE I'M HEARING THIS...

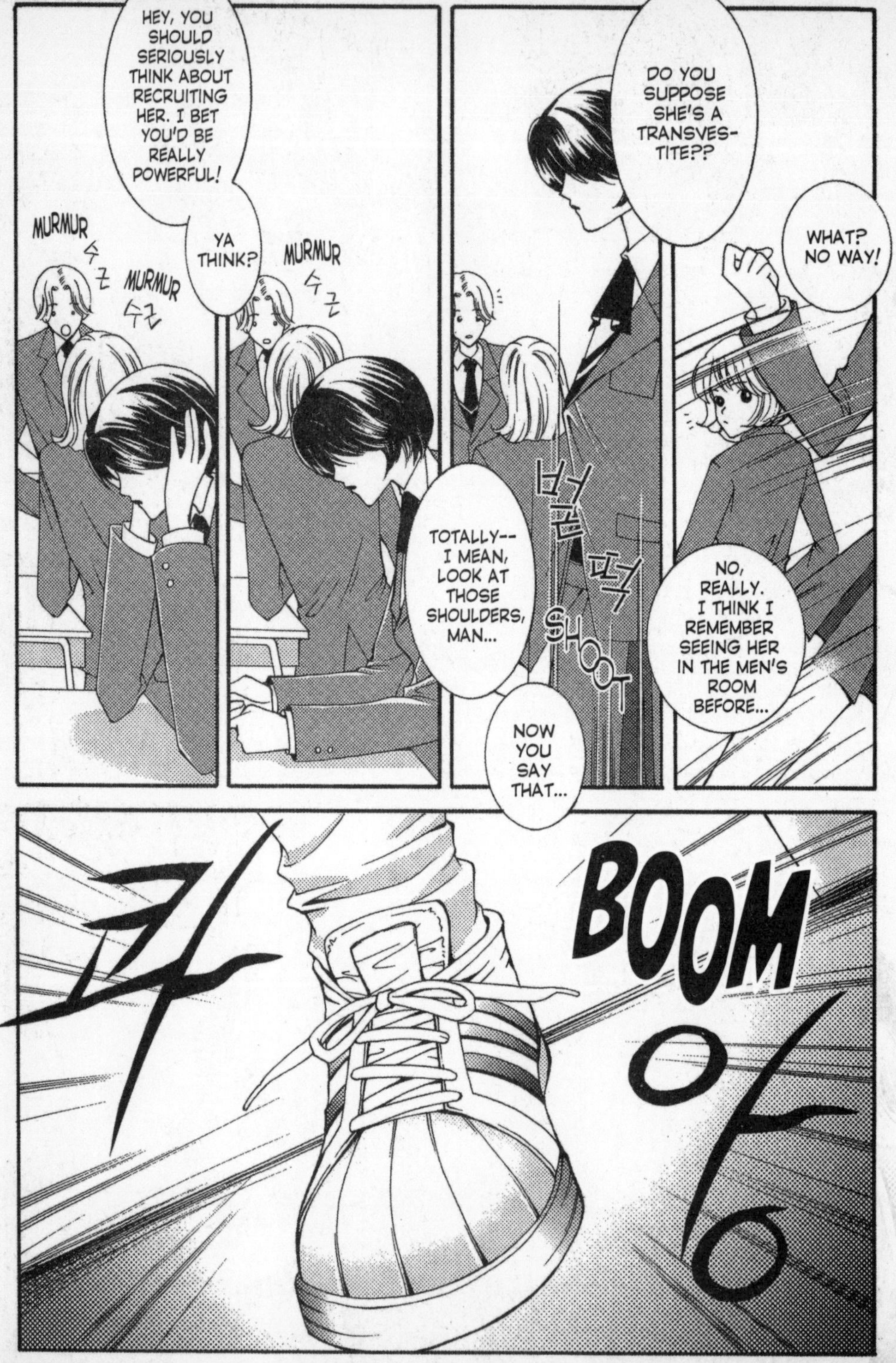
HEY, YOU SHOULD SERIOUSLY THINK ABOUT RECRUITING HER. I BET YOU'D BE REALLY POWERFUL!
MURMUR 수군
MURMUR 수군
YA THINK?
MURMUR 수군
TOTALLY-- I MEAN, LOOK AT THOSE SHOULDERS, MAN...
DO YOU SUPPOSE SHE'S A TRANSVES-TITE??
벌떡 SHOOT
NOW YOU SAY THAT...
WHAT? NO WAY!
NO, REALLY. I THINK I REMEMBER SEEING HER IN THE MEN'S ROOM BEFORE...
쾅
BOOM

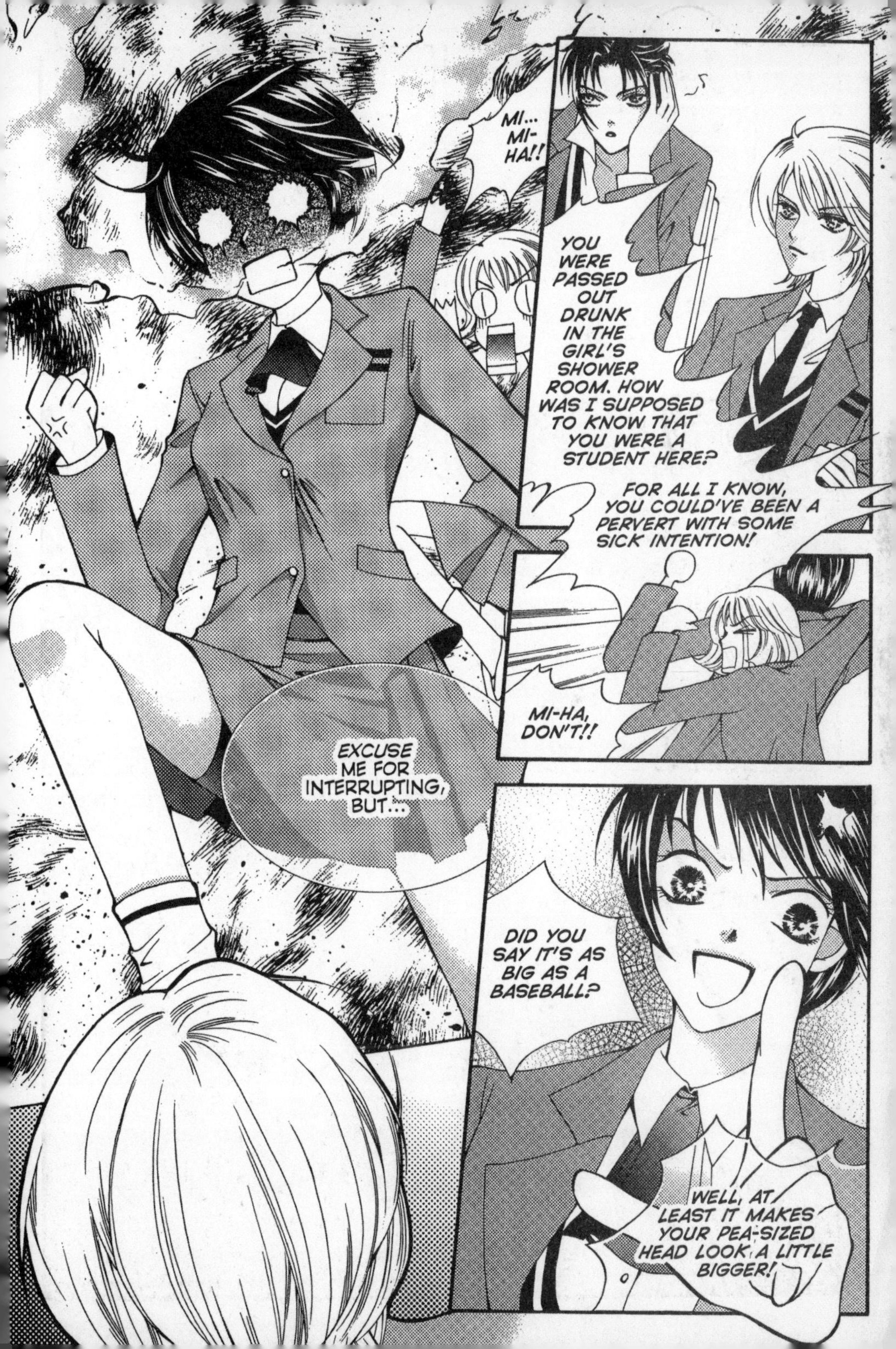
MI... MI-HA!!
EXCUSE ME FOR INTERRUPTING, BUT...
YOU WERE PASSED OUT DRUNK IN THE GIRL'S SHOWER ROOM. HOW WAS I SUPPOSED TO KNOW THAT YOU WERE A STUDENT HERE?
FOR ALL I KNOW, YOU COULD'VE BEEN A PERVERT WITH SOME SICK INTENTION!
MI-HA, DON'T!!
DID YOU SAY IT'S AS BIG AS A BASEBALL?
WELL, AT LEAST IT MAKES YOUR PEA-SIZED HEAD LOOK A LITTLE BIGGER!

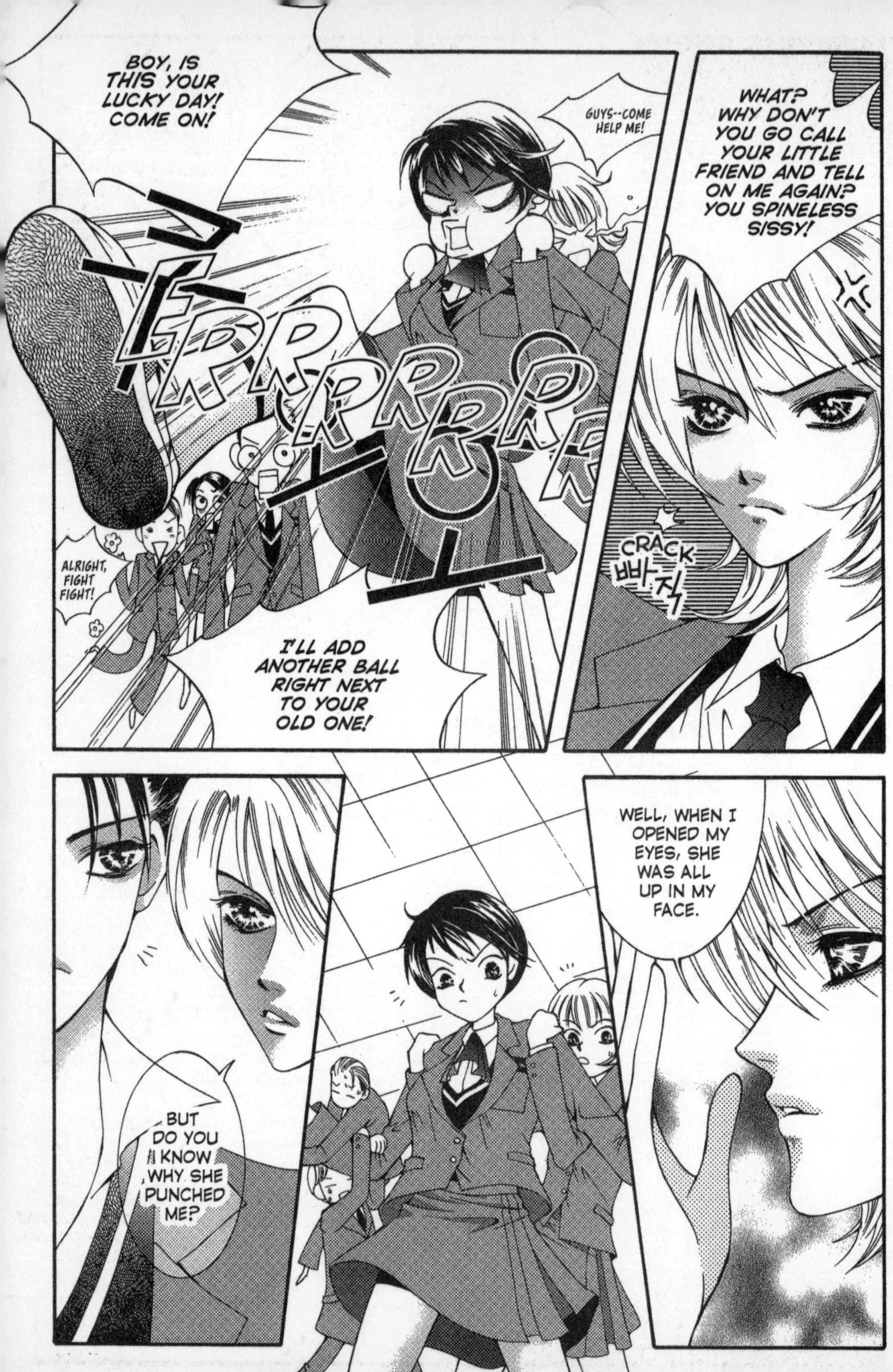
BOY, IS THIS YOUR LUCKY DAY! COME ON!
GUYS--COME HELP ME!
ALRIGHT, FIGHT FIGHT!
I'LL ADD ANOTHER BALL RIGHT NEXT TO YOUR OLD ONE!
WHAT? WHY DON'T YOU GO CALL YOUR LITTLE FRIEND AND TELL ON ME AGAIN? YOU SPINELESS SISSY!
CRACK
빠직
BUT DO YOU KNOW WHY SHE PUNCHED ME?
WELL, WHEN I OPENED MY EYES, SHE WAS ALL UP IN MY FACE.

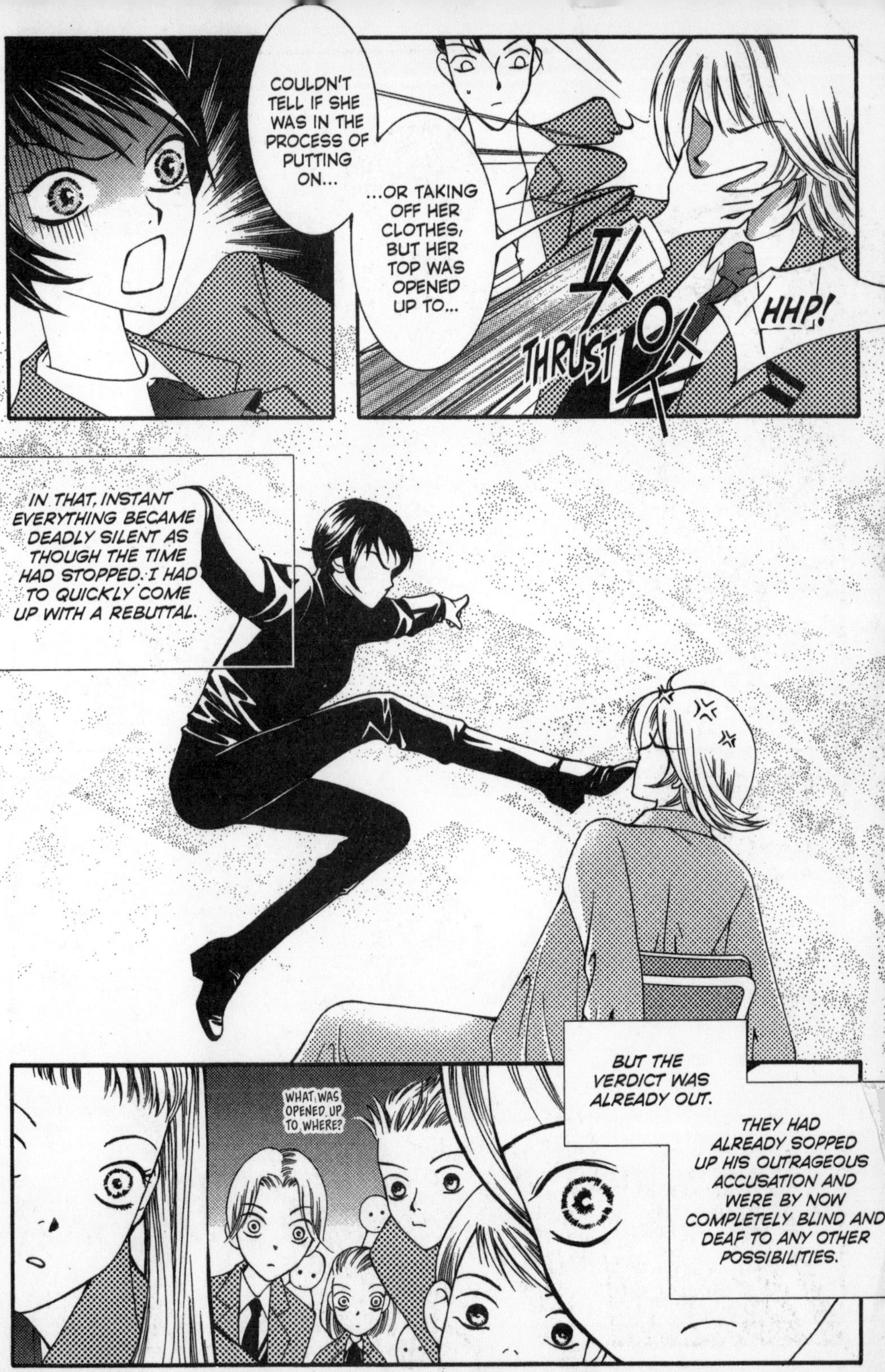
COULDN'T TELL IF SHE WAS IN THE PROCESS OF PUTTING ON...
...OR TAKING OFF HER CLOTHES, BUT HER TOP WAS OPENED UP TO...
THRUST
HHP!
IN THAT, INSTANT EVERYTHING BECAME DEADLY SILENT AS THOUGH THE TIME HAD STOPPED. I HAD TO QUICKLY COME UP WITH A REBUTTAL.
WHAT WAS OPENED UP TO WHERE?
BUT THE VERDICT WAS ALREADY OUT.
THEY HAD ALREADY SOPPED UP HIS OUTRAGEOUS ACCUSATION AND WERE BY NOW COMPLETELY BLIND AND DEAF TO ANY OTHER POSSIBILITIES.

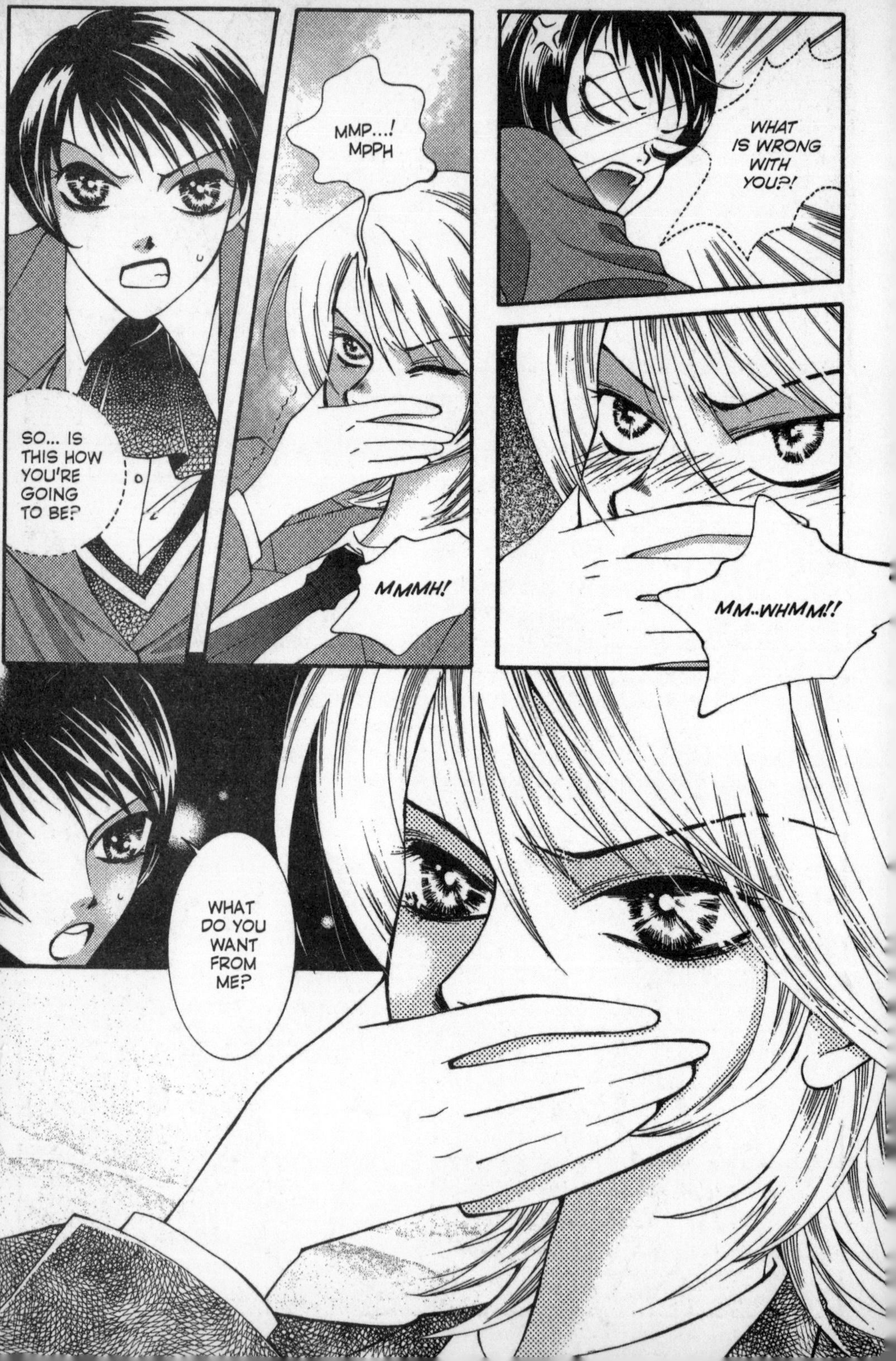
SO... IS THIS HOW YOU'RE GOING TO BE?
MMP...! MPPH
MMMH!
WHAT IS WRONG WITH YOU?!
MM..WHMM!!
WHAT DO YOU WANT FROM ME?

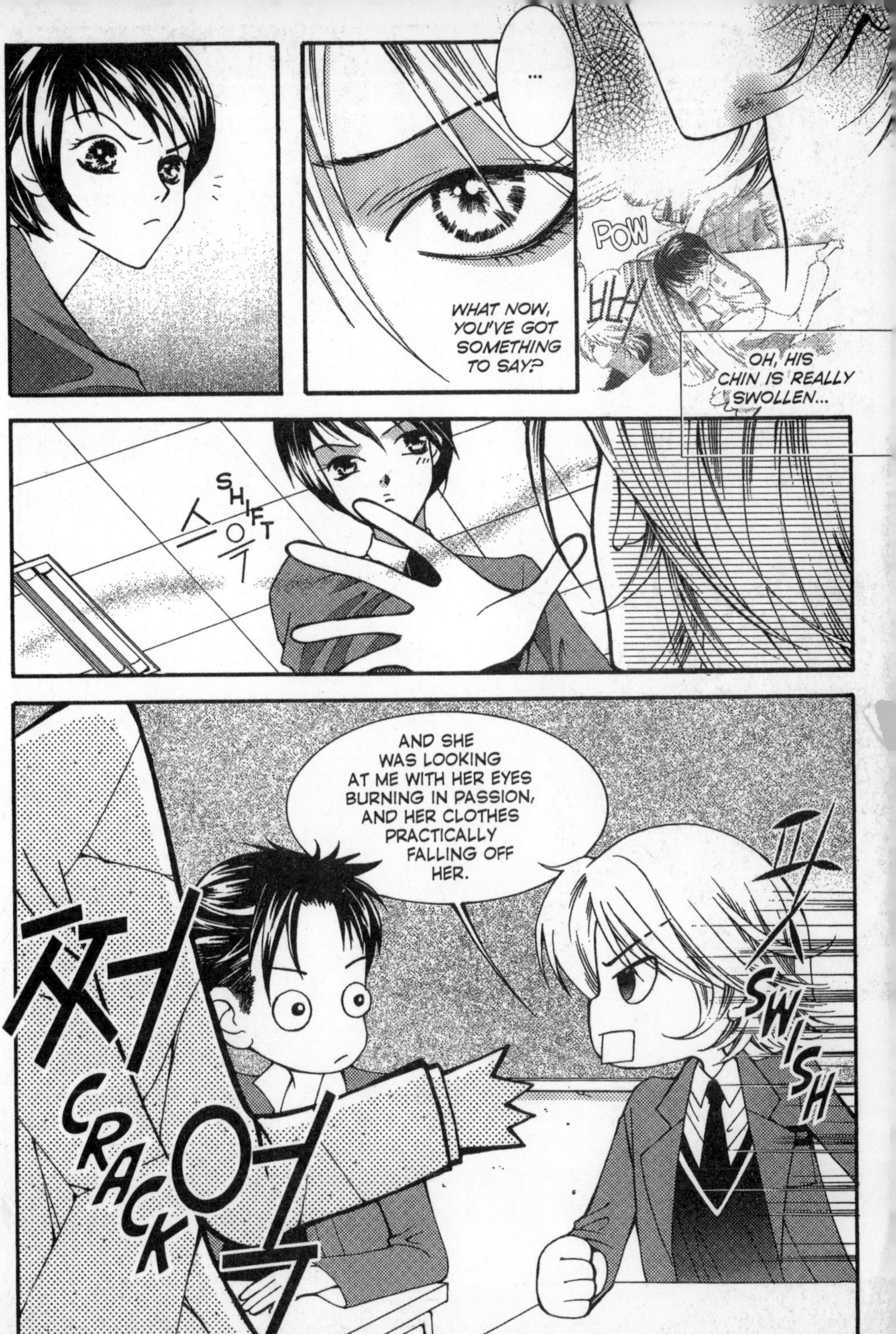
...
WHAT NOW, YOU'VE GOT SOMETHING TO SAY?
POW
OH, HIS CHIN IS REALLY SWOLLEN...
SHIFT
AND SHE WAS LOOKING AT ME WITH HER EYES BURNING IN PASSION, AND HER CLOTHES PRACTICALLY FALLING OFF HER.
CRACK
SWISH

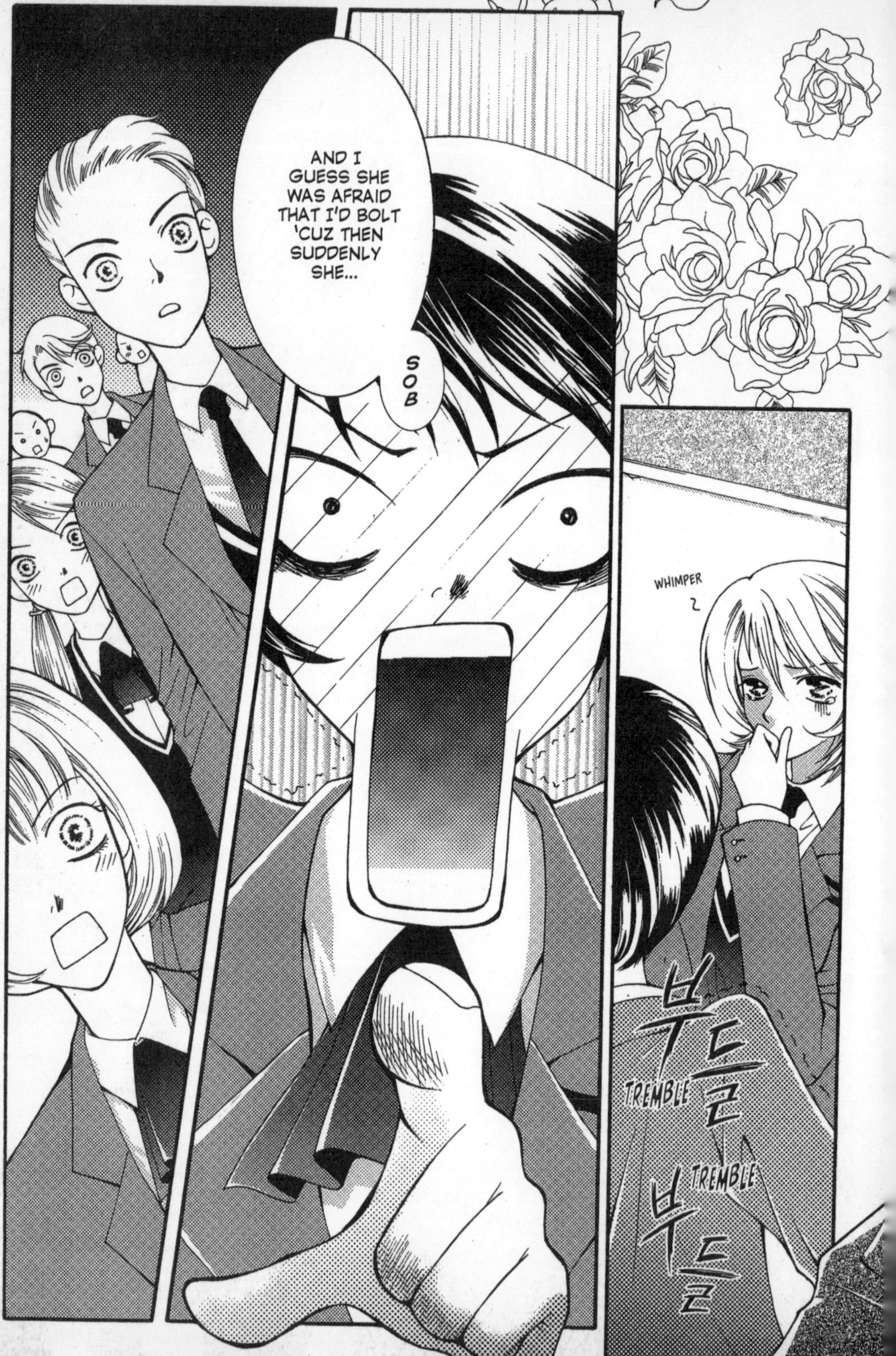
AND I GUESS SHE WAS AFRAID THAT I'D BOLT 'CUZ THEN SUDDENLY SHE...
SOB
WHIMPER
부들
TREMBLE
TREMBLE
부들

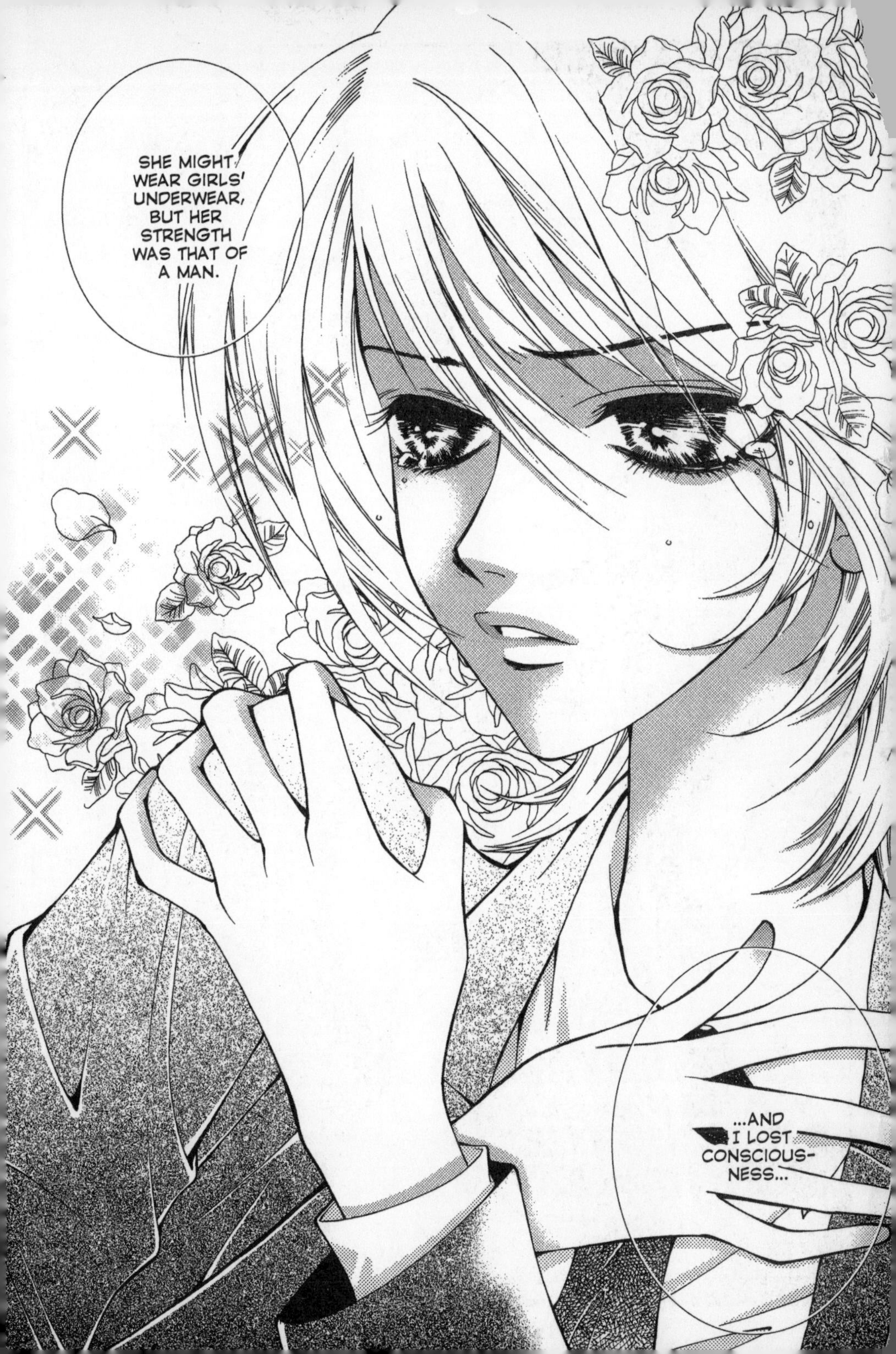
SHE MIGHT WEAR GIRLS' UNDERWEAR, BUT HER STRENGTH WAS THAT OF A MAN.
...AND I LOST CONSCIOUS-NESS...

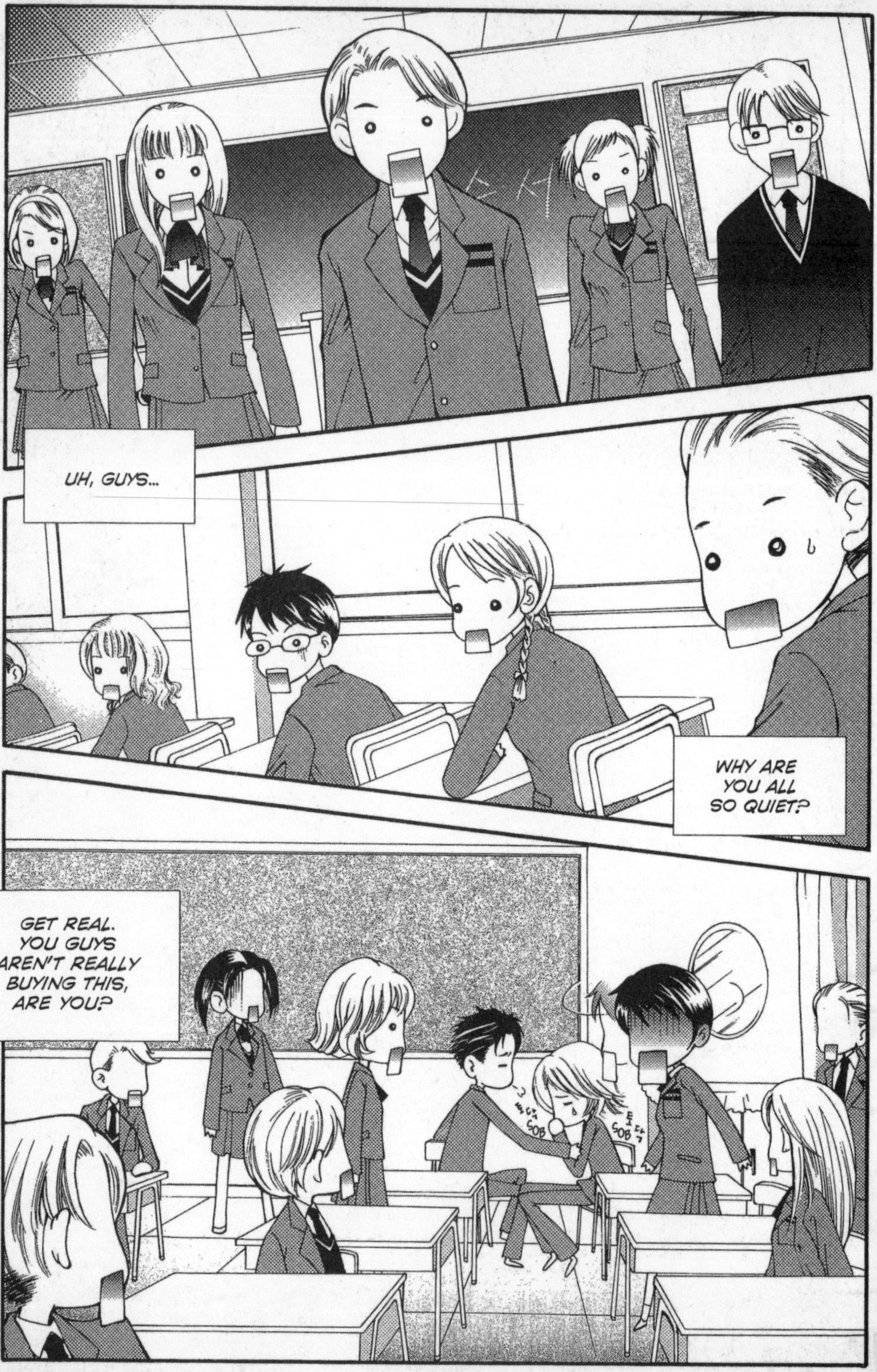
UH, GUYS...
WHY ARE YOU ALL SO QUIET?
GET REAL. YOU GUYS AREN'T REALLY BUYING THIS, ARE YOU?
SOB
SOB

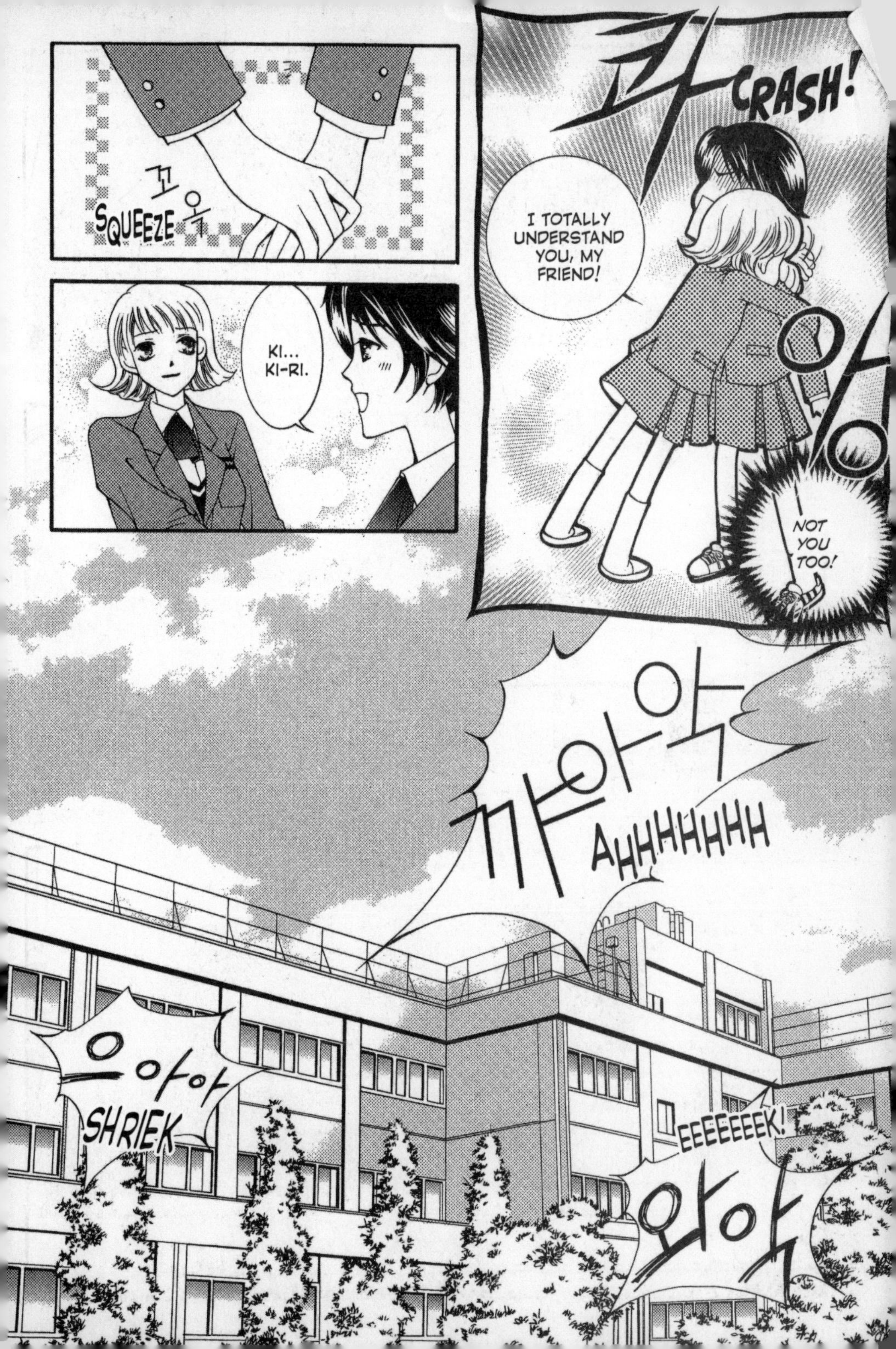
꼬옥
SQUEEZE
KI... KI-RI.
콰
CRASH!
I TOTALLY UNDERSTAND YOU, MY FRIEND!
NOT YOU TOO!
꺄아악
AHHHHHHH
SHRIEK
EEEEEEEK!

Danbi Original

Chocolat vol.1

Story and art by JiSang Shin · Geo

Translation Sunny Kim
English Adaptation Sunny Kim
Touch-up and Lettering Marshall Dillon
Graphic Design EunKyung Kim · YoungAh Cho
Assistant Editor Jackie Oh · Audra Furuichi
Editor JuYoun Lee

ICE Kunion

Project Manager Chan Park
Marketing Manager Erik Ko
Editor in Chief Eddie Yu
Publishing Director JeongHyun Chin
Publisher and C.E.O. JaeKook Chun

Chocolat © 2005 JiSang Shin · Geo
First published in Korea in 2002 by SIGONGSA Co., Ltd.
English text translation rights arranged by SIGONGSA Co., Ltd.
English text © 2005 ICE KUNION

Published by ICE Kunion
SIGONGSA 2F Yeil Bldg. 1619-4, Seocho-dong, Seocho-gu, Seoul, 137-878, Korea

ISBN : 89-527-4453-5

First printing, October 2005
10 9 8 7 6 5 4 3 2 1
Printed in Canada

www.ICEkunion.com/www.koreanmanhwa.com